teach yourself...

GeoWorks Pro

ARNOLD SHULMAN
EDITH SHULMAN

MIS:PRESS

A Subsidiary of
Henry Holt and Co., Inc.

Copyright © 1992 by Management Information Source, Inc.
a subsidiary of Henry Holt and Company, Inc.
115 West 18th Street
New York, New York, 10011

All rights reserved. Reproduction or use of editorial or pictorial content in any manner is prohibited without express permission. No patent liability is assumed with respect to the use of the information contained herein. While every precaution has been taken in the preparation of this book, the publisher assumes no responsibility for errors or omissions. Neither is any liability assumed for damages resulting from the use of the information contained herein.

First Edition—1992

ISBN Book 1-55828-189-4

Printed in the United States of America
10 9 8 7 6 5 4 3 2 1

MIS:Press books are available at special discounts for bulk purchases for sales promotions, premiums, fund-raising, or educational use. Special editions or book excerpts can also be created to specification.

For details contact: Special Sales Director
MIS:Press
a subsidiary of Henry Holt and Company, Inc.
115 West 18th Street
New York, New York 10011

TRADEMARKS

AllType is a trademark of ATech Software (also known as Ancier Technologies)
SoftType is a trademark of ZSoft Corporation
LANtastic is a trademark of Artisoft Inc.
LAN Manager is a trademark of MicroSoft Corporation
PC-NFS 3.5 is a trademark of Novell is a trademark of Novell, Inc.
Apple Laserwriter is a trademark of Apple Computer Company
QMS is a trademark of QMS, Inc.
HP is a trademark of Hewlett-Packard Company
PostScript is a trademark of Adobe Systems, Inc.
Quattro Pro SE is a trademark of Borland International, Inc.
Lotus 1-2-3 is a trademark of Lotus Development Corp.
Cakewalk is a trademark of Twelve Tone Systems, Inc.
Finale is a trademark of Coda Music Software, a Wenger Company
GEOS, GeoWorks, GeoWorks Pro, GeoComm, GeoDex, GeoDraw, GeoManager, GeoPlanner, and GeoWrite are trademarks of GeoWorks Corporation
MS-DOS is a trademark of MicroSoft Corporation
The Norton Utilities is a trademark of Symantec Corporation
PC Tools is a trademark of Central Point Software, Inc.
Sprint is a trademark of Borland International, Inc.
URW Roman, URW SAns, URW SymbolPS, and URW Mono are trademarks of URW, GmbH.

NOTE: The GeoWorks Pro software contains Nimbus Q from Digital Typeface Corporation and typefaces from URW, GmbH. Certain images and backgrounds are copyrighted works of Comstock, Inc.

Acknowledgments

We want to thank the staff of GeoWorks who were especially helpful in spite of the numerous tasks involved with bringing out the GEOWORKS PRO program. In particular we appreciate the interest and assistance of Jim Kilpatrick and Matthew Loveless.

Nan Borreson of Borland International has always taken the time to be of help even beyond our expectations.

A special thanks to Steve Berkowitz at MIS:Press. It has been an enjoyable experience working with the editorial staff he assigned to this project. In particular, it has always been a pleasure talking to Pansy Sapp and Cary Weinberger. Their comments have proved especially useful.

In the end we do feel the book has been considerably improved by all their contributions.

Contents

INTRODUCTION xxi
   About this Book xxiii
      Additional Information xxiv

CHAPTER 1: Installing GeoWorks Pro 1
   Configuring GeoWorks Pro 6
      Selecting the Monitor 6
      Selecting a Different Monitor 6
      Selecting the Mouse 7
      Selecting the Printer 8
      Entering Your Serial Number 8
   Summary 8

Contents

CHAPTER 2: The Beginner Workspace—The Appliances 9

Running GeoWorks Pro 10
Welcome Basics 10
Moving Around in GeoWorks Pro 11
    Icons 11
    Mouse Pointers 11
    Mouse Buttons 12
Using the Appliances 14
    Planner 15
    Address Book 17
    Banner 18
    Solitaire 21
    Calculator 21
    Notepad 22
Summary 24

CHAPTER 3: The Intermediate Workspace 25

Getting Started in Workspaces 26
Moving Around the Intermediate Workspace 26
    File Cabinet Window 28
    The File Cabinet Icons Display 28
    The File Menu Commands 32
    Menu Selection With the Mouse 34
    Keyboard Commands for Menus 35
Overview of the File Cabinet Window 37
    Top Row of File Cabinet Buttons 39
    The File Cabinet Information Line 44
    Bottom Row of File Cabinet Buttons 45
A Sample Document 49
Summary 51

CHAPTER 4: The Advanced Workspace 53
Moving Around the Advanced Workspace 54
GeoWorks Pro Windows 54
- Accessing the GeoDraw Window 54
Exiting an Application 59
Creating and Saving Documents (Files) 59
- DOS and GeoWorks Files 60
- DOS Document Filenames and Icons 60
- GEOS Document Filenames and Icons 60
- About Subdirectories 61
- Importing and Exporting DOS/GEOS Files 62
Opening the GeoComm Application 64
Opening the GeoWrite Application 66
Moving Around Subdirectories 67
Importing a DOS file into GeoWrite 69
Saving a GEOS Document as a DOS Document 69
- Verifying the DOS File Export 70
Summary 71

CHAPTER 5: GeoManager 73
The GeoManager Screen 74
Control Line 75
- Control Button 75
- Express Button 76
- Title Bar 80
Menu Bar 81
- File Menu 81
- Tree Menu 88
- View Menu 90
- Options Menu 92

vii

Contents

    Disk Menu 95
        Window Menu 98
Information Line 99
Main Display Window 99
Bottom Line Icons 100
Summary 101

CHAPTER 6: The Preferences Application and the Extras Directory **103**

The Preferences Application 103
Accessing the Preferences Application 104
    Date & Time 107
    Background..107
    Sound 110
    Printer..111
    Computer 112
    Video 114
    International 115
    Keyboard...119
    Mouse 121
    Modem 122
PC/GEOS 125
GeoManager Extras Folder 126
Summary 140

CHAPTER 7: The GeoWrite Application **141**

Starting GeoWrite 142
    Application Window Elements 143
    The Menu Bar 143
    The Ruler Bar 143
    The Format Bar 144

Main Text Window 147
    Headers and Footers 147
    Typing Mode 148
Selecting and Editing Text with the Mouse 148
    Selecting by Dragging 148
    Selecting by Specifying 148
    Selecting Words 149
    Selecting Lines 149
    Selecting Larger Units 149
    Adjusting Range Selected 150
    Deleting Selected Text 150
    To Replace a Range of Text 150
Keyboard Editing and Typing Cursor Movement 150
Summary 152

CHAPTER 8: GeoWrite Menus 153

File Menu 154
    The Pin Symbol 154
    New 154
    Open 155
    Close 156
    Save 156
    Save As 157
    Revert 157
    Text File Commands 158
    Print 160
    Exit (F3) 163
Edit Menu 163
    The Pin Symbol 164
    Cut (Shift+Del) 164

Contents

    Copy (Ctrl+Ins) 164
    Paste (Shift+Ins) 164
    Store Style 165
    Recall Style 165
    Insert Page Break 165
    Insert Page Number 165
    Check Spelling (F5) 166
View Menu 171
    Correct for Aspect Ratio 171
Options Menu 171
    Draw Graphics 171
    Align Ruler with Page 172
    Snap to Ruler Marks 172
    Show Ruler Top 172
    Show Ruler Bottom 172
    Show Horizontal Scroll Bar 173
    Show Vertical Scroll Bar 173
    Show All 173
    Hide All 173
    Measurement Units 173
    Spell Check Options 173
    Save Options 173
Paragraph Menu 173
    The Pin Symbol 174
    Paragraph Color 174
    Border 176
    Default Tabs 178
    Tab Attributes 178
    Left (Ctrl+L) 179
    Center (Ctrl+C) 180
    Right (Ctrl+T) 180
    Full (Ctrl+F) 180

Single (1) (Ctrl+1)	180
One and a Half (Ctrl+2)	180
Double (2) (Ctrl+5)	180
Paragraph Spacing	181
Fonts Menu	182
More Fonts	183
Sizes Menu	184
Standard Font Sizes	184
Make Existing Text Font Smaller or Larger	184
Make New Text Smaller or Larger	185
Custom Size	185
Character Spacing	185
Styles Menu	186
Plain Text (Ctrl+P)	186
Bold (Ctrl+B)	186
Italic (Ctrl+I)	186
Underline (Ctrl+U)	187
Strike Thru	187
Superscript (<)	187
Subscript (>)	187
Text Color	187
Window	187
The Pin Symbol	188
Previous Page (Ctrl+V)	188
Next Page (Ctrl+N)	188
Go to Page	188
Redraw (Shift+Ctrl+R)	188
Overlapping	189
Full-Sized (Ctrl+F10)	189
Page Listing and Select Page	189
Summary	190

Contents

CHAPTER 9: GeoWrite Operations And Tutorial 191

Accessing GeoWrite 192
Exercise 1 192
Create and Save a Document 192
Setting Options 193
Setting a Center Tab 193
Selecting Text 194
Changing Font of Existing Text 195
Changing the Size of Existing Text 195
Changing Text Styles of Existing Text 196
Closing Pinned Menus 196
Removing Text Highlighting 197
Creating a Blank Line 197
Changing Font, Size, and Style for New Text 197
Typing Text 197
Making a Header 198
Changing Header Size 200
Inserting a Graphic Image in the Document 200
Saving the Document 204
Exercise 2 205
Creating a Page Break 205
Creating a Table 205
Setting the Table Margins 206
Setting Decimal Tabs 208
Drawing a Border Around the Table 210
Saving the Document 213
Exercise 3 213
Creating a First-line Indented Paragraph 213
Creating an Indented Margin Paragraph 214
Creating a First-line Outdent Paragraph 214
Saving the Document 214

Using Documents Created in Quattro Pro SE or Lotus 1-2-3 215
Summary 217

CHAPTER 10: The GeoDraw Application.....................................219

Accessing the GeoDraw Application..220
File Menu 220
   Import...220
Edit Menu...222
   Fuse Objects 223
View Menu...224
   Correct for Aspect Ratio...225
Options Menu 225
   Drag As Rectangle 225
   Drag As Outline 226
   Show Tool Box 226
Modify Menu 226
   Nudge 226
   Flip Horizontal 227
   Flip Vertical 227
   Rotate 45° Left 227
   Rotate 45° Right...228
   Rotate to Any Degree 228
   Line Properties 228
   Area Properties..229
   Text Properties..230
Arrange Menu 230
   Bring To Front 230
   Send To Back 231
   Move Forward 231
   Move Backward 231
Text Menu...231

Contents

Justification 231
Left 232
Right 232
Center 232
Full 233
Text Properties 233
Window Menu 234
Overlapping (Ctrl+F5) 234
Full-Sized (Ctrl+F10) 234
Document Listing 234
Tool Box 234
Arrow Pointer Tool 235
Text Tool 235
Line Tool 237
Connect Line Tool 237
Rotate Pointer 238
Rectangle Tool 238
Circle Tool 238
Polygon Tool 239
Summary 239

CHAPTER 11: The GeoPlanner Application **241**
Using GeoPlanner 242
Selected Year 243
Current Time 243
Selected Day and Date 243
Calendar 243
Schedule of Events 244
Scheduling an Event 244
Viewing Scheduled Events 245
The Menu Bar 245

xiv

File Menu	245
Edit Menu	247
View Menu	249
Options Menu	250
Quick Menu	253
Utilities Menu	253
GeoDex Lookup	255
Summary	257

CHAPTER 12: The Calculator Application 259

Using the Calculator	260
Delete	261
Parentheses (Standard Configuration)	261
Clear	262
Error	262
Order of Operations (Standard Configuration)	262
Memory Use	263
The Calculator Menu Bar	263
File Menu	263
Edit Menu	263
Options Menu	264
Memory Functions	267
Summary	268

CHAPTER 13: The Notepad Application 269

Accessing the Notepad Application	269
Using Notepad for Notes	270
Using Notepad as a DOS Text Editor	271
The Notepad Menus	271
File Menu	271
Edit Menu	273

Contents

    Sizes Menu 274
  Summary 274

CHAPTER 14: The Scrapbook Application **275**

  Accessing the Scrapbook 276
  The Scrapbook Window 276
    Go to Page Button 277
    Previous and Next Buttons 278
  The Menu Bar 278
    File Menu 278
    Edit Menu 280
    View Menu 282
  Changing the Default Scrapbook 283
    Opening More Than One Scrapbook at a Time 284
    Cutting or Copying Between Scrapbooks 285
  Summary 286

CHAPTER 15: The GeoDex Application **287**

  Accessing the GeoDex Application 287
  The GeoDex Window 288
    Next 289
    Previous 289
    New 289
    Quick Dial 291
    GeoPlanner 292
  The Menu Bar 292
    Edit Menu 292
    View Menu 293
    Option 294
  Dialing a Phone Number 296
  Summary 296

Contents

CHAPTER 16: America Online **297**
America Online Installation 298
The Menu Bar 298
    Help Menu 299
    File Menu 299
    Edit Menu 305
    Go To Menu 305
    Mail Menu 314
    Members Menu 319
    Window Menu 321
Summary 322

CHAPTER 17: The GeoComm Application **323**
Accessing the GeoComm Application 324
File Menu 325
    Type from Text File 325
    Capture to Text File 327
    Send XMODEM 327
    Receive XMODEM 328
    Save Buffer 330
    Exit 330
Edit Menu 331
    Message 331
View Menu 333
    Small/Large Font 333
    Window Size 333
Options Menu 334
    Protocol Settings 335
    Terminal Settings 337
    Modem Settings 339
Dial Menu 341

Contents

    Scripts 341
    Quick Dial 346
    Hang Up 347
  Summary 347

CHAPTER 18: The Games Applications 349

  The Solitaire Application 350
  Game Menu 351
    Options Menu 351
    Card Layout 353
    Playing the Game 354
  The Tetris Application 355
    Moving Pieces 356
    Scoring 357
    Game Menu 358
    Options Menu 359
  Summary 362

CHAPTER 19: Spreadsheet Viewer 363

  Quattro Pro SE 365
  Spreadsheet Viewing 365
    Specifying a File from GeoManager 367
  Quattro Pro Viewer Menus 369
    File Menu 369
    Edit 372
    Options 374
    Fonts 381
    Sizes 381
    Help 381
    Window 381
  Summary 383

CHAPTER 20: The DOS Programs Application 385
   Accessing the DOS Programs Application 386
   The DOS Programs Window 386
      Options Menu 387
      Command Line Options...391
   Summary 394

INDEX..395

Introduction

GeoWorks Pro is an exciting new multitasking graphical environment for all IBM and compatible PCs. The GeoWorks applications all utilize the same user interface and they all can share information. GeoWorks Pro is completely compatible with MS-DOS 5.0 and it works with the task swapping feature. This allows you to switch between DOS programs.

GeoWorks Pro allows you to print with a PostScript printer (including Apple Laserwriter and QMS printers, and HP printers with PostScript cartridges). You also get a wide choice of dot-matrix printer drivers.

The GeoWorks Pro package supports networks such as Novell, LANtastic, LAN Manager, and PC-NFS 3.5. Therefore, you can use network drives in the same way you use your local hard disk. It is also possible to print on a network printer if you redirect your printer port (refer to your network manuals for details on setting up a network printer).

GeoWorks Pro has the flexibility to adjust to the user's level of expertise. The *Beginner Workspace* is friendly enough for novices to "get their feet wet" before going on to more advanced functions. In the *Intermediate Workspace*, you are able to work with many of the powerful Advanced applications, but with the convenience of template documents. These make it easy for the user to produce professional-looking results without spending hours practicing.

The *Advanced Workspace* is suited for the user who needs the power and convenience of integrated, graphical applications. Finally, the *DOS programs* facility lets you assign icons to all your favorite DOS programs.

When you first enter GeoWorks Pro, you are asked which of the four GeoWorks environments you wish to use: Beginner, Intermediate, Advanced, or DOS.

The Beginner Workspace contains basic versions of the GeoWorks programs, called *Appliances*. These are intended to acquaint the new user with GeoWorks Pro with a minimum of fuss. The programs in this area are remarkably simple to use, but still produce fine and satisfying results.

In the Intermediate section, you will find many applications to help you create documents, produce drawings, manage your schedule, and keep track of addresses among other things. Many of the documents in the Intermediate Workspace are what are called *templates*. These are models in which the formatting choices have been set; all you have to do is add your own material. This section also contains many other template documents to help you create such things as banners, business cards, and newsletters.

The Advanced Workspace provides a collection of applications that rival the power of stand-alone programs. It includes *GeoWrite*, a powerful word processor/desktop publisher with a "what-you-see-is-what-you-get" display, advanced font technology, sophisticated formatting capabilities, and the ability to insert graphics into your documents. *GeoDraw* is a versatile drawing package that allows you to create complex images, fuse and scale objects, rotate images, and scale images to any size. Among the other features are a calendar, address book, and file manager. The Advanced Workspace allows for multitasking—you can run as many applications at a time as you wish.

Lastly, DOS program mode allows you to easily exit GeoWorks Pro and load a DOS program by simply clicking a button. When you are ready to return, just exit the DOS program and you are returned to GeoWorks Pro exactly where you left it.

Furthermore, you can import items into GeoWorks Pro from the viewer. This gives you the ability to include any of these items in documents you write, and to transmit your data to others by modem and/or fax (if your computer has a modem and/or fax board or you have a fax machine).

About this Book

This book recreates the working environment of your computer screen by discussing each pull-down menu in the order in which it would be encountered. This allows you to view your screen and proceed through each application in order. Topics are addressed in the same sequence, and each command is discussed, menu by menu. A complete set of menu maps gives the user a graphic overview of the structure of GeoWorks Pro and the relationship between its applications and external programs.

Chapter 2 covers the use of the Beginner Workspace in detail. These programs are specifically designed for the novice user, and they are simplified versions of some of the applications found in the Advanced Workspace.

Chapter 3 describes the Intermediate Workspace and introduces the reader to some of the applications found in the Advanced Workspace.

Chapters 4 through 19 deal with the applications found in the Advanced Workspace. They cover each of the programs thoroughly, showing every menu and discussing the use of each command. All the special features found in the Advanced mode are described, as well as the interaction of the various programs.

Finally, Chapter 20 deals with DOS programs. You are shown how to assign icons to your DOS programs as well as how to create your own batch files without having to leave GeoWorks Pro.

For the beginning user, this book serves as a step-by-step guide to using the features of GeoWorks Pro. Each application is discussed in detail—what it does, how to use its features and how it relates to other GeoWorks Pro programs. This book explains the use and function of every command and provides easy-to-understand examples. The basic procedures, such as moving and resizing screens, selecting, copying, or moving objects, and working with multiple documents, are covered in detail.

The experienced computer user will find the book an easy way to become familiar with the fine points of the GeoWorks Pro Advanced applications. It also serves well as a handy reference for checking on specific commands. The format of the book makes finding specific information from any menu extremely simple.

Additional Information

When references are made to keys of the PC keyboard, such as Enter or Return, this book will use **Enter**. A key combination such as holding down the Alt key while pressing the F10 function key, will be indicated as **Alt-F10**. Other combinations, such as **Ctrl-Alt-Del** (which reboots your computer), means press and hold the Control key, press and hold the Alt key, and while holding down these two keys, press the Delete key.

Throughout the book there will be sections that require special attention. The following icons will be used to mark these sections:

NOTE — Indicates that you should take note of the information. This symbol may indicate a helpful hint or a special condition.

WARNING — Indicates cautionary information or warnings. This symbol often provides a warning that you may lose data if you incorrectly perform an action.

Chapter 1

Installing GeoWorks Pro

Before you can use GeoWorks Pro, you must install it on your hard drive using the GeoWorks Pro automated installation program. The installation program creates a subdirectory on your hard drive, copies files from the floppy disks, then steps you through configuring GeoWorks Pro for your computer system. During the installation and setup program you will need to:

- Tell GeoWorks Pro where to install the program files
- Decide whether GeoWorks Pro should modify two system files on your hard drive—the AUTOEXEC.BAT and CONFIG.SYS files—so they will work correctly with GeoWorks Pro
- Tell GeoWorks Pro what kind of monitor, mouse, and printer are connected to your computer.

NOTE GeoWorks Pro takes up more than 6MB of hard disk space. If you don't have this much room, you can still use GeoWorks Pro. You can take advantage of the Selective Install option to install only the parts of GeoWorks Pro you need.

The GeoWorks Pro package includes a set of installation disks. If you do not have all of the disks, contact the manufacturer. The automated installation procedure takes you through the installation steps and helps you make the necessary choices. The following steps describe the installation procedure.

1. Insert **Disk 1** into drive A: (or drive B:) and close the drive door.

2. Go to the drive A: DOS prompt, A> (or B: prompt, B>) by typing:
   A: (or B:).
   Press: **Enter**.
   At the DOS prompt, type SETUP.
   Press: **Enter**.
   The program displays an introductory screen saying that you will be asked to answer some questions about your computer.

3. Press: **Enter** to continue.
   In this and all other steps, pressing **Esc** takes you back to the previous screen; pressing **F3** takes you back to the DOS prompt.

4. Press: **Enter** to continue.
   The program displays a notice stating SETUP will install GeoWorks Pro in the drive and directory shown **(C:\GEOWORKS)**. To accept the default drive and directory—also called the path,
   Press: **Enter**.
   If you want to install GeoWorks on a different drive (for example, drive D:) or in a different subdirectory (for example, \GE),
   Press: **Backspace** to delete as much of the path as necessary. Type the new path.
   Press: **Enter** to accept the new path.

5. The program displays a screen similar to that shown in Figure 1.1.

Installing GeoWorks Pro • **3**

```
                    G E O W O R K S      P R O      S E T U P
GeoWorks Pro, with all its applications, sample documents, clip art, and
outline fonts, takes up a lot of hard disk space.  You can, however, save space
by leaving certain parts out during the installation process
(although you won't get to use those items when you run GeoWorks Pro).

Choose one of the options listed below to learn more about and install that
configuration of Pro on your hard disk. Should you decide to install a
different configuration, press ESC to return to this screen. Note that
in addition to the sizes listed below, Pro requires 0.5 Meg of free space
on your hard disk for working files.

Options:
     Standard Install (needs 6.5 Meg)
     Minimal Install  (needs 4 Meg)



     Press ENTER if the highlighted answer is OK.
     Press ESC to return to the previous screen.
     Press the UP and DOWN arrows to change the answer.
     Press F3 to quit the installation program.
```

Figure 1.1. Message Screen for Choosing Installation Size Option.

This tells you that GeoWorks Pro takes up a lot of hard disk space and informs you that you don't have to install all parts of the program. You are asked to choose either:

- Standard Install (6.5 Meg)
- Minimal Install (4 Meg)

(In fact, you will need half a meg (.5MB) more than stated in the message, 7MB and 4.5MB respectively, because GeoWorks Pro needs .5MB to work with while it is running.)
Select the one you want. Press: **Enter**.
If you selected Minimal Install, you see a screen that recommends you do a Standard Install because you can always delete the parts you don't need later. The rest of this chapter describes the Standard Installation.
If you select the Standard Installation, and press **Enter**, the message shown in Figure 1.2 is displayed.
Press: **Enter** to continue.

6. The installation program displays a screen similar to Figure 1.3 asking if you want to be able to start GeoWorks Pro from any DOS prompt.

If you want this, GeoWorks Pro must add a statement to your computer's AUTOEXEC.BAT file.
Press: **Enter** to select Yes. GeoWorks Pro modifies the AUTOEXEC.BAT file.
If you do not want GeoWorks Pro to modify the AUTOEXEC.BAT file:
Press: **RightArrow** to highlight **No**.
Press: **Enter**.

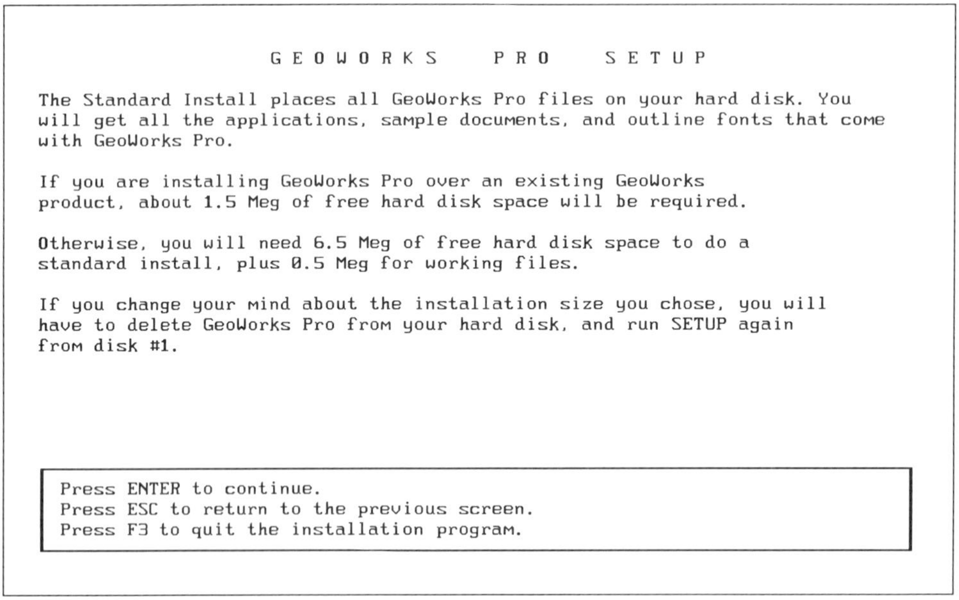

```
                   G E O W O R K S    P R O    S E T U P

The Standard Install places all GeoWorks Pro files on your hard disk. You
will get all the applications, sample documents, and outline fonts that come
with GeoWorks Pro.

If you are installing GeoWorks Pro over an existing GeoWorks
product, about 1.5 Meg of free hard disk space will be required.

Otherwise, you will need 6.5 Meg of free hard disk space to do a
standard install, plus 0.5 Meg for working files.

If you change your mind about the installation size you chose, you will
have to delete GeoWorks Pro from your hard disk, and run SETUP again
from disk #1.




  Press ENTER to continue.
  Press ESC to return to the previous screen.
  Press F3 to quit the installation program.
```

Figure 1.2. Message Screen for Standard Installation Option.

7. Press: **Enter** to start the installation. A notice is displayed indicating that you have chosen to be able to start GeoWorks Pro from any directory.
   Type: GEOS
   Press: **Enter**.

8. GeoWorks Pro begins copying the first disk to the drive and directory you specified. The program keeps you informed of the progress of the procedure and displays a notice, similar to that in Figure 1.4, when you need to insert the next disk.

```
                    G E O W O R K S    P R O    S E T U P
  Would you like to be able to start GeoWorks Pro no matter
  what directory you are currently working in?

  If you say "Yes", the path in your AUTOEXEC.BAT file will be changed
  to contain C:\GEOWORKS.  A copy of the original file will be
  kept in C:\GEOWORKS\SYSTEM\AUTOEXEC.OLD.

  Changes to the AUTOEXEC.BAT file don't take effect until the next
  time you restart your machine.

  Options:
     Yes
     No



     ┌─────────────────────────────────────────────────────────┐
     │ Press ENTER if the highlighted answer is OK.            │
     │ Press ESC to return to the previous screen.             │
     │ Press the UP and DOWN arrows to change the answer.      │
     │ Press F3 to quit the installation program.              │
     └─────────────────────────────────────────────────────────┘
```

Figure 1.3. Message Screen for Adding GeoWorks Pro to the AUTOEXEC.BAT File.

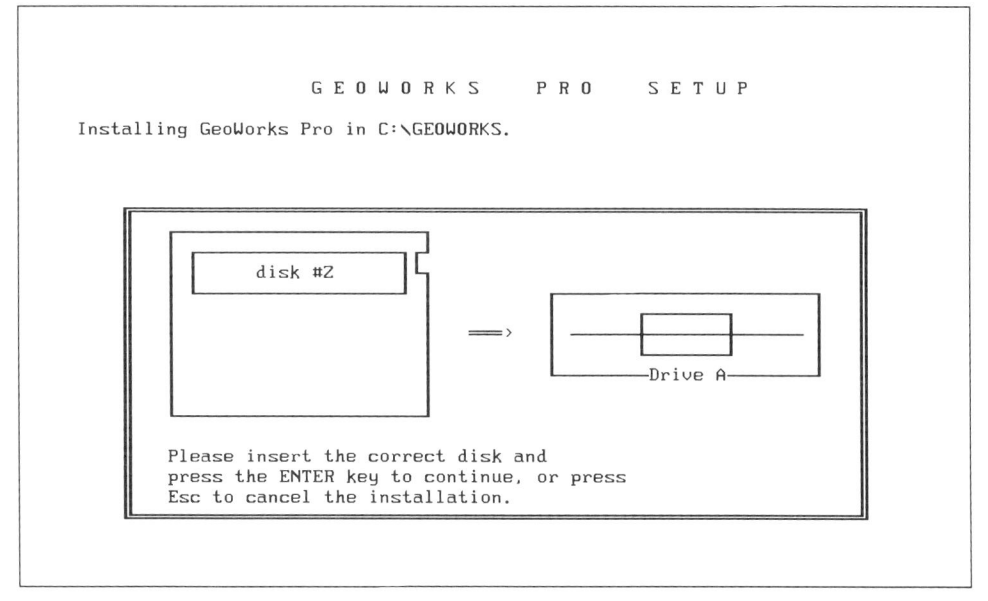

```
                    G E O W O R K S    P R O    S E T U P
  Installing GeoWorks Pro in C:\GEOWORKS.




                ┌──────────────────┐
                │  ┌────────────┐  │
                │  │  disk #2   │  │         ┌─────────────────────┐
                │  └────────────┘  │         │                     │
                │                  │   ═>    │   ┌───────────┐     │
                │                  │         │───┤           ├─────│
                │                  │         │   └───────────┘     │
                │                  │         │         Drive A     │
                │                  │         └─────────────────────┘
                │                  │
                │ Please insert the correct disk and
                │ press the ENTER key to continue, or press
                │ Esc to cancel the installation.
                └──────────────────────────────────────────┘
```

Figure 1.4. Insert Next Disk Screen.

9. Insert the next disk.
   Press: **Enter** to continue.
   After all the disks have been copied, the program flashes an Installation Complete message. Remove the disk from the floppy drive. You now have a choice.

   - You can press **Enter** to continue.
   - You can press **F3** to return to the DOS prompt.

Configuring GeoWorks Pro

If you press **Enter**, you see a notice stating that on the next few screens you will verify that your display, mouse, and printer work properly with GeoWorks Pro.

Selecting the Monitor

The Setup program displays the *monitor* (video display device) it senses is connected to your computer. To accept this choice for your monitor, press **Enter**. A test screen with four arrows at the corners is displayed. These arrows should be sharp and clear. If not, you need to select a different monitor.

If you do not want to accept the SETUP choice, or if the test screen is not sharp, press **F10** to make another choice.

Selecting a Different Monitor

If you press **F10**, the Setup program displays a list of monitor choices. Use the **UpArrow** and **DownArrow** or **PgUp** and **PgDn** keys to scroll through the list. When your choice is highlighted, press **Enter** to select it.

You can move quickly through the list by typing the first letter of your selection. The highlight bar jumps to the first name beginning with this letter. This can be repeated as necessary until your selection is highlighted. Once highlighted, you can select it by pressing **Enter**.

When you select a different monitor, the next screen states that GeoWorks Pro must be restarted before it can use the new monitor. After you restart, the program returns you to the test screen with the four arrows. If you cannot see the arrows clearly, press **F10**. GeoWorks Pro reloads the original monitor. Select another monitor, restart the program and check your selection. When you are satisfied with the appearance of the test screen, press **Enter** to continue.

Selecting the Mouse

Now you can specify your mouse type. The program displays a list of choices with the default choice, No Idea, highlighted. Select the default if you do not know the type mouse you have, or scroll through the list to highlight your choice. To select your highlighted choice, press **Enter**.

If you have named a mouse, the next screen shows the type of mouse you selected (serial or parallel) and prompts you for the port to which it is connected. The available ports are shown with the most likely port highlighted. If you aren't sure which port is correct, press **Enter** to accept the default. Otherwise, highlight your selection, then press **Enter**.

The program displays a mouse test window. Move the mouse cursor (which looks like an arrow) to the test box. Click (press and release) the left mouse button. If the mouse type and port are selected correctly, a beep sounds and the test box flashes. If not (or if no mouse cursor appears), you may have:

- Selected the wrong mouse from the list. Press **F10** to make a new choice
- Chosen the wrong port. Press **Esc** to change your selection
- Selected No Idea when asked which kind of mouse you have, and the default mouse settings do not work. If you know your mouse software is already installed and the mouse works correctly with other software, read your mouse software documentation to determine the correct selection. Then press **F10** to make the change.

If you have not installed the mouse software yet, press **F3** to go to the DOS prompt. Install the mouse driver (software). To return to the Setup program:

Type: `GEOS`

Press: **Enter**.

Selecting the Printer

The next screen prompts you to specify your printer type. Scroll through the displayed list to highlight your printer type (or highlight None, if appropriate). Press **Enter** to select your choice. If you select None, the Setup is complete. If you specify a printer, the program displays a list of serial and parallel ports. Highlight the one to which your printer is connected, then press **Enter**.

The program displays the printer test window. Turn on your printer. Click the mouse button in the test box. If the printer type and port are set correctly, you will print a test page. If nothing prints, you may have chosen the wrong port. Press **Esc** to choose a different port. If you printed a test page but it doesn't look right, you may have specified the wrong printer model. Press **F10** to select the correct model from the list.

When the test is successful, press **Enter** to continue.

You have successfully configured GeoWorks Pro for your computer. Congratulations!

Entering Your Serial Number

You are now asked to type your 16-digit serial number (see your Customer Support Handbook). After you type the number, highlight OK and press **Enter**. GeoWorks Pro displays the main screen. If you do not want to enter the number at this time, you can highlight Enter Later and press **Enter** to begin the GeoWorks Pro program.

Summary

In Chapter 1 you learned how to install GeoWorks Pro on your hard drive and how to configure the program for your computer. You are now ready to begin working. In the next chapter you will learn how to navigate in the program and use the appliances.

Chapter 2

The Beginner Workspace— The Appliances

GeoWorks Pro offers six handy, easy-to-use applications in the Beginner Workspace. These are called *appliances*. Appliances are simplified versions of programs in the Advanced Workspace. Use the appliances to get acquainted with GeoWorks Pro: make notes (*Notepad*), plan your schedule (*Planner*), organize names and addresses (*Address Book*), do quick calculations (*Calculator*), create large banners (*Banner*), and play a challenging game in your free time (*Solitaire*). As you use them, you will become familiar with moving around the screen and performing basic operations.

This chapter describes:

- How to start GeoWorks Pro from the DOS prompt
- How to use the six items included in the Appliances section
- How to move around the program using the mouse.

Running GeoWorks Pro

To start GeoWorks Pro from the C:> DOS prompt:

> Type: `GEOS`
> Press: **Enter**.

If you get the message "Bad command or file name", the GeoWorks subdirectory may not be in your AUTOEXEC.BAT file path statement. Change your default subdirectory to the subdirectory in which you installed GeoWorks Pro:

> Type: `CD \GEOWORKS`
> Press: **Enter**.

If you specified a different subdirectory during the installation, then use the subdirectory you specified.

Then run GeoWorks Pro by typing the run command:

> `GEOS`
> Press: **Enter**.

The GeoWorks Pro program displays the Welcome screen.

Welcome Basics

From the Welcome screen you can directly access EXIT, HELP, the Beginner, Intermediate, or Advanced Workspaces, and DOS Programs. The last four items are the main work areas of the program.

At the top left of the Welcome screen is the EXIT button, one of the ways you can exit the program. Selecting the EXIT button displays a prompt asking if you really want to leave GeoWorks Pro. Selecting Yes returns you to the DOS prompt. Selecting No returns you to the Welcome screen.

At the top right of the Welcome screen is the HELP button. Selecting the HELP button displays help screens that briefly describe features or operations—a quick way to refresh your memory.

The center portion of the Welcome screen displays four panels: Beginner, Intermediate, Advanced, and below these, DOS Programs. Clicking on a panel accesses the features within the program area. For example, clicking on the Beginner panel selects it and displays the screen shown in Figure 2.1.

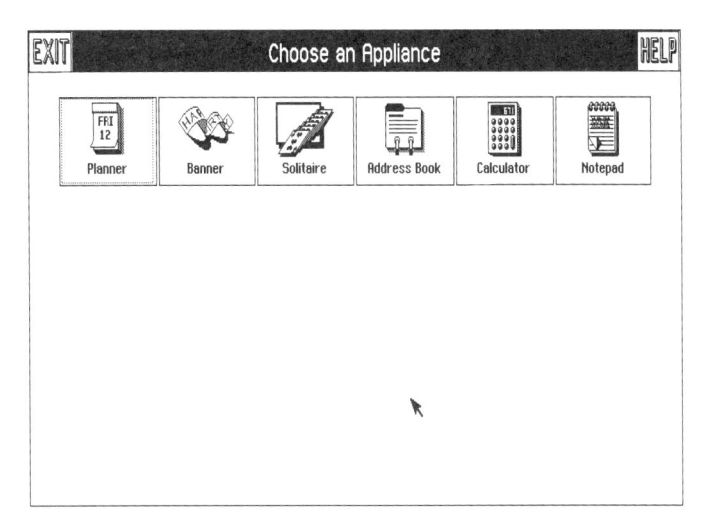

Figure 2.1. The Choose an Appliance Screen in the Beginner Workspace.

From the Beginner screen you can access the EXIT and HELP buttons, and the six applications (appliances): Planner, Address Book, Banner, Solitaire, Calculator, and Notepad.

Moving Around in GeoWorks Pro

Except when entering text from the keyboard, you can use a mouse for all operations in GeoWorks Pro. In the Beginner Workspace you can use the mouse to select appliances, access help screens, use the features of an appliance, cut, copy and move text, and exit the appliance. You can use the mouse in the same way to move about in the Intermediate and Advanced Workspaces and the DOS Programs sections of GeoWorks Pro.

Icons

An icon is a small picture that represents something you can work with, such as a file, a directory, or an appliance.

Mouse Pointers

As you move the mouse around the screen you see a pointer that corresponds to the motion of the mouse. Depending on what is occurring, the pointer takes one of four shapes:

Arrow Pointer

The normal mouse pointer.

Hourglass Pointer

It indicates that an operation is in progress and you must wait for the operation to complete.

Circle/Slash Pointer

If you move the pointer outside the active area of the screen, the pointer changes to this shape.

I-beam Pointer

It indicates the position of the text cursor for entering text from the keyboard.

Mouse Buttons

You perform actions with the left and right mouse buttons. Use the left button for most functions; if a button is not specified, use the left one. Use the right mouse button to move things around on the screen in a procedure called *direct manipulation*. This book always notes that the right mouse button is required whenever it is needed for an operation.

Pointing and Clicking

To select an item, move the mouse pointer around the screen until it is on the item you want, for example, an icon, a selection button, or a menu option, then press and release (click) the left button. The selected item is highlighted.

Multiple Clicking

Items such as appliance icons require a second click to execute the option. You can select and execute an item in one step by double-clicking. Position the pointer on the item and then rapidly press and release the left button twice. It may take a little practice, but once you master this, you can go on to triple-clicking, quadruple-clicking, and even quintuple-clicking. (You will use these multiple clicks to select text in the Advanced Workspace Applications. See Chapter 4.)

Dragging

Pressing and holding a mouse button while moving the mouse at the same time is called *dragging*. Drag while pressing the left mouse button to highlight text in the appliances and to move and resize windows. If you press and hold the right mouse button when dragging, you can move items around on the screen. Often you can also do this with the left mouse button.

Scrolling

Use scroll bars when the contents of a window are wider or longer than the window itself. A window has two scroll bars: a vertical one at the right and a horizontal one at the bottom. If you move the mouse pointer to one of the end arrows on a scroll bar and click on it, the window information moves in small steps in the opposite direction of the arrow.

For example, when you click on a down arrow button, the window text scrolls up, revealing text that was below the window. When you click on a left arrow button, the window text scrolls to the right, revealing text that was to the left of the window.

In text documents, the document scrolls one line or column at a time. With other items, each click moves the display a specific amount. To scroll continuously, press and hold the mouse button on one of the end arrows.

To scroll one complete window at a time, move the pointer to the dark area of a scroll bar (the paging area) and click. To scroll continuously one window at a time, press and hold the mouse button on the paging area.

To scroll to a specific location, move the pointer to the light-colored section of a scroll bar (the slider). This area indicates the location of the part of the document currently visible in the window, relative to the entire document. Press and hold the mouse button and drag the slider to the desired position on the bar, scrolling the document. Continue until you reach the part of the document you want to see.

Selecting

Often when you want to work with something such as a file, directory, graphic or other item, you will first have to *select* it. You can tell when an item is selected because it is highlighted on the screen. Some objects display *handles* when selected. **Handles** are small rectangles in the corners and centers of sides of selected objects (see Chapter 10, "The GeoDraw Application"). Text can also be selected (see Chapter 7, "The GeoWrite Application").

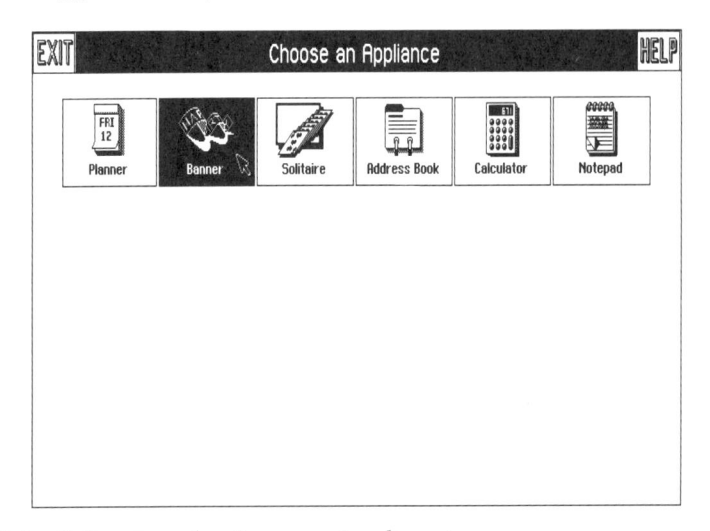

Figure 2.2. Selecting the Banner Application.

Although different applications have different ways of highlighting an item, the most common way is to reverse the colors (white becomes black). In any case, it will always be easy to tell when something has been selected. Figure 2.2 shows the Banner button being selected. Notice the reversed colors of this button.

NOTE The difference between an appliance button and an icon is that when you click (i.e., single-click) an appliance button, it is selected and opens the appliance immediately. When you click an icon, it is selected. You must then click the selected icon to open whatever it represents (you can use the shortcut of double-clicking to do both at once).

Using the Appliances

At the Choose an Appliance window (Figure 2.1 and 2.2), click on one of the six appliance buttons to select the appliance you want to run. For help using the active appliance, click on the **HELP** button. To quit the appliance and return to the Choose an Appliance window, click on the **EXIT** button.

Select **Exit** from the Choose an Appliance window to return to the Welcome window.

Planner

Select the Planner button from the Choose an Appliance window to display the screen shown in Figure 2.3. Planner is a combination desk calendar and date book.

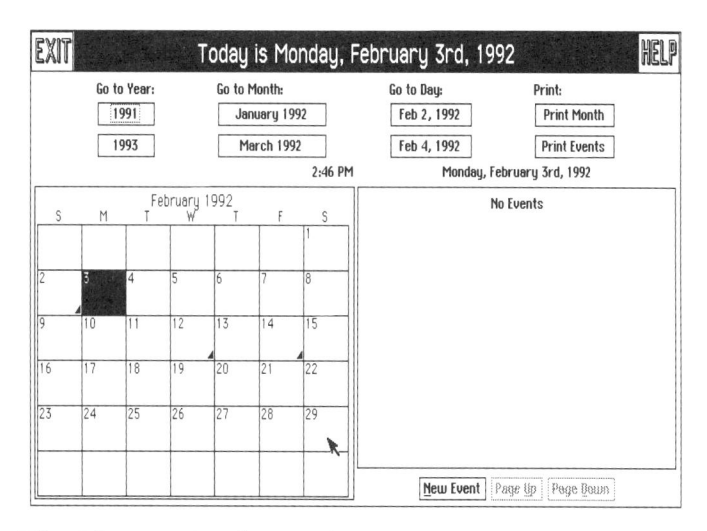

Figure 2.3. The Planner Appliance Screen.

The Planner Screen

At the top of the screen Planner displays the current day of the week and date. To the left is a calendar page for a whole month. Each time you activate Planner it displays the current month with the current day highlighted. Above the calendar is the current time. The right panel contains any scheduled events for the highlighted day. Above the events panel is the day and date corresponding to the highlighted day in the calendar. Above the calendar and events list are four items: Go to Year, Go to Month, Go to Day, and Print.

Go to Year	The two **Go to Year** buttons display the year preceding and the year following the currently displayed year. For example, if the displayed year is 1995, the top button would read 1994 and the bottom button would read 1996. Click on a year button to change the calendar display to the selected year.

Go to Month/Day	The Month and Day items work the same way. For example, each click on the **Next Day** button advances it one day. The day highlighted on the calendar page changes accordingly (although the current day remains outlined until you move to another month). Click on the preceding or following month buttons to change the displayed month.

Print	This option offers you two choices: you can print a monthly calendar or a schedule.

Events	At the bottom of the screen is the **New Event** button. Click on this button to enter a time block in the events panel. You can change the default time of 8:00 a.m. by typing the time you want. To enter a note about the event, use the mouse to move the text cursor (I-beam pointer) to the right of the time and type the note.
You can keep entering time blocks by clicking the New Event button, changing the times to suit your schedule. When you have more than one page of events, the **Page Up** and **Page Down** buttons become active. Click on these to scroll your schedule.

You can make entries for any date(s) you want by clicking the Go to Year, Month and Day buttons until you have the date you want. A small triangle in the lower right corner of a day's box on the calendar indicates a scheduled event. Clicking on that day in the calendar brings up its list of events.

Click on the **EXIT** button to return to the Choose an Appliance screen.

Address Book

Select Address Book from the Choose an Appliance window to display the screen shown in Figure 2.4.

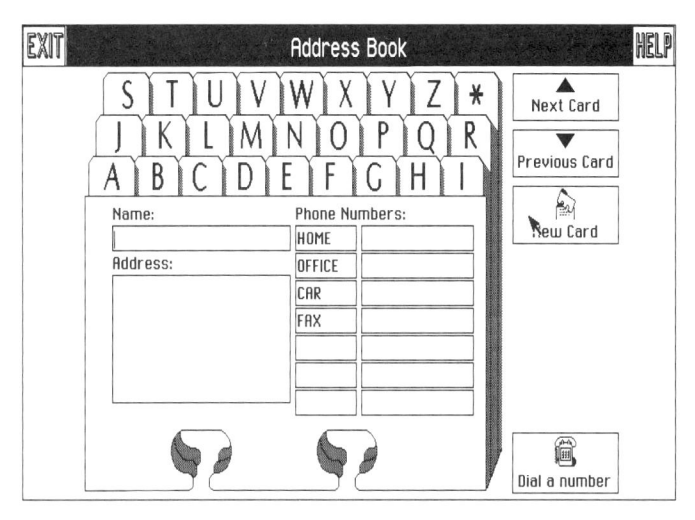

Figure 2.4. The Address Book Screen.

The Address Book is similar to a card file with a separate card for each name and address, sorted alphabetically by the first word in the name box. If you want to sort alphabetically by last names, type the last name first in the name box.

Beneath the name is the address box. To the right of the address is a box for entering phone numbers—you can include home, office, car, and fax numbers. You can create other phone number categories by entering them in a blank phone box.

Click on a letter at the top of the Address Book window to bring up the first card sorted by that letter. Flip backward or forward through the cards by clicking on the **Next Card** and **Previous Card** buttons at the far right of the window.

You can create a new card by clicking on the **New Card** button. Enter the information you want and the new card becomes part of the card file. If you have a modem connected to your computer, you can dial the currently displayed phone number on the selected card by clicking the **Dial a Number** button. For a detailed discussion of Address Book features, see Chapter 15, "The GeoDex Application."

Click on the EXIT button to return to the Choose an Appliance screen.

Banner

Select the Banner appliance from the Choose an Appliance window to display the screen shown in Figure 2.5.

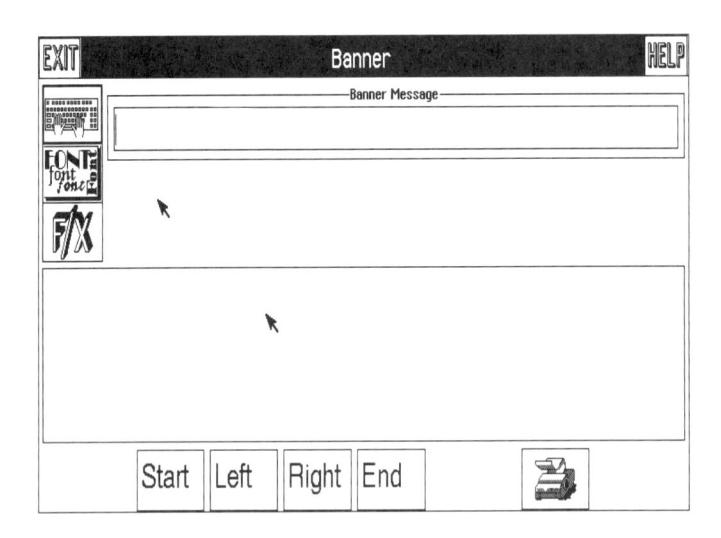

Figure 2.5. The Banner Screen.

With this appliance you can create banners up to 100 feet long with a choice of nine fonts, four text styles, five special effects, and four border styles.

Begin typing in the banner text window at the blinking text cursor. As you type, the text is also displayed in the bottom portion of the window as it will appear in print. Note that each square in this display represents an 8 1/2 x 11–inch page. The dots at the top and bottom represent the line feed holes in the paper and do not appear in the banner printout. Figure 2.6 illustrates how the window appears as you create a banner.

If you choose double-height letters from the F/X menu box, each letter occupies two boxes (or pieces of paper) as shown in Figure 2.7.

Figure 2.6. Typing Banner Text.

When you are finished entering the text, you are ready to select the font type and size you want for your banner text. At the top left of the Banner window are three icons: Type, Font, and F/X.

Type After you have created a banner and selected a font, you may want to view the line as it will appear. However, the actual banner text will be too large to see the whole line. You can click on the **Type** icon (a keyboard with hands) in the upper-left corner to view a lot more of the text. It will appear in the top box in the font you selected (special effects won't be shown on this line).

Font Click on the **Font** icon in the upper-left corner to display a box containing nine font choices. Click the font you want to try. The banner text at the bottom changes to reflect your choice. Keep trying fonts until you see one you like. Now you are ready to select the special effects you want on your banner.

F/X Click on the **F/X** icon to display a box with three columns of choices, as shown in Figure 2.7. You can select any or all of the items in the left column:

Bold, Italic, Underline, or Double Height letters. You can choose only one option at a time from the middle column: No Effect, Small Shadow, Large Shadow, Fog, or 3D Effect. You can choose only one option at a time from the right column: No Border, Thin Border, Thick Border, or Double Border. The banner text display changes with the effects you choose.

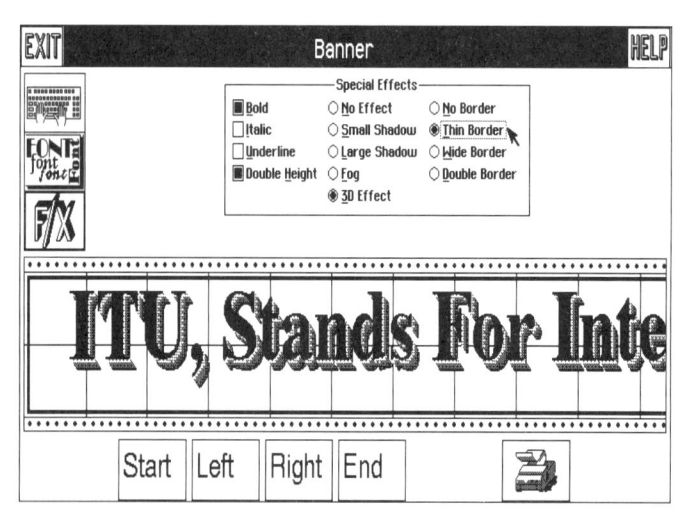

Figure 2.7. Typing a Double-Height Banner.

Moving Around the Banner

At the bottom of your screen are four direction buttons you use to view banner text too long to fit on the screen. To see the Start or End of the text, click on those buttons. Click on the Right or Left button to scroll the banner text.

Printing the Banner

At the bottom right of the appliance window is a **Print** icon. Click this to print the banner.

Click on the EXIT button to return to the Choose an Appliance screen.

Solitaire

If you're looking for a bit of diversion, select Solitaire from the Choose an Appliance window to play the solitaire game Klondike. Unfortunately, it does not let you cheat; otherwise, play it using the standard game rules. When you select a card to move, the program displays all the acceptable destination cards in reverse video. You cannot move a card if there is no appropriate destination. See Chapter 18 for more on the Solitaire appliance.

Click on the EXIT button to return to the Choose an Appliance screen.

Calculator

Select Calculator from the Choose an Appliance window to display the screen shown in Figure 2.8.

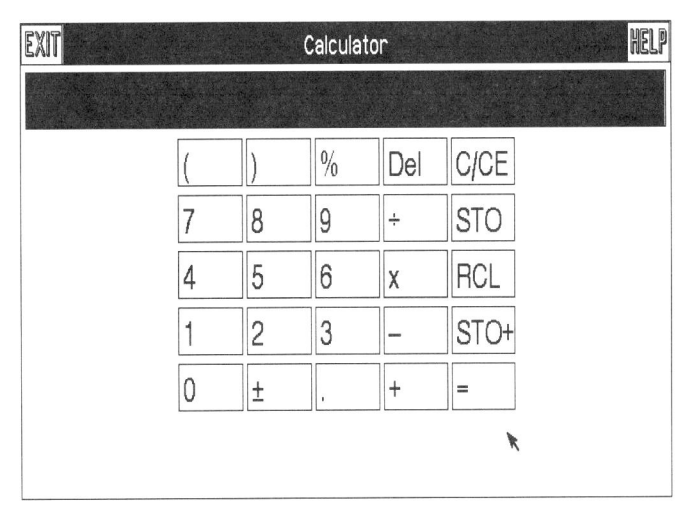

Figure 2.8. The Calculator Screen.

This appliance is a handy on-screen calculator that performs standard computations. For example, suppose you want to multiply 5 by 3. Click on the **5** button to enter that number. Next, click on the **x** (times) button. Then click on the **3** button. Finally, click on the = (equals) button for the answer.

To store the displayed number, overwriting any previously stored value, click the **STO** button. Click the **STO+** button if you want to add the displayed number to the stored value. Clicking the **RCL** button recalls (displays) the stored value.

To subtract a number from the stored value, you must change the number (to be subtracted) into a negative, using the ± button. Then use **STO+** to add the negative number to the stored value. Adding a negative to a positive is the same as subtracting.

Clicking the **DEL** button removes digits from a displayed number one digit at a time. Clicking the **%** button divides the displayed number by 100.

Clicking the **C/CE** button clears the displayed number. To clear the storage memory, click **0** (zero) and then click **STO** (stores zero).

You can perform an operation such as 5x(3+4), by using the parentheses (and) buttons. Try it yourself:

1. Click **5**
2. Click **x**
3. Click **(**
4. Click **3**
5. Click **+**
6. Click **4**
7. Click **)**
8. Click **=**

Your answer should be 35. For a more detailed discussion of the Calculator see Chapter 12.

Click on the EXIT button to return to the Choose an Appliance screen.

Notepad

Select Notepad from the Choose an Appliance screen to display the screen shown in Figure 2.9. Use Notepad to save, recall, and print notes.

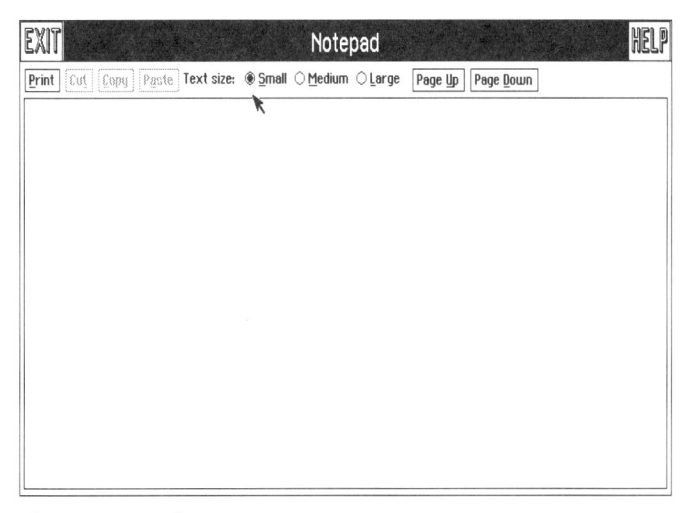

Figure 2.9. The Notepad Screen.

The program automatically displays the last note saved on the Notepad.

Entering Text in a Note

Enter text by typing it in the note area. Text wraps automatically to the next line as you type. Press Enter only when you want to begin a new paragraph. Use Backspace to delete the character to the left of the cursor, or Del to delete the character on the right. You can remove a block of text by using Cut (see below).

The blinking I-beam pointer (text cursor) indicates where the next character will be placed. To reposition the text cursor, move the mouse cursor to the new location, then click the left mouse button. Notes longer than one page activate the scroll bar buttons.

Printing a Note

Click the print button in the upper-left corner of the appliance window to print your note.

Using Cut, Copy, and Paste

You can cut text out of the note, copy text, and paste it where you want. Select the text to cut or copy by pressing and holding the left mouse button on the first character of the text, then dragging the mouse cursor to the last character you want to include. Release the button. The selected text is highlighted.

Click on the **Cut** or **Copy** button in the edit box at the top of the window. Cut removes the selected text from the Notepad and moves it to the clipboard. Copy puts a copy of the selected text on the clipboard. Position the mouse cursor where you want to insert the text now on the clipboard and click the left mouse button. Select **Paste** in the edit box to move the clipboard text to the text cursor location.

Changing Text Size

You can change the size of the letters in the note display window by clicking one of the Text Size buttons: **Small**, **Medium**, or **Large**. Changing the display, however, does not affect the size of the characters printed in the note.

Summary

In Chapter 2 you learned how to move around the GeoWorks Pro program, and how to use the six applications in the Beginner Workspace.

Chapter 3

The Intermediate Workspace

The *Intermediate Workspace* has more capabilities than the Beginner Workspace. It not only contains more applications, but also has menus that allow you to make choices and tailor output exactly as you want it. Many of the applications are in the form of *template documents*. These make your job easy; the formatting has been done so you can produce a professional-looking document by just adding your text (and graphics if you want).

This chapter describes:

- The Intermediate Workspace and how to move around it
- The File Cabinet and all the file management functions it can perform
- Menu bars and how to work with them
- The creation of a sample document and the use of GeoWorks Pro's template documents.

Getting Started in Workspaces

When you first start GeoWorks Pro, you enter the Welcome screen. From there, click on the **Intermediate** button to display the main window of the Intermediate Workspace, called the File Cabinet.

Windows

In GeoWorks Pro, *windows* are rectangular areas of the screen in which information is displayed. In the Intermediate Workspace, these windows fill the screen, unlike in the Advanced Workspace, where you can change the size and overlap windows.

Icons

The center of the File Cabinet window contains icons representing directories and files. *Directory icons* are pictures of manila folders; *file icons* are pictures of a stack of papers.

There is a minor difference between a button and an icon. You click on a button only once to select the item. You must *double-click* on an icon to select the item. So when we refer to clicking on an icon, this means you must double-click on it to select it.

Dialog Boxes

Sometimes GeoWorks Pro may need more information or alerts you that there is a problem. Such displays are called *dialog box*es. Some of these can be kept open and you can switch between them if you want. Others require you to respond before you can continue. Figure 3.1 illustrates a typical dialog box.

Moving Around the Intermediate Workspace

See Chapter 2 for a basic discussion about using the mouse in GeoWorks Pro. In the Intermediate Workspace you use the mouse to select the directories and files with which you want to work, to scroll displays that are bigger than one screenful, and to access the buttons that surround the main display.

The ways of selecting (and deselecting) items using the mouse are described below:

Click Item Selection

To select an icon, move the mouse cursor to that icon and click on it. The icon is highlighted to indicate it is selected. If you then position the mouse pointer over another object and click, the second object becomes selected and the first object becomes deselected.

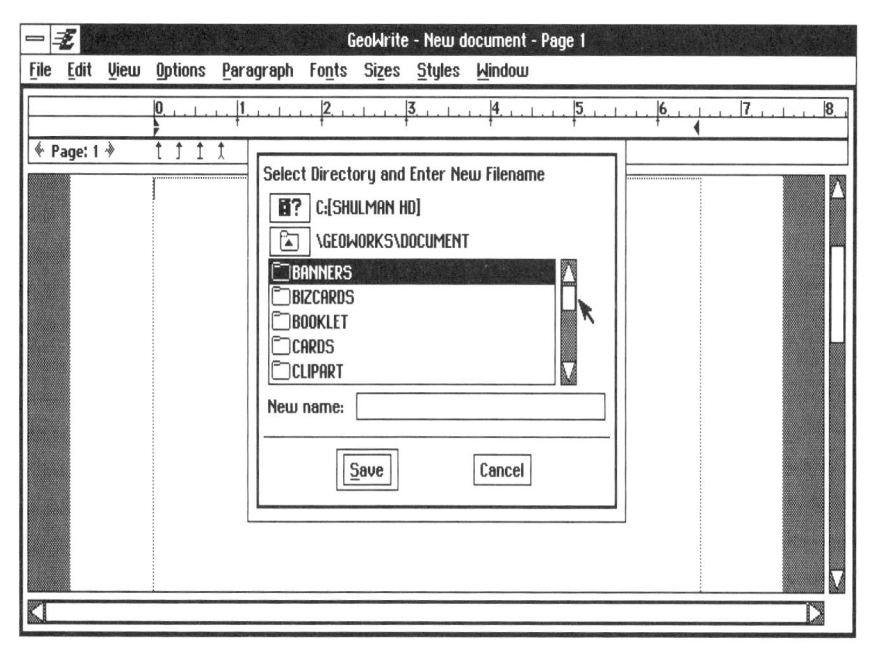

Figure 3.1. A Typical Dialog Box.

If you want to deselect an item without selecting another one, you can click on the empty space outside the icon.

A handy way to select more than one object by clicking is to hold down **Ctrl** while clicking the mouse button. When you release **Ctrl**, the object is added to the selection group. Repeat for each object you want to include. This is especially useful if the objects are not near each other.

NOTE

If you have a group of items selected and you want to remove individual objects from the group, you can move the mouse pointer to the object. Press and hold **Ctrl** and click the mouse button. That individual object is now unselected.

Drag Item Selection

You can also select several icons at once by *dragging to* highlight. As you look at the File Cabinet window, imagine a rectangle large enough to cover the objects you want to select. Position the mouse pointer at one corner of the imaginary rectangle.

Click and hold the left mouse button while dragging diagonally to the opposite corner of the imaginary rectangle. As you drag, a dotted selection box circumscribes the dimensions you set. When the dotted selection box surrounds all the objects you want to select, release the button. If you miss an object, you can repeat the process, or use the Ctrl-click method to add the item to the group.

In some applications, the selected object is displayed with handles. *Handles* are small rectangles in the corners and at the center of each side of the object. These handles are used to resize the object.

File Cabinet Window

The File Cabinet window is shown in Figure 3.2. You perform document tasks (e.g., opening and closing files and directories and formatting disks) in this window. It consists of a main center area where all the directories and files are displayed as icons. Above and below this area are rows of buttons that allow you to perform a variety of management tasks. The line directly under the top row of buttons displays information about the current status.

In general, the top and bottom buttons require you to first choose something from the center area of the window. The following discusses the center area of the window:

The File Cabinet Icons Display

The center area of the window contains icons representing all the directories and files with which you can work.

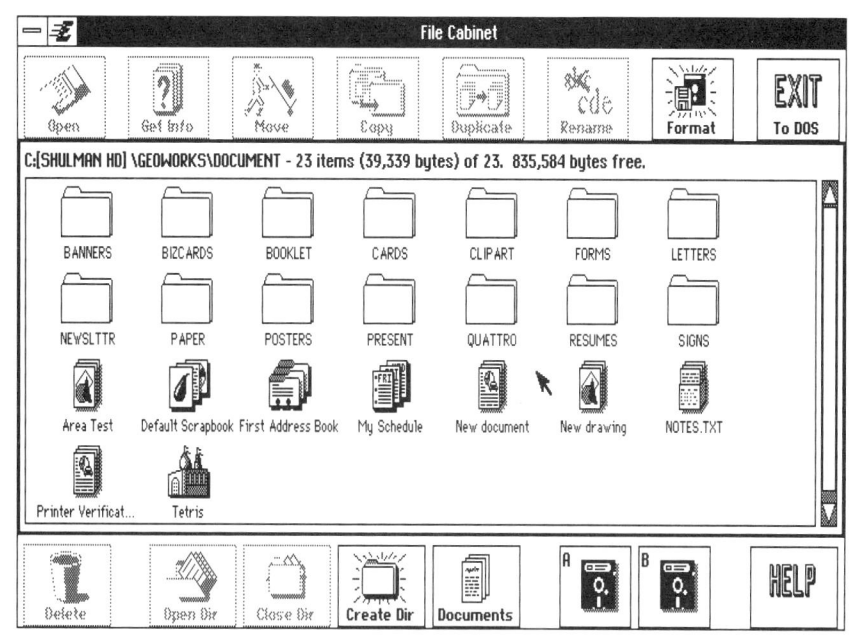

Figure 3.2. The File Cabinet Window.

Directories

Initially there are 14 directory icons (manila folders) in the Intermediate Workspace. If you create others they will also appear here. Each directory contains several files, usually template documents that can help you produce professional-looking results. For example, the CARDS directory contains files to help you make a variety of greeting cards. When you open this directory, you see these files, as shown in Figure 3.3.

Some of the template documents in the CARDS directory have already been finished—all you have to do is add your own touches. Others are *blank templates*, i.e., blank areas where the formatting has been done so your text and graphics will fit onto a card. You are free to be as creative with the contents as you want.

When you select one of these files, you will see a message like the one in Figure 3.4 telling you that it is a *Read-Only* template document. You must save it with a different name if you want to change it for your use.

30 • *Teach Yourself GeoWorks Pro*

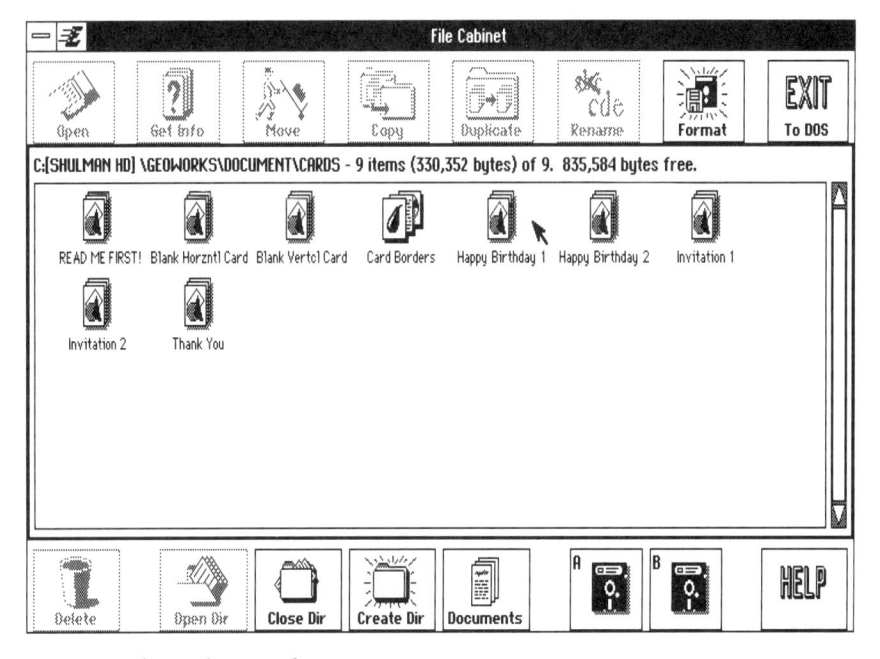

Figure 3.3. The Files in the CARDS Directory.

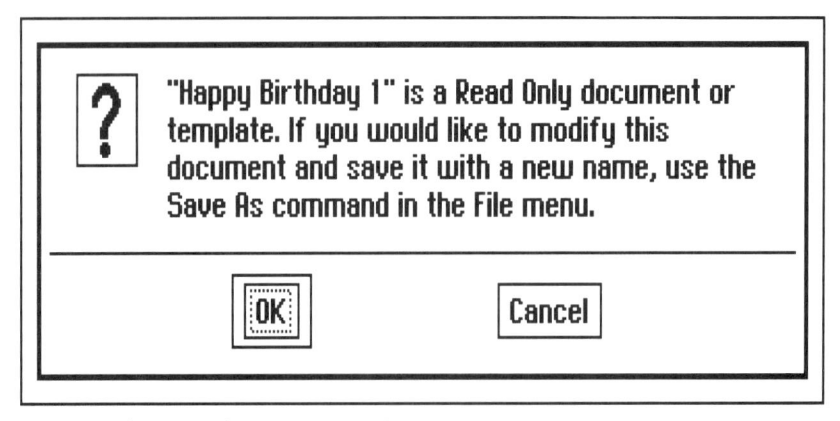

Figure 3.4. The Read-Only Template Screen.

If you click **OK** to indicate you want to use the template, you go to an application (program) to make your changes. This includes changing the text, selecting different fonts and type sizes, adding graphics, and many other things. The application you end up in will depend on the type of template document you are using. For example, selecting a template for making banners places you in the GeoDraw screen, while a newsletter template places you in the GeoWrite screen.

Files

The next group of icons in the center section of the File Cabinet represents files (documents). Each of these icons is represented by a picture of a small stack of paper. Most of the stacks represent GEOS files. Icon symbols help you distinguish between types of files. The filename is shown beneath each icon. GEOS files can have up to 32 characters (counting spaces and punctuation).

If you look closely, you can see that one of the icons shows the papers in a box labeled DOS. The name, NOTES.TXT, appears below it. Notice that this name has a different format than the others. DOS filenames must conform to the standard DOS naming conventions:

- The filename cannot be more than eight characters long
- A period separates the filename from the extension
- The extension is optional and can have up to three characters.

There are nine files in the window (unless you have created others). Many of these file icons represent applications that you start when you open that document. These applications are the same as those in the Advanced Workspace. You will find a discussion of each these applications in the appropriate Advanced Workspace chapters.

There are icons representing the Scrapbook, GeoDex Address Book, GeoPlanner, GeoWrite, GeoDraw, and Notepad. The GeoWrite and GeoDraw files are Read-Only templates; in order to use these you must save them with a different name. Then you can modify that new document.

Two other icons, Area Test and Printer Verification, are Read-Only template applications for testing your printer. They can be used "as is" to check your printer. The Area Test file shows how your printout conforms to the page size you have specified (this is the size you select in the Change Options dialog box accessed from the Printer Options box). The Printer Verification file lets you print the sample page to see how your printer's output looks. If you have saved the document as a separate file, you can add notes relating to settings you used. You can also change the font and the type size.

The last icon represents the game Tetris; you will find a discussion of Tetris in Chapter 18, "The Games Applications."

The File Menu Commands

Notice a menu bar at the top of each of the application screens. The menu bar contains the titles of pull-down menus. The menus that appear on the menu bars of these applications are the same as the menus in the corresponding Advanced Workspace applications. In general, you are referred to the chapter that discusses the corresponding Advanced Workspace application. The File menu commands are probably the most basic and important menu commands, however, so they are discussed now.

Open

If you are already working and want to open a file, select **Open**. A dialog box similar to Figure 3.5 is displayed allowing you to select the file you want to open.

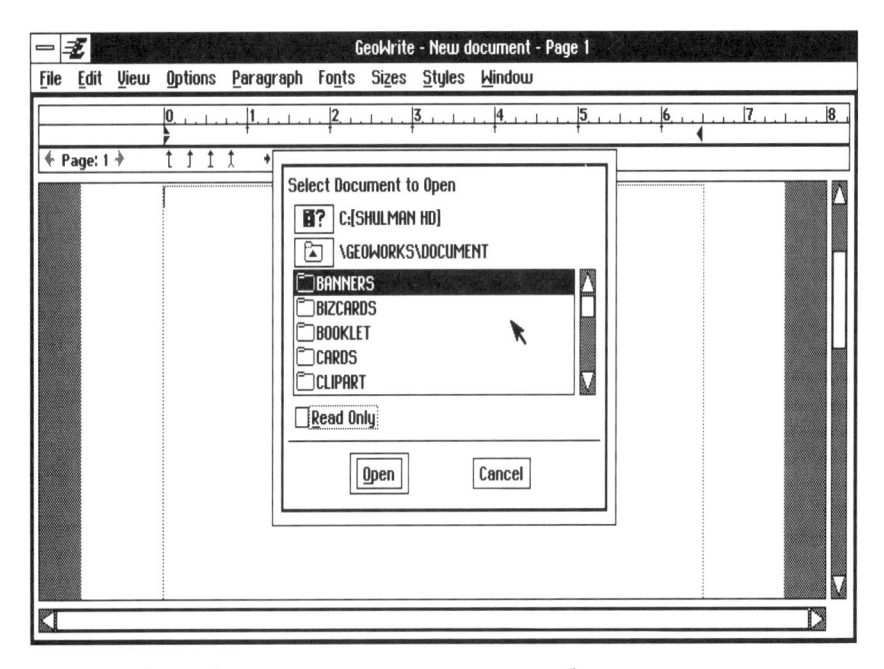

Figure 3.5. The Select Document to Open Dialog Box.

The top line of the dialog box shows the drive icon at left; the text next to it indicates the current drive and the volume label of the disk. The next line shows the directory icon at left and displays the current directory path. In this figure, the path is \GEOWORKS\DOCUMENT. This means the current directory is DOCUMENT, which is a subdirectory of the GEOWORKS directory.

The window underneath lists the contents of the current directory. In Figure 3.5 this list shows the contents of the DOCUMENT subdirectory (BANNERS, BIZCARD and three other subdirectories are shown). You can use the scroll bar at right to view the rest of the contents of the DOCUMENT directory (more subdirectories and some files).

If you want to go to a different drive, click the disk icon on the top line. This displays a list of available drives in the list box. Click on the drive you want and click on **Open** to select it.

Clicking on the directory icon takes you up one level in the directory tree. For example, in Figure 3.5, the Directory line reads: \GEOWORKS\DOCUMENT. If you click on the directory icon next to it, you will move up one level, to the \GEOWORKS directory. Clicking this icon again takes you back to the parent directory and displays the \ symbol; this is the *root directory* of the drive. If you click again, you end up with a list of available drives.

You can select a subdirectory by clicking on it and then clicking on **Open** to select it from the list; this allows you to move to different subdirectories to select a file.

Save

After you have created a document, you can save it by clicking this option. A dialog box prompt for a file name. Enter a name and click **Save**. The file is saved with the name you specified. If you want to save the file to a different directory or drive, follow the procedure discussed under Open to switch to that location before you save the file.

If the file has been saved and you just want to save an updated version, selecting Save will save it immediately (you are not prompted for a filename).

Use Save As instead of Save to save the file with another name while retaining the original file and name.   **NOTE**

Revert

This option allows you to recover the last saved version of a document. This is handy if you have made changes and then decided you don't want the changes after all. Select **Revert** from the File menu and click **Yes** in the dialog box. The document is restored to the previous version and the changes are lost.

Close

When you are finished working on a document, select **Close** to close that file and return to the application screen. You do not leave the application, just the document you were working on.

Exit

If you want to close the document and leave the application, select **Exit** from the File menu. You can also do this by double-clicking on the **Control** button, located in the extreme upper-left of the screen, a box with a thin horizontal bar in it.

Menu Selection with the Mouse

There are two methods for selecting items from a menu. The click or the drag method.

Click Item Selection

Move the mouse cursor on the menu you want to select. Click the left mouse button to display the menu. Move the mouse cursor to the desired menu item and click the left mouse button again to select the menu item and close the menu.

Drag Item Selection

Move the mouse cursor to the menu you want to select. Press and hold the left mouse button while you drag the highlight to the desired menu item. Release the mouse button to select the item and close the menu.

If you miss an object, you can repeat the process, or use the Ctrl method described next to add the item.

Keyboard Commands for Menus

To access menus and make menu selections from the keyboard:

1. Press: **Alt** to highlight the first menu across the top of the active window.

2. Press: **LeftArrow** or **RightArrow** to move along the menu bar.

3. Press: **DownArrow**, **Spacebar**, or **Enter** to display the highlighted menu. If you want to move to a different menu, press **LeftArrow** or **RightArrow**.

4. Press: **UpArrow** and **DownArrow** to highlight the item you want in the pull-down menu. Three dots following the item name indicate that the option opens a dialog box. A cascading menu (a submenu of the highlighted option) is indicated by a right-facing arrow next to the item. To access a cascading menu press **RightArrow**, then use **UpArrow** or **DownArrow** to highlight a submenu item. Press **LeftArrow** to close the cascading menu and return to the previous menu.

5. Press: **DownArrow**, **Spacebar**, or **Enter** to select a menu item and close the menu.
Press: **Enter** to close the menu without making a selection.

6. To access the Control button or Express button menus use **LeftArrow** or **RightArrow** to move the highlight off the menu bar and position it on the Control button or Express button, displaying its menu. Make your selection from the Control menu or Express menu in the same way as on other menus.

Mnemonic Commands for Menus

When a menu name includes an underlined character, you can use the character to select the option from the keyboard. The character can be a letter or number. Follow these steps to access a menu bar menu using the mnemonic method:

1. Press: **Alt** and hold it down while you press the letter key (mnemonic) associated with that menu. For example, in all

Advanced Workspace applications, the letter F is the mnemonic for the File menu. To select the File menu, press **Alt-F**.

2. After a menu is open, select menu items by pressing the mnemonic key alone. For example, to select the New option in the File menu, press **N**.

Hotkey Commands for Menus

You can instantly access some menu items, bypassing the menus, using *hotkeys* (also called *keyboard accelerators*). Hotkey combinations are displayed beside the corresponding option in the pull-down menus.

For example, suppose you have copied text to the clipboard in the Notepad application. You reposition your text cursor where you want to insert the copied text. Now, instead of using the mouse or the mnemonic keys to access the Paste option in the Edit menu, you could simply use the Paste hotkey combination: **Shift-Ins**. The Paste hotkey is the same in all GeoWorks Pro applications that let you cut or copy and paste text.

Pinning a Menu

The first option in each pull-down menu is a *pin symbol*. Select the pin option to keep the menu open after you make a selection. The menu display changes to include a title bar and Control button. Although you can select the pin option using keyboard commands, you must subsequently use the mouse to make a selection within a pinned menu.

Moving a Pinned Menu

To move a pinned menu, press and hold the left mouse button over the menu's title bar while dragging the menu to its new location. Release the left mouse button to relocate the menu. (As you drag the menu, the mouse cursor changes to two small perpendicular arrows with arrowheads at each of the four ends.)

Closing a Pinned Menu

To close and unpin a menu, double-click on the **Control** button in the upper-left corner of the menu. The menu unpins and closes.

Overview of the File Cabinet Window

A brief tour of the File Cabinet window will help familiarize you with its important features. Beginning at the very top, in the left corner, you see:

Control Button

The Control button is a small rectangular button with a horizontal bar in it located in the extreme upper-left corner of the window. It is found in all the windows of the Intermediate Workspace.

A single click on the **Control** button displays the Control menu. Note that in the menu display of the File Cabinet Control button, all but one of the items are dimmed. Even though this button has all the items found in the Advanced Control menu, you cannot use them because they relate to changing the size and location of the window and you can't do this in the Intermediate Workspace.

Consequently, the only item that you can use is Close (which closes the application and returns you to the previous window). Double-clicking the left mouse button on the **Control** button does the same thing, i.e., exits the application and returns you to the previous window.

Don't bother trying to access a dimmed menu item—it cannot be done.

Express Menu Button

The Express menu button is found just to the right of the Control button; it is generally the same on all application windows. Clicking on the **Express** button displays the Express menu, which will look similar to the one shown in Figure 3.6.

The top section of the Express menu lists open applications, indicating the current application with a filled circle to the left of the item. You can open as many applications as you want in the Intermediate Workspace. The Express menu does not display applications not currently open.

You can switch between open applications by clicking on the one you want; that window will appear on the screen (it was really there all along, just underneath the other windows). You may see the same application listed several times in the list. This is because each time you create a document in that application it is listed separately. If you have opened the same application several times, you may have to select from the Express menu list until you find the one you want.

NOTE You can go back to the Welcome screen by pressing the **F2** key. This is quicker than going to the Express menu and selecting Welcome.

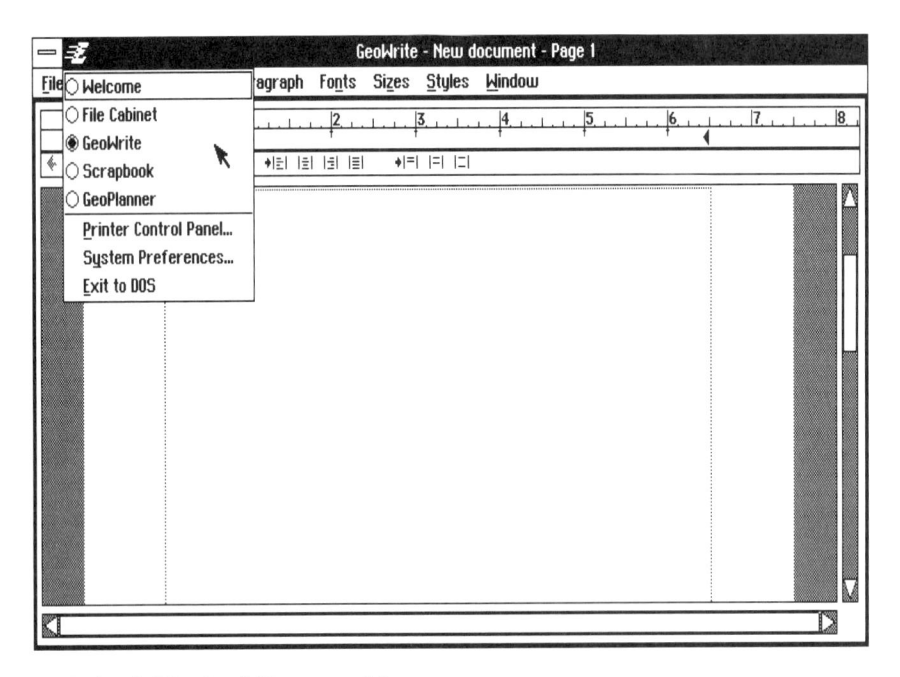

Figure 3.6. A Typical Express Menu.

Printer Control Panel

This item allows you to view the currently selected printer and also a list of documents waiting to print.

Preferences

When you select the **Preferences** option, the Preferences screen appears. This contains exactly the same items as the Preferences application in the Advanced Workspace, described in Chapter 6. Refer to this chapter for a discussion of this screen.

Exit to DOS

If you click on **Exit to DOS**, GeoWorks Pro closes and you return to DOS. A screen prompts you if you are sure you want to return. Selecting **Yes** takes you to DOS. If you select **No**, you return to the window where you were.

Title Bar

The title bar occupies the rest of the top line of the window. In the File Cabinet window, it displays the title File Cabinet, as shown in Figure 3.2. In other application windows, The title bar displays the application name and the name of the current document.

Top Row of File Cabinet Buttons

The next section of the File Cabinet window contains eight buttons: Open, Get Info, Move, Copy, Duplicate, Rename, Format, and Exit. Most of these are shown dimmed (unavailable) until you select a directory or file from the main area by clicking on the icon. Exit and Format are always available, however.

Open

This button becomes available after you select a directory or file in the File Cabinet window. Once you make a selection, clicking on the **Open** button will open that item.

Get Info

You can get information on a selected item by clicking on the **Get Info** button. You see information on the name and path to the directory or file. The attributes and time of last modification are given. If the item is a file, you also see the size, GEOS file type, and the creator of the file (the application used to create the file).

Move

There are two ways of moving a file in the Intermediate Workspace:

- You can use the mouse to drag the item to the icon where you want to move it
- Use the Move button.

Moving by Dragging

The easiest way to move an item is to use the mouse. The following steps outline the procedure:

1. Click: On the item or items you want to move.

2. Keep the mouse pointer on a selected item. Press and hold the **Right mouse** button. The pointer will change to a single sheet of paper or a stack of papers to indicate whether you are dragging one item or several.

3. Drag: The pointer to one of the following places:
   - A directory (folder icon)
   - The Close Directory button at the bottom of the window

If you drag the item(s) to a directory folder, they are moved to that directory.

When you drag them to the Close Directory button, they are moved to their parent directory (one level up in the directory tree).

To move a file or group of files to a floppy disk, refer to the Floppy button discussion.

Moving Using the Move Button

You can also move items using the Move button. When you click **Move**, the Move Selected File To dialog box appears, as shown in Figure 3.7. This dialog box works the same way as the Select Document to Open dialog box, described at the beginning of this chapter.

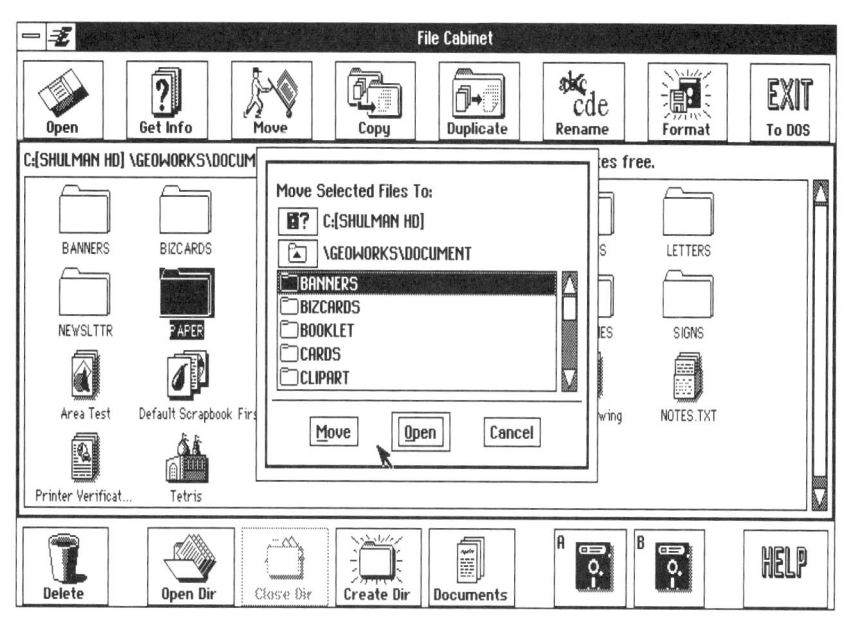

Figure 3.7. The Move Selected File To Dialog Box.

Drive Icon   The top icon represents a disk drive. The current drive and its label are shown to the right of the icon. You can change to another drive by clicking on this icon. This displays a list of your disk drives; double-click on the drive you want or click on it and then click the Open button at the bottom. Below that is the directory icon. To its right is the path to the current directory. In Figure 3.2, the path is \GEOWORKS\DOCUMENT. Clicking on this icon takes you back one level in the directory path and displays a list of the contents of that directory. If you keep clicking on the icon, you eventually end up at the root directory (\). If you click again, you see a list of available drives.

A list of the subdirectories contained in the current directory (DOCUMENT) is shown in the box. You can scroll the list to select the directory you want as the destination.

Open	Clicking the **Open** button adds the subdirectory to the path shown and displays a list of its contents. You can select an item from this list and add it to the path.
Move	If you click **Move**, the items you selected are moved to the destination directory you specified. If you are moving several items, a box appears listing the progress of the move. To halt the operation, click **Stop**.
Cancel	This button returns you to the previous screen with no changes made.

Copy

This button operates the same way as the Move button just described, except that it places a copy of the selected item(s) in the destination directory you specify. The original items remain where they were. Select a destination from the dialog box which appears and click the **Copy** button at the bottom of the box.

There is no dragging method for copying an item to another location (except for copying to a floppy disk—see the discussion of the Floppy button).

Duplicate

You can duplicate a file within the *same directory* by clicking the **Duplicate** button. A dialog box appears suggesting a new name. You can accept this name or enter your own filename in the box. Click the **Duplicate** button at the bottom of the dialog box to perform the operation.

Rename

If you want to change the name of a file or directory, you can use the Rename button. First select the item(s) you want to rename, then click on **Rename**. The Rename dialog box appears, showing the current name of the item. Figure 3.8 shows a typical rename dialog box.

The current name is shown highlighted. When you begin to type in the new name, it will overwrite the old name. In this example, the new name has been entered as *art work*. (GeoWorks Pro allows filenames that DOS would not, like this one with a space. See Chapter 4 for more on naming files.)

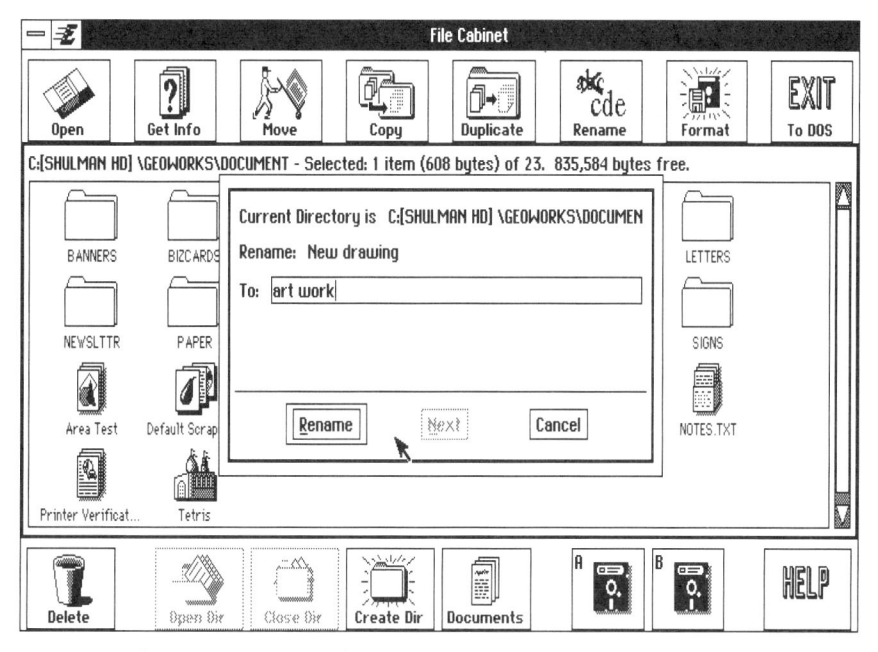

Figure 3.8. The Rename Dialog Box.

If you want to modify only the current name, you can click on it to remove the highlighting. You can then add the changes without over writing the name.

Click on the **Rename** button at the bottom of the box. The item appears in the File Cabinet window with the new name.

If you have selected more than one item, the Next button becomes active. Click on it to see the next item to be renamed. Follow the same procedure to rename it.

Format

The handy Format button, allows you to format disks from the Intermediate Workspace. You may have a disk you have used and wish to remove all the data it contains. One way to do this is to reformat it. If you have a new disk, it *must* be formatted before you can use it.

You can check if a disk has been formatted by inserting it in a floppy drive and clicking the button for that drive. If you get a message that the disk is unreadable, you probably need to format the disk.

44 • *Teach Yourself GeoWorks Pro*

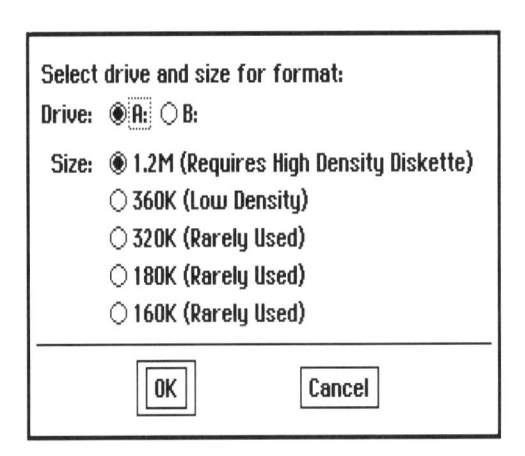

```
Select drive and size for format:
Drive:  ⦿ A:   ○ B:
 Size:  ⦿ 1.2M (Requires High Density Diskette)
        ○ 360K (Low Density)
        ○ 320K (Rarely Used)
        ○ 180K (Rarely Used)
        ○ 160K (Rarely Used)

              [ OK ]     [ Cancel ]
```

Figure 3.9. The Disk Format Dialog Box.

The process of formatting a floppy disk is quite simple. All you have to do it supply a little information about your disk.

1. Insert: The disk you want to format in one of the floppy drives.
2. Click: **Format** button. The dialog box seen in Figure 3.9 appears.
3. Click: Icon for the drive with the disk in it.
4. Click: The correct size for the disk you are formatting.
5. Click: **OK**. A dialog box appears asking you to enter a name for the disk.
   Type in a name and click the **Format** button at the bottom of the box. The formatting begins. You see a message keeping you posted about the progress of the formatting and when it is finished.

Exit

This button at the top right of the window is used to return to DOS. When you click this button, you see a message asking if you are sure you want to return to DOS. Click **Yes** to shut down GeoWorks Pro and go to DOS.

The File Cabinet Information Line

This line displays the current drive with its label (its name) and the path to the currently open directory. It also shows the number of items in the

File Cabinet, the number of bytes used, and the number of free bytes. For example, Figure 3.2 shows C:[SHULMAN HD] as the current drive and label. The path is \GEOWORKS\DOCUMENTS, and there are 23 items displayed in the window. These 23 items use 39,339 bytes and there are 835,584 bytes free.

Bottom Row of File Cabinet Buttons

There are eight buttons in this row: Delete, Open Dir, Close Dir, Create Dir, Documents, Floppy icon A:, Floppy icon B:, and Help. Many of these buttons are dimmed until you select an item.

Delete

A dimmed button becomes active only after you make a selection. You can get rid of files and directories you no longer want by using this button. First select the item(s) you want to delete, then click the **Delete** button. A dialog box appears asking if you are sure you want to delete the item(s). If you click on **No** or **Cancel**, you return to the screen with no change. If you select **Yes**, the item(s) are deleted.

Make sure of what you are deleting. Once an item is deleted you cannot recover it using GeoWorks Pro. **WARNING**

Open Dir

In order to view or work with the contents of a directory, you must first open it. To do this, you can click on the icon of the directory (the folder icon) of the directory you want. The Open Dir button now becomes active; click on it to open the selected directory. The contents of the directory are displayed in a new window.

A quick way to open a directory is to double-click on its icon. This opens it immediately, saving a step. **NOTE**

If you want to open a directory on a floppy disk, follow these steps:

1. Insert the floppy in a drive. Click the appropriate Floppy button (icon(s) at the bottom right) corresponding to that drive. (For

example, if you put the floppy disk in drive B:, click on the icon labeled **B:**.)

2. The File Cabinet window shows the contents of the root directory of the disk. Double-click on the icon you want to open.

NOTE If the disk contains DOS files, you will not be able to open these.

Close Dir

This button is used to close the current directory and return you to the previous directory. In other words, it takes you back to the parent directory (one level up in the directory tree). For example, if you are in a directory called PINES which is a subdirectory of the directory TREES, clicking Close Dir returns you to the TREES directory.

You can continue the process until you reach the DOCUMENT directory (this is the directory where you usually store all the GeoWorks Pro documents you create with the various applications—including those you create in the Advanced Workspace). The button is then dimmed, indicating that you cannot go any higher.

Create Dir

You can create a new directory in any open directory. In order to do this, the parent directory (the one where you want the new directory to go) must be visible in the File Cabinet window. This may require you to change directories until the parent directory is displayed.

Next, double-click on the icon of the parent directory to open it. Then, click on the **Create Dir** icon. The dialog box shown in Figure 3.10 is displayed.

Enter the name for the new directory. The directory name must be a legal DOS filename, but you don't have to enter an extension if you don't want one (see the File Cabinet icons discussion above for details on naming files and directories). In this example, the name of the new directory is ITU_WORK.

Click the **Create** button at the bottom of the box. The new directory is created and its icon appears in the File Cabinet window.

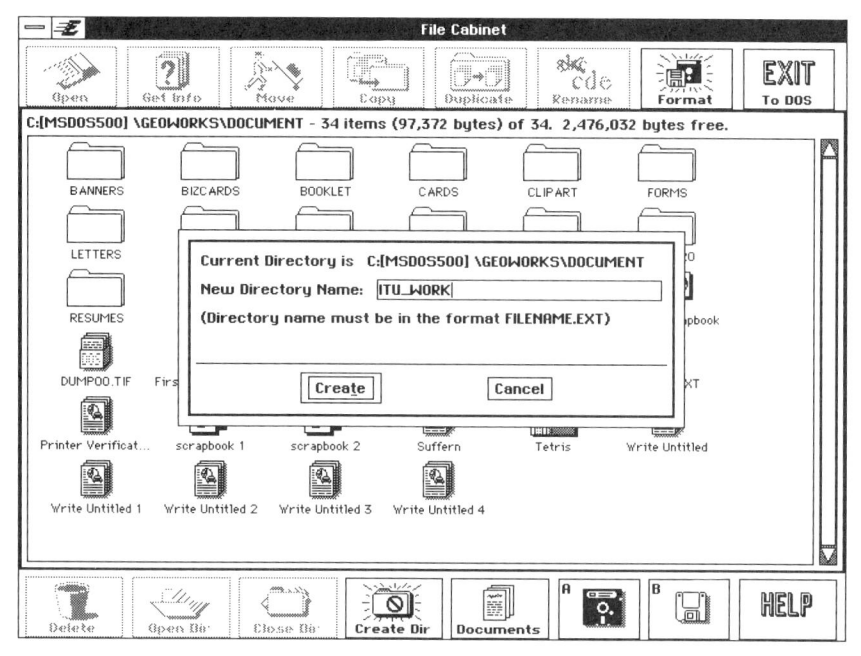

Figure 3.10. The Create Dir Dialog Box.

Documents

This button opens the DOCUMENTS directory of GeoWorks Pro. The DOCUMENTS directory is where you normally store all the documents you create in GeoWorks Pro. The DOCUMENTS directory lets you access all the subdirectories and files within it. If you are already in the DOCUMENTS directory, clicking this button does nothing.

Floppy Buttons

These buttons represent the available floppy drives. The number of buttons depends on the configuration of your computer. The button indicates the type of drive, 3-1/2-inch or 5-1/2-inch, and the letters in the upper-left corner indicate the drive. You can use these buttons to display the contents of a floppy disk, to move or copy files from the File Cabinet window to a floppy disk, and to copy files from a floppy to the hard disk.

48 • *Teach Yourself GeoWorks Pro*

Viewing the Contents of a Floppy Disk

If you want to see what is on a floppy disk, insert it into a floppy drive. Click the appropriate Floppy button. The contents are displayed.

Copying a File or Directory to a Floppy Disk

1. Insert: The floppy disk in the drive you want.
2. Select: The items you want to copy from the File Cabinet window.
3. Press and hold: The right mouse button and drag the items to the appropriate floppy icon.

Moving a File or Directory to a Floppy Disk

1. Follow steps 1 and 2 above.
2. Press and hold: The **Alt** key. While holding the key, drag the items to the appropriate floppy icon.

Copying from a Floppy Disk to the Hard Disk

1. Insert: The floppy disk in the drive you want.
2. Click: The appropriate **floppy** button. The contents of the disk are displayed.
3. Select: The file you want. Drag the icon to the **Documents** button. The file is copied to the hard disk.

Moving a File from a Floppy Disk to the Hard Disk

1. Follow steps 1 and 2 above.
2. Select: The file you want.
   Press and hold the **Alt** key while dragging the icon to the **Documents** button. The file is moved to the hard disk.

NOTE You can move multiple files and even whole directories by selecting all the items before performing the copy or move operation.

Help

When all else fails, you can click this button to get help. A screen appears displaying information about all the features of the File Cabinet. Scroll the screen to view the topic you want.

A Sample Document

The document shown in Figure 3.11 demonstrates the results you can obtain by using some of the template documents supplied in the Intermediate Workspace. It was created by opening two different template files from the CLIPART directory and inserting pictures from them into a document opened in the New Document template file and saved as BEXAR'S LOOT. (GeoWorks Pro allows filenames that DOS would not, like this one, which is too long and has both a space and an apostrophe. See Chapter 4 for more on naming files.)

A brief description of the steps involved is given below.

First, open the New Document file on the File Cabinet screen. The Read-Only message is displayed. Click **OK**; the GeoWrite application is opened with a blank document. Select **Save As** from the File menu and save the file with the name BEXAR'S LOOT.

Next, select File Cabinet from the Express menu to return to the File Cabinet screen. Then, open the CLIPART directory and double-click on the **Clip Art** file to open it. The Read-Only message screen appears. Click **OK** to display the screen with a message about the Clip Art file.

Click on the **Go To Page** button at the bottom. The Go To Page dialog box appears, as shown in Figure 3.12.

Scroll the list to find the Treasure Chest and select it. Click **View Page** to display that picture. Click **Close** to remove the dialog box.

From the Edit menu, select the **Copy** option. The picture is copied to the Clipboard.

Click on the **Express** button and click on the **GeoWrite** button to go to the BEXAR'S LOOT document. Select the **Paste** option from the Edit menu. The treasure chest picture is pasted into the BEXAR'S LOOT document.

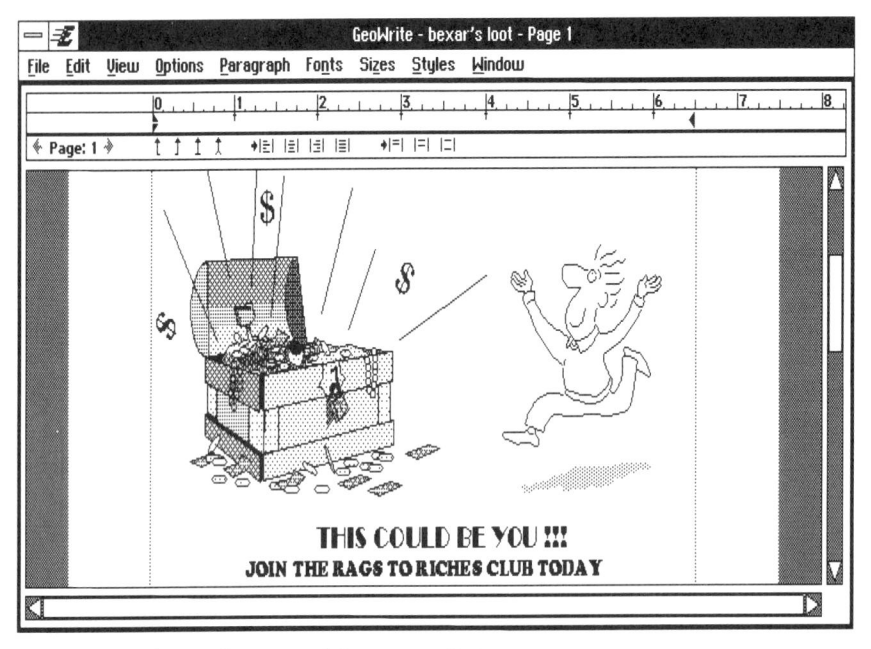

Figure 3.11. The "This Could Be You" Document.

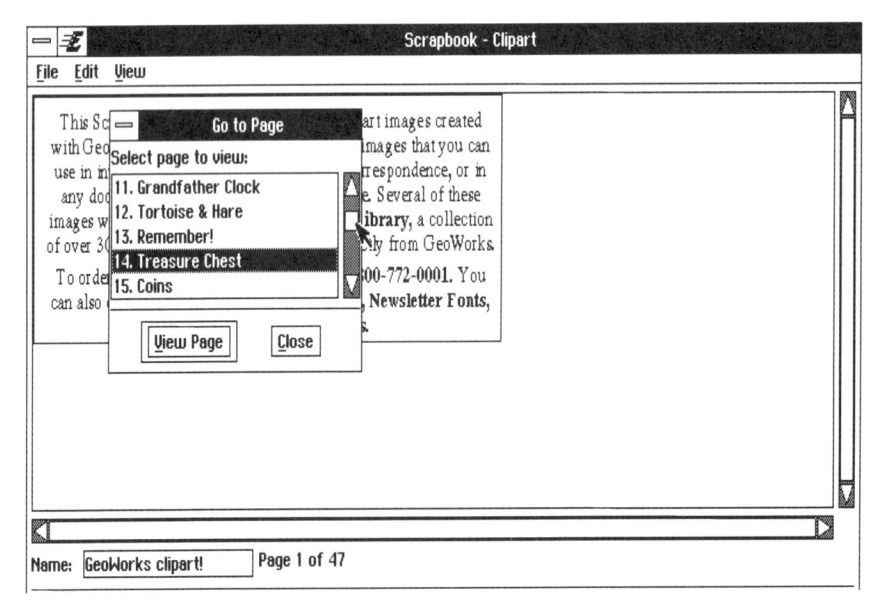

Figure 3.12. The Go To Page Dialog Box.

Repeat this procedure by opening the T/Maker file from the CLIPART directory, choosing the Running Man cartoon and copying it into the BEXAR'S LOOT document.

Position the cursor underneath the pictures and type the text you want. If you want to change the font or type size, you can highlight the text you want and change it. In the picture shown in Figure 3.11, each line of text has a different font and type size.

Summary

This chapter presented an overview of the Intermediate Workspace and the File Cabinet window. It discussed the features of the File Cabinet window and the tasks you could perform in it.

Chapter 4

The Advanced Workspace

The Advanced Workspace, a more advanced section of the GeoWorks Pro program, contains 16 applications (programs designed to perform particular functions). These are among the many things you can do in the Advanced Workspace:

- Make notes
- Schedule appointments
- Write and edit lengthy documents
- Make drawings and insert them into documents
- View and/or import various spreadsheets and chart files.

Some of the applications are similar to the appliances and the applications found in the Intermediate Workspace, but they are more advanced and more powerful.

Moving Around the Advanced Workspace

See Chapter 2 for a general discussion about using the mouse in GeoWorks Pro. In the Advanced Workspace you can use the mouse, keyboard commands, and hotkeys to access menus and make menu selections. Displayed next to many menu items in the Advanced Workspace applications there are keyboard commands—hotkeys such as Alt-F5 or Ctrl-L—that provide quick access to the pull-down menu items.

See the middle of Chapter 3 for a complete discussion of using the mouse and (or) the keyboard, including hotkeys, to work with menus.

GeoWorks Pro Windows

Windows in GeoWorks Pro are rectangular areas of the screen in which information is displayed. You can move windows around the screen, stack them up like sheets of paper or overlap them. You can change the size of a window so that it fills the screen or displays only a line or two, or you can reduce the window to an icon.

This section gives you an overview of a typical window—the GeoDraw application window. Other application windows are quite similar.

Accessing the GeoDraw Window

Select the **Advanced** panel from the Welcome screen, displaying the GeoManager screen. Select the **GeoDraw** icon, displaying the window shown in Figure 4.1.

Descriptions of GeoDraw window items follow. Starting at the top-left corner of the window, the features are explained in the following sections:

Control Button

The Control button is a small rectangular button with a horizontal bar in it located in the upper-left corner of the window. Double-clicking the left mouse button on the Control button exits the application and returns you to the GeoManager window.

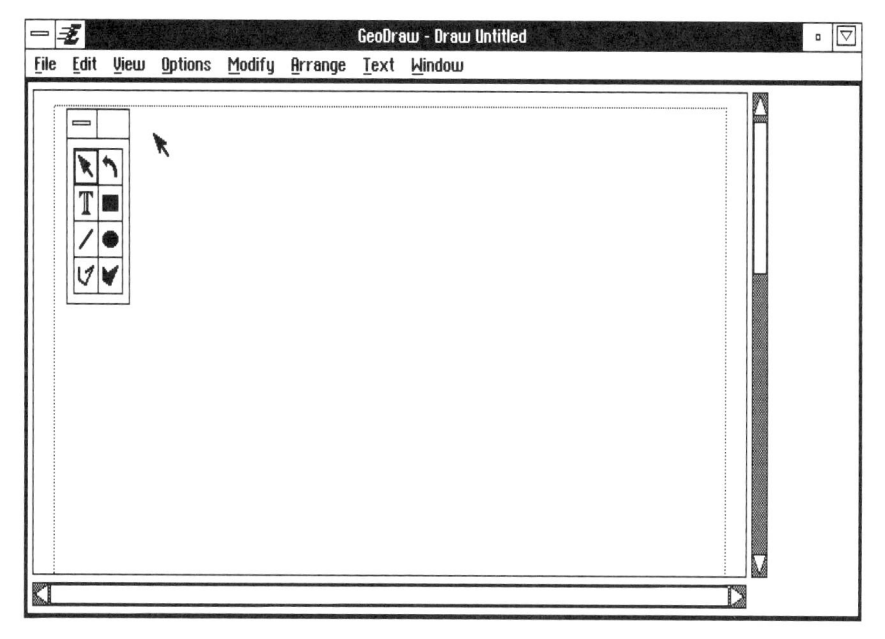

Figure 4.1. The GeoDraw Window.

Single-clicking on the **Control** Button displays the Control menu. You cannot access a dimmed menu item until some specific action activates it. Don't bother trying to access a dimmed item—it cannot be done.

When you display the GeoDraw Control menu immediately after starting the application, the only available options are Minimize, Maximize, and Close; all other options are dimmed.

Select **Minimize** to reduce the application to an icon placed at the bottom of the screen. Restore it by double-clicking on the icon.

Select **Close** to close the application and return to the GeoManager screen.

Select **Maximize** to expand a window so it fills the entire screen. Any Minimized icons at the bottom of the screen will be covered by a Maximized window. To restore a Maximized window to its original size, select **Restore** from the Control menu.

Express Menu Button

The Express menu button is located immediately to the right of the Control button. The Express menu, which is generally the same on all application windows, lets you move around GeoWorks Pro without closing an application. For example, when you select GeoManager from the GeoDraw Express menu you go directly to the GeoManager screen. The GeoDraw application—now an icon at the bottom of the screen—is still active, waiting in the background for you to return to it. You could open another application, then use the Express menu to leave it open (as an icon) and return to the GeoManager screen.

The Express menu lists all open applications, indicating them with a filled circle to the left of the item. To return to an open application, select it from the Express menu or double-click on the application icon at the bottom of the screen. If you try to select an already-open application from the GeoManager screen, GeoManager tells you it is already open. You may have to close or minimize a window that covers the icon.

The Express menu does not display applications not currently open. To open an application using the Express menu, select **Startup**. Then select the application you want from the displayed list.

Title Bar

The title bar is centered in the top line of the window. The title bar displays the application name and the name of the current document.

Maximize/Restore Button

In the top-right corner of the application window is the rectangular Minimize/Maximize Restore button.

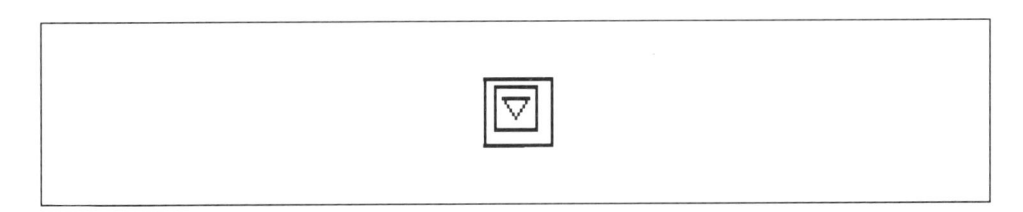

Figure 4.2. The Maximize/Restore Button.

The Minimize/Maximize Restore button is empty when the window display is less than the full screen. Selecting an empty **Minimize/Maximize Restore** button maximizes the application window so it fills the screen. Remember, a maximized window covers any icons at the bottom of the screen. When the application window is maximized, the Minimize/Maximize Restore button has a small triangle in it. Selecting the button with a triangle in it reduces the application window size to less than the full screen, uncovering icons at the bottom of the screen.

Minimize Button

Near the top-right corner of the application window, next to the Minimize/Maximize Restore button is the Minimize button. This rectangular button always has a small square in it. Selecting the **Minimize button** reduces the application window to an icon (the same as selecting the Minimize option in the Control menu).

Some applications, such as GeoDraw and GeoWrite, let you open several documents within the application, each with its own window. Document windows can be minimized or maximized in the same way application windows can be. You cannot open multiple copies of an application itself.

Menu Bar

The second line of an application window (in this case the GeoDraw window) contains the menu bar. In GeoDraw the menu bar shows eight menu options: File, Edit, View, Options, Modify, Arrange, Text, and Window.

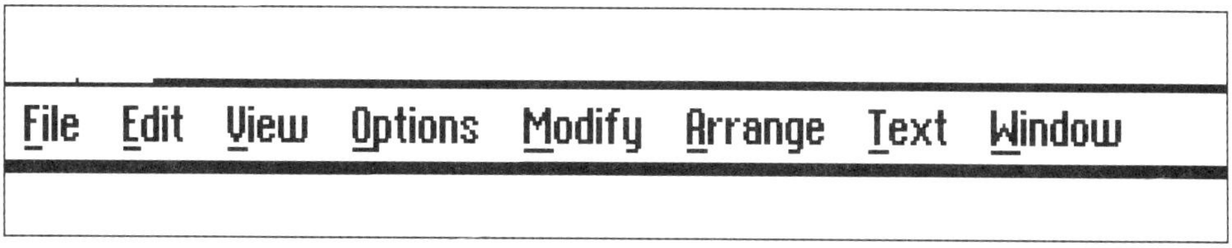

| File | Edit | View | Options | Modify | Arrange | Text | Window |

Figure 4.3. A Menu Bar.

Scroll Bar

Use scroll bars when the contents of a window are wider or longer than the window itself. A window has two scroll bars: a vertical one at the right of the window and a horizontal one at the bottom. If you move the mouse pointer to one of the end arrows on a scroll bar and click on it, the window information moves in small steps in the opposite direction of the arrow.

For example, when you click on a scroll bar down arrow, the window text scrolls up, revealing text that was below the window.

Dialog Boxes

Sometimes GeoWorks Pro may need more information or must alert you of a problem. In such cases, a display called a *dialog box* appears. Some of these can be kept open and you can switch between them if you want. Others require you to give a response before you can continue. Figure 4.4 illustrates a typical dialog box.

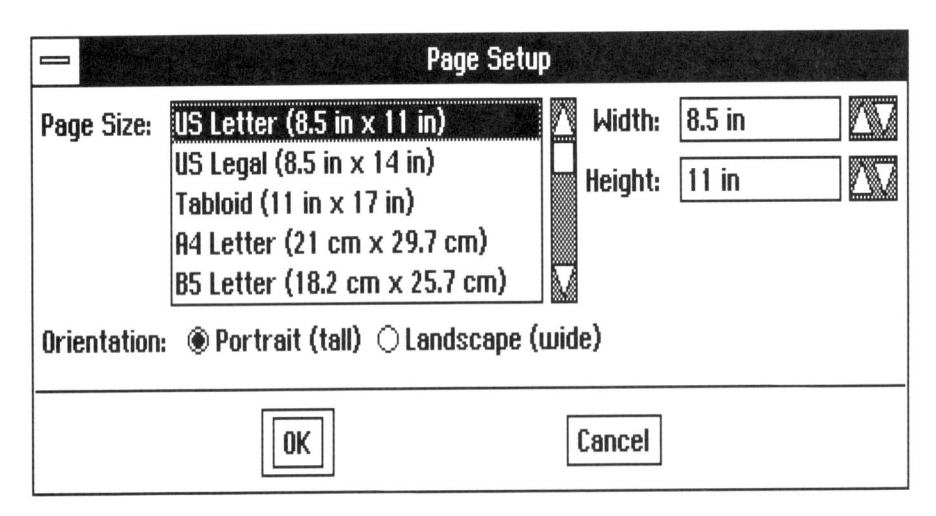

Figure 4.4. A Typical Dialog Box.

Icons

An *icon* is a small picture that represents something you can work with, such as an application, a file or a directory. Figure 4.5 shows the GeoManager window. All the icons in this window represent applications except for the top-left icon; it represents a directory.

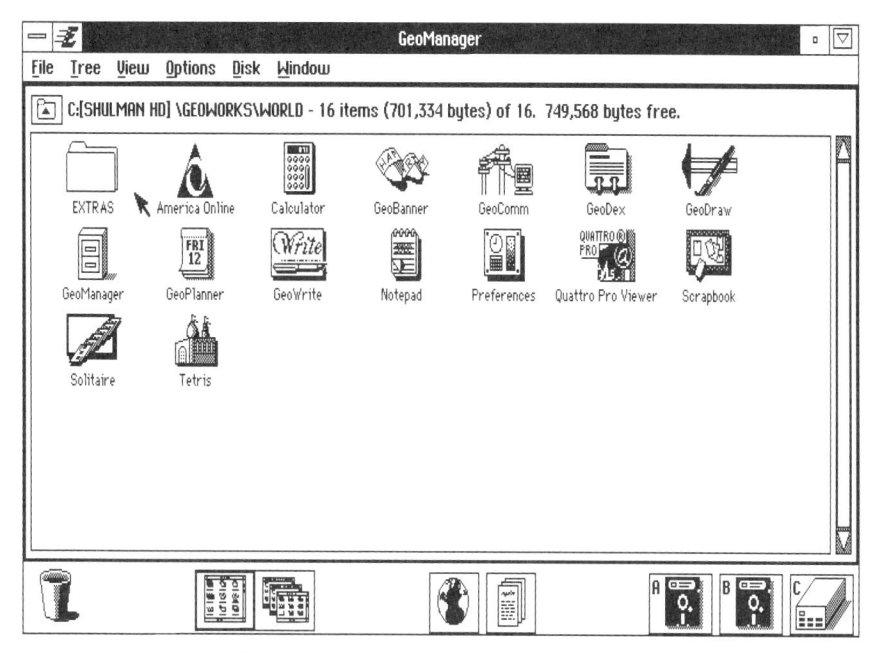

Figure 4.5. Icons on the GeoManager Screen.

Exiting an Application

There are several ways to close an application and return to the GeoManager screen:

- By selecting the **Close** option from the File menu.
- By selecting the **Close** option from the Control button menu.
- By double-clicking on the **Control button**.

You can also close the application and exit to DOS by selecting **Exit to DOS** on the Express menu.

Creating and Saving Documents (Files)

Most applications in the Advanced Workspace create an untitled document when you first start the application. You can also create an untitled document when you are already working in an application by selecting **New** from the application's File menu. As you work in a document, your data is stored in temporary memory in your computer. Any data not saved to the hard disk or a floppy disk will be lost when you close the application or exit GeoWorks Pro. To save your work, select **Save** from the File menu. If the document is untitled, you will be asked to give it a name. You can save the document in any subdirectory (and drive) you want, although you may find it most convenient to save it in the GeoWorks DOCUMENT subdirectory.

As a precaution, GeoWorks Pro periodically copies your work to disk to keep it safe. Use the Preferences application to specify the time interval between saves. If you make changes to a document and then decide you don't want those changes, you can go back to the last saved version by selecting **Revert** from the File menu.

DOS and GeoWorks Files

Depending on the application, GeoWorks Pro creates one of two kinds of documents. Most GeoWorks Pro applications work with and create DOS documents. A notable exception is the GeoWrite application, which creates "GEOS" documents—documents with file-naming and other conventions different from DOS documents.. GEOS and DOS documents are not compatible.

DOS Document Filenames and Icons

A DOS filename is always one to eight characters (with no spaces). It may be followed by a period and an extension of one to three characters. For example: COVERLTR.DOC is a valid DOS file name.

A DOS document icon is a small file box with the word DOS on it (which can be hard to read when blown up to a large size.) Below the document icon is its filename. A typical DOS file is shown in Figure 4.6.

GEOS Document Filenames and Icons

GEOS file names can be up to 32 characters long (including punctuation and spaces). For example: RESUME.COVER.LETTER is a valid GEOS file name.

Figure 4.6. A DOS File Icon.

GEOS document icons display a symbol representing the originating application. Each type of GEOS application has a unique icon, so you can easily find a particular type of file. Below the GEOS document icon is its file name. Two GEOS file icons and names are shown in Figure 4.7.

About Subdirectories

Think of a *directory* as a folder that can hold files and/or other directories called *subdirectories* (the icon GeoWorks uses for a directory or subdirectory is actually a picture of a manila folder). The directory that contains a subdirectory is called the *parent directory*. Thus, a directory called BEARS might contain subdirectories named POLAR, PANDA, and KOALA. BEARS is the parent directory of the other three.

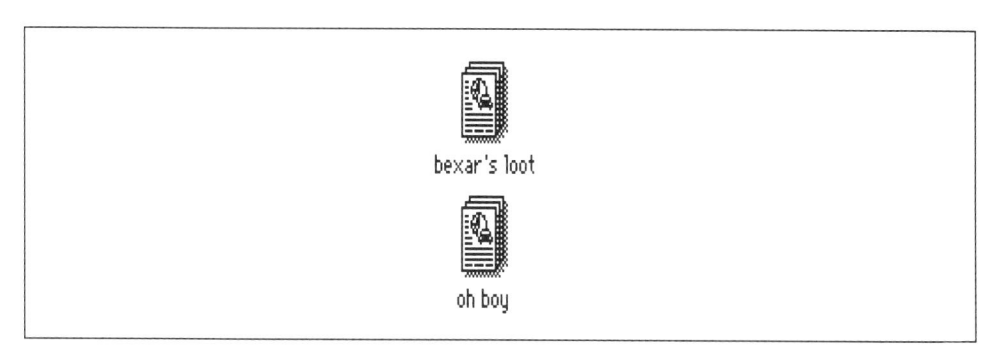

Figure 4.7. GEOS File Icons.

The *root directory* is designated by the symbol (\); it is the primary or topmost directory level and does not have a name. All directories on a disk branch from the root directory; that is, they are subdirectories of the root directory.

GeoWorks Pro uses two main directories, WORLD and DOCUMENT. The WORLD directory stores applications (programs you can run), and the DOCUMENT directory stores data files (files you can use). In order to locate a directory or a file, you have to specify the path, i.e., the drive and a list of directories, and/or subdirectories that lead to the item.

For example, suppose that on your C: drive you have a subdirectory called DOCUMENT under the root directory. Under the DOCUMENT directory is a subdirectory called TREES. In the TREES subdirectory is a file called SPRUCE. The path to the SPRUCE file is:

```
C:\DOCUMENT\TREES\SPRUCE
```

You must include a colon after the drive letter and a backslash (\) between each level in the path name.

To select this same file graphically, choose the DOCUMENT icon, then choose the TREES folder. The contents of the TREES subdirectory will be displayed (including the SPRUCE file). Note that the full path to the TREES directory is indicated next to the directory button.

If you are in a DOS application, the subdirectory file display shows only DOS documents, even if GEOS documents are also stored in the subdirectory. If you are in a GEOS application, the subdirectory file display shows only GEOS documents, even if a DOS document is stored in the subdirectory.

Importing and Exporting DOS/GEOS Files

You cannot directly retrieve a DOS document into a GEOS application document (or vice versa). However, using special import/export options within applications you can share data between document types. The following exercise will teach you how to import and export DOS and GEOS documents. In it, you will:

1. Exit GeoWorks Pro and return to the DOS prompt (if you are currently running the program).

2. Run GeoWorks Pro from the DOS prompt.

3. Open GeoComm (which uses DOS documents) and verify the names of two GeoComm script files.

4. Open GeoWrite (which uses GEOS documents) and import a GeoComm script DOS document, converting it to a GEOS file.

The Advanced Workspace • 63

5. Save the new GEOS document, then export and save the same document as a DOS file.

The purpose of the following exercise is to exchange file types between applications. To accomplish this, you will be asked to perform actions you may not now understand. These will be fully explained in later chapters, but for now, please take them on faith.

1. If you are currently running the GeoWorks Pro program, select **Exit to DOS** from the Express menu. You will return to the DOS prompt. Or, if you would rather not exit, close any open applications and return to the GeoManager screen. Skip to step 4.

2. Run the GeoWorks Pro program.
   Type: `GEOS` at the DOS prompt.
   Press: **Enter**.
   GeoWorks Pro displays the Welcome window.

3. Select: The **Advanced** icon by clicking on it once.

   If this is the first time you have run GeoWorks Pro, the program will display the GeoManager window showing all the applications available in the Advanced Workspace. Proceed to Step 4.

   If you previously used the Advanced Workspace, then the program displays the window you were in when you exited GeoWorks Pro. Close any open applications except GeoManager by activating the application window and selecting **Close** from the Control menu.

4. At the bottom center of the GeoManager screen is a World button—an icon with a globe in it.
   Select: **World** button to be certain the GeoManager screen is displaying application icons. If the World button was not already active, your screen will change to the display shown in Figure 4.5. If the World button was already active, your display was already similar to that shown in Figure 4.5.

5. The Document button is located just to the right of the World button.
   Select: **Document** button to display a screen similar to the one shown in Figure 4.8.

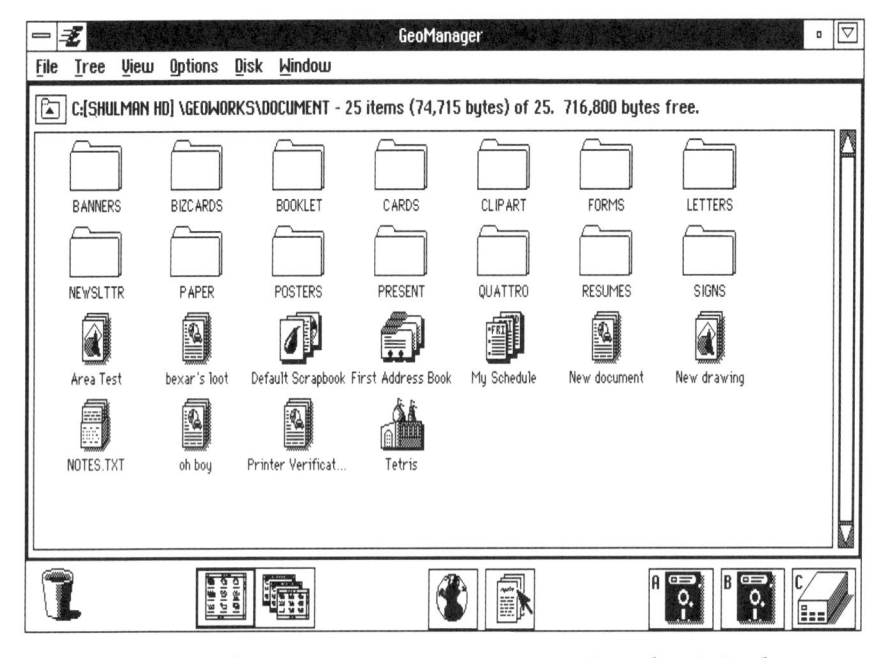

Figure 4.8. The GeoManager Document Display Window.

Notice that the Information line now includes \DOCUMENT as part of the path statement.

A shortcut method to open a document from the Document window is to click on a document icon, then select **Open** from the GeoManager File menu.

GeoWorks Pro opens the application in which the document was created and also opens the document itself, ready for you to use.

6. Select: **World** button again to return to a display similar to that in Figure 4.5.

The World directory displays applications; the Document directory displays subdirectories and files.

Opening the GeoComm Application

Next you will open the GeoComm application. You already know that you could simply double-click on the GeoComm icon to open the application, so let's try another method: the Express menu.

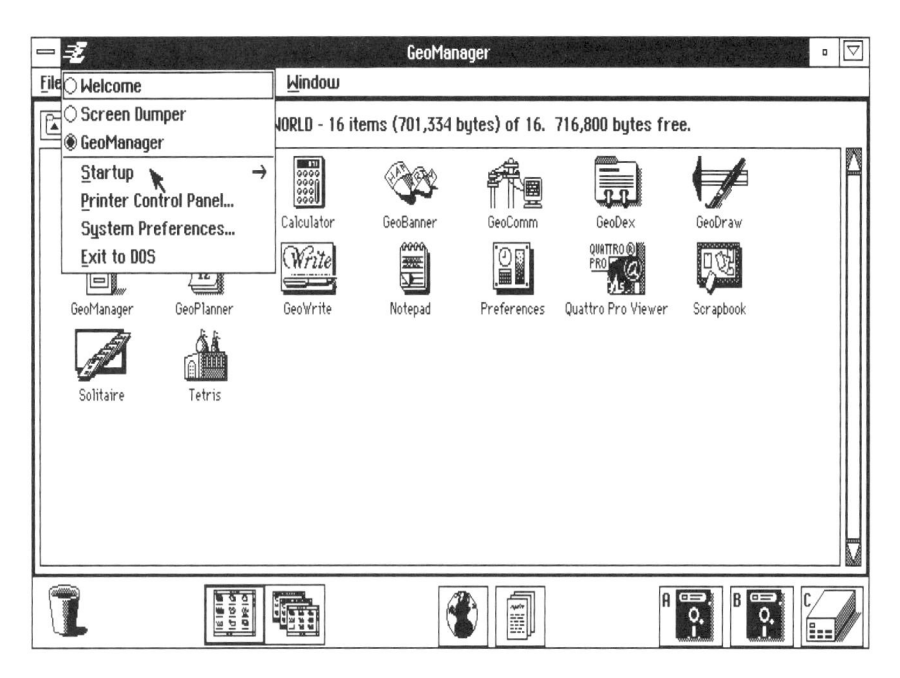

Figure 4.9. The Express Menu.

1. Select: **Express** button at the top of the GeoManager screen to display the screen shown in Figure 4.9.

2. Select: **Startup** on the Express menu. The Startup menu lists all the Advanced Workspace applications.

3. Select: **GeoComm** from the Startup menu to open the GeoComm application.

4. Select: **Dial** from the GeoComm application window.

5. Select: **Scripts** from the Dial menu.

Figure 4.10 shows the Dial menu and the Scripts dialog box with two script files (DOS documents) COMPU.MAC and GENIE.MAC available for selection.

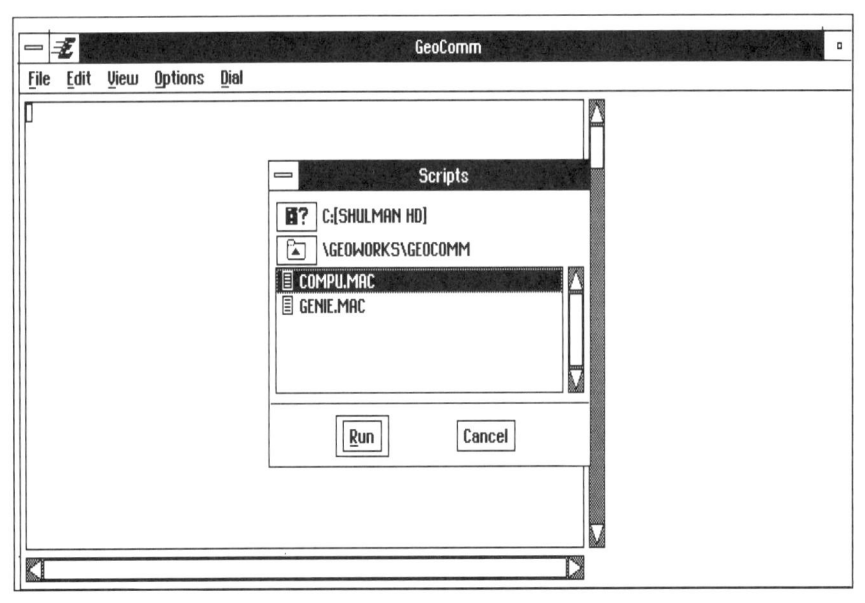

Figure 4.10. Script (DOS) Files Available for Selection.

The line next to the drive icon in Figure 4.10 shows drive C: and a volume label, SHULMAN.HD. A volume label is the name you have assigned to the disk (using the DOS volume label command).

Script files (DOS documents) must have the extension .MAC as part of the file name. A script file without the extension will not display in the Scripts dialog box.

Opening the GeoWrite Application

The next few steps illustrate how to open the GeoWrite application, leaving the GeoComm application open as an icon.

1. Select: **Cancel** to close the Scripts dialog box.

2. Select: **Minimize** button (the rectangular button with a small box in it, top right) to keep GeoComm open but reduce it to an icon as shown at the bottom left of Figure 4.11.

3. Double-click on the **GeoWrite** icon in the GeoManager window to open the application.

4. Select the File menu.

5. Select **Insert From Text File** from the File menu to display the Insert From Text File dialog box.

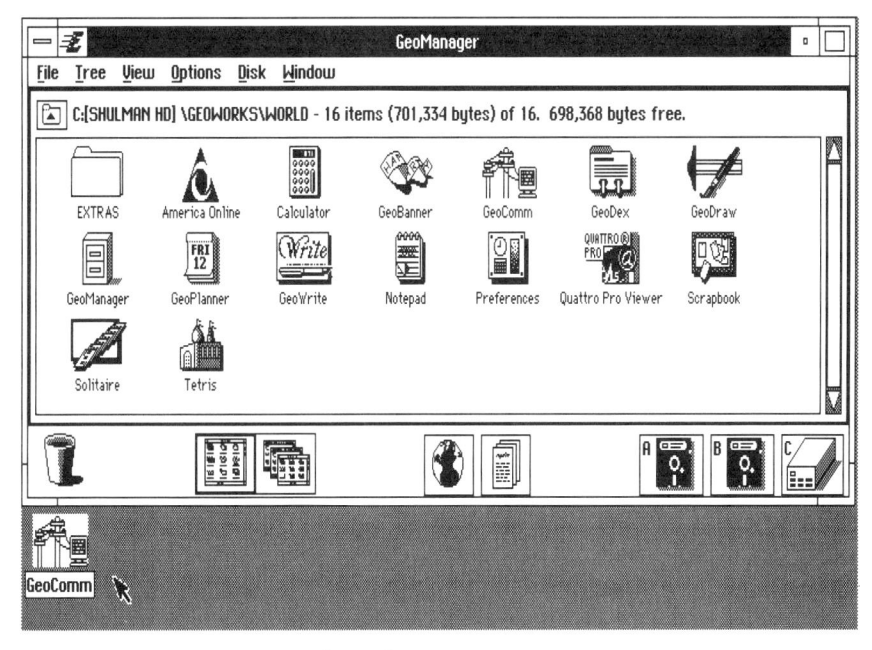

Figure 4.11. GeoComm Reduced to an Icon.

Use the Insert From Text File option to import a DOS file into GeoWrite. The command converts a copy of the original DOS file into a GEOS file; the DOS file remains unchanged.

Moving Around Subdirectories

In this section, you will learn about subdirectories and how to move around them in GeoWorks Pro. The first button in the Insert From Text File dialog box is the Drive button. Beside it is the current drive designation. (In Figure 4.12, drive C: is the current drive and the volume label is SHULMAN.HD.)

```
Insert From Text File
  ■?  C:[SHULMAN HD]
  📁  \GEOWORKS
  📄  DOCUMENT
  📄  ENSEMBLE.BAT
  📄  FIG4_13.TIF
  📁  FONT
  📄  GEO.HLP

      [ Insert ]    [ Cancel ]
```

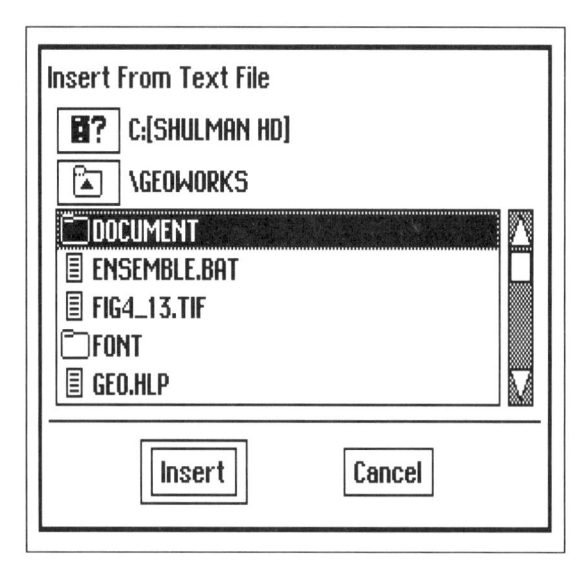

Figure 4.12. The Insert From Text File Dialog Box.

Below the Drive button is the Move Up One Directory Level button. Beside the Move Up One Directory Level button is an information line displaying the path to the current subdirectory. It should read \GEOWORKS. The listing in the panel below the buttons displays the subdirectories (file folders) and files in the current subdirectory.

1. Click: **Move Up One Directory Level** button. The current drive root directory—always identified by a \ (backslash)—becomes the current directory. The files in the root directory and subdirectories under the root directory are now shown in the panel.

2. Double-click on the GEOWORKS subdirectory line in the panel. The current subdirectory now changes to \GEOWORKS. The GEOWORKS subdirectory contents are again displayed in the panel.

3. Double-click on the GEOCOMM subdirectory line in the panel. The current subdirectory changes to \GEOWORKS\GEOCOMM and the subdirectory contents are displayed in the panel—the same two filenames you saw from within the GeoComm application: COMPU.MAC and GENIE.MAC.

NOTE Because these are DOS documents, you would not find them listed if you tried to open them using the Open command in the GeoWrite File menu. GeoWrite would show that the \GEOWORKS\GEOCOMM subdirectory is empty because it does not recognize DOS files.

Importing a DOS File into GeoWrite

Now you will import a DOS document into GeoWrite and save it as a GEOS document and a DOS document (while keeping the original DOS document).

1. Highlight: The document named COMPU.MAC in the Insert From Text File dialog box.

2. Click: the **Insert** button (below the list of files) to import the highlighted file into GeoWrite. The Import From Text File dialog box closes. The program displays page 2 of the two-page file COMPU.MAC in the GeoWrite window. The title bar displays the file name: Write Untitled 1. The displayed document is a GEOS file.

Saving a GEOS Document as a DOS Document

Suppose you have a GEOS document and want to save it as a DOS file. Let's say you want to save it in the \GEOCOMM subdirectory and keep the original unchanged.

1. Select: **Save As Text File** from the File menu, which displays the Save to Text File dialog box. The path information line reads \GEOWORKS.

2. Double-click on the GEOCOMM line in the panel. The information line now reads \GEOWORKS\GEOCOMM.

3. Move: Mouse cursor to the File Name box and click the left mouse button to activate the text cursor.

4. Type: `MYCOMM.MAC`. Remember, if you create a GeoComm script file in GeoWrite, and then save it as a DOS file in the \GEOWORKS\GEOCOMM subdirectory, you must use the .MAC extension.
   Remember that any time you are saving a GEOS file as a DOS text file you must use the DOS file-naming convention described earlier in this chapter.

5. Click: **Save** button to save the DOS file in the \GEOWORKS\GEOCOMM directory with the file name MYCOMM.MAC. The Save As Text File dialog box closes and you return to the GeoWrite application window.

6. Select: **Save** (or **Save As**) from the GeoWrite File menu to display the Select Directory and Enter New File Name dialog box.

7. Move: Mouse cursor into the File name box and click the left mouse button to activate the text cursor.

8. Type: `MY COMM SCRIPT FILE`
   Press: **Enter**.

The program saves the file to the \GEOWORKS\DOCUMENT directory with the file name MY COMM SCRIPT FILE and closes the dialog box. The title bar (the top line of the GeoWrite application window) displays the new filename.

When saving a GEOS file in GeoWrite, follow the GEOS file-naming conventions described earlier in this chapter.

Verifying the DOS File Export

Now you will return to the GeoComm application to make sure the exported file is there.

1. Verify that the MYCOMM.MAC file was saved correctly to the \GEOWORKS\GEOCOMM subdirectory.
   Select: **GeoComm** from the Express menu to return to the already-open GeoComm application.

2. Select: **Scripts** from the Dial menu.
   You now see three script files; one of them is MYCOMM.MAC.

Summary

In Chapter 4 you learned:

- How to move around the Advanced Workspace using the mouse, keyboard commands, and hotkeys
- The basic features of an application window
- The difference between DOS documents and GEOS documents and how to recognize them by their icons and filenames
- The basics of subdirectory structure
- How to import a DOS document into a GEOS application
- How to export a GEOS document to a DOS application
- How to save DOS and GEOS documents

You also reviewed the ways to open an application in the Advanced Workspace. Take a few moments to review the several ways to open an application in the Advanced Workspace:

- Double-click on the application icon in the GeoManager screen.
- Select **Startup** from the Express menu, then select the application name.
- Click on a document icon (in the Document directory display), then select **Open** from the GeoManager File menu.

Chapter 5

GeoManager

The GeoManager Application is the nerve center of the GeoWorks Advanced Workspace. In GeoManager you can perform file and disk management functions easily without having to remember any DOS commands. Specifically, you can:

- Open GEOS applications and documents, as well as DOS programs (non-GeoWorks Pro programs) and batch files
- View the directory structure of a disk as a directory tree. You can expand or shrink branches of the tree to view more or less detail
- View the contents of a directory by name, size, or date and time of last modification
- Open and view more than one directory at a time
- Perform disk management tasks such as formatting, copying, and renaming disks
- Copy and move both files and directories by using the mouse to highlight and then drag them to other disks and directories
- Delete files and directories by using the mouse to highlight and then drag them to the Wastebasket.

The GeoManager Screen

When you start GeoWorks Pro, it displays the Welcome screen. Click the **Advanced** button to display the GeoManager screen shown in Figure 5.1.

When you exit the Advanced Workspace, GeoWorks Pro remembers what programs were open and what documents were on your screen. The next time you run the Advanced Workspace, GeoWorks Pro restores the screen to the way it was when you exited. If you have been using the Advanced Workspace, your screens may vary somewhat from the figures in this book. Don't worry. Any differences will not significantly impact your ability to follow the discussions in this book.

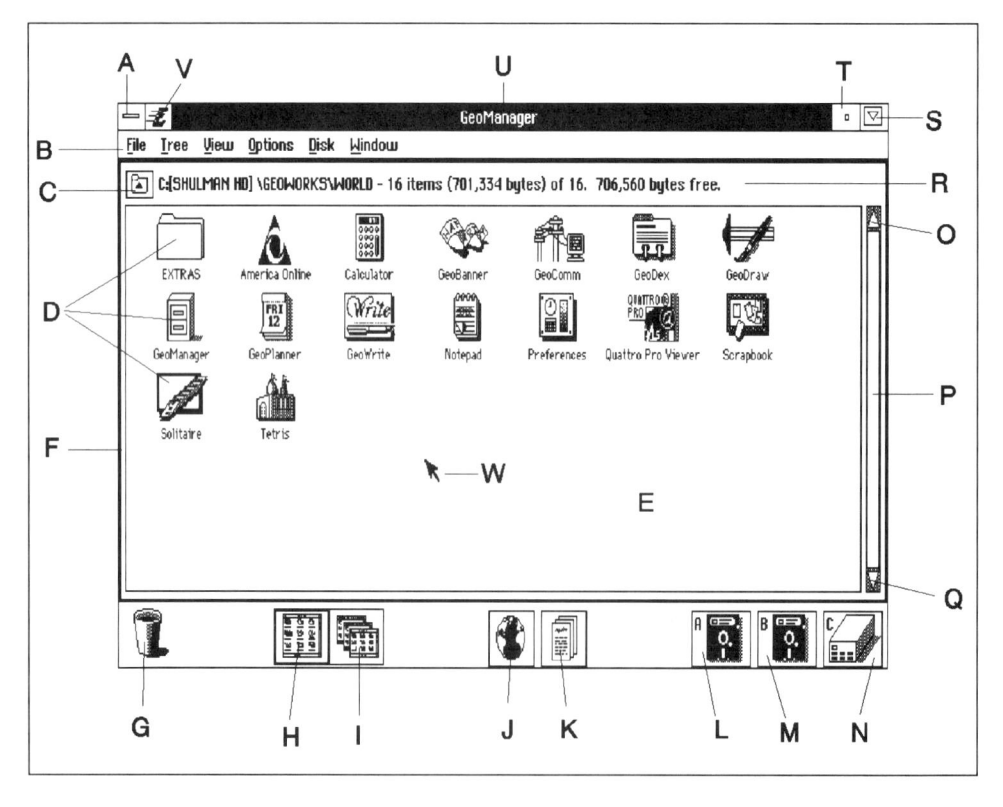

Figure 5.1. Important GeoManager Screen Features.

GeoManager • 75

A. Control button
B. Menu bar
C. Directory button (icon)
D. Icons
E. Main display window
F. Resize border
G. Wastebasket
H. View directories/full-sized windows
I. View directories /overlapping windows
J. WORLD directory button
K. DOCUMENT directory button
L. Floppy disk (5-1/4-inch)
M. Floppy disk (3-1/2-inch)
N. Hard disk drive C:
O. Scroll up arrow
P. Scroll bar
Q. Scroll down arrow
R. Information line
S. Maximize button
T. Minimize button
U. Title bar (active
V. Express menu button
W. Mouse Cursor

Control Line

The top line of the GeoManager screen is divided into five sections (from left to right): the Control button, the Express button, the title bar, the Minimize button, and the Maximize/Restore button.

Control Button

The small rectangular box on the extreme left with the bar through it is the **Control** button (see Figure 5.1, A). All application windows and most menu windows also have a Control button. Its function is always the same: to access the Control menu (with a single click), or to immediately close the application window (with a double-click).

Anytime GeoManager is the only application open, using the Control button to close the GeoManager screen will leave you on the Background screen with no icon or menu to select. If you find yourself stranded in this way, you can:

WARNING

- Press **F2** to return to the Welcome screen, then select the EXIT button to return to the DOS prompt. From here, you can run

GeoWorks Pro again. (You will not be able to select the Advanced box because GeoManager is still running.)

- Press **Ctrl-Alt-Del** to exit to the DOS prompt. (This does not reboot your computer, it simply drops you back to the DOS prompt.) You could also use the reset button if your computer has one (this will reboot your computer).

NOTE Any time GeoWorks Pro exits abnormally it will present you with a Reset screen the next time it is started. This screen will give you the choice to start GeoWorks Pro normally (the Welcome window) or to restart the Advanced Workspace.

Beside each Control menu option is a shortcut command you can use from the keyboard instead of using the Control menu. Every option in the Control menu has a corresponding shortcut command. Not all options in all menus have shortcuts.

Restore (Alt+F5)	Restore is unavailable until you maximize the window. Select **Restore** to return the window to its original size.
Move (Alt+F7)	Move is unavailable until you select an application window you want to reposition.
Size (Alt+F8)	Size is unavailable until you select an application window you want to resize.
Minimize (Alt+F9)	Minimize reduces the window to an icon at the bottom of the screen.
Maximize (Alt+F10)	Maximize expands the window to fill the entire screen. When you select Maximize, Restore becomes active.
Close (Alt+F4)	Select **Close** to exit an application window.

Express Button

The Express button (see Figure 5.1, V) is immediately to the right of the Control button.

Sometimes when you move from one application window to another, the Express button and title bar may not be visible. Simply click the mouse cursor anywhere in the application window to display the Express button and title bar.

The Express menu is divided into three item groups: Welcome, Reopen an Application, and Go To a New Application.

Welcome (F2)

When you select Welcome from the Express menu, both the Express menu and the GeoManager screen close and you return to the GeoWorks Welcome screen. Or you can press **F2** from the GeoManager screen to close GeoManager and return to the Welcome screen without using the Express menu.

Reopen an Application

The middle section of the Express menu gives you instant access to any application that is already open. As the number of open applications increases, the Express menu lengthens to include those applications. You can quickly switch to any open application by selecting it from the Express menu.

You can open multiple applications and move among them easily within the Advanced Workspace. Only one application window is active at a time—the one in which you are working at the moment. Every open application has either a window or an icon visible on the Advanced Workspace screen.

When you select an application from the Express menu, the Express menu closes and the selected application becomes the active window. To switch from one application to another, open the Express menu and click on the desired application program. The current program becomes inactive and the selected program becomes the active window, overlapping other windows on the screen. The active window title bar is highlighted; an inactive window title bar is dimmed.

Applications that do not create documents, such as GeoManager and America Online, will not allow more than one open window at a time for that application.

Applications that create documents, such as GeoWrite and GeoPlanner, allow many open windows for the same application. For example, you could open multiple GeoWrite windows, each displaying a different GeoWrite document. Creating several documents from within the same window does not create separate windows for each document. To create separate windows you must open the application from GeoManager each time.

The Express menu lists every open application window in the order it was created. The only way to distinguish among multiple GeoWrite applications in the Express menu is to remember the order in which you created them.

Startup

Select the **Startup** option when you want to open an application. The program displays a cascading menu, similar to that shown in Figure 5.2, showing the available applications.

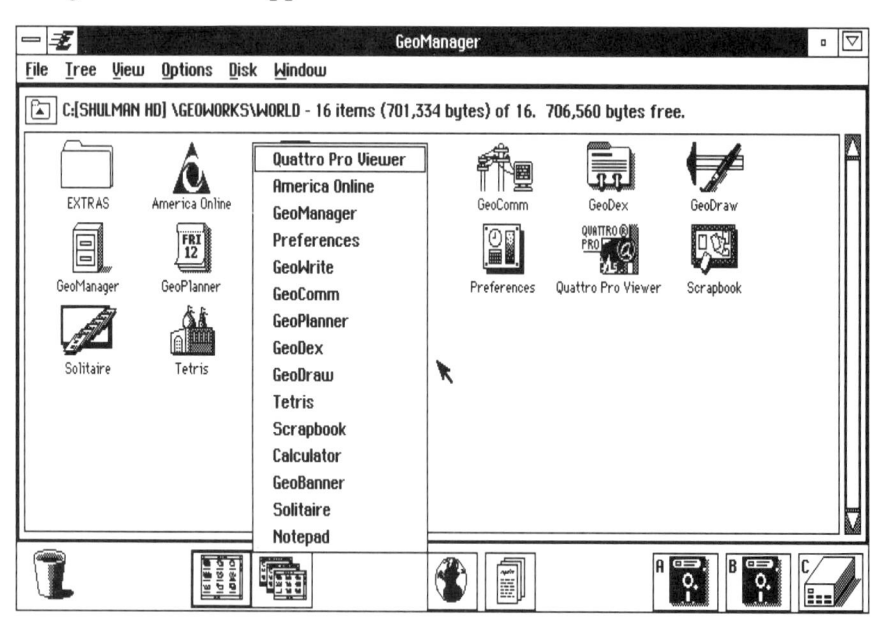

Figure 5.2. The Startup Cascade Menu.

Clicking on an application opens an application window, which becomes the active window. The Express menu adds the new application to its list of open applications. You can start as many applications as you want in the Advanced Workspace.

Printer Control Panel option

If you have several documents to print, GeoWorks Pro lets you put the documents to be printed in a "stack." You can view this stack by choosing **Printer Control Panel** from the Express menu. Figure 5.3 shows a typical Printer Control Panel display.

The top line shows the printer currently being used. To the right of this is the **Other Printer(s)** button. If you have more than one printer, you can click Other Printer(s) on the Printer Control Panel dialog box to view the documents waiting to print on that printer.

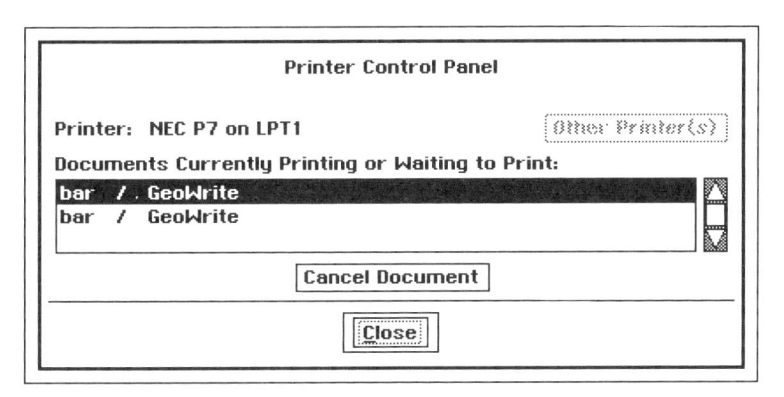

Figure 5.3. A Printer Control Panel Display.

The middle section displays a list of documents, with the document that is currently printing at the top and the documents waiting listed below it. Documents near the beginning of the list print before those farther down.

You can cancel any document if you wish, including the one that is currently printing. Click on the name of the document in the list that you wish to cancel, then click the **Cancel Document** button. If the document you cancel is the one that is currently printing, the printer may continue for a short time before stopping.

If you have a list of documents to be printed and you exit to DOS, when you return you are asked if you want to continue printing.

Exit to DOS

Selecting the **Exit to DOS** option closes both the active window and the Express menu, returning you directly to the DOS prompt.

Another, slightly longer way to exit to DOS is to select Welcome from the Express menu (or press **F2**) to return to the Welcome screen. Then click the **EXIT** button to return to the DOS prompt. No matter which method you use, when you return to the Advanced Workspace the next time, it will be exactly as it was just before you left it.

Title Bar

The center portion of the top line of a window is the title bar (see Figure 5.1, U), which identifies the window's application. Applications that create documents, such as GeoWrite and GeoComm, will also display a document name in the title bar.

Relocating a Window

You can relocate an active window by placing the mouse cursor over the title bar, then pressing and holding the left mouse button. The mouse cursor changes to a small cursor with four arrowheads, one pointing up, one down, one left and one right. As long as you hold down the left mouse button you can drag the window around the screen. Release the mouse button to "set down" the window in its new location. Moving and resizing windows allows you to arrange the workspace to suit your preferences.

Resizing a Window

The outer edge of most windows is divided into eight resizing sections—each corner of the window and the sides between the corners. You cannot resize a window if it doesn't have these resizing sections. Moving the mouse cursor onto any of these sections changes the mouse cursor's appearance. Its new shape indicates the border(s) you can resize.

Press and hold the left mouse button to display an outline of the window. Drag the window edge in the direction of the mouse pointer to change the outline size (larger or smaller). Release the mouse button when the window is the size you want. You will not be able to shrink a window beyond its minimum size.

Repositioning an Icon

Place the mouse cursor on the icon you want to reposition, then press and hold the left mouse button while you drag the icon to its new location. Release the left mouse button.

Unshrinking an Icon

To restore a window from an icon, double-click the left mouse button on the icon.

Menu Bar

The GeoManager menu bar, the second line at the top of the window (see Figure 5.1, B), contains six options: File, Tree, View, Options, Disk and Window.

File Menu

Select File to display the File menu. The File menu contains the following menu items:

Pin

Select (click on) the pin symbol to keep the menu open after you have made your selection. Notice that the pin disappears and a Control button appears in the upper-left corner of the menu. Once a menu is pinned, you can relocate it wherever you want.

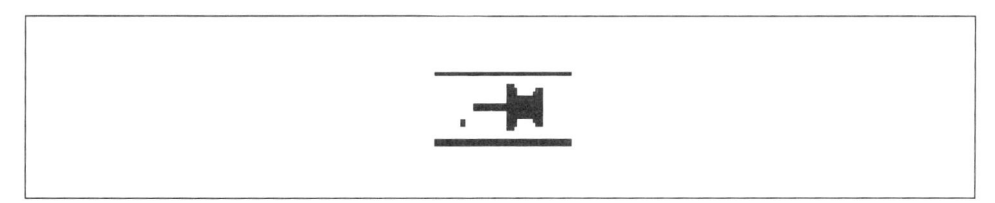

Figure 5.4. The Pin Symbol.

Open

Before you can use this menu option, you must first select an item. If you select an application icon, you will open that application. If you want to open a subdirectory or a file, you must be in the DOCUMENT directory. Click on the **Document** button at the bottom of the GeoManager window (Figure 5.1, K) to display the documents and subdirectories.

Click on a document icon, then select **Open** from the File menu. You can also double-click on a document icon to select it directly from the GeoManager window. If you selected a GEOS document, the program displays the document in an application window. If you selected DOS document, GeoManager alerts you that the file cannot be opened.

Get Info

Click on a document icon to highlight it. Select **Get Info** from the File menu to display the Get Info dialog box. Figure 5.5 shows a typical GEOS document Get Info dialog box (with a pinned File menu at the left).

If the read-only attribute is not set, you can enter and edit text in the User Notes box shown in Figure 5.5 (as it is here.) Click the **OK** button to save the notes with the file. If you selected more than one document, click the **Next** button to display the next selected document. Click the **Cancel** button to close the dialog box.

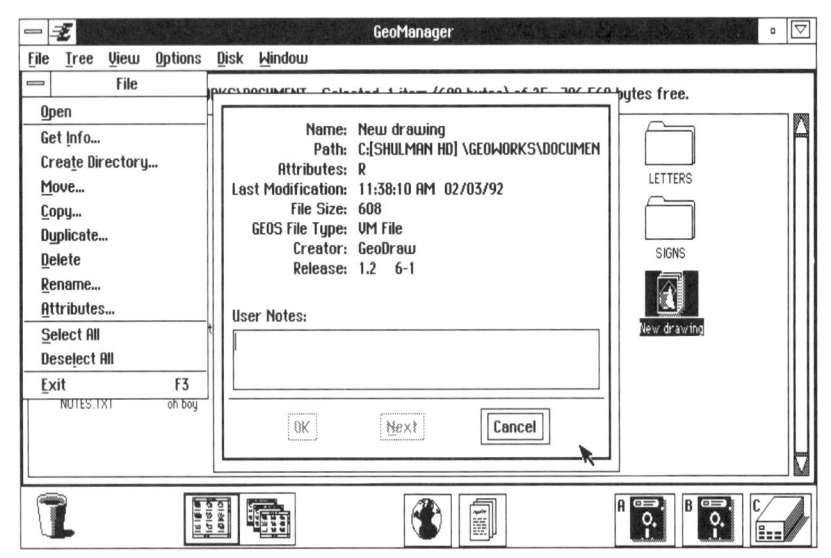

Figure 5.5. Get Info Dialog Box for a GEOS Document.

Create Directory

Select **Create Directory** on the File menu to create a new directory. You will usually use this option when the Tree menu is displayed (see below). Figure 5.6 shows the Create Directory dialog box displayed over the directory tree for drive C:.

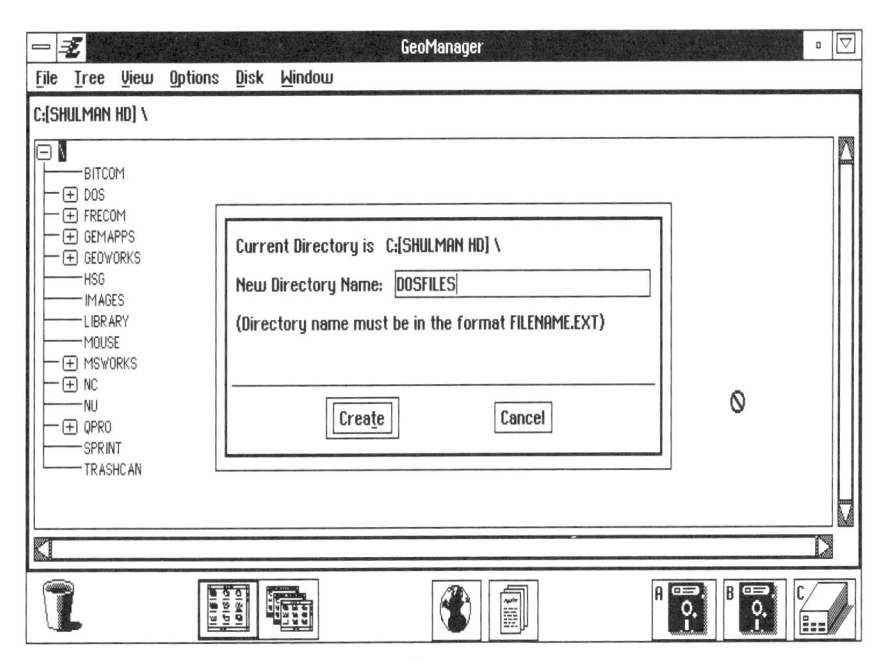

Figure 5.6. Create Directory Dialog Box.

Suppose you have a subdirectory called MUSIC on your hard drive. You want to create a subdirectory under MUSIC called JAZZ. To create the new directory, first open the MUSIC directory. Select **Create Directory** from the File menu. Enter the new subdirectory name in the dialog box, then click the **Create** button. GeoWorks Pro creates the new subdirectory. MUSIC is now the parent directory of JAZZ. Directories must follow the DOS conventions for naming files.

Move

The Move command deletes the item from its current location and relocates it. Highlight the item you want to move by clicking on it, then select **Move** from the File menu to display the Move dialog box.

GeoManager's move functions just as Move does in the Intermediate Workspace, discussed in Chapter 3.

Copy

The steps to copy an item are almost identical to moving the item. However, when you copy an item, the original item remains in its current location and a copy of it is made at the new location. See Chapter 3 for a full discussion of Copy.

NOTE When you highlight a subdirectory and select **Copy**, the program copies the subdirectory and all its contents in the same operation.

Duplicate

Use the Duplicate command to make a copy of the file under a different name in the same directory or subdirectory. (Remember, copying a file results in two identical files with the same name, but in different locations.) Highlight the items you want to duplicate, then select Duplicate from the File menu. See Chapter 3 for a full discussion of Duplicate.

Delete

Use the Delete command to delete items. Highlight the files or subdirectories you want to delete, then select **Delete** from the File menu. If the Confirm Delete option is set in the Options menu (discussed later), then the program displays a dialog box asking you to confirm each deletion: click **Yes** to delete, **No** to not delete.

WARNING If the Confirm Delete option is *not* set in the Options menu, you will confirm, once that you want to proceed, then the program will delete all selected items. Click on **Cancel** to close the dialog box without deleting any more files.

When you select multiple items to delete, a progress box tells you what is happening. Click on **Stop** in the progress box to stop the delete operation after the current file.

Delete by dragging

You can delete selected items by dragging them (using the *right* mouse button) to the Wastebasket icon at the bottom of the GeoManager screen. If the Confirm Delete option is set in the Options menu, the program displays a dialog box asking you to confirm each delete. Click on **Cancel** to close the dialog box without deleting any more files.

If Confirm Delete is *not* set on the Options menu, you will not receive a request to confirm the delete. The items are deleted as soon as you release the right mouse button on the Wastebasket icon.

WARNING

Rename

To change the name of directories or files, highlight the items, then select **Rename** from the File menu to display a dialog box. Click on the **To** box and type the new name for the first item. Click on **Rename**. To skip an item, click on **Next**. Click on **Cancel** to close the dialog box without renaming any additional files. If you type a name that conflicts with an existing file or subdirectory, a dialog box prompts you to select a different name.

Attributes

There are four types of attributes you can assign to DOS files:

R	Read-only
H	Hidden
S	System
B	Archive.

An attribute is either on or off. Attributes are used only with DOS files (non-GEOS files); a file can have any combination of attributes. Perhaps the most useful attribute is Read-only, which protects a file against accidental changes or deletion. You can see file attributes by selecting **Names and Details** from the View menu. The far-right column displays file attributes. Figure 5.7 shows a Names and Details file listing for drive C.

```
                         GeoManager
File  Tree  View  Options  Disk  Window
  C:[SHULMAN HD] \ - 42 items (589,531 bytes) of 52. 759,808 bytes free.
  EPSON100.SYS      42,156 02/28/88   6:57:46 AM
  EPSONLQ.SYS       45,288 03/01/88   5:04:18 PM
  FRECONFG.EXE      81,992 09/17/90   3:49:12 PM A
  GOMOUSE.BAT          123 10/21/89  12:20:20 AM
  GS.BAT                13 03/26/91  12:35:40 PM A
  HERCBW.SYS        35,596 02/28/88   6:58:06 AM
  HIMEM.SYS         11,304 05/01/90   3:00:00 AM A
  IBMBW.SYS         32,976 02/28/88   7:05:58 AM
  IMAGE.DAT         47,616 11/16/91   8:39:16 PM R A
  KEYDES.COM        45,024 11/07/86   1:16:00 AM
  LOG.COM            1,807 12/09/88   9:51:58 PM
  NDOS.COM          11,845 06/06/91   6:00:00 AM A
  NDOS.LOG           7,128 02/05/92  12:20:44 PM A
  NDOS.OVL          73,612 06/06/91   6:00:00 AM A
  QUIKMEM2.SYS       3,628 01/28/88   8:26:28 AM
  SCAN.BAT              36 10/25/91   3:05:08 PM A
  TREEINFO.NCD         411 02/03/92  10:48:08 AM A
  WINA20.386         9,349 04/09/91   5:00:00 AM R
```

Figure 5.7. A Names and Details Display.

Highlight the file or files whose attributes you want to change. If you want to change attributes on a consecutive group of files, press and hold the left mouse button on the first file, then drag the highlight to include all the files you want to affect. Release the button. To select multiple individual files, hold down Shift then click on the files you want to select.

Select **Attributes** from the File menu to display the Change File Attributes dialog box, similar to Figure 5.8.

Click on the attributes you want to select for the file named in the Change File Attributes dialog box. Clicking an attribute toggles it on and off. Click on **Change** to assign the attributes to the current file. Click on **Next** to go to the next file without changing the current file's attributes. Click on **Cancel** to close the dialog box without making any additional file attribute changes. To see the file attribute changes, select **Names and Details** from the View menu.

If Show Hidden Files is set in the View menu, files with hidden or system attributes will display. If Show Hidden Files is not set in the View menu, you will not see any files with the Hidden or System attributes.

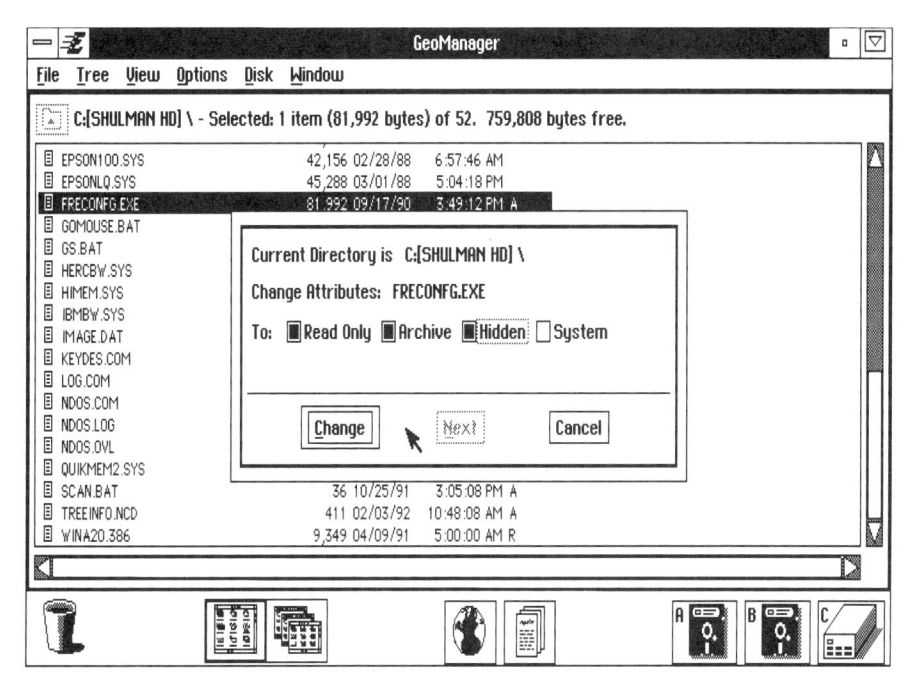

Figure 5.8. The Change File Attributes Dialog Box.

Select all

Use this option to select (highlight) all items (subdirectories and files) in a directory.

Deselect all

Use this option to deselect (remove the highlight from) all selected items in a directory.

Exit (F3)

Select **Exit** from the File menu to remove the application from memory and close the window. You can also exit an application by double-clicking on the **Control** button.

If GeoManager is the only open application, closing it returns you to the Welcome screen.

NOTE Normally you do not exit GeoManager. If you are running several applications and you notice that your system is running slowly, you can exit GeoManager to free memory.

Tree Menu

Use the Tree menu to view the subdirectories on a disk. The Tree menu displays the directory structure as an organization tree. The root directory (\ ) is at the top of the tree. Directories and subdirectories are shown with branch lines, indicating their relationship to the root directory and to each other. You can control how much of the tree to display by expanding or collapsing the directories. A plus sign (+) beside a directory name means the directory can be expanded to display subdirectories. A minus sign (-) indicates a subdirectory is fully expanded. Double-click on a directory to look at its files.

The Tree menu contains the following menu items:

Pin

Select the pin symbol to keep the menu open after you have made your selection from it. Once a menu is pinned, you can relocate it wherever you want.

Show Tree Window

Select this option when you want to display the directory contents of the current drive in tree form. Figure 5.9 shows the structure of a typical directory tree with GEOWORKS selected.

Drive

Select this option to change the tree display to a different drive. Select the new drive (for example, drive D:) from the cascading menu.

Expand All

Select this option when you want to Expand All directories shown in the directory tree, displaying the entire subdirectory structure, as shown in Figure 5.10.

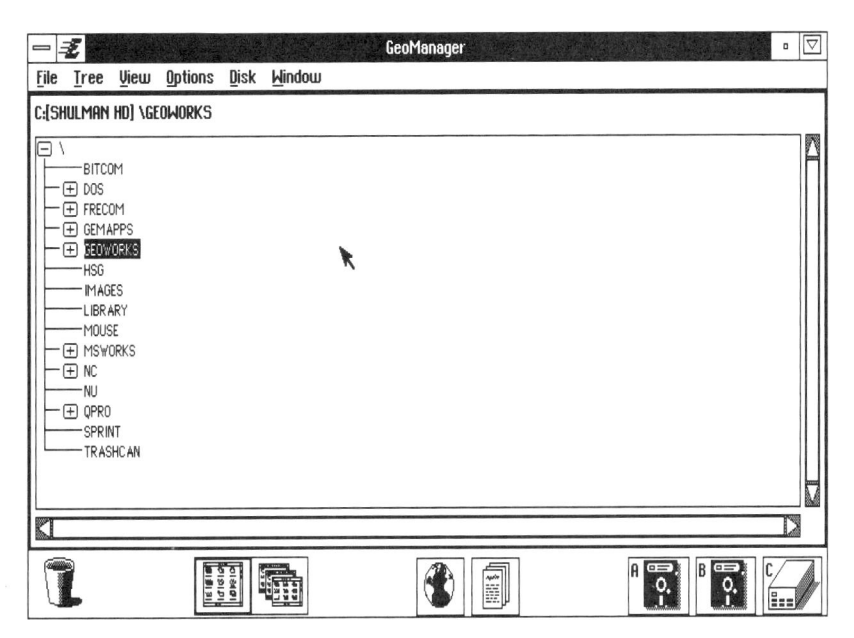

Figure 5.9. A Directory Tree.

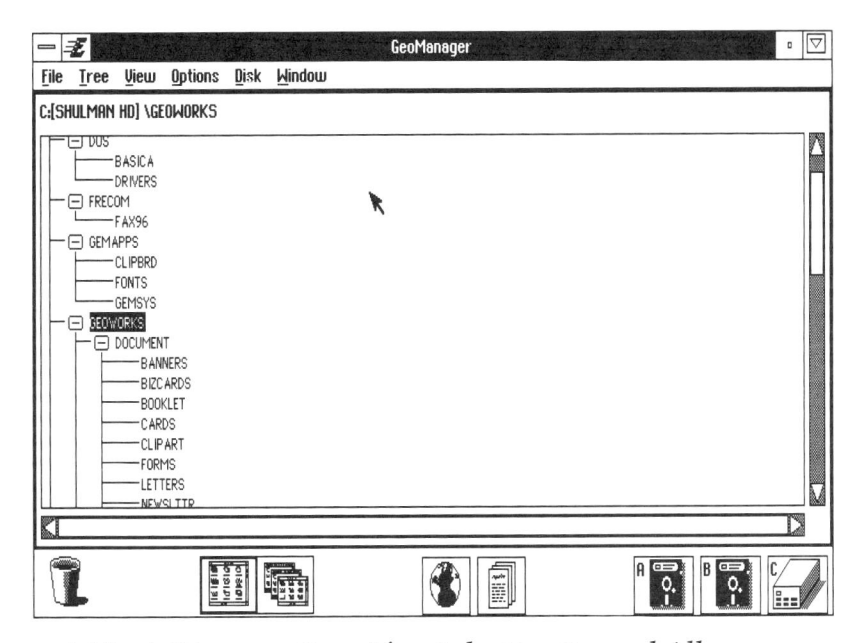

Figure 5.10. A Directory Tree After Selecting Expand All.

Expand One Level

To expand only one level, click the plus sign (+) next to the directory you want to expand. The next subdirectory level displays.

You can also click on the name of the directory you want to expand (do not click on the plus or minus sign) to highlight the directory. Then choose Expand One Level from the Tree menu. The selected branch expands one subdirectory level.

Expand Branch

To expand all directories and subdirectories within a branch, click on the name of the directory you want to expand (do not click on the plus or minus sign). Then select Expand Branch from the Tree menu. The selected branch expands to display the complete structure of that directory.

Collapse Branch

To collapse all directories within a branch, click on the name of the directory you want to collapse (do not click on the plus or minus sign). Then select Collapse Branch from the Tree menu. The selected branch collapses. Compare Figure 5.10 and Figure 5.11 to see the difference between the expanded and collapsed displays for the GEOWORKS directory.

Click on the minus sign beside a subdirectory to collapse that directory branch.

View Menu

The items in the GeoManager directory window are usually represented by small icons arranged alphabetically by name. Use the View menu to change the GeoManager display. Select the subdirectory you want to view, then select one of the View menu options.

Pin

Select the pin symbol to keep the menu open after you have made your selection from it. Once a menu is pinned, you can relocate it wherever you want.

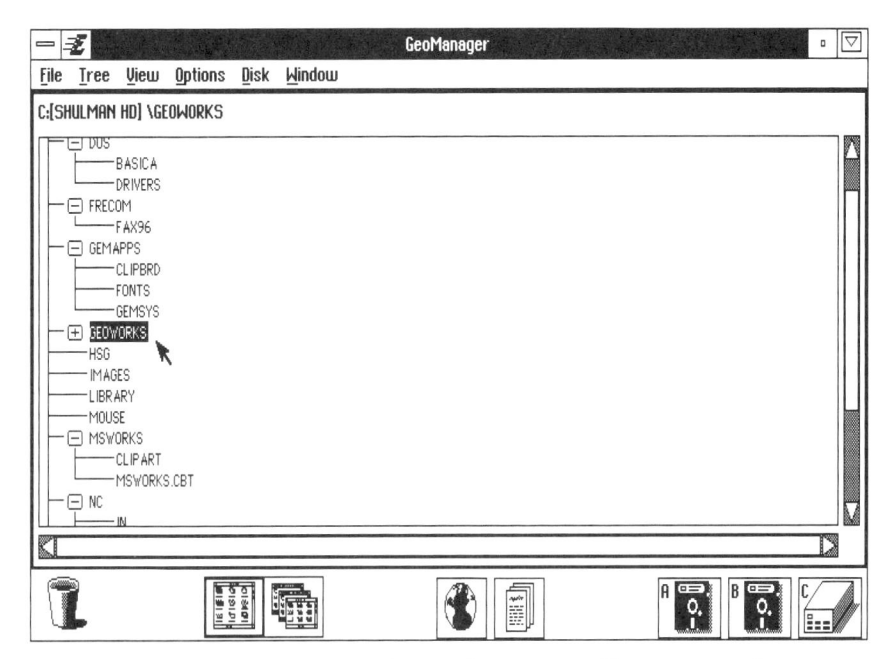

Figure 5.11. A Directory Tree After Selecting Collapse Branch.

Names Only

Select this option to display the contents of the window as a list of small icons with the name to the right of the icon. Use this view if you have numerous files and you want to see as many of them as possible at one time.

Names and Details

Select this option to display the contents of the window as a list of small icons with the name, size, last modification date, and attributes to the right of each icon. The modification date for a directory is the date it was created.

Icons

Select this option to show the contents of the active directory as icons, with the name below the icon.

Sort By

To change the way files are sorted in a subdirectory, first select the subdirectory, then select **Sort By** in the View menu. Select the sort option you want from the cascading menu. Directories are always displayed before files no matter what sorting method is used.

The Sort By cascade menu gives you three choices:

Name	Sorts alphabetically by file name
Date and Time	Sorts files by date and time of last modification, displaying the most recently modified files first
Size	Sorts files by size, displaying the largest file first

Show Hidden Files

Toggle this option to display or hide files that have Hidden or System attributes. If the Show Hidden Files menu item is not selected, Hidden or System files are not listed in the active directory display.

Compress Display

When you select this option, the directory display compresses, displaying as much as possible on the screen at one time. Figure 5.12 shows an uncompressed display. Figure 5.13 shows the same directory in compressed format.

Options Menu

Pin

Select the pin symbol to keep the menu open after you have made your selection from it. Once a menu is pinned, you can relocate it wherever you want.

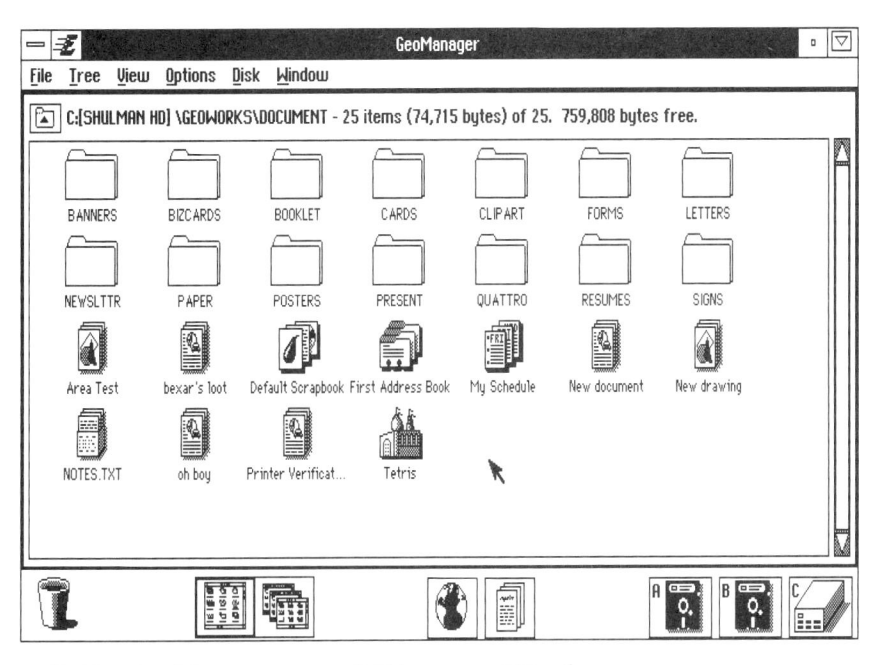

Figure 5.12. An Uncompressed Directory Display.

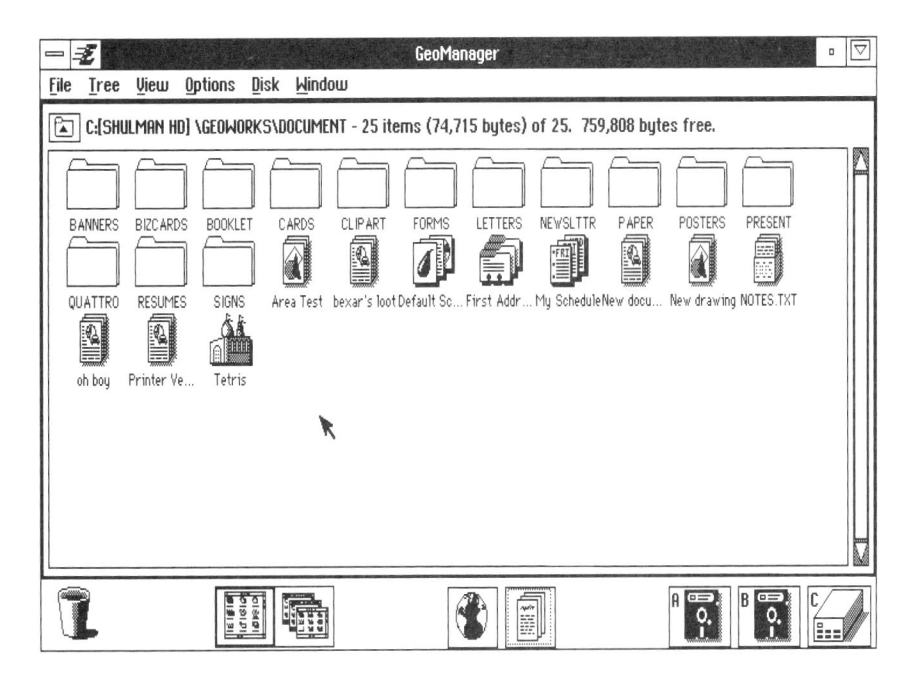

Figure 5.13. A Compressed Directory Display.

The next three items in the Options menu determine whether a confirmation message will display when you delete or replace a file.

Confirm Delete

Select this option to always display a confirmation box when you delete a file of any kind. If the Confirm Read-only option is set, you will get a separate confirmation box when you are about to delete a read-only file.

Confirm Read-Only

Select this option if you want a confirmation box when you delete a read-only file, regardless of whether Confirm Delete is set or not.

Confirm Replace

Select this option to display a confirmation box when you copy or move a file to a directory that contains another file with the same file name. If Confirm Replace is toggled off, the file you are moving or copying will automatically—without confirmation—overwrite (replace) the existing file.

Minimize on Run

Select this option if you want GeoManager to shrink to an icon when you run another GeoWorks application. If Minimize on Run is off, GeoManager remains open when you switch to another application.

Ask Before Returning to GeoWorks Pro

If you have this option on, and you start a DOS program or batch file from GeoManager, when the batch file finishes or you are ready to quit the DOS program, you will be asked to press either **Enter** to return to GeoWorks Pro or **Esc** to go to DOS. This gives you time to read any output on the screen before returning to GeoWorks Pro.

If the option is off, GeoWorks Pro will restart immediately.

You can verify this by selecting the Show Tree Window option from the GeoManager Tree menu. Select your DOS directory and then double-click on CHKDSK.EXE. You return to DOS and a display of the disk's contents is displayed.

Save Options

Select this option to save the current selections in the Options menu. The new menu settings become the default settings and are used whenever you run GeoWorks Pro.

Disk Menu

Use the Disk menu to make a copy of a floppy disk, format a disk, rename a disk, or rescan a drive to update a directory display. Figure 5.14 displays the Disk menu. The menu is pinned so it will remain open after you select a menu item (in this case, Rename Disk).

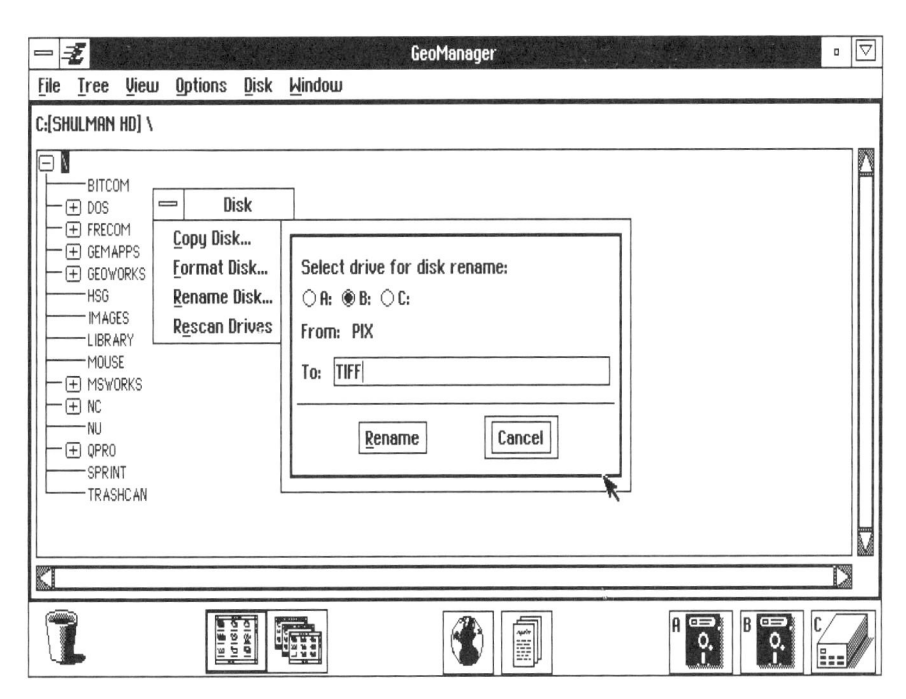

Figure 5.14. The Disk Menu.

Copy Disk

This option is similar to using the DOS DISKCOPY command. It duplicates an entire floppy disk onto another floppy disk. The source (original) and target (destination) disks *must be the same size*, and the drives *must be the same type,* for example, 360K floppy disk to 360K floppy disk. You cannot use Copy Disk to copy files from a 360K floppy disk to a 1.2M floppy disk nor from a 3-1/2-inch disk to a 5-1/4-inch disk.

If you have two similar floppy drives, you can copy the disk in one drive to the disk in the other. If you do not have two like drives, you will be instructed to exchange disks as the copy is made.

It is a good idea to label the disks before you start a disk copy so you don't get them mixed up during the exchanges.

Select **Copy Disk** from the Disk menu to display a dialog box similar to Figure 5.15. In this figure you can see that when drive A: is selected as the source, drive B: is not an available drive destination; the destination is shown as A:. In this case, drive A: is a 5-1/4-inch drive and drive B: is a 3-1/2-inch drive.

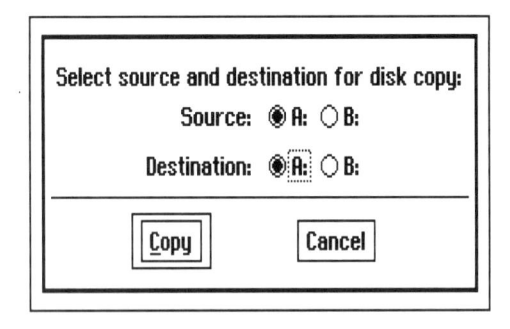

Figure 5.15. The Copy Disk Dialog Box.

Select the source by clicking on the drive you want to use. Select the destination drive. Select **Copy** from the Copy Disk dialog box. Screen instructions tell you when and where to exchange disks (if necessary) and when the copy is complete.

Format Disk

Disks must be formatted before you can use them. Use the Format Disk command to format (or reformat) a disk.

If you want to know if a disk is formatted, insert it in a drive and click the drive icon in the right corner of the GeoManager window. If the disk is formatted, the program displays a disk directory. If the disk is not formatted, the disk drive is empty, or the drive door is open the program displays the message, **Couldn't find a formatted disk in drive.**

To format a floppy disk, place it in a disk drive, then select **Format Disk** from the Disk menu to display the Format Disk dialog box. Click on the drive that contains the disk you want to format. A selection box displays the format options for the selected drive.

Click on the size selection (floppy disk capacity) you want. Note that options indicate when high-density floppy disks are required. These store more data but are more costly.

It is best to select the highest capacity you can for the floppy disk and drive you are using. For example, it is possible, but not recommended, to format a 1.2M diskette (which holds 1,200,000 bytes of data) at the lower 360K density (so it holds only 360,000 bytes). However, it isn't a good idea to format a 1.2M disk as a 360K diskette.

After you select the size of a disk, another dialog box prompts you for an optional disk volume label (disk name). A volume label can be up to 11 characters long. Type a volume label if you want one. Click **Format**. The program formats the disk according to your selections.

A summary screen tells you when formatting is complete and displays the total bytes of disk space, bytes in bad sectors, and bytes available on the disk.

Rename Disk

Use Rename Disk when you want to name an already-formatted disk or change an existing volume label. You can label floppy diskettes and your hard drives. Figure 5.14 shows the Rename Disk dialog box. The volume label in drive B: is PIX. A new volume label, TIFF, has been typed in the box. Clicking the **Rename** button in the dialog box changes the volume label in drive B: from PIX to TIFF. Clicking the Cancel button closes the dialog box without changing the label.

Rescan Drives

If you change a floppy disk in a drive, select **Rescan Drives** from the Disk menu to update the directory display. The program rereads all displayed drives (floppy and hard drives) and updates the GeoManager display.

Window Menu

Pin

Select the pin symbol to keep the menu open after you have made your selection from it. Once a menu is pinned, you can relocate it wherever you want.

Close

Select **Close** to close the active window.

Close All

Select **Close All** to close all currently open windows.

Overlapping (Ctrl+F5)

Select **Overlapping** from the Window menu if you want to overlap open windows. You can also use the Overlapping icon at the bottom of the GeoManager window. Figure 5.16 shows three overlapping window displays.

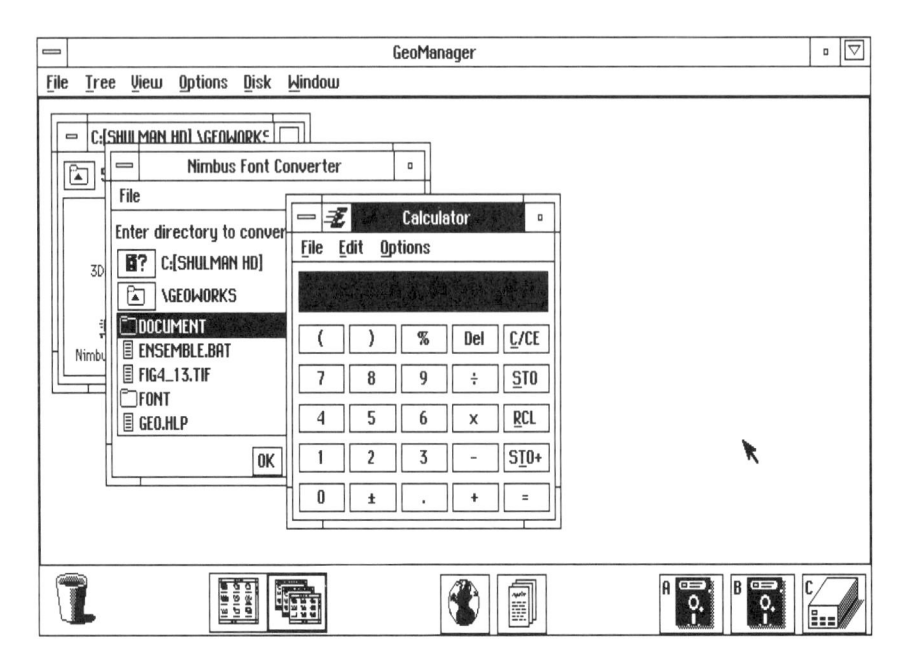

Figure 5.16. Overlapping Windows Display.

You can maximize the active window, drag the active window to a new location, or resize the active window in an overlapping display.

Full-Sized (Ctrl+F10)

Select this option to view the active window in an overlapping display as a full-sized window.

Listing and Selection

The bottom portion of the Window menu lists open directory windows. A filled-in circle indicates the active directory window. If you select another directory from this menu, it becomes the active window (and the filled-in circle is displayed next to it).

Information Line

The third line of the GeoManager window, the Information line (see Figure 5.1, R), displays the current directory and the path to the current directory. It tells you the total number of files in the subdirectory, how many of those files are visible (not hidden files), how much disk space the visible files use, and how much free space is available on the disk.

At the extreme left end of the Information line is a small index-card icon with an upward-pointing arrowhead. Click on this button to move up one directory level.

Main Display Window

The Main Display Window in the GeoManager window is the primary work and display area (see Figure 5.1, E). When you are viewing the contents of the World directory, you see icons representing the Advanced Workspace applications. These are representative of the functions the applications perform.

Bottom Line Icons

Wastebasket

You use the Wastebasket to permanently delete files and directories. To do this, place the mouse cursor over the file or directory you want to delete and press and hold the *right* mouse button. Drag the selected file or directory to the Wastebasket and release the right mouse button. The program asks you to confirm that you want to delete the item. (Once deleted, the item cannot be recovered.)

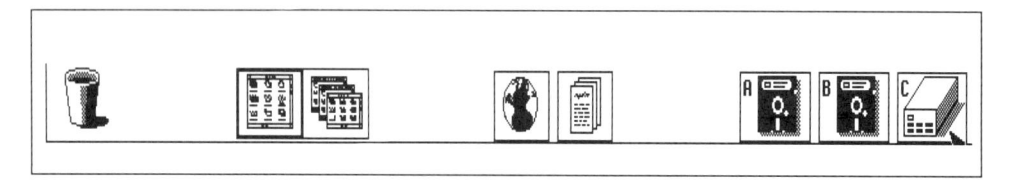

Figure 5.17. The GeoManager Screen Bottom Line Icons.

Full-sized/overlapping Buttons

Use these buttons to toggle between full-sized (see Figure 5.1, H) and overlapping window (see Figure 5.1, I) displays. You can switch between viewing one directory at a time, or simultaneously viewing multiple directories.

The two main subdirectories in GeoWorks Pro are WORLD and DOCUMENT. (The DOCUMENT subdirectory is discussed next.) The World directory contains applications—programs you can run—displayed as icons.

Document Button

The DOCUMENT directory contains your data files, the files you create and use while working in a GeoWorks Pro application. File icons represent both DOS and GEOS files. (See Chapter 4 for a discussion on the difference between GEOS and DOS files, their icons, and file-naming conventions.)

A folder icon represents a subdirectory under the current directory. A subdirectory can contain files and other subdirectories. The folder name (subdirectory name) must adhere to the DOS file-naming convention of one to eight characters for the name and an optional one to three-character extension.

Drive Buttons

In the lower-right corner of the GeoManager window are the drive buttons (see Figure 5.1, L-N), one for each available drive on your computer, including RAM disks, ROM disks, or other disk-drive types. Click on a drive button to change the GeoManager display to that drive.

Summary

In this chapter you learned how to use the GeoManager application. Each of the GeoManager menus and menu options was explained in detail, including a discussion on subdirectory structure and floppy-disk-capacity options.

Chapter 6

The Preferences Application and the Extras Directory

The Preferences Application

When you installed GeoWorks Pro, you selected monitor, mouse, and printer settings for your computer. You can change these and other settings at any time by using the Preferences application in the Advanced Workspace. You can change:

- The look and feel of the program
- The computer's date and time settings
- The background image over which windows are displayed
- Whether Sounds are on
- The settings for your monitor, mouse, printer, modem, and keyboard
- Formats for Currency, Quotes, Date, and Time
- Settings for the internal operations of GeoWorks Pro.

Accessing the Preferences Application

You can start the Preferences application two ways:

- Double-click on the **Preferences** icon in the GeoManager World window.
- Choose **Startup** from the Express Menu and select **Preferences** from the cascading menu.

Figure 6.1 shows the Preferences window after accessing it from the GeoManager World window.

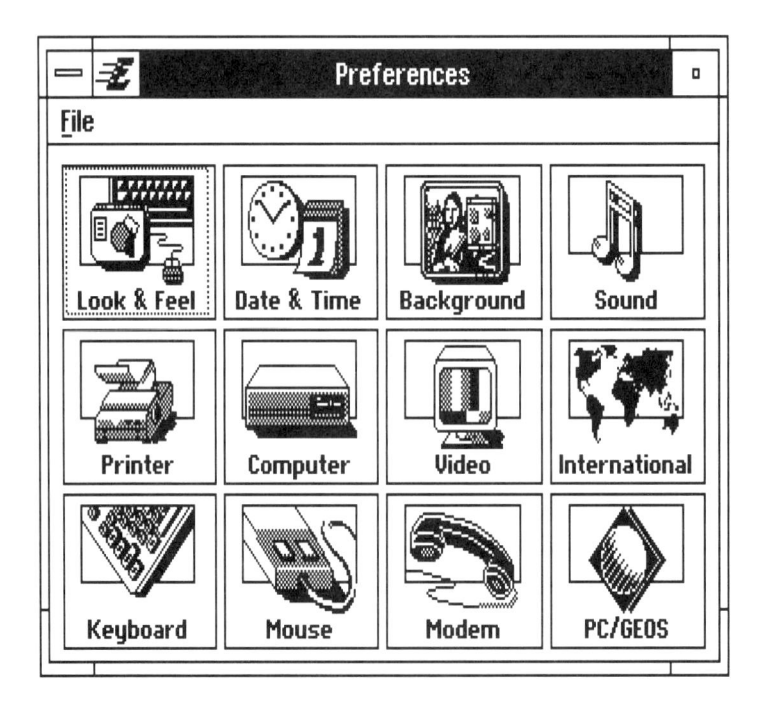

Figure 6.1. The Preferences Window.

The Preferences window includes the standard application window features: Control button, title bar, Minimize button and menu bar. File is the only menu option on the menu bar. Use the nine Preferences icons to configure GeoWorks Pro on your computer to your needs and preferences.

Look & Feel

Use this option to:

- Set the size of text in menus and dialog boxes
- Specify how often an application should safeguard (back up) your open documents
- Set the Overstrike Mode
- Decide which part of the program you want to enter automatically when you start GeoWorks Pro (bypass the Welcome screen if you wish).

Selecting **Look & Feel** displays the dialog box shown in Figure 6.2. Filled-in circles indicate the active options.

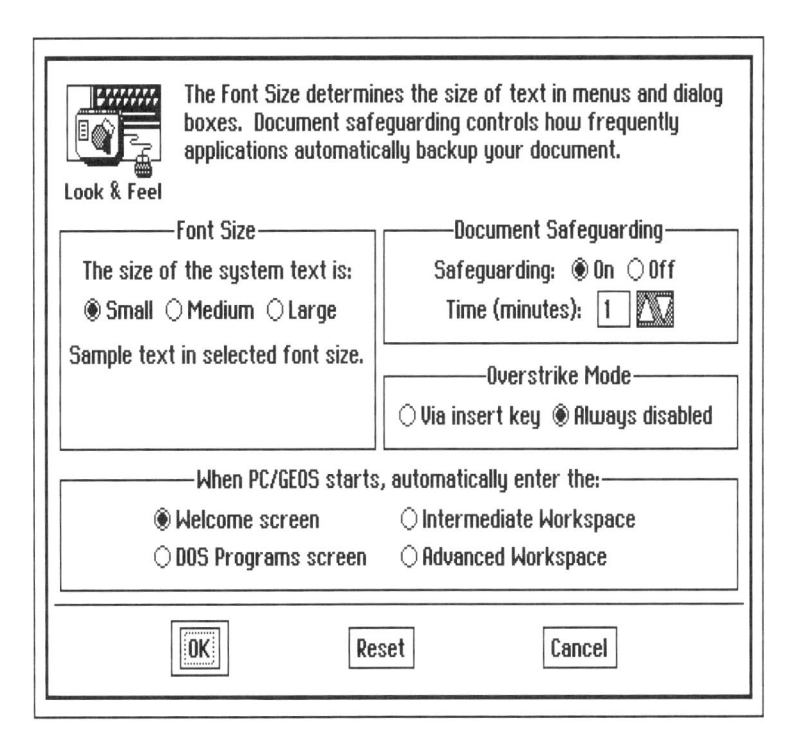

Figure 6.2. The Look & Feel Dialog Box.

Font Size

You can select one of three options for the font size displayed in menus and dialog boxes: small, medium, or large. When you click on an option, the sample text in the Font Size box changes to demonstrate the active setting. (This setting does not affect your printed documents.)

Document Safeguarding

As you modify a document, your changes are stored in the computer's temporary memory until you save the document. If you turn off your computer before saving your modified document, the changes will be lost. With Safeguarding On, changes stored in temporary memory are periodically and automatically stored on disk, although not as part of your document. When you save a document, safeguarded changes and changes in temporary memory become a permanent part of the document.

Click on the up and down triangles to specify the time interval (in minutes from 1 to 18) between saves.

NOTE Under certain circumstances, you can undo changes to a previously saved document. Select the **Revert** option in the GeoManager File menu to restore to the screen the last-saved version of your document. All changes in temporary memory and safeguarded changes are erased.

Overstrike Mode

You can choose to have the overstrike mode always disabled or to have it invoked when you use the Insert (Ins) key.

Opening Screen

In the bottom panel of the Look & Feel dialog box you can select which part of GeoWorks Pro you want to enter automatically when you start the program: the Welcome screen, the Intermediate Workspace, the Advanced Workspace, or the DOS Programs screen. Click the one you want.

OK, Reset, and Cancel

Click the **OK** button when you are satisfied with your Preferences selections. The document safeguarding changes take effect immediately.

The Font Size and Opening Screen settings will not be effective until you exit and re-enter GeoWorks Pro.

Click the **Reset** button to return the settings you changed to the way they were when you opened the dialog box.

Click the **Cancel** button to close the dialog box and return to the Preferences window without saving any changes.

Date & Time

Use this handy feature to set the current date and time in your computer's internal clock.

Date

Position the mouse cursor in the Date box, then click to activate the text cursor. You can type the date in two ways: `3/26/92` or `3/26/1992`.

Time

Position the mouse cursor in the Time box, then click to activate the text cursor. Enter the time using the 12-hour format. Be sure to include A.M. or P.M. after the time (separated by a space). For example: `12:06 P.M.` or `9:47 A.M.`

OK, Reset, and Cancel

Click the **OK** button to update the clock.

Click the **Reset** button to revert to the date and time settings active when you opened the dialog box.

Click the **Cancel** button to return to the Preferences window without making any changes.

Background

The background is the area behind all windows in your workspace. This fun item lets you change the background from a solid gray to either a pattern or a picture (graphic). Select **Background** to display the dialog box shown in Figure 6.3. Note that this is the dialog box you see if you have a black-and-white monitor. If you have color, there will be a color bar located just above the Get Background from Clipboard button.

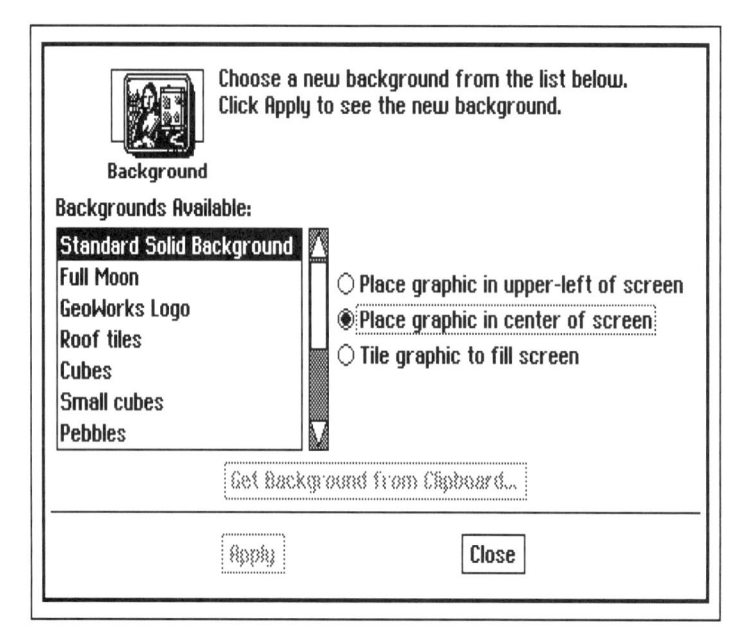

Figure 6.3. The Background Dialog Box.

Selecting a Background

GeoWorks Pro comes with 12 background options listed in the left panel. You can create your own background and add it to the list (discussed later in this chapter). Use the scroll bar to view the list, then click on your selection.

Display Options

Click on your preference to display the background one of three ways:

- Upper-left of the screen
- Center of the screen
- Tiled (repeated) across the screen to fill it.

Click **Apply** to view the selected background. (You may have to reduce application windows to icons to adequately view the screen.)

Changing the Background Color

If you have a color monitor, you can add some color to your black-and-white background. Click on one of the color buttons shown on the color bar. Next, click on the **Apply** button to put your choice into effect. The black background is replaced with your selected color.

Creating a Custom Background

You don't have to settle for the standard selections in the background list. Any image you create in GeoDraw can become a background image. Furthermore, anything you can import into GeoDraw can be used. This includes any image in the Clip Art file, any text, colored shapes, TIFF (Tag Interchange File Format) images, or PCX images (created with PC Paintbrush).

The procedure for creating your own custom background is quite simple:

1. Create or import a picture in GeoDraw.

2. Select: All the objects you want in the picture. You can do this by dragging the pointer or holding **Ctrl** and clicking on the individual objects.

3. Select: **Copy** from the Edit menu. The image is copied to the Clipboard.

4. Switch to Preferences.
   Click: **Background** option to display the Background dialog box.

5. Click: **Get Background From Clipboard**. A dialog box appears where you must enter a filename.
   Enter the name you want.
   Click on **OK**.

6. The picture is copied from the Clipboard to the new file, and the name is displayed in the Backgrounds Available list. It also becomes the new background display.

7. When you are satisfied with the choice of background, click **Close** to return to the Preferences window. The new background is in effect.

Figure 6.4 shows the Preferences application displayed over a customized cartoon clip art (titled Zoomer) background.

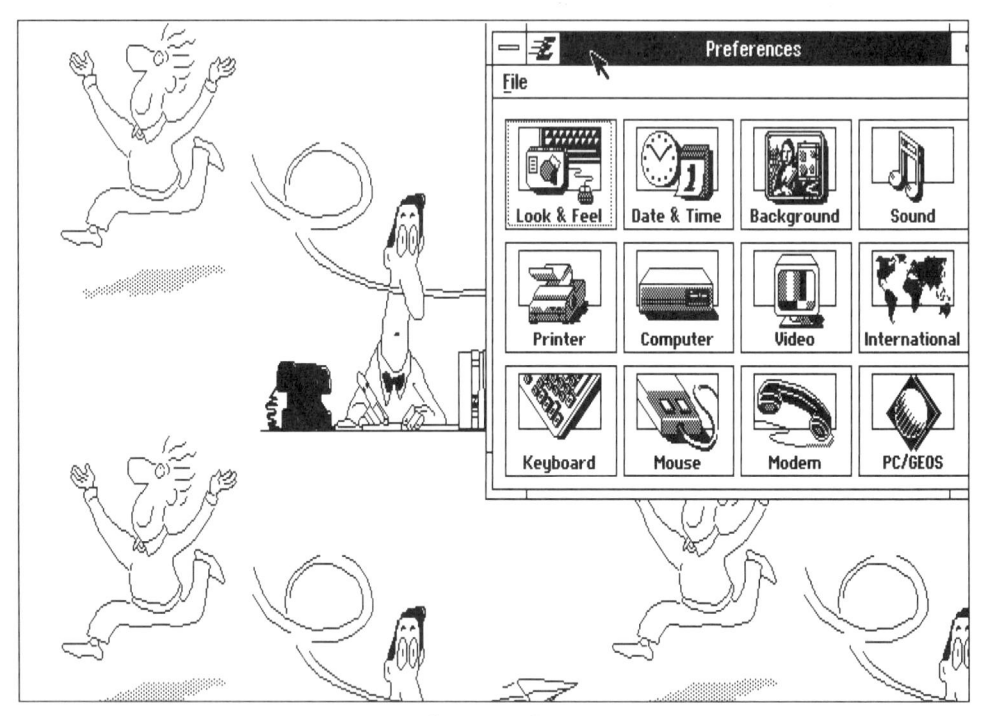

Figure 6.4. Zoomer Cartoon Background.

Sound

This option allows you to turn off the GeoWorks Pro sounds. When you select this option, the Sound dialog box appears. It contains On or Off buttons (the default is On). Click the **Off** button if you want to turn off the sounds, then click **OK**. This setting is put into effect immediately; you don't have to restart GeoWorks Pro.

NOTE Be aware that the Sound Off setting affects sounds throughout Geoworks Pro. This could cause some problems, such as turning off any alarms you set in GeoPlanner.

Printer

Before you can print any documents, you must configure GeoWorks Pro so that it works with your printer(s). Selecting this option displays a dialog box that lists any printers you selected during the automatic installation program.

Use the vertical scroll bar to view the list, if necessary. Across the bottom of the dialog box are five buttons: Install New, Edit, Delete, Test, and Close. The options Edit, Delete and Test are not available until you select an installed printer from the list of available printers.

Install New

Selecting the option to install a new printer displays another dialog box listing all printers supported by GeoWorks Pro. Scroll through the list to highlight your printer name, then click on it. The printer name displays in the Printer Name box. You can change the printer name to any text you want to identify that printer.

Select the appropriate port from the Port box on the right. Each port on the list corresponds to a possible connection at the back of the computer (not all computers have a connection for every port on the list). Usually, parallel printers plug into LPT1, while most serial printers plug into COM1.

Parallel port

When you select a parallel port, no additional configuration is required.

Serial port

When you select a serial port, the Serial Port Options button becomes activated. Clicking on it displays the Serial Port Options dialog box with the six settings for a serial port. Check your printer manual to determine the correct settings.

Baud rate	Indicates the speed at which data will transmit between your computer and the printer, for example: 1200, 2400, 4800, etc.
Word Length	Signifies the amount of data the computer can process at one time (word). Most personal computers process eight bits (a byte) at one time.

Stop Bits	Are inserted during the transmission to mark the end of each word. Specify the number of stop bits your printer uses.
Parity	Specifies the type of error detection used to check the accuracy of data transmission to the printer.

When you are satisfied with the printer settings, click the **OK** button to add the new printer to the Printers Installed list.

See "Modem" section in this chapter for additional information.

Edit

Click the **Edit** button to change the settings for an installed printer. Click the OK button to accept the new settings.

Click the **Reset** button to return the settings to what they were when you opened the dialog box.

Click the **Cancel** button to return to the Printer dialog box with no changes made.

Delete

Click the **Delete** button to delete a highlighted printer from the list of installed printers.

Test

You can test a printer after you install it by selecting **Test**. The printer should begin printing a test page immediately. If nothing happens, or if you get nonsense as a printout, you can try changing the printer's configuration by selecting Edit.

Close

Click the **Close** button to return to the Preferences window, saving your printer settings.

Computer

Use this option to take advantage of any computer memory beyond 640K. Selecting **Computer** displays the Computer dialog box shown in Figure 6.5.

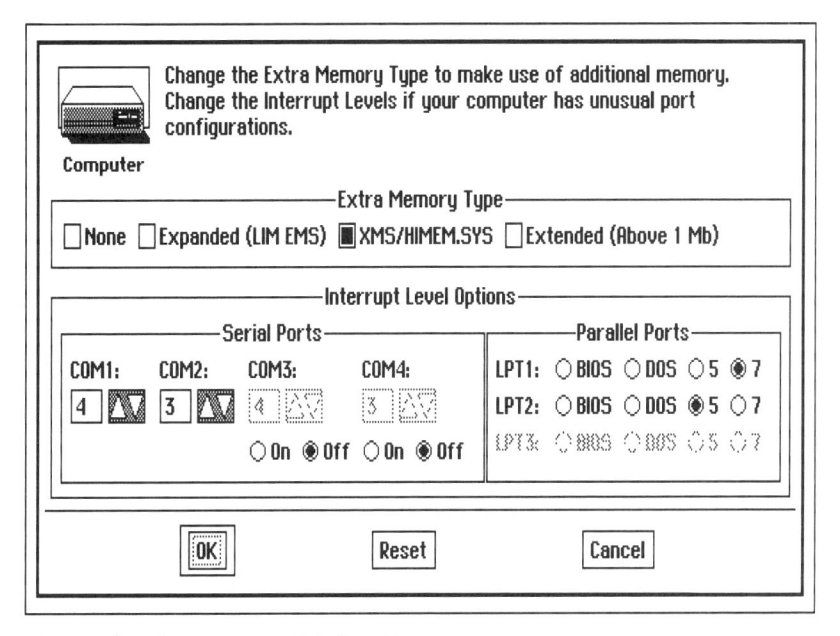

Figure 6.5. The Computer Dialog Box.

Select the type(s) of memory you have: None, Expanded Memory (LIM EMS), Managed Extended Memory, and Extended Memory.

None

Select this option if your computer does not have extended or expanded memory.

Expanded Memory

This is additional memory accessed through a window in the 640K memory area. If you have an original PC or XT-type computer with more than 640K, you have *expanded memory*. It is also possible to install expanded memory boards for other computers. Expanded memory is defined by the Lotus/Intel/Microsoft Expanded Memory Specification (LIM EMS).

Extended Memory

If you have an IBM 286 or 386 (or compatible) computer with more than 640K, you probably have *extended memory*. You may also have expanded memory.

Managed Extended Memory

If you have an extended memory driver such as HIMEM.SYS, you have *managed extended memory*.

Interrupt Level Options

Change the Interrupt Level settings only if your computer has unusual port configurations. You can click the up or down triangles to enter interrupt numbers for up to four serial ports. You can choose from three settings for each of three parallel ports.

WARNING: You should not change the interrupt levels unless you are very familiar with the inner workings of the computer. See the "Modem" section in this chapter for a discussion about setting interrupt levels.

Video

Select the **Video** option if you change your monitor after installing GeoWorks Pro or if you want to enable the screen blanking feature. Selecting Video from the Preferences window displays the dialog box shown in Figure 6.6.

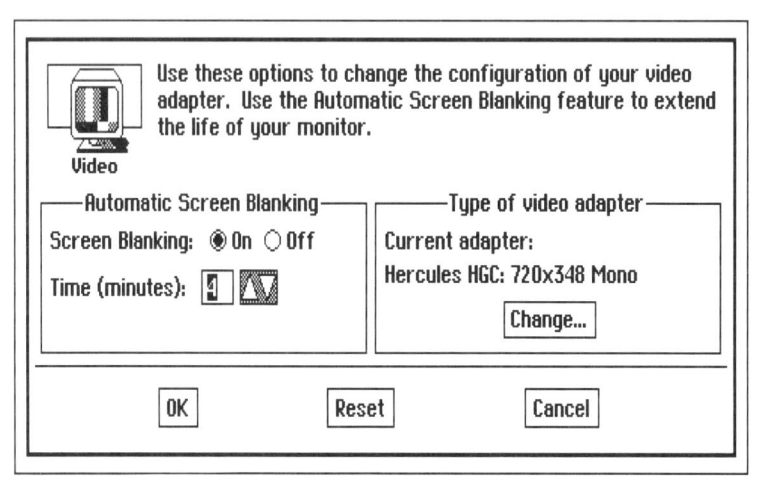

Figure 6.6. The Video Dialog Box.

Type of Video Adapter

Click the **Change** button to display a list of video monitors supported by GeoWorks Pro. Scroll the list to find the correct monitor, then click on it to select it.

Automatic Screen Blanking

Automatic screen blanking may prevent damage to your monitor. If the same image is left on the screen for a long time, the image may become "burned in" so that a ghost outline of the image is always visible, even when the screen is turned off. With automatic screen blanking active, the picture is automatically blanked after a specified period of inactivity.

After you select **On**, you can specify the length of time before the screen blanks—from 2 minutes to 30 minutes.

> **NOTE:** Automatic screen blanking does not work with all computers.

International

This option allows you to choose the way the currency symbol, decimal points, quotation marks, date, and time are displayed. When you select International from the Preferences screen, the International Dialog box appears.

Scroll the box at left to find the item you want to change and click on it then click on **Edit**. The appropriate dialog box will appear as detailed below. Change to the formats you want (your choices are shown the *Example* section in the lower-left of the box. When you are satisfied, click on **OK** to accept your changes. The dialog box then disappears. If you have made any changes, GeoWorks gives you the option of shutting down then and restarting so the changes take effect right away.

Currency

The Edit Currency dialog box is shown in Figure 6.7.

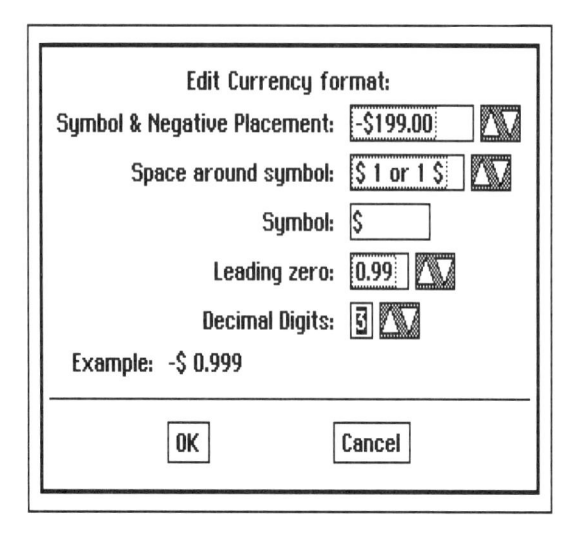

```
          Edit Currency format:
Symbol & Negative Placement: [-$199.00] ▲▼
      Space around symbol: [$ 1 or 1 $] ▲▼
                  Symbol: [$]
             Leading zero: [0.99] ▲▼
           Decimal Digits: [3] ▲▼
    Example: -$ 0.999

              [ OK ]   [ Cancel ]
```

Figure 6.7. The Edit Currency Dialog Box.

You can change most of the items by clicking on the up or down arrows at the right. In the case of the currency symbol, you must delete the current symbol and type the one you want. Note that your keyboard must contain the symbol, since you can't enter it with the ASCII code number. You have the following choices:

- Placement of the currency symbol and the minus sign
- Set the space around the symbols
- Choose a different currency symbol
- Turn on/off the leading zero
- Set the number of decimal places (from 0 to 9).

As you make your choices, they are shown in the Example section of the dialog box. Click **OK** to accept the changes.

Number Format and Measurement Units

Selecting **Number** from the International dialog box and clicking on Edit displays the Numbers dialog box shown in Figure 6.8.

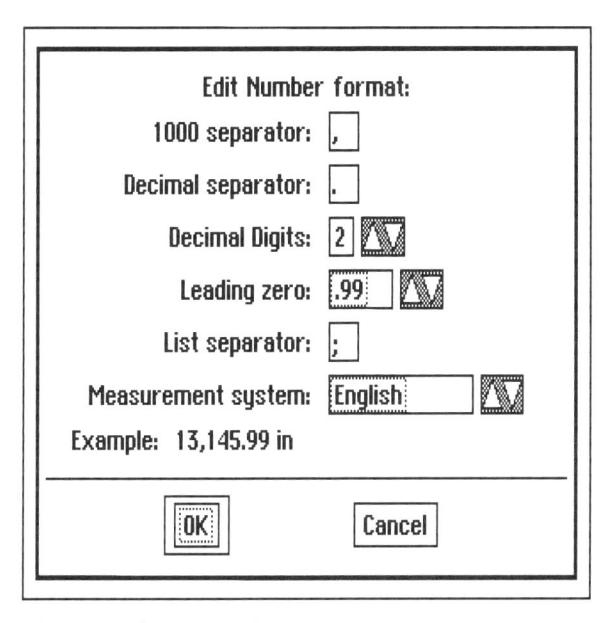

Figure 6.8. The Numbers Dialog Box.

This dialog box allows you to specify how numbers are presented in GeoWorks Pro as well as specifying the units of measurement. You can delete the present symbol and type the one you want. Your choices appears in the Example section in the lower-left of the dialog box. You have the following choices:

- Change the character used to separate thousands (e.g., 1,000,000). A comma is the default.
- Change the character used for the decimal place. Some countries use a comma instead of a period (2,45, not 2.45).
- Change the number of decimal places displayed (from 0 to 9) by clicking on the up or down arrows. (Note that this has no effect on the Calculator tool.)
- Turn on or off the leading zero by clicking on the up or down arrows. For example, a number could be shown with the zero, as 0.556, or without it.as .556
- Enter a different list separator (the semicolon is the default: 1;2;3).
- You can select the measurement system used in GeoWorks Pro. The choices are English (inches) or Metric (centimeters).

Quotation Marks Format

You can choose the kind of quotation marks used in GeoWorks Pro. Typographer's quotation marks give your documents a more polished, typeset appearance than the straight up and down marks found on a typewriter keyboard. Straight marks are often used to indicate measurements in feet and inches (7"4' long) or minutes and seconds of arc (S 21° 5' 12"). Delete the current symbol and type the symbol you want in the box at the right. You can change the marks for:

- opening single quote
- closing single quote
- opening double quote
- closing double quote.

Long Date Format

Selecting this item displays a list of possible long date formats at the right side. If you click **Edit**, the Long Date Format dialog box is displayed. It is seen in Figure 6.9.

You can enter symbols in the small squares to indicate the type of separator you want. In the rectangular fields, you click the up or down arrows to select the formats. The first rectangle lets you choose to spell out the weekday or abbreviate it (Monday or Mon). The next three rectangles can display either the month, day, or year; there are several format selections for each (e.g., for the day, 8th, 08, or 8).

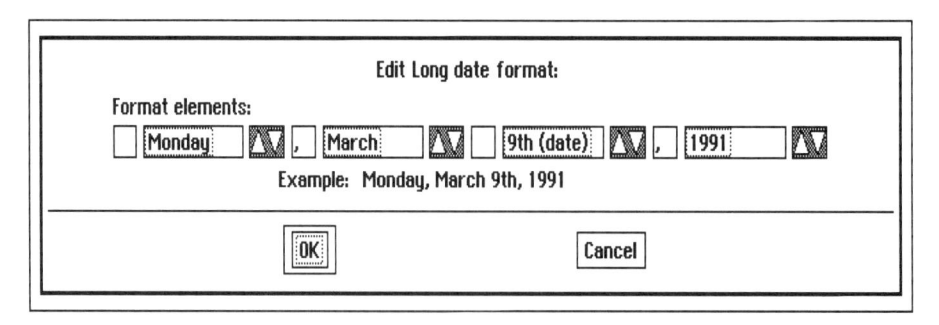

Figure 6.9. The Long Date Format Dialog Box.

Clicking the up or down arrows changes the selection displayed. This allows you to choose which element of the date display comes first, and so on. For example, you could show the day first and then the month as in: Monday, 10 May (European style) or vice versa as in: Monday, May 10.

Short Date Format

If you select this option, a list of examples of the short date format is shown at right. Clicking **Edit** displays the Short Date Format dialog box. This works the same as the Long Date Format dialog box described above, except that it does not show the weekday. You can choose the separator characters, and how and in what order the month, day and year are displayed.

Time Format

This option shows a list of examples of time formats at the right. Click **Edit** to display the Time Format dialog box. This dialog box works like the Date Format boxes described above. You can enter the separator characters you want in the small squares. The rectangular fields allow you to choose either a 12-hour or a 24-hour format.

Keyboard

This option allows you to change some aspects of keyboard response as well as the way GeoWorks Pro maps the keyboard keys to the characters they produce. When you select this option and click **Edit**, the Keyboard dialog box, shown in Figure 6.10, is displayed.

Keyboard Delay

You can change how long you must hold down a key before it begins repeating. The choices are: short, medium, and long.

Keyboard Repeat Rate

This sets the speed at which the key repeats. You can specify slow, medium, or fast.

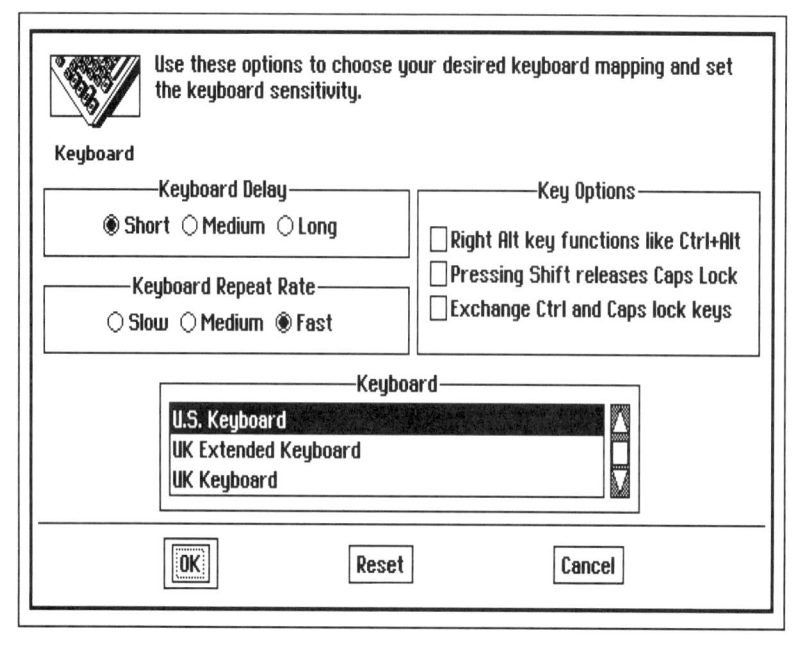

Figure 6.10. The Keyboard Dialog Box.

Key Options

In this section, you can turn on or off three items:

- Right **Alt** key functions like **Ctrl+Alt**. This can save you some keystrokes.
- Pressing **Shift** releases **Caps Lock**. If this option is on, Caps Lock is turned off whenever you press Shift. When this option is off, Caps Lock acts the way it does in DOS: it stays on until you press Caps Lock again.
- Exchange the **Ctrl** and **Caps Lock** keys. If you select this item, your Ctrl key acts like a Caps Lock key and vice versa. This can be useful if you are accustomed to a keyboard layout where Caps Lock is above the Shift key and Ctrl is below and happen to use a keyboard where this arrangement is reversed.

Keyboard

This item offers a choice of three types of keyboard "mapping":

U.S. Keyboard This is the typical keyboard used in the United States.

UK Extended Keyboard This keyboard changes the characters produced by various keys. Among these changes: **Shift+3** produces the pound sterling symbol (£), **Shift+"** (the quotation mark key) produces an @ symbol, and the backslash key (\) produces a # symbol.

UK Keyboard This is almost identical to the UK Extended keyboard. There are differences in the symbols produced by the key at the very left of the top row of the keyboard.

Mouse

Use the Mouse option when you change your mouse type after installing GeoWorks Pro, or, if you want to modify the mouse sensitivity—that is, how quickly the mouse reacts to your motion and clicks. Selecting Mouse displays the Mouse dialog box.

Double Click Time

You can specify Slow, Medium, or Fast as the double-click time. The new speed takes effect immediately. You can test the setting by double-clicking on the **Double Click Test** button. When you double-click quickly enough for the current setting, the box flashes and beeps.

Mouse Acceleration

Use this option to set how fast the pointer moves across the screen as you move the mouse—Slow, Medium, or Fast.

Type of Mouse

Click the **Change** button if you want to specify a different mouse type or port than the ones specified during installation. In the dialog box that appears, scroll the list of mouse types supported by GeoWorks Pro to select your mouse type. If it is a serial mouse, click the appropriate serial port button. An interrupt setting option may become available, depending on the mouse you select. If it does, check your mouse's documentation to be sure the interrupt level is correct. If not, enter the correct setting. There are only a few mouse types where this will be required; if your mouse is not one of the ones that require an interrupt setting, just forget about that setting. Click the **OK** button to accept your mouse settings.

GeoWorks Pro displays a box asking if you want to restart the program in order to activate the new mouse. Click **Yes** to restart GeoWorks Pro. You can then test your mouse choice.

Click the **Reset** button to return the mouse settings to those in effect when you opened the dialog box.

Click the **Cancel** button to return to the Preferences window with no changes made.

Modem

Use this option to set your modem parameters: the serial port, transmission speed, and format of the transmission. Selecting the Modem option displays the dialog box shown in Figure 6.11.

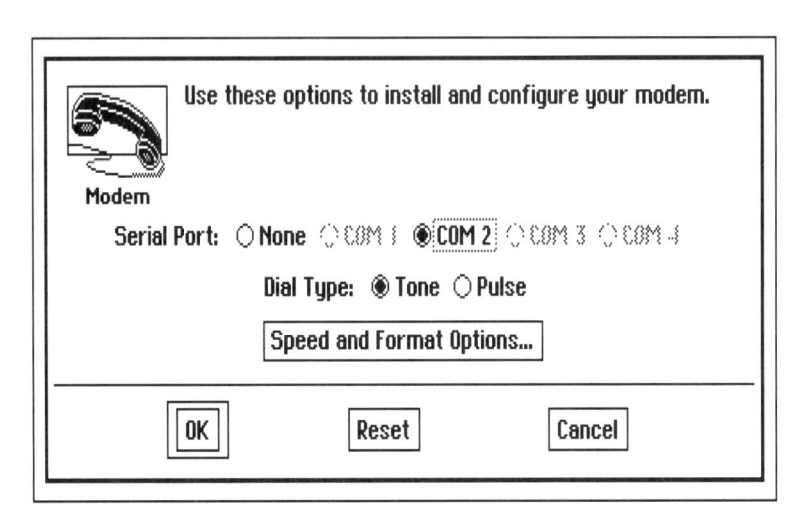

Figure 6.11. The Modem Dialog Box.

Click on the serial port to which your modem is connected, usually COM1. If you have a serial mouse connected to COM1, you can probably use COM2. Make sure you do not select the same port for your serial mouse and the modem. (See "Printer Selection" in this chapter for additional information.)

Check your modem's manual to determine the dial type: tone or pulse. Click the appropriate type for your modem.

Click the **Speed and Format Options** button to display the Modem Options dialog box, shown in Figure 6.12. Change the options in the dialog box to match the capabilities of your modem (check your modem's manual). The Speed and Format Options dialog box contains the following items:

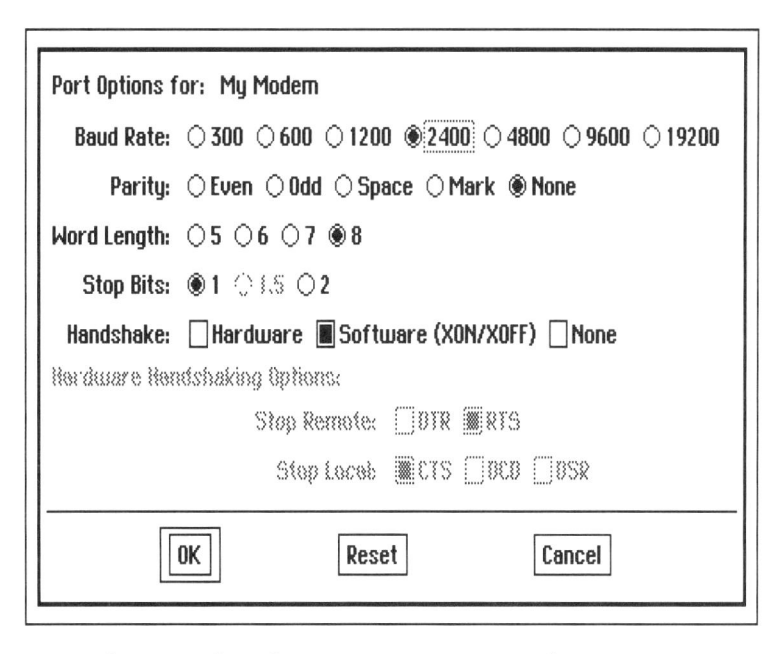

Figure 6.12. The Speed and Format Options Dialog Box.

Baud Rate

Baud is the number of signal changes per second; it indicates the speed at which communications take place. For modems, some common settings are 300, 1200, and 2400. For peripheral devices such as serial printers connected directly to the computer, settings are 4800 or 9600. Baud rate is not the same as bits per second. At low speeds they are close, but at higher rates the difference becomes significant.

Parity

An error-detection technique used to check the accuracy of the digital data transmission. It uses the final bit of a byte to check accuracy. There are five choices for this item:

None	No parity. The last bit is ignored. This is the most common setting.
Even parity	When a character is transmitted, the sending terminal adds up the bits in the character. If the sum of the 1-bits in the character is even, the terminal adds a zero as the last (parity) bit. If the sum is odd, the terminal adds a 1 as the last bit, so the sum of the 1-bits is always kept even.
Odd parity	Works in a similar manner, except that in odd parity, the sending terminal adds a zero as the last bit if the sum of 1 bits in the character is odd. When the sum is even, a 1 is added as the last bit, to keep the sum of the 1-bits always odd.
Mark	In mark parity, the last bit is always set to 1 (on).
Space	In space parity, the last bit is always set to zero (off).

Word Length

A PC serial port transmits one byte (character) at a time. The transmission sequence is: start bit (always a zero), character bits (7 or 8), parity bit (if used), and stop bit. (Seven bits are needed to represent the Standard ASCII character set, and eight bits are needed for the IBM Extended character set.)

The Word Length option lets you choose the number of data bits in each data character transmitted. The most common are 7 or 8. If parity is set to Space (None), then a setting of 8 is needed, otherwise 7 is used. Some peripherals, however, require settings of 5 or 6, although this is very rare. The appropriate parity bit (or check bit) is then added to the data bits by the sending terminal during transmission.

Stop Bits

The end of each character is set off by a stop bit. This is a 1 bit which indicates the end of that segment. More than a single stop bit can be used. You can specify the number of timing units (stop bits) between characters. Inserting more slows down the flow of data. You can choose 1 or 2 stop bits.

Handshake

This refers to the signals transmitted back and forth to establish a valid connection between the two parties.

Usually these items are specified by the documentation supplied with the device, however, in some cases you can change these. Microcomputers commonly transfer one character (byte) at a time. They use a 7-bit ASCII code to represent Standard ASCII. An eighth bit can be used to represent the IBM Extended ASCII set. An additional bit (the check or parity bit) is added to detect transmission errors.

Click the **OK** button to accept your selections and return to the Modem dialog box.

PC/GEOS

Selecting this option displays the PC/GEOS dialog box shown in Figure 6.13.

You should not change any settings in this area unless instructed to do so by an authorized GeoWorks customer support technician. The PC/GEOS settings control internal options; incorrect settings can adversely affect performance, even prevent GeoWorks Pro from working at all. (In this case, you may have to reinstall the program.)

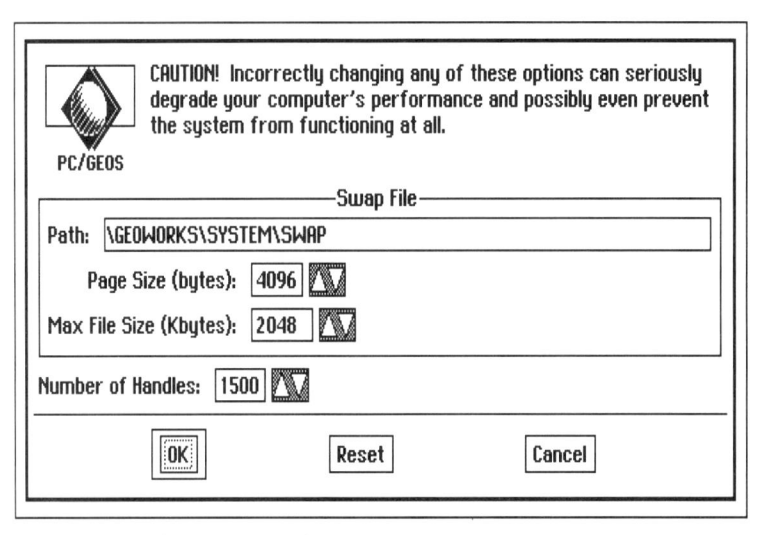

Figure 6.13. The PC/GEOS Dialog Box.

GeoManager Extras Folder

This directory contains five items: 3D font demo, Bounce, Nimbus Font Converter, Perf, and Screen Dumper. Two are just for display; the others give you information about your computer's performance, allow you to capture screens (print what appears on your computer screen), and convert native Nimbus-Q fonts into PC/GEOS Nimbus fonts.

When you open GeoManager your screen resembles that shown in Figure 6.14. If you are in GeoManager and your screen does not resemble that shown in Figure 6.14, click the **WORLD** button in the bottom center of the GeoManager window.

The first icon on the GeoManager main screen is the Extras Folder. Selecting this folder displays the screen shown in Figure 6.15. The following items are available:

3D Font Demo

This is a 3D font demo that just spins a font. It is used by GeoWorks Pro at trade shows to attract attention.

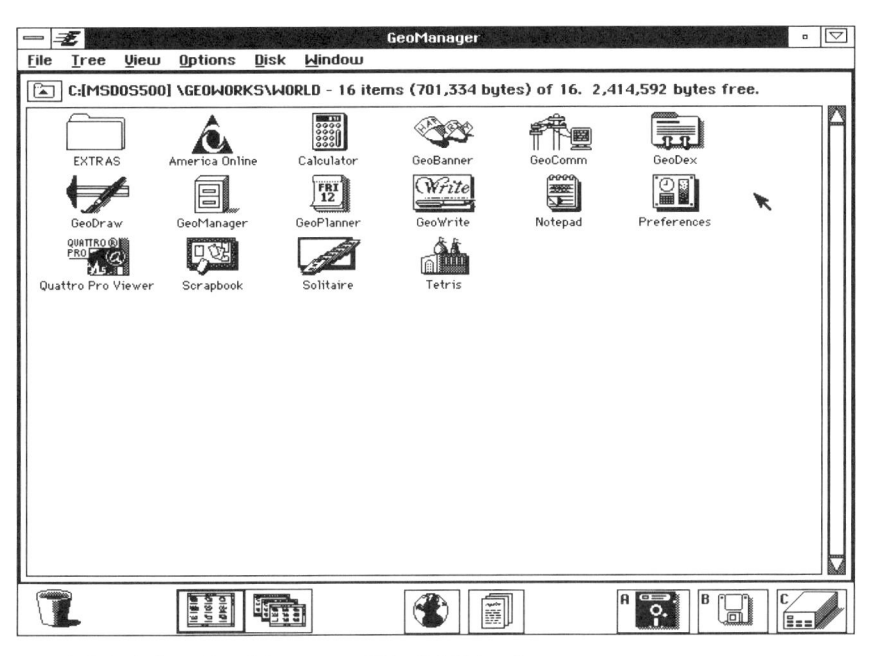

Preferences Applications and the Extras Directory • **127**

Figure 6.14. The GeoManager World Display.

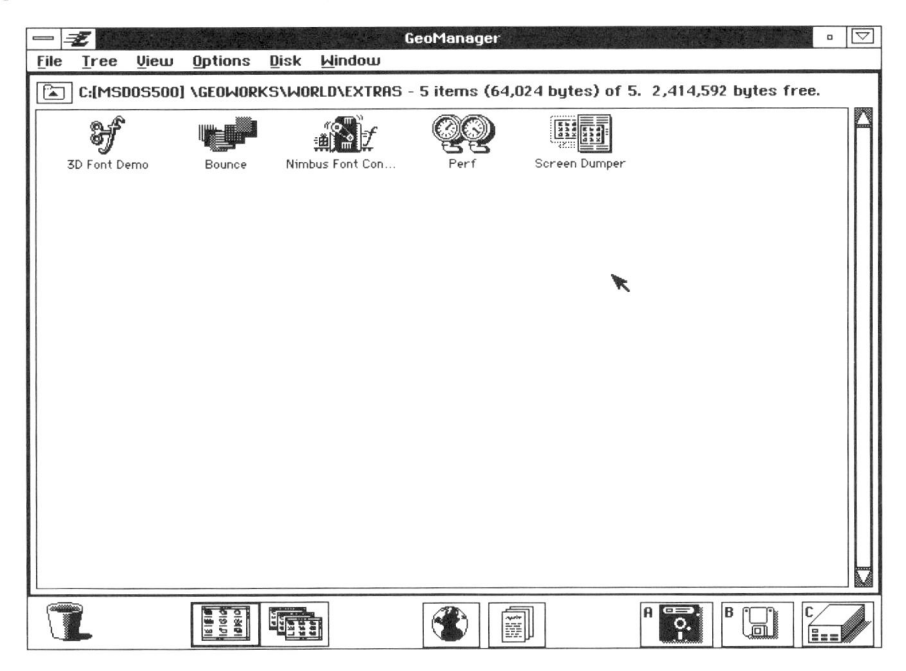

Figure 6.15. The GeoWorks\World\EXTRAS Window.

Bounce

Bounce just bounces. Like the 3D font demo it is used by GeoWorks Pro to attract attention.

Nimbus Font Converter

PC/GEOS uses a font format that is a derivative of Nimbus-Q, not the native Nimbus-Q font. GeoWorks Pro includes outlines for nine typefaces. In addition, you can get additional fonts through GeoWorks font packages, including Fun Fonts, Newsletter Fonts, and Business Fonts. All of these fonts are designed for use exclusively with PC/GEOS products.

You can get native Nimbus-Q fonts by purchasing an application that uses them. One such application is SoftType from ZSoft Corporation. Currently, there is no way to buy these fonts directly.

Because PC/GEOS does not use native Nimbus-Q fonts, a special program is included with GeoWorks Pro to convert these native Nimbus-Q fonts into PC/GEOS fonts. The program which converts the fonts is called Nimbus Font Converter.

NOTE You can buy font packages from other sources that include font conversion programs. These can usually convert the fonts into the format used by PC/GEOS. There is also a specific conversion program called AllType which converts a large number of formats, including Adobe Type 1, into the PC/GEOS format.

When you select **Nimbus Font Converter**, a dialog box appears where you can select the file you want to convert. Clicking **OK** activates the conversion, if the file contains a font that can be converted.

Perf

This extra gives you a report on your computer's performance; you can watch the results as you perform various tasks. When you select this item, you get the screen shown in Figure 6.16.

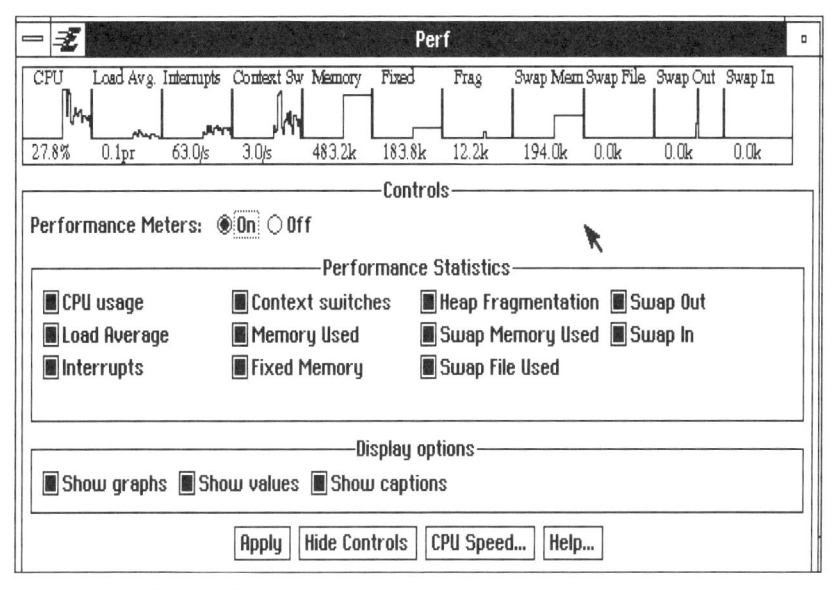

Figure 6.16. The Perf Screen.

Performance Display At the top of the screen is a bar displaying up to 11 performance categories (the number shown depends on what you have selected). You can display a graph, a value and a caption for each category. The categories are: CPU Usage, Load Average, Interrupts, Context Switches, Memory Used, Fixed Memory, Heap Fragmentation, Swap Memory Used, Swap File Used, Swap Out, and Swap In.

Controls The next area of the screen allows you to turn the performance meters on and off. If you choose **Off**, and click the **Apply** button at the bottom, the display no longer reflects any changes in the categories. The default setting is On.

Performance Statistics The 11 performance categories are displayed in this area, along with a button to select/unselect each one. Click on the button for an item and then click Apply to change the setting. The default is for all items to be selected.

Display Options   In this area are selections that allow you to choose whether to show the graphs, the performance values, and the captions, or not. The default is to show all three.

At the bottom of the screen are four buttons. After you make your selections, clicking **Apply** puts your choices into effect.

If you click **Hide Controls**, only the performance bar at the top is displayed. You can drag this window to the bottom of the screen and then watch the performance statistics as you work with other applications. This is demonstrated in Figure 6.17.

To return to the full display, click on any graph in the bar.

If you select the **CPU Speed** button, you can get a rating for your computer's CPU speed. Performance window's relative to a base XT.

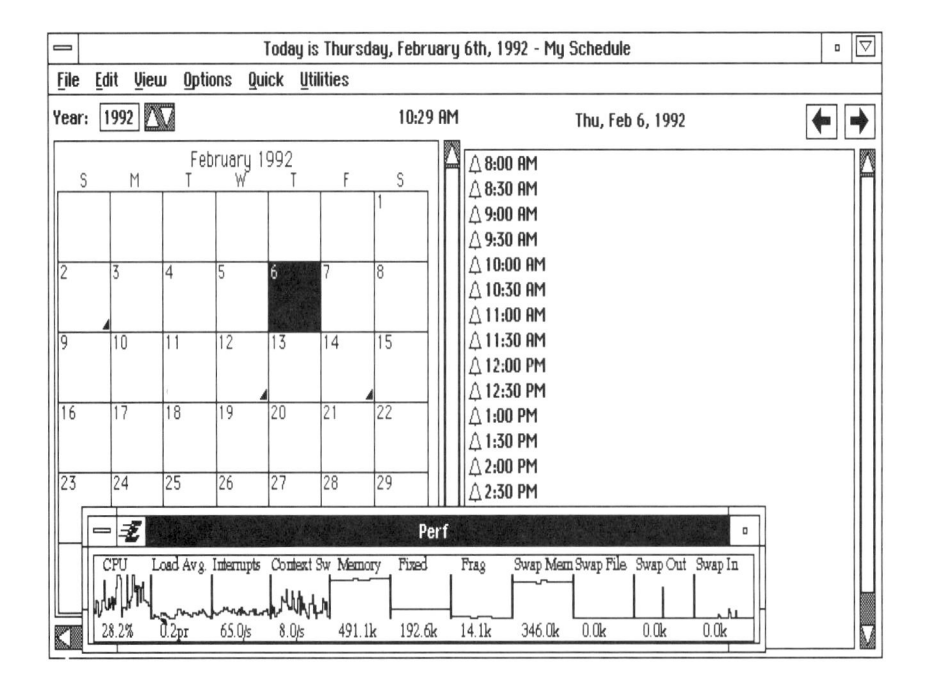

Figure 6.17. The Performance Bar and the GeoPlanner Application.

Preferences Applications and the Extras Directory • **131**

The **Help** button gives you access to a series of help screens. These explain in detail the meaning of each of the performance categories.

If you reduce the Performance screen to an icon (either select **Minimize** from the Control menu, or click the **Minimize** button), you will be able to view the leftmost performance area (CPU is the default) as you work. Click on it to display the performance screen again.

Screen Dumper

The Screen Dumper utility allows you to capture images of GeoWorks Pro screens. In fact, the Screen Dumper was used to capture the screen images for this book.

The Screen Dumper gives you the option of capturing the entire screen, a selected window, or a portion of the screen. Color as well as black-and-white screen images can be captured. You also have the option of including the cursor in the captured image if you want it.

The main Screen Dumper screen typically looks like Figure 6.18.

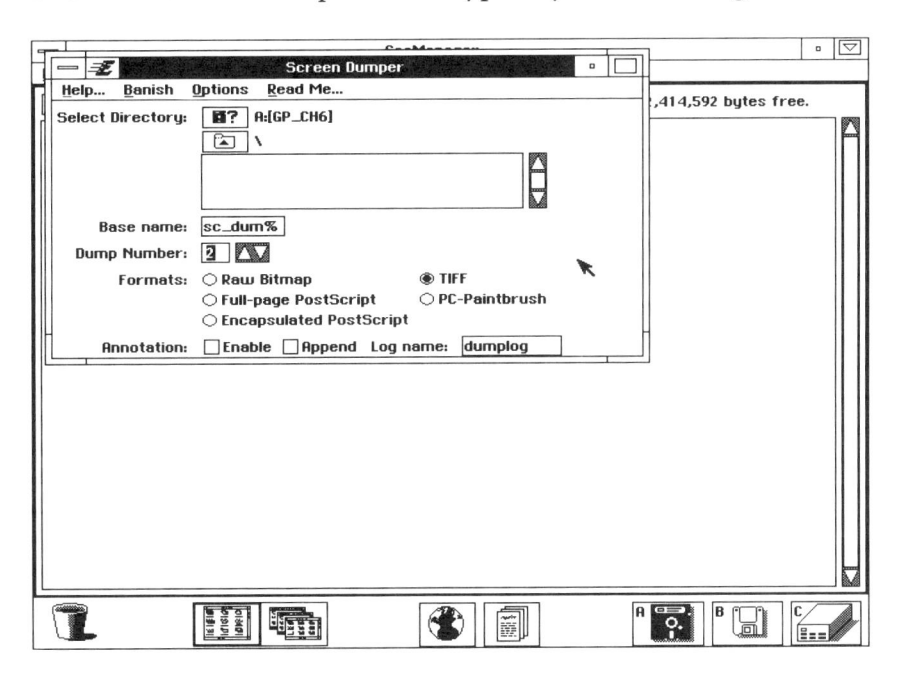

Figure 6.18. A Typical Main Screen Dumper Menu Screen.

Select Directory

The drive icon to the right of Select Directory is used to specify the drive to be used to save the captured images. In Figure 6.18 this icon has been clicked and drive A: has been selected. This is the drive where the captured image files will be stored. The Directories line below the drive icon shows that the root directory (\) of drive A: will be used to store the captured images. The box below this is empty, indicating there are no subdirectories in drive A:.

Base Name

The Base name line below the Directories box is used to specify the name of the captured file. The % (percent) sign is a representation of the number of images you capture during a session. When you start, the number is 00 (zero zero). Each time you capture an image, the number increases by one.

For example, in Figure 6.18 the base name specified is SC_DMP%. Assume you are capturing .TIF files (as indicated in Figure 6.18). The first image you capture will be named SC_DMP00.TIF. As you capture more images they will automatically be sequentially named SC_DMP01.TIF, SC_DMP02.TIF, SC_DMP03.TIF, etc. All the files will be saved in the root directory of drive A:.

NOTE A DOS format is used for the name, so you can only use a maximum of eight characters. The % (percent) sign represents two characters. The three-letter extension is automatically added, according to the format you click in Formats.

Dump Number

The number shown in the Dump Number window is the number that will be used for the next image captured. You can change this number by clicking on the up/down arrows to the right of the box, or click in the box and then type a new number. In Figure 6.18 the Dump Number is 2, an therefore the next captured image will be stored in A:\SC_DUMP02.TIF.

When capturing a great many files you will probably find you often would like to overwrite the last file you captured, or some other previously captured file. You can overwrite an existing file (with the same base name) by changing the dump number to make it correspond to the filename of the file you want to overwrite.

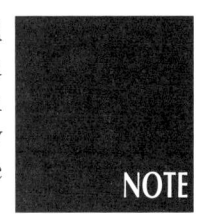

Formats

The format for the captured image file can be selected by clicking on the format type you want. The following formats are available:

Raw Bitmap	This format was used by GeoWorks to produce slices of the screen dump in an internal bitmap format used to convert to PostScript (a popular printing language) prior to the use of the Screen Dumper for creating PostScript images.
Full-page PostScript	Creates single-page full-screen captures and can work with any of the other options below. The Full-page PostScript option produces a showpage command at the end of the dump, and the dump is centered in the indicated page space.
Encapsulated PostScript	This format is used to create a file of the screen capture that can be printed on a PostScript printer.
TIFF	This format can create a black-and-white, a 16-color, or a grayscale TIFF file in Intel byte-order.
PC-Paintbrush	This format produces a standard PCX format in either black-and-white or color PCX files.

Annotation

The last line of the Screen Dumper contains the following options:

Annotation Enable This option allows you to create a log of the screen files created by the Screen Dumper. Clicking **Enable** causes the Screen Dumper to display a dialog box each time a screen is captured. The text you enter is saved with the filename to the log file.

Append Selecting this option allows you to save the log in one continuous file. If you do not select this option the file from the current session will overwrite the previous session's file.

NOTE With append off, you can change the log name to prevent overwriting the previous session's log.

Log Name In the box to the right of Log Name you may specify the name for the file where the annotation entries are saved. The log file is saved in the same directory as the directory you specified for saving the captured image files.

Screen Dumper Menu Bar

There are four selections on the menu bar as follows:

Help

Selecting this option displays a scrollable Help screen. You can scroll the window to display additional help information.

Banish

The Screen Dumper can be removed from the window by choosing Banish, but the program remains functioning and usable. If you want to have the banished screen returned, press Ctrl-Shift and then press Tab. Pressing F1 brings the Screen Dumper back on screen.

When you are capturing a great many screens you will find yourself returning to the Screen Dumper frequently. There you can check the current screen number and filename that is to be saved. You can also change the location where the files are saved.

Preferences Applications and the Extras Directory • **135**

You can use the Minimize button to reduce the Screen Dumper to an icon. This gives you convenient access to it. Alternately, you can use the Express menu to return to the Screen Dumper.

NOTE

Options

Choosing either of the PostScript selections or the TIFF selection in Formats allows you to set additional parameters from the Options menu. Figure 6.19 shows the Options menu after a TIFF format was specified in the main menu. Notice that the PostScript option is dimmed.

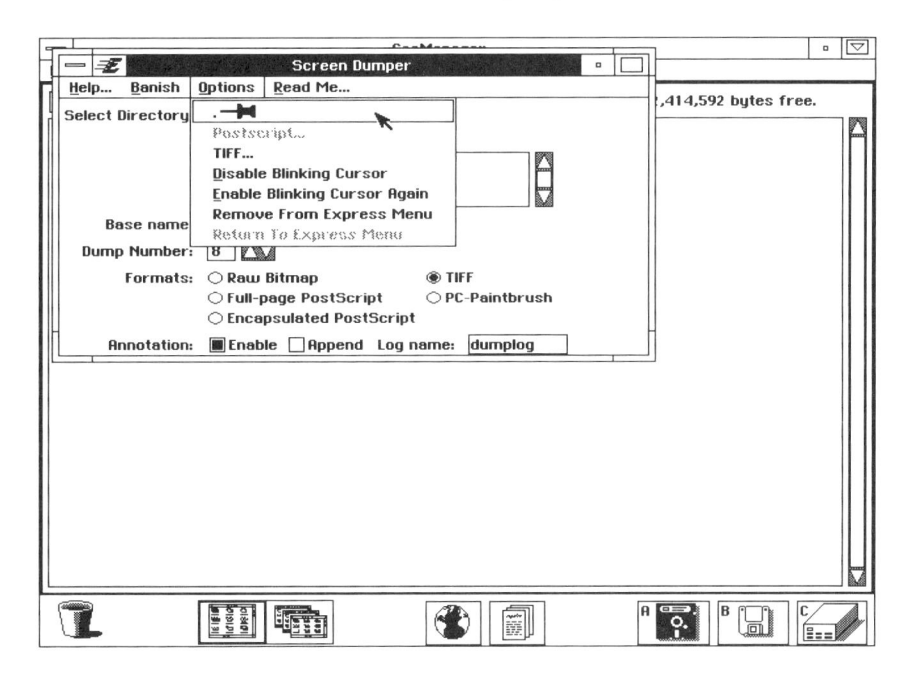

Figure 6.19. The Options Menu.

PostScript

This option is available only if you have specified one of the two available PostScript formats from the main Screen Dumper menu. The following options are available on the PostScript Dialog Box:

Image Name	This box allows you to enter a name to represent the PostScript image in a desktop-publishing program (e.g., PageMaker). This name has no effect on the captured image, or the filename where it is in place. The name documents only the screen-capture file, and should help orient you by displaying the name in the Postscript Parameters box.

Color	This option allows you to specify the color selection best suited for your equipment:

> **RGB**	For image viewing on color monitors
> **CMYK**	For use with color printers
> **Grayscale**	For black-and-white printers and monitors.

NOTE	RGB and CMYK use PostScript color extensions (colorimage operator). Use Grayscale if your printer does not support this.

Number of Copies	Allows you to specify the number of copies to be printed each time you print the file. If you need more than one copy it is faster to specify the number rather than print one copy over and over.

Orientation	Portrait is the normal way paper is oriented for printing. Landscape more closely resembles the monitor's width-to-height ratio. Use Landscape for printing full-screen displays.

Width, Height	This is the size of the image in inches. The width and height are always relative to the image (not the page orientation). The image is made to print this size even if it has to be stretched to fit. The Screen Dumper does not automatically size the width and height to match the image.

Paper Size	This represents the size of the paper you will use to print the image. The image is centered in this space.

TIFF

This option is available only if you have TIFF from the main Screen Dumper menu. The following options are available on the TIFF dialog box:

Dump Color As Color   Use this option when viewing on a color monitor. This option has no effect if you are dumping to a monochrome monitor.

Dump Color As Grayscale   Use this option when viewing on a monochrome monitor or printing in black and white.

Image Compression   Not available.

Using the Screen Dumper

The following outlines how to use the Screen Dumper:

1. Access the screen dumper from the main GeoManager screen (see Figure 6.14).

2. Double-click on the **Extras** folder. Figure 6.15 shows the Extras items you can select.

3. Select: **Screen Dumper**. The screen shown in Figure 6.18 is displayed.

4. Specify: The drive and directory where you want the captured files to be saved.

5. Specify: The base name you want for the files and the starting Dump Number.

6. Specify: The **Format** to be used for the captured image files.

7. Specify if you want to **Enable** annotation and if it is to be an **Appended** file. If you specified annotation also specify a **Logname**.

8. Open the **Options** menu.
   Specify: The parameters you want for the captured image (e.g., color).

9. Display the window you want to capture.

10. Use one of the commands in the following table to capture the image you want.

11. If you have Annotation on, enter a description of the captured image.

NOTE Using the Express menu is an easy way to go to the desired window. You can also use the Express menu to return to the Screen Dumper.

Table 6.1. Capturing Images.

Keys	Action
Shift+PrtSc	Freezes GeoWorks Pro and writes the entire screen image to a file.
Ctrl+Shift+Tab (hold Ctrl and Shift and then press Tab.)	Temporarily freezes GeoWorks Pro.
F8	Writes the entire screen image to a file.
Ctrl+Shift+Tab	Temporarily freezes GeoWorks Pro.
F3	Writes window without pointer to a file.
Ctrl+Shift+Tab	Temporarily freezes GeoWorks Pro.
F4	Writes window with pointer to a file.
F11 (if available)	Writes window without pointer to a file. Same as **Ctrl+Shift+Tab F3**.
F12 (if available)	Writes window with pointer to a file. Same as **Ctrl+Shift+Tab F4**.
Ctrl+Shift+Tab	Temporarily freezes GeoWorks Pro.
F5	Displays a *dump rectangle*. You can use this rectangle to outline the area of the screen you want to capture. Use the mouse to drag the outline where you want it or use the keys on the numeric keypad to size and position the rectangle. Refer to Table 6.2 for use of the numeric keypad.
F6	Writes the portion of the screen surrounded by the rectangle to a file.

To capture the same portion of the screen to a new file you can issue the command **Ctrl+Shift+Tab F6**. This captures the same area again but writes it to a new file.

If you have pressed **Ctrl+Shift+Tab** and frozen the display but decide you do not want to capture an image, press **Esc**. **NOTE**

Table 6.2. Keypad Use.

Keypad Key	*Action*
Keys 7,8,9 4,5,6 1,2,3	Moves the dump rectangle one pixel in the direction of the key (e.g., pressing the 7 on the numeric keypad moves the dump rectangle one pixel up and one pixel to the left).
Alt+Keypad key	Moves the dump rectangle eight pixels in the direction of the key.
Shift+Keypad key	Enlarges the dump rectangle one pixel in the direction of the key. *Also* holding down the **Alt** key enlarges the dump rectangle eight pixels at a time.
Ctrl+Shift+Keypad key	Shrinks the dump rectangle one pixel in the direction of the key. If you *also* hold down the **Alt** key you can shrink the dump rectangle eight pixels at a time.

In the above tables, after you press **Ctrl+Shift+Tab** move the pointer to the title bar of the window you want to capture. (This is not required if you are capturing only a portion of the screen using **F6**.) The Screen Dumper captures the window directly under the pointer. Sometimes a window is built up from several small ones that don't look like windows. This helps you capture the window you actually want.

NOTE If you are capturing images in different sessions of GeoWorks Pro, make sure to verify that the Screen Dumper is set to save the files in the drive and directory you want. Also verify that the Dump Number is the one you want, to avoid overwriting files you want to keep.

NOTE Before using the Screen Dumper you must turn the blinking cursor off. When you do this GeoWorks Pro will shut down and automatically restart (with text cursor not blinking). After you are finished capturing screens, re-enable the blinking cursor.

Summary

In Chapter 6 you learned how to use the GeoManager Preferences application. Each of the Preferences menu options was explained in detail. In addition, the Extras directory was discussed. The Screen Dumper, the Perf, and the Nimbus Font Converter were outlined in detail.

Chapter 7

The GeoWrite Application

The GeoWrite application is the GeoWorks Pro word processor. In this chapter—which is designed to be first an introduction and then a reference—you will learn about the main elements of the GeoWrite main screen:

- The ruler bar
- The format bar
- Justification settings
- Line spacing settings
- Scroll bars
- Main text window
- Typing modes
- Selecting and editing text with the mouse
- Keyboard editing and typing cursor movement.

142 • *Teach Yourself GeoWorks Pro*

    This chapter and the next two discuss the GeoWrite application. In this chapter, you will find an overview of the GeoWrite screen and editing techniques. Chapter 8 discusses the GeoWrite menus and Chapter 9 provides a GeoWrite tutorial in which you can practice using most of the features discussed in this chapter and in Chapter 8.

Starting GeoWrite

Double-click on the GeoWrite application icon in the GeoManager window to display the GeoWrite main screen. GeoWorks Pro starts with a blank, untitled document. Figure 7.1 identifies the important elements of the GeoWrite main screen.

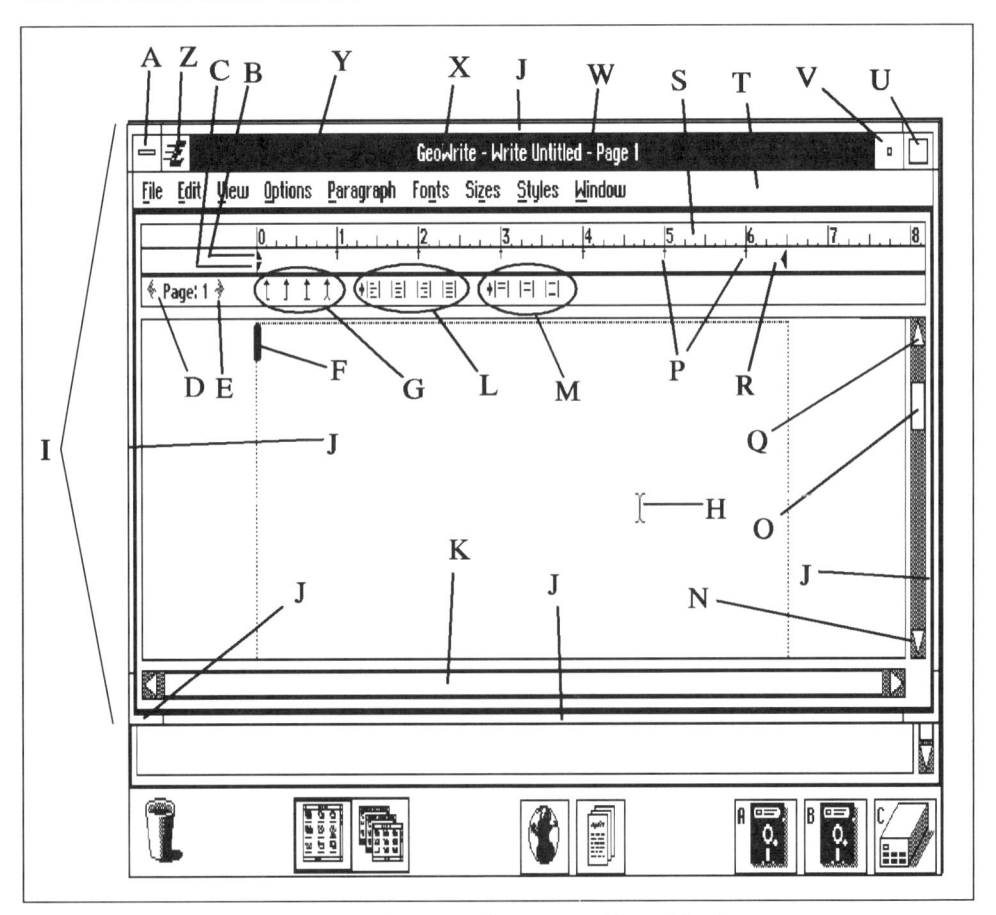

Figure 7.1. GeoWrite Main Screen Elements Identified.

A.	Control menu button	N.	Scroll down arrow
B.	Left indent	O.	Scroll slider
C.	Left margin	P.	Small tab arrows
D.	Previous page	Q.	Scroll up arrow
E.	Next page	R.	Right margin
F.	Text cursor	S.	Ruler
G.	Tabs	T.	Menu bar
H.	Mouse cursor	U.	Maximize/Restore button
I.	Main text window	V.	Minimize button
J.	Resize border	W.	Document Name/Page
K.	Horizontal scroll bar	X.	Application name
L.	Justification	Y.	Title bar
M.	Line spacing	Z.	Express menu button

Application Window Elements

At the top of the GeoWrite main screen are five elements common to all application windows: Control menu button, Express menu button, Title Bar, Minimize button, and Maximize/Restore button. These items, along with the horizontal and vertical scroll bars, are discussed in Chapter 4.

The Menu Bar

The second line of the GeoWrite main screen is the menu bar (see Figure 7.1, T) with nine menu options, which are discussed in Chapter 8.

The Ruler Bar

The ruler bar consists of two lines (see Figure 7.1, B, C, P, R and S). The top line is an actual ruler showing the horizontal page measurements. Use the ruler as a guide when changing margins, indenting paragraphs, and setting tabs. Below the ruler is a line showing the current margins, indents, and tabs.

Left Margin and Indent

The left margin marker and indent marker are displayed initially as a split arrowhead (see Figure 7.1, B and C). Changing these markers affects only the paragraph in which the text cursor is currently located or any highlighted paragraphs. To set the left margin and indent for the entire document, choose **Page Setup** from the File menu. (See Chapter 8.)

You can move the indent marker or the left margin marker by placing the mouse cursor on it, then pressing and holding the left mouse button while dragging the marker to the desired location along the ruler.

You can move the left margin and indent markers together by pressing **Shift** while dragging the markers (as a unit) to the new location.

Right Margin

The right margin marker looks like an arrowhead pointing left (see Figure 7.1, R). Changing the right margin marker affects only the paragraph in which the text cursor is currently located or any highlighted paragraphs. To set the right margin for the entire document, choose **Page Setup** from the File menu. (See Chapter 8.)

To relocate the right margin, drag the marker to the desired location.

Tabs

The tab types (see Figure 7.1, P) and locations are also displayed on the lower portion of the ruler bar. Placing and removing tabs is described below in the Tab section of the format bar discussion.

Ruler Settings

When you highlight a range of text, the ruler turns gray and shows only those settings that are common to all highlighted paragraphs.

The Format Bar

Use the line immediately below the ruler bar to select the displayed page, tabs, justification, and line-spacing settings.

Paging Arrows

Click on the small arrow before the Page number to display the previous page; click on the small arrow after the Page number to select the next page.

Tabs

When you open GeoWrite there are small tab arrows below each of the unit markers on the ruler line (1", 2", 3", etc. see Figure 7.2, P). When you press **Tab** the text cursor moves to the nearest tab to the right of its current position. A line tab setting remains in effect for all subsequent lines until you set a new line tab. You could set different tabs for every line of the document.

You can position the text cursor in any line of the document and change the tab setting for that line. The new tab setting will affect only that line. Text that wraps (automatically flows) to the next line falls back to the left margin. A carriage return at the end of a line forces the text cursor to the next line, starting a new line or paragraph at the left margin.

The tabs shown in the lower portion of the ruler bar (see Figure 7.1, P) are relevant to the line in which the text cursor is currently located (or the currently highlighted text).

Selecting a Tab Type

You can select four tab types. The tab symbols are each represented by an up-pointing arrow, but with a different arrow base. Select a tab type by placing the mouse cursor over it, then pressing and holding the left mouse button. The mouse cursor changes to the selected tab type and jumps to the line below the ruler markings. Drag the tab to the desired location and release the mouse button. The program removes the original small tab arrows at the ruler unit markers.

Left-justified Tab

From the tab, the text you type moves to the right with every character, as if the tab were a left margin. If you press **Tab** within a line, all of the text to the right of the cursor position shifts right to start at the next tab location. If the following text needs to wrap and flow to accommodate the relocated text, the document adjusts the text as necessary.

Right-justified Tab

As you type, the text cursor remains at the tab location, but the characters you type move to the left of the tab.

Center-justified Tab

As you type, the text cursor moves to the right with every other character; alternate characters move to the left. The result is centered text at the tab location.

Decimal Align Tab

Use this tab on each line of a column of numbers to align the numbers on the decimal point. As you type, the tab operates like a right-justified tab until you type a period (decimal point). Then the tab operates like a left-justified tab.

Copy a Tab

You can copy an existing tab on the lower line of the ruler bar by pressing and holding **Ctrl** while dragging the tab to a new location.

Remove a Tab

To remove a tab (delete it) from the lower line of the ruler bar, place the mouse cursor over it, then press and hold the left mouse button while dragging the tab off the ruler bar in any direction. Release the mouse button.

Justification Settings

Four symbols—Left, Center, Right, or Full justification—represent text between the left and right page borders. The active symbol for currently highlighted text, the text in which the text cursor is located, is identified by a small arrow next to it (see Figure 7.2, L).

Align Left

Use this option to align text along the left margin with a ragged-right margin, as indicated in the symbol.

Center Align

Use this option to center text lines, regardless of line length, between the left and right margins.

Align Right

Use this option to align text along the right margin with a ragged left margin.

Fully Justified

Use this option to justify text along both the left and right margins.

Line Spacing Settings

Select a line spacing option to set single spacing, line-and-a-half spacing, or double spacing.

Main Text Window

The Main Text Window (see Figure 7.1, I) displays one page or portion of one page at a time. (You cannot display the bottom of one page and the top of another page at the same time in one window.) This is the area where you create your document.

Headers and Footers

You can create a unique header and/or footer for each page of your document. Or, you can create one header or footer for odd pages and one for even pages. Headers are located at the top of the page, footers at the bottom. The header and footer text can be centered, flush against the left margin or flush against the right margin. A typical header or footer includes chapter titles, page numbers and names you want repeated on every page. See Chapters 8 and 9 for additional information on headers and footers.

A header or footer, including text and graphics, appears on every page that follows (including the current page) until you set a new header or footer.

Notice that when you open a window the slider is not at the top of the scroll bar. Rather, it is positioned so that the panel displays the top of the text area. To see the header area, drag the vertical slider to the top of the scroll bar. You will see the header area boxed off separately, above the main text window. When you want to see the footer area, drag the vertical slider to the bottom of the scroll bar. You will see the footer area boxed off separately, below the main text window.

Typing Mode

There are two typing modes: Insertion and Overwrite. Press **Ins** to toggle between them.

Insertion Mode

In Insertion mode, characters are inserted at the text cursor position, pushing to the right any existing text. The Insertion cursor moves one space to the right with each character you type.

Overwrite Mode

In Overwrite mode, a typed character overwrites the existing character at the text cursor position. The Overwrite cursor moves one space to the right with each character you type.

Selecting and Editing Text with the Mouse

To change format settings for a block of text, you must first select the block.

Selecting by Dragging

You can use the mouse to select (highlight) a block of text. Position the mouse cursor at the beginning of the text you want to select. Press and hold the left mouse button while dragging the cursor to the end of the text you want to block. Release the mouse button. The program displays the selected text in reverse video—white text on a black background.

Selecting by Specifying

Another method of selecting text is to place the text cursor to the left of the first character you want selected. Position the mouse cursor at the end of the block you want to select. Press and hold **Shift** while you click the left mouse button to select the block.

To adjust the selected area, redefining the block of text, press and hold **Shift** while you move the mouse cursor to a new end position for the block. You can redefine a block larger or smaller. Click the left mouse button. The new block is selected.

Selecting Words

Double-click the left mouse button to select the word under the mouse cursor. To select a range of words, double click but don't release the left mouse button on the second click. Drag the mouse cursor to highlight the desired words.

You can also use the Selecting by Specifying technique. Place the text cursor at the beginning of the text you want to select. Then move the mouse cursor to the end of the block. Press and hold **Shift** while you click the left mouse button. The specified text is selected.

Selecting Lines

To select a line, triple-click the left mouse button with the cursor anywhere over the line you want to select.

You can also use the Selecting by Specifying technique. With the text cursor in the line and the mouse cursor at the end of the line you want to select, press and hold **Shift** while you click the left mouse button.

Selecting Larger Units

Each time you add a click to a multiple-click sequence, a larger unit of text is specified. For example, double-click specifies words, triple-click selects lines, quadruple-click (four clicks) specifies paragraphs, and six clicks specifies pages.

You can extend a selection by clicking but not releasing the mouse button on the last click, then dragging the highlight to include additional text. For example, you could triple-click to select a line but not release the mouse button on the third click. Then drag the highlight to include several more lines or a paragraph or a page.

You can also use the Selecting by Specifying technique to select larger units of text.

Adjusting Range Selected

If you want to adjust a still-highlighted block, press and hold **Shift** while you move the mouse cursor to a new location. Click the left mouse button to lock the selected area to the newly specified range.

Deleting Selected Text

After highlighting an area, press **Del** or **Backspace** to delete the selected area.

To Replace a Range of Text

After highlighting an area, type the new text you want to appear in the highlighted area. The program deletes the original block of text and inserts the new text in the same location.

Keyboard Editing and Typing Cursor Movement

Proficient typists often prefer to do editing from the keyboard instead of using a mouse. The following table describes keyboard editing commands.

Table 7.1. Keyboard Editing Commands.

Text Cursor Movement	*Keyboard Equivalent*
One character/line in any direction	Arrow keys
One word backward	Ctrl-LeftArrow
One word forward	Ctrl-RightArrow
One paragraph backward	Ctrl-UpArrow
One paragraph forward	Ctrl-DownArrow
To beginning of line	Home
To end of line	End
To beginning of text (page)	Ctrl-Home
To end of text (page)	Ctrl-End

Table 7.1. continued...

Selecting Text	Keyboard Equivalent
Select left	Shift-LeftArrow
Select right	Shift-RightArrow
Select up	Shift-UpArrow
Select down	Shift-DownArrow
Select to beginning of word	Shift-Ctrl-LeftArrow
Select to end of word	Shift-Ctrl-RightArrow
Select whole word	Ctrl-Space
Select to beginning of line	Shift-Home
Select to end of line	Shift-End
Select whole line	Ctrl-Home followed by Shift-Ctrl-End

Selecting Text	*Keyboard Equivalent*
Select to beginning of paragraph	Shift-Ctrl-UpArrow
Select to end of paragraph	Shift-Ctrl-DownArrow
Select whole paragraph	Ctrl-UpArrow followed by Shift-Ctrl-DownArrow
Select to beginning of column/page	Shift-Ctrl-Home
Select to end of column/page	Shift-Ctrl-End
Select whole column/page	Ctrl-Home followed by Shift-Ctrl-End

Adjust Text Selected	*Keyboard Equivalent*
Adjust up	Shift-UpArrow
Adjust down	Shift-DownArrow
Adjust left	Shift-LeftArrow
Adjust right	Shift-RightArrow

Table 7.1. continued...

Adjust Text Selected	Keyboard Equivalent
Adjust to previous word	Shift-Ctrl-LeftArrow
Adjust to next word	Shift-Ctrl-RightArrow
Adjust to beginning of line	Shift-Home
Adjust to end of line	Shift-End

Adjust Text Selected	Keyboard Equivalent
Adjust to beginning of paragraph	Shift-Ctrl-UpArrow
Adjust to end of paragraph	Shift-Ctrl-DownArrow
Adjust to beginning of column/page	Shift-Ctrl-Home
Adjust to end of column/page	Shift-Ctrl-End

Deleting Text	Keyboard Equivalent
Delete character to right	Del
Delete character to left	Backspace
Delete to end of word	Ctrl-Backspace
Delete to beginning of word	Ctrl-Del
Delete to end of line	Shift-Ctrl-Del
Delete to beginning of line	Shift-Ctrl-Backspace
Delete selection	Del or Backspace

Summary

In this chapter you learned about the elements of the GeoWrite application screen, the basics of formatting text, and how to move the text cursor and select text using keyboard commands.

Chapter 8

GeoWrite Menus

This chapter—which is designed to be first an introduction and then a reference—teaches you how to use the options in the nine GeoWrite menus:

- File
- Edit
- View
- Options
- Paragraph
- Fonts
- Sizes
- Styles
- Window.

Chapter 9 provides a GeoWrite tutorial in which you can practice using most of the features discussed in Chapters 7 and 8. See Chapter 4 for a discussion on the different ways to select menus and menu items in an application window.

To run the GeoWrite application, start GeoWorks Pro in the usual way, then select the GeoWrite icon from the Advanced Workspace. The program displays the GeoWrite main screen, as shown previously in Chapter 7. Figure 7.1, which identifies the important elements of the GeoWrite main screen.

File Menu

The File menu is the first option on the GeoWrite menu bar.

The Pin Symbol

The first option in each of the GeoWrite menus is the pin symbol. Select this menu option to keep the menu open after you have made your selection from it. Once a menu is pinned, you can relocate it wherever you want by dragging the pinned menu title bar to a new location. You can then make repeated selections from a pinned menu without reopening it each time.

Figure 8.1 shows a pinned File menu that has been moved to the lower left corner of the window.

To close (unpin) a pinned menu, double-click on the **Control** button in the upper-left corner of the menu. Or, single-click on the **Control** button, then select **Close**. (You can also place the mouse cursor on the Control button, then press and hold the left mouse button while dragging to highlight **Close**. Release the mouse button.)

New

Use this option to create a new, untitled document. When you enter GeoWrite from the GeoManager window, the title of the open document (on the title bar) is "Untitled." The document title remains the same until you Save the document and specify a different file name.

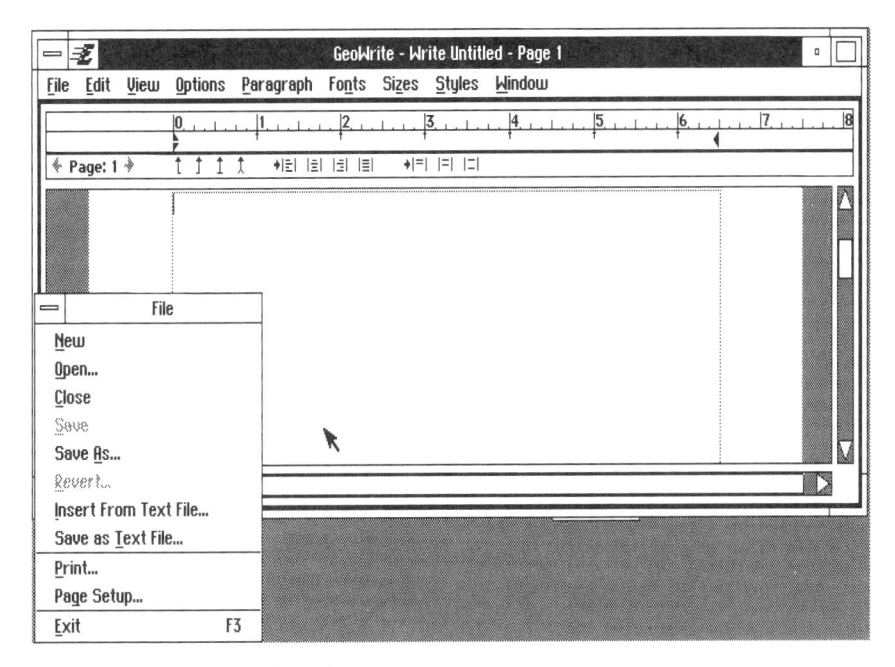

Figure 8.1. A Pinned File Menu.

Suppose you have an open document named "Untitled." You select **New** to create a second document. The program displays a new blank page (the second document is now active) and the new document title bar displays the text: **Write Untitled—1 Page 1**. You are now ready to start typing in the second document. You have two documents open (Untitled, and Untitled 1).

If you were to continue opening new documents, each new document would be given a unique name by adding 1 to the assigned number (e.g., Untitled 2, Untitled 3). When you save an untitled document and give it a new name, the untitled file's name and number become available for assignment to other new documents.

Open

Use the Open command to open (locate and display) a previously saved file. When you select **Open**, the Select Document to Open dialog box is displayed. For a full explanation of the Open menu, see the discussion of the application file menus in Chapter 3.

Close

Use the Close command to close the active document. If you have made changes to the document, the program asks whether you want to save the modifications. If you do not elect to save the changes, they will be lost when you close the document.

Save

The Save command saves the active document, storing it to disk to preserve your work. A saved document means you can return to the last-saved version if you subsequently make changes and then decide you don't want to incorporate those changes in the document. To restore the previously saved version, select the **Revert** option.

The first time you select Save for an active document, the program displays the Select Directory and Enter New Filename dialog box, similar to that shown in Figure 8.2.

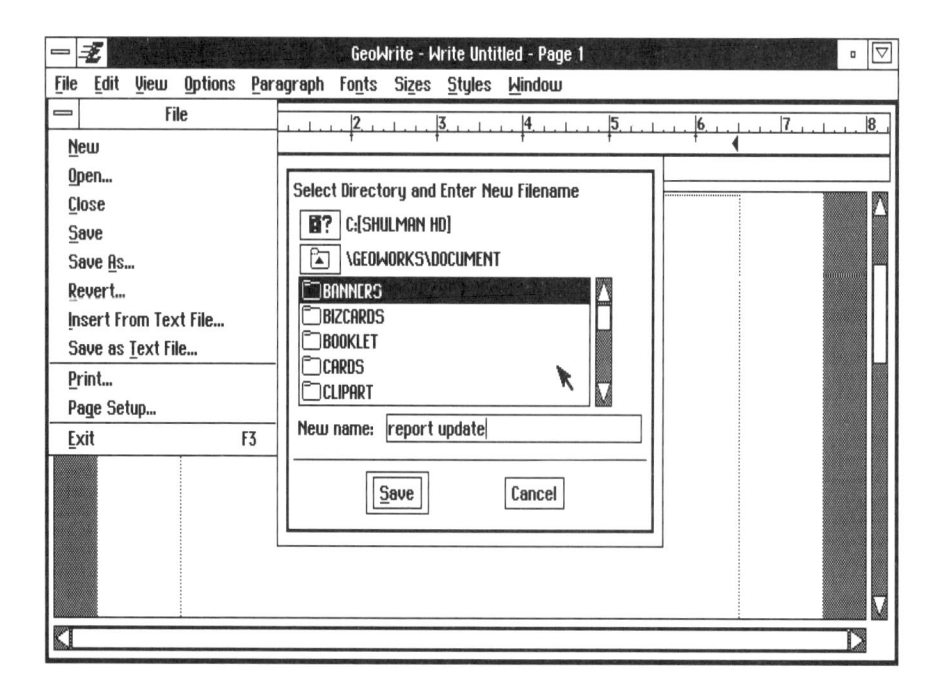

Figure 8.2. The Select Directory and Enter New Filename Dialog Box.

Note that the File Menu in Figure 8.2 is pinned. You can accept the current drive and subdirectory, or you can select a different drive and/or subdirectory in which to save the document. Then position the text cursor in the New Name box and type a document filename.

GeoWrite documents are saved in GEOS file format, so you can use up to 32 characters in the file name. A GEOS filename is case-sensitive (uppercase and lowercase letters are considered different characters). You can use spaces between words in a GEOS filename. This allows you to use more descriptive filenames for your documents than you can with DOS—one of the seemingly small things that can make a big difference.

After typing the new filename, you can complete the save command in one of three ways:

- Press **Enter**.
- Click the **Save** button.
- Press **Alt-S** (the mnemonic method).

The dialog box closes, and you return to the now-saved document which displays the new filename on the title bar.

Whenever you select Save for a previously saved document, the program saves it to disk immediately and automatically in the same location and under the same filename (overwriting the older version).

Save As

Use this option to save an active, previously saved document under a different filename. You can accept the current drive and subdirectory, or you can select a different drive and/or subdirectory. Enter a filename that is different from the existing document name in the New Name box. The original document remains as last saved. You can use the Save As feature to save several versions of a file as you work.

Revert

The Revert option retrieves the last-saved version of the current document. Any changes made to the current document after the last save are lost. When you choose **Revert**, the program asks you to confirm that you want to revert to the last saved version. Click the **Yes** button if you are certain you want to revert.

Text File Commands

The next two menu options allow you to import files *from* other word processors and to export GeoWrite documents *to* other word processors. These useful options give you great flexibility; there may often be times when you want to use a document in your GeoWrite document that was created with another word processor. Conversely, someone may want to use your GeoWrite document in a file created with a different word processor.

Insert From Text File

You cannot open a document in GeoWrite if it was created with another word processor. Conversely, other word processors cannot open GeoWrite documents. The reason is that each word processor has its own way of indicating the internal formatting of its documents and this information cannot be understood by other word processors.

All is not lost, however. It is possible to transfer documents from other word processors to GeoWrite, and vice versa, but first you must get rid of all the formatting information. This creates what is known as a text file (or ASCII file); such a file contains all the letters, numbers, and some special characters as the original document but no formatting characters. When all the formatting characters are removed, the text file has no paragraph spacing, boldface, colors, or other special features.

Fortunately, most word processors, page layout programs, and even some spreadsheets have the capability of translating a document into a text file so it can be exported as well as the capability of translating it to a form GeoWrite can use.

Importing a Text File

Since GeoWrite can directly use only files it creates, the GeoWrite dialog boxes lists only those files. If you want to work with a DOS file, i.e., one created by another word processor and exported from that word processor as a text (ASCII) file. you must import it into GeoWrite. To do this:

1. First open a GeoWrite file or create a new one by selecting **New File** from the File menu.

2. Next, click on the location in the file where you want the imported file inserted. this places the cursor. If the cursor is located on a space, the file will be inserted there. If you highlight a section of text, the imported file will replace that section of text (the whole imported file will be inserted, even if it is longer than the highlighted section of the GeoWrite file).

3. Select the **Insert From Text File** option on the File menu. The Insert From Text File dialog box appears.

4. Change to the drive and directory (if necessary) where the file is located. Locate the file you want and double-click on the name. The contents of that file are inserted in the location you specified in step 2.

The imported file takes on the formatting style of the text at the insertion point in the GeoWrite file.

NOTE

Save as Text File

If you decide that a document you created in GeoWrite is going to be used with another word processor, you can save it as a text file. This will permit the other word processor to import it.

This text file won't look exactly like the original because most of the formatting symbols will be gone (tabs and special characters will remain). The text file will not have carriage returns at the end of each line. The returns will occur only where you pressed Enter, for example, at the end of a paragraph.

To save the document as a text file, use the following procedure:

1. Have the GeoWrite document open.

2. Select: **Save as Text File** from the File menu. The Save as Text File dialog box appears, as shown in Figure 8.3.

3. Enter a DOS filename in the filename field. You must give the file a legal DOS filename (refer to Chapter 4 for a discussion of DOS and GEOS filenames).

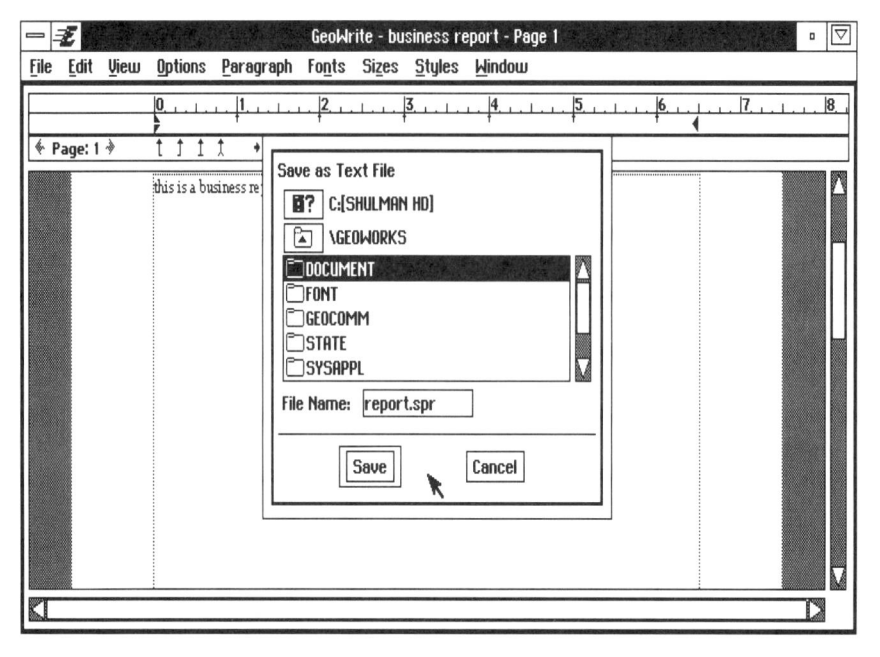

Figure 8.3. The Save As Text File Dialog Box.

4. Click: **Save** button. GeoWrite saves a text file version of the document. The original document remains as it was with its original GeoWrite name. In this example, the original GEOS file, BUSINESS REPORTS, was saved as a DOS file with the name REPORTS.SPR.

Print

Use the Print command to specify the quality of your printed file: draft (for fast printing), high quality (for the final copy) or medium (for an in between combination of print quality and speed). You can print all or selected pages and specify the number of copies you want to print. The Printer Options dialog box is shown in Figure 8.4.

The upper portion of the dialog box identifies the current printer. Select the print quality and number of copies you want.

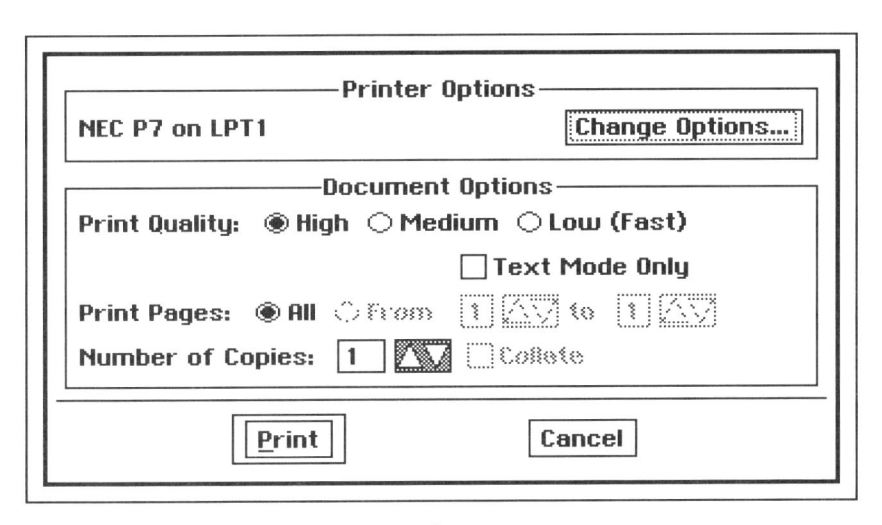

Figure 8.4. The Printer Options Dialog Box.

Change Options

Click the **Change Options** button to select another printer (if you installed more than one), and to change paper size and paper source.

Use the **Print** option on the GeoManager Preferences Application menu to install a new printer so you can select it from the GeoWrite Change Options dialog box. **NOTE**

Page Setup

Before you can print a document, you must specify the paper size (or envelope size, if you want to print envelopes) as well as the paper orientation. Select the **Page Setup** option from the File menu; this displays the dialog box shown in Figure 8.5.

You can scroll the list of paper and envelope sizes in the box at the upper-right. Click on the size you want to select. If nothing there suits your fancy, you can customize the paper size by scrolling through the page widths and heights at the left side. Both the width and the height can range from 2 inches to 45 inches (the size changes in half-inch increments). It is thus possible to have a paper size as small as 2"x 2" or as large as 45"x 45".

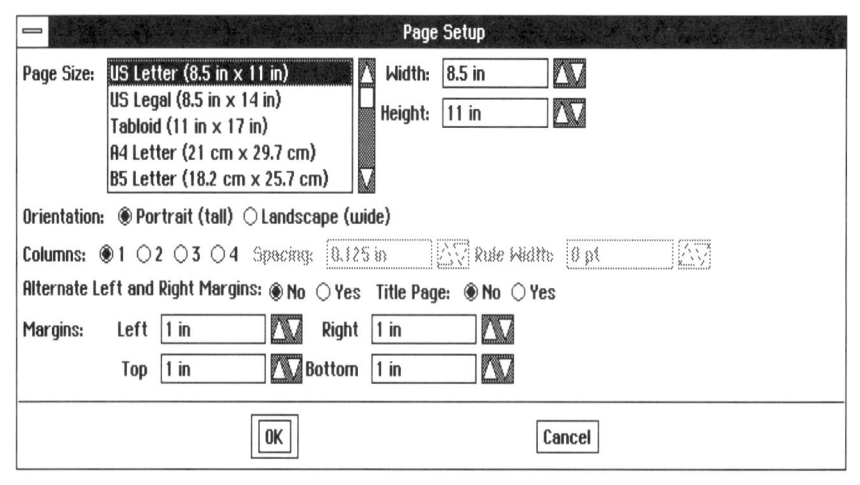

Figure 8.5. The Page Setup Dialog Box.

You can change the units displayed with these lists to metric (centimeters—cm) by selecting **Measurement Units** from the Options menu. A dialog box appears where you can specify metric units; the page sizes will then be given in metric units.

Printing a Document

You can view a list of documents waiting to print by selecting the **Printer Control Panel** option from the Express menu.

Follow these steps to print a document.

1. Select: **Page Setup** from the File menu and verify that the paper size and page orientation settings are what you want. Make any changes required.

2. Click: **OK** to close the Page Setup dialog box. Note: The number of columns affects the whole document. You must create different documents if you want a different number of columns on different pages of your final document.

3. Select: **Print** from the File menu.
   Set the print quality: **High**, **Medium**, or **Low** resolution. (Not all options are available for all printers.)

4. (Optional Step) Select: **Text Mode Only** for faster printing at any print-quality setting. This option does not print graphics and it uses only the internal printer fonts. Documents printed in Text Mode Only can look considerably different than the screen display.

5. Set: **From** and **To** range values to print selected pages. Select: **All** if you want to print all pages of the document.

6. Specify the **Number of Copies** you want to make.

7. Select: **Print**. The printer starts printing.

Exit (F3)

Use the Exit option to close all open documents and exit GeoWrite. If any documents were modified since the last save, the program asks if you want to save the changes.

While a document is printing, you can open another file or even a different application and continue working. This gives you an excuse to play one of the games!

Edit Menu

Selecting **Edit** from the GeoWrite Menu Bar displays the Edit menu shown in Figure 8.6.

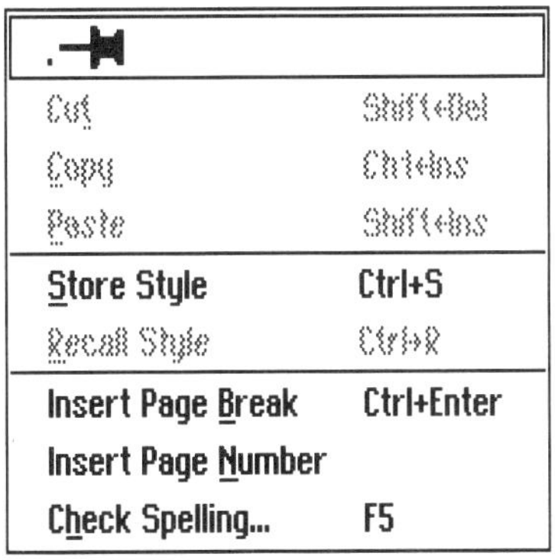

Figure 8.6. The Edit Menu.

The Pin Symbol

See the Pin Symbol section of the File menu discussion earlier in this chapter.

Cut (Shift+Del)

Use the Cut option to remove selected text from a document, moving it to another location in the same document or to another document. Select (highlight) the text you want to move, then select **Cut** from the Edit menu. The Cut option moves the highlighted text to the Clipboard, where it is saved until you save something else to the Clipboard. Use the Paste command to copy the Clipboard information to a document.

Copy (Ctrl+Ins)

Use the Copy option to copy text from one location of your document to another or to another document. Copy is very much like Cut except that the selected material is not removed from its original location in the document.

Select the text you want to copy. Select **Copy** from the Edit menu. The highlighting disappears. Although it seems as if nothing has happened, Copy places a copy of the highlighted text on the Clipboard. Use the Paste option to copy the Clipboard contents into a document.

Paste (Shift+Ins)

Use the Paste option to copy Clipboard contents to your document. Position the text cursor where you want to insert the Clipboard contents. Select **Paste** to copy the text.

Paste does not remove the information from the Clipboard. You can paste the Clipboard information into multiple locations in multiple documents, if you wish.

Clipboard contents are saved automatically each time you Cut or Copy text. Even if you turn off your computer, the next time you return to GeoWrite the last Clipboard contents are intact, ready to be pasted into a document.

Store Style

You can save a combination of format settings (margins, indent, tabs, and fonts) as a style that can be used to format new or existing text.

For example, suppose you have set up a special heading in your document that is centered (Paragraph menu), 24 point (Sizes menu), with special character spacing (Sizes menu), a particular font (Fonts menu), and both bold and italic (Style menu). To save these settings, place the cursor anywhere in the heading and select **Store Style** from the Edit menu.

Recall Style

Use this option to recall a style to format new text. Position the text cursor at the location where you want to start using the stored style. Select **Recall Style** from the Edit menu, then type the text you want affected by the style.

You can also recall a style to format existing text. Highlight the text you want to restyle then select **Recall Style** from the Edit menu. The highlighted text is reformatted to the stored style.

Insert Page Break

Select this option to start a new page at the current cursor position. Any text to the right of the cursor position is carried (with the cursor) to the next page.

Moving Between Pages

The format bar below the ruler bar displays the current page number. To the left of the page number is a LeftArrow; to the right of the page number is a RightArrow. Click on the LeftArrow to go to the previous page (if one exists). Click on the RightArrow to go to the following page.

You can also use the Window menu to move to another page. Select the page you want from the list of current pages in the document.

Insert Page Number

Select this option to insert the current page number into the text at the text cursor position. When you use this command in a header or footer, the page number is automatically set (updated) for each page of the header or footer.

Check Spelling (F5)

GeoWrite provides help for those whose spelling and/or typing leaves something to be desired. By selecting the **Check Spelling** option, you have access to the System Dictionary.

Even though the System Dictionary contains over 100,000 words, that is still just a fraction of all the words in the English language. For that reason, GeoWrite also has a User Dictionary that allows you to add other words you use frequently.

You can then scan your document (or selected parts of it) to locate misspelled words, and correct their spelling, or check on unknown words and add them to the User Dictionary if you wish.

The first thing to do is specify which part of your document you want to check. There are three ways you can conduct a spell check:

- On a single word or an isolated section of text
- From the current cursor position to the end
- On the entire document.

To check a single word, double-click the mouse on that word. If you want to check only a single paragraph of text, triple-click the mouse on that paragraph. To designate any other section of text, click and hold the mouse button; drag the mouse pointer to select the text you want. After the text is selected, choose **Check Spelling** from the Edit menu.

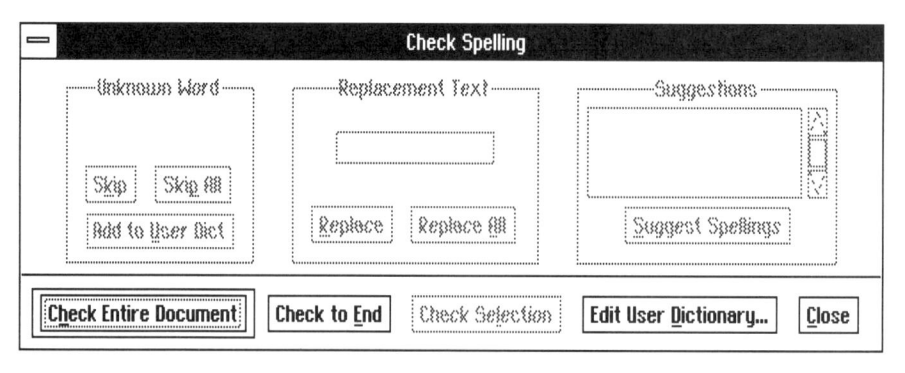

Figure 8.7. The Check Spelling Dialog Box.

When you select Check Spelling, the Check Spelling dialog box appears, as shown in Figure 8.7. The three boxes at the top are shown dimmed (inactive) until a misspelled word is found.

- If you have highlighted any text, the spell checking begins automatically after the dialog box appears. The spell checker stops on the first misspelled (or unknown) word in the selected text.
- You can check the document from the cursor position to the end by clicking someplace in the document to position the cursor there. Do not highlight text. Next, select **Spell Checking** from the Edit menu and click on the **Check to End** button at the bottom of the dialog box.
- If you want to check your entire document, first be sure no text is selected (highlighted). Then select **Check Spelling** from the Edit menu and click on the **Check Entire Document** button at the bottom of the dialog box.

Once you have carried out one of the steps above, the spell checking begins. If the spell checker finds a word that is not in either the System or User Dictionary, it highlights the word (you may have to move the dialog box to see this). It also places the word in the Unknown Word box (at the upper-right of the dialog box) which becomes active.

You have a choice of how to treat the word:

- **Ignore the word.** If you are sure it is correct and you don't want to add it to the User Dictionary, click on the **Skip** button to skip the word *just this once*. If the word occurs throughout the text, the checker will keep stopping at each occurrence of the word unless you check **Skip All**. This causes the checker to ignore the word for the current checking session (i.e., until the Check Spelling dialog box closes).
- **Correct and replace it.** If you know the correct spelling, type it in the Replacement Text box (in the middle of the dialog box). Next, click **Replace** to change the current word. Check **Replace All** if you want to change every instance of the misspelled word in the document immediately.

- **Let the Spelling Checker suggest a replacement.** If you click **Suggest Spellings**, the checker will check the System Dictionary for words that are similar to the unknown word. It displays all the words it finds in the Spelling Suggestions box (upper-right of the dialog box).

    You can use the scroll bar to scan the list of words to see if the correct word is listed. If it is, select the word by clicking on it. The word appears on the Replacement box on the left. You can change the word or use it as is. When you are satisfied, click **Replace** to change only the current occurrence of the word or **Replace All** to change all occurrences of the word.

    If the word you want is not listed, you can click on the **Suggest From User Dictionary** button. The checker then looks in the User Dictionary for similar words. Follow the procedure above to replace the misspelled word.

- **Add the word to the User Dictionary.** If you know the word is correct, you can keep the spell checker from stopping on that word in the future by adding it to the User Dictionary. Click the **Add to User Dictionary** button; the word is added to that dictionary.

Editing the User Dictionary

The User Dictionary was created to permit you to add words not in the System Dictionary. You add words from documents by the procedure described in the previous section.

If you want to add a word that is not in a document, you can still add it to the User Dictionary. Suppose, for example, you have just coined the word "maximinize" (perhaps to replace that bureaucratic favorite, counterproductive). Just click the **Edit User Dictionary** button at the bottom of the Check Spelling dialog box and the Words in User Dictionary dialog box appears.

Type `maximinize` in the New Word field and click on the **Add New Word** button. The word is added to the dictionary and you can use it without worrying about the spell checker.

If you stop using a particular word or if you realize you added a misspelled word by mistake, it is easy to remove it from the User Dictionary. Click on the **Edit User Dictionary** button to open the Edit User Dictionary dialog box. Scan the list of words in the dictionary; click on the one you want to remove, then click the **Delete Selected Word** button. The word is removed and the spell checker will stop on that word in the future.

Customizing the Spelling Checker

There are some features of the spelling checker that you can change to customize its behavior. This is done from the GeoWrite Options menu, but the procedures are described here for continuity with the spell-checking section.

When you select the **Spell Check Options** from the Options menu, another menu appears. As illustrated in Figure 8.8, this menu has three options.

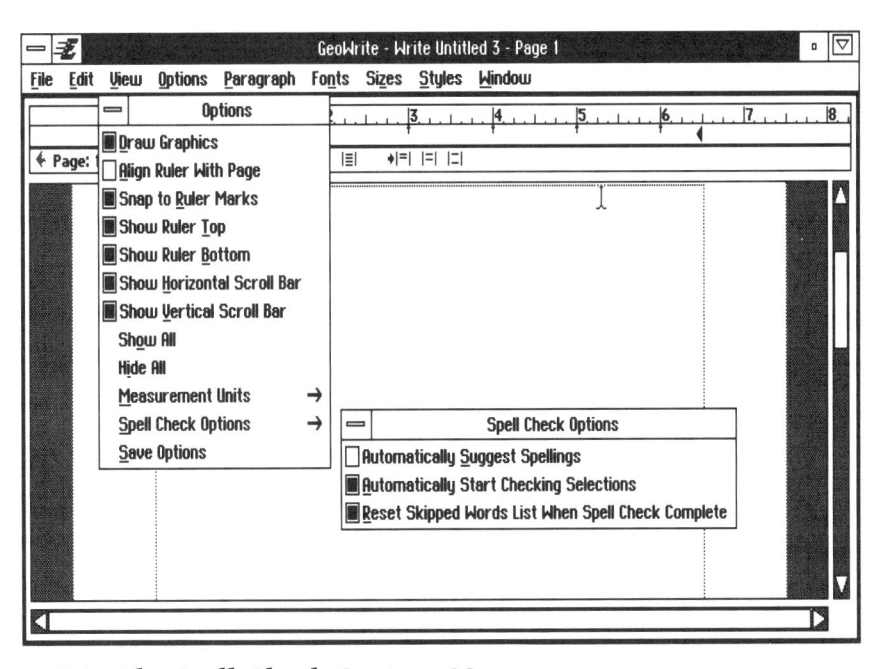

Figure 8.8. The Spell Check Options Menu.

Automatically Suggest Spellings

The Spell Check Options dialog box allows you to specify whether or not to automatically suggest spellings. The default is off. If the Automatically

Suggest Spellings box is on, the checker automatically checks the System Dictionary and suggests spellings. This can be useful as it saves a step, and you can often find the correct word in the list.

If you have a slow computer, you might find this process takes a long time. When the Automatically Suggest Spellings box is off, the checker won't automatically search the dictionary for words. You will have to click **Suggest Spellings** whenever you want to see a list of words.

Automatically Start Checking Selections

This option is normally on (the default). This means that when you select text to be checked and choose **Check Spelling** from the Edit menu (or press **F5**), the spelling checker automatically goes to work without waiting for you to click the **Check Selection** button.

If you turn this option off, you will have to click the **Check Selection** button before it will begin.

Reset Skipped Words List When Spell Check Complete

You can instruct the spell checker to skip every occurrence of a word that it has located by clicking **Skip All** in the Check Spelling dialog box. Usually, this only causes the spell checker to skip the word for the current session because the Reset Skipped Words option is set to On (the default). Once the spell check is complete, the word will once again join the ranks of the hunted.

If you set the option to Off, the spell checker will continue to skip the word even in checking other documents that were open in GeoWrite. It continues to skip the word until you close GeoWrite. It will be reset to On when you open GeoWrite again. However, if you shut down GeoWorks Pro without closing GeoWrite, the option will still be set to Off the next time.

You may want to check a document frequently and you don't want the checker stopping on the same words every time but you don't want to store them permanently in the User Dictionary. If so, you can set this option to Off. That way you won't have to keep telling the checker to skip those words.

View Menu

Use the View menu to change the magnification of the page within the window. You can view the entire page at once (reduced magnification) or a small portion of it (enlarged magnification). Larger magnifications may help reduce eyestrain.

NOTE: Magnification settings do not affect the font size or printed text on a page.

Correct for Aspect Ratio

You may want to use this option if you have a monochrome monitor (these are usually used with a Hercules or Hercules-compatible graphics card) or a CGA monitor. These monitors use rectangular pixels rather than square ones. (A pixel is the smallest dot your monitor can display.) As a result, images tend to look squashed—too short and too wide. Selecting the **Correct for Aspect Ratio** option changes the way a document displays so it more closely represents the way it will print. If you select this option and your screen dims, your monitor already has square pixels and no correction is necessary. Selecting this option toggles it on or off.

If your screen writes too slowly with Correct for Aspect Ratio turned on, try using this option only when you want to preview your document.

Options Menu

Figure 8.9 shows the Options menu.

Draw Graphics

GeoWrite documents can contain text and graphics. Select **Draw Graphics** to see the actual graphic images on the screen. Graphics images, however, will slow down scrolling speed as you move through the document. When you turn off Draw Graphics, a graphic image placeholder indicates the image location without slowing down scrolling.

```
                    ┌─────────────────────────────┐
                    │            ·-■-             │
                    ├─────────────────────────────┤
                    │ ■ Draw Graphics             │
                    │ ☐ Align Ruler With Page     │
                    │ ■ Snap to Ruler Marks       │
                    │ ■ Show Ruler Top            │
                    │ ■ Show Ruler Bottom         │
                    │ ■ Show Horizontal Scroll Bar│
                    │ ■ Show Vertical Scroll Bar  │
                    │   Show All                  │
                    │   Hide All                  │
                    │   Measurement Units       → │
                    │   Spell Check Options     → │
                    │   Save Options              │
                    └─────────────────────────────┘
```

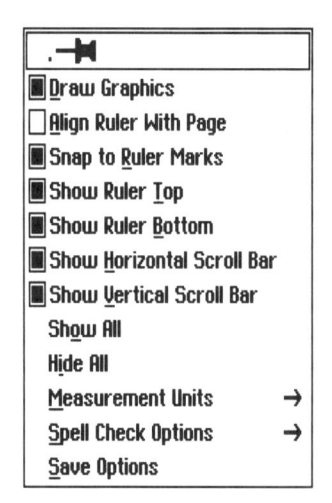

Figure 8.9. The Options Menu.

Align Ruler With Page

When you select Align Ruler With Page, the zero on the ruler line aligns with the edge of the page. If you do not set this option, the zero of the ruler line aligns with the text's left margin.

Snap to Ruler Marks

When you select this option, the tabs, indents, and margin markers snap to the nearest 1/8-inch mark on the ruler. As long as this option is turned on, you cannot set tabs, indents and margins at any increment smaller than 1/8-inch (such as a 1/16-inch mark).

Show Ruler Top

You can choose to show or hide the top line of the ruler bar by toggling the **Show Ruler Top** option. As you learned in Chapter 7, the top line of the ruler bar displays a ruler image with scale gradations.

Show Ruler Bottom

You can choose to show or hide the bottom line of the Ruler Bar by toggling the Show Ruler Bottom option. As you learned in Chapter 7, the bottom line of the ruler bar displays the tab, indent and margin markers.

Show Horizontal Scroll Bar

You can choose to show or hide the horizontal scroll bar by toggling this option.

Show Vertical Scroll Bar

You can choose to show or hide the vertical scroll bar by toggling this option.

Show All

Select this option when you want all screen display options turned on. This option is not a toggle—selecting it activates **Show All** every time.

Hide All

Select this option when you want all screen display options turned off. This option is not a toggle—selecting it activates **Hide All** every time.

Measurement Units

When you select this option, a dialog box appears in which you can specify the measurement units that will be used in the page setup dialog box. You can select English (inches), Metric (centimeters—cm), or the System default, which is inches in the U.S.

Spell Check Options

This menu option displays a submenu that allows you to customize the way the spell checker behaves by setting these items on or off. Refer to the discussion of spell checking.

Save Options

Select this option to save the current Options menu settings and close the menu.

Paragraph Menu

Figure 8.10 shows the Paragraph menu.

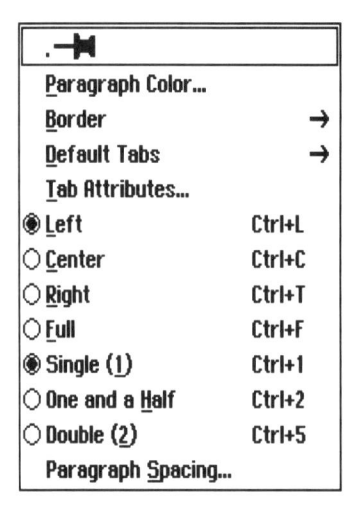

```
      ┌─────────────────────────┐
      │         📌              │
      │ Paragraph Color...      │
      │ Border             →    │
      │ Default Tabs       →    │
      │ Tab Attributes...       │
      │ ◉ Left          Ctrl+L  │
      │ ○ Center        Ctrl+C  │
      │ ○ Right         Ctrl+T  │
      │ ○ Full          Ctrl+F  │
      │ ◉ Single (1)    Ctrl+1  │
      │ ○ One and a Half Ctrl+2 │
      │ ○ Double (2)    Ctrl+5  │
      │ Paragraph Spacing...    │
      └─────────────────────────┘
```

Figure 8.10. The Paragraph Menu.

The Pin Symbol

See the Pin Symbol section of the File Menu, discussed earlier in the chapter.

Paragraph Color

You can use Paragraph Color settings, which will display as colors or patterns, depending on your monitor, to modify the way your document looks on the screen. Colors always print as black on a black-and-white printer. A multicolor document created on a monochrome monitor will print multicolor on a color printer.

On a monochrome monitor, patterns of varying intensity represent colors. You cannot apply these patterns to paragraph backgrounds or borders.

Selecting **Paragraph Color** displays a dialog box similar to the one in Figure 8.11, which shows the dialog box for a monochrome monitor. The patterns representing colors start on the left with black and progress to white on the right.

The dialog box color scale for an EGA or VGA monitor looks slightly different, but functions in the same way as the monochrome dialog box.

Halftone

The Halftone setting controls color intensity—the concentration of color—in text, paragraph backgrounds, and borders on color and monochrome monitors. Select **Solid** for 100%, **Dark** for 50%, **Medium** for 25%, or **Light** for 15% color concentration. Halftones print on color and black-and-white printers. You will learn how to create halftone fonts in Chapter 10.

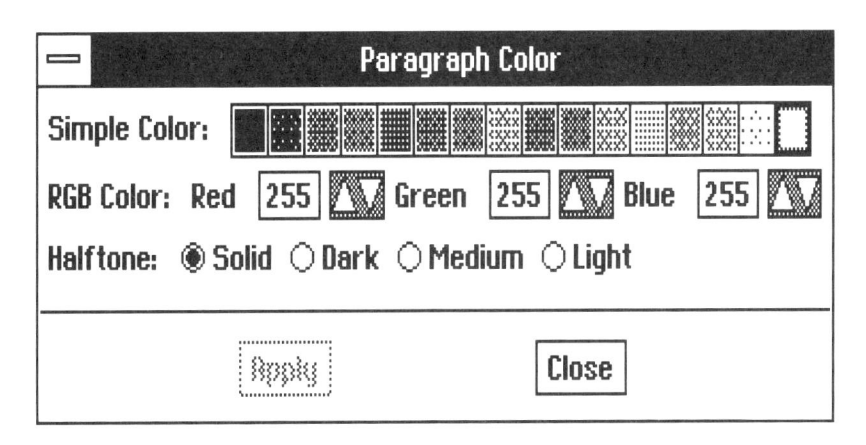

Figure 8.11. The Paragraph Color Dialog Box.

RGB Color

To change the color mix, select a color box (or pattern box) and vary the amount of red, green, or blue for that box, click on a **DownArrow** to decrease the color amount (down to 0), or click on an **UpArrow** to increase the color amount (up to 255).

Apply

Click the **Apply** button to see the new color settings.

Close

Click the **Close** button to close the dialog box and return to the GeoWrite window.

Border

The Border cascading menu contains options to let you use colors and halftones in borders.

None

You must select None when you want to exit a border box and continue typing in your document outside the border. For example, suppose you create a double-line border box for a one-line title. After typing the title text, you must press **Enter** to insert a blank line in the box, then select **None** from the Border menu to exit the box.

One Line

Select this option when you want to create text surrounded by a one-line border.

Two Line

Select this option when you want to create text surrounded by a two-line border.

Shadow Top Left

Select this option when you want to create text surrounded by a border box that appears to cast a shadow from an imaginary light source at the top left corner of the screen. The shadow extends from the right and bottom edges of the box.

Custom Border

Select this option to custom-design a border. Select a border type—Normal, Shadow, or Double line—as a basis for your custom border. The program displays the Custom Border dialog box ,similar to the one shown in Figure 8.12.

Sides to Border

You can determine which sides of the box are to have borders by using the Sides to Border option.

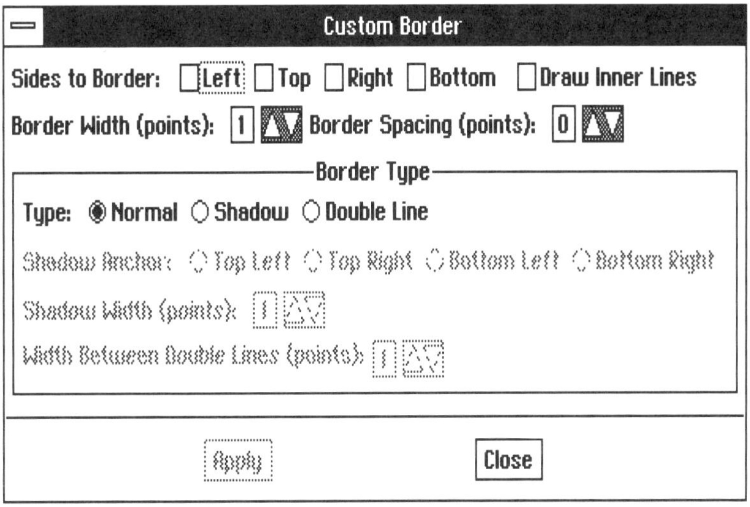

Figure 8.12. The Custom Border Dialog Box.

Draw Inner Lines

When the Draw Inner Lines option is active, pressing **Enter** draws a line within the border. When Draw Inner Lines is not active, pressing **Enter** inserts a blank line within the border.

Border Width

Select **Border Width** to adjust the width of the border.

Border Spacing

You can adjust the space between the text and border by selecting this option.

Shadow Anchor

If your custom border includes a shadow, you can change the shadow position by selecting **Shadow Anchor**. Remember, the shadow appears on the side of the box opposite the light source.

Shadow Width

Select this option to adjust the width of the box shadow.

Border Color

The Border Color dialog box of the Border menu item is almost identical to the Paragraph Color dialog box of the Paragraph menu..

See the Halftone, RGB Color, Apply, and Close sections under "Paragraph Color" above for a discussion of the Border Color dialog box features.

Default Tabs

In the Default Tabs cascading menu you can select one of four options as the default tab setting: None, Half inch, One inch, or Two inches.

Tab Attributes

Suppose you want to change a left-justified tab to a right-justified tab with dot leaders. Click on the tab in the ruler bar, then select **Tab Attributes** in the Paragraph menu to display the Tab Attributes dialog box. (Or you can double-click on the tab to select it and display the dialog box in one operation.) Figure 8.13 shows the Tab Attributes dialog box.

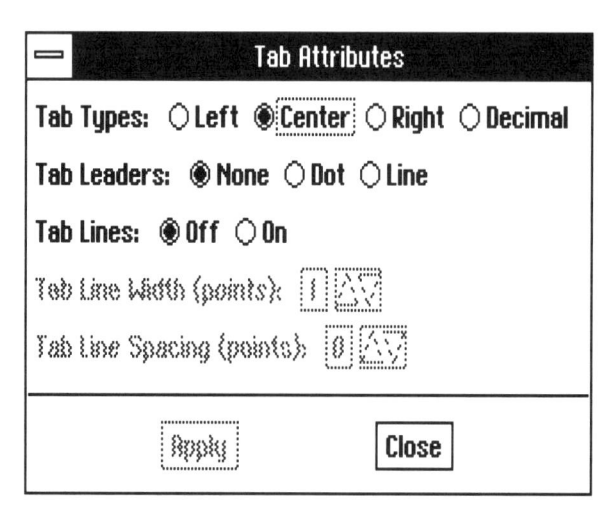

Figure 8.13. The Tab Attributes Dialog Box.

If you do not first select a tab before displaying the Tab Attributes dialog box, options are dimmed and unavailable.

Tab Types

Select the tab type you want: left-justified, right-justified, centered, or decimal-aligned.

Tab Leaders

Select the tab leader option you want, line or dots. Use tab leaders to insert a line or a row of dots between the text and the leader tab. For example, a table of contents often uses dot leaders to fill the space between the content descriptions and the corresponding page numbers.

Tab Lines

Toggle on the Tab Lines option to draw vertical lines at the tab location for columns and tables. You can also use it to mark portions of a document that have been changed.

A Tab Line tab is indicated in the ruler bar by a vertical line. You can set multiple Tab Line tabs in a document. When you press **Enter** to start a new line in the document, the program draws vertical lines at the Tab Line positions.

Tab Line Width

Select this option to specify the width of the vertical tab line (from 1 to 3 points).

Tab Line Spacing

Select this option to specify the spacing between the text and the tab line (from 1 to 3 points).

Left (Ctrl+L)

Select this option on the Paragraph menu to left-justify the paragraph in which the cursor is located or a currently highlighted paragraph. Left-justification aligns the left edge of the text at the left margin and leaves the right margin ragged.

Center (Ctrl+C)

Select this option to center-justify the paragraph in which the cursor is located or a currently highlighted paragraph. Center-justification centers each line of text between the left and right margins.

Right (Ctrl+T)

Select this option to right-justify the paragraph in which the cursor is located or a currently highlighted paragraph. Right-justification aligns the right edge of the text at the right margin and leaves the left margin ragged.

Full (Ctrl+F)

Select this option to fully justify the paragraph in which the cursor is located or a currently highlighted paragraph. Full justification adds spaces between words so that both the left and right text edges align at the margins.

> **NOTE** You can achieve the same justification results by selecting the left, center, right or full justification icons below the ruler bar.

Single (1) (Ctrl+1)

Use this option to single-space lines in selected text or the paragraph in which your text cursor is located.

One and a Half (Ctrl+2)

Use this option to space lines one-and-a-half lines apart in selected text or the paragraph in which your text cursor is located.

Double (2) (Ctrl+5)

Use this option to double-space lines in selected text or the paragraph in which your text cursor is located.

You can achieve the same spacing results by selecting the Single spacing, One-and-a-half spacing, or Double spacing icons below the ruler bar (on the right).

NOTE

Paragraph Spacing

Select this option to change the spacing above, below, and within a selected paragraph or the paragraph in which the text cursor is located. This is a particularly useful tool. For example, you can add space before or after a heading, stretch columnar text to fill a larger space, or squeeze text to fit a smaller space. Figure 8.14 shows the Paragraph Spacing dialog box.

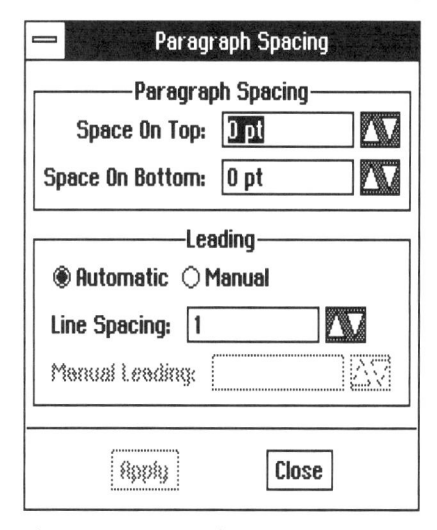

Figure 8.14. Paragraph Spacing Dialog Box.

Paragraph Spacing

Click on the up and down arrows to set the amount of space above or below the affected text (0 to 3 points).

Leading

Use this option to control precisely the distance between lines (leading) in the selected paragraph. Manual leading adds the Line Spacing value as a constant to the space between lines, regardless of the font sizes used in the lines. Manual leading is most appropriate when you use one font size. Automatic leading determines the largest font in a line then multiplies the font size by the Line Spacing value. Use automatic leading when you combine font sizes in a document.

GeoWorks Pro dialog boxes display values in inches, but you can enter values in any of the following units: in (inches), pi (picas), pt (points), cm (centimeters), mm (millimeters), ci (Ciceros), or ep (European points).

Line Spacing

Click on the up or down arrows to select the line spacing value you want to use or position the text cursor in the Line Spacing box and type a value. (You can use fractions.)

Apply

Select **Apply** to see how your selection affects the selected paragraph or the paragraph in which your text cursor is located.

Close

Select **Close** to accept the paragraph spacing settings, close the dialog box, and return to the GeoWrite window.

Fonts Menu

To set a new font for existing text, highlight the text, then select the Fonts menu. Select the font you want to use from the Fonts menu. The menu closes and you return to the GeoWrite window. The selected text displays in the new font.

To set a font for new text, position the text cursor where you want to begin typing with the new font. Select the Fonts menu. Select the font you want to use from the Fonts menu. The menu closes and you return to the GeoWrite window, ready to type with the new font.

See the Pin Symbol section of the File Menu, discussed earlier in the chapter.

More Fonts

To see a sample of a font before activating it in the document, select the **More Fonts** option from the Fonts menu. The More Fonts dialog box is displayed.

> **NOTE:** The More Fonts dialog box is already pinned when it is displayed. Since it is pinned, you can move it to one side by clicking the right mouse button on the menu bar and dragging to the new location.

When you have the More Fonts dialog box displayed at one side of the screen, you can go back to your document and highlight any text you want to change, then go to the dialog box and select the font you want. The sample text below the font list changes to display your font selection.

Click the **Apply** button to see how that font will look in your document. If you don't like that choice, you can go back to the dialog box and choose another font. When you are satisfied with the font selection, click the **Close** button to return to the GeoWrite window.

Figure 8.15 shows a sample of the available fonts. Notice that the Fonts menu has been pinned and moved to the upper-right corner.

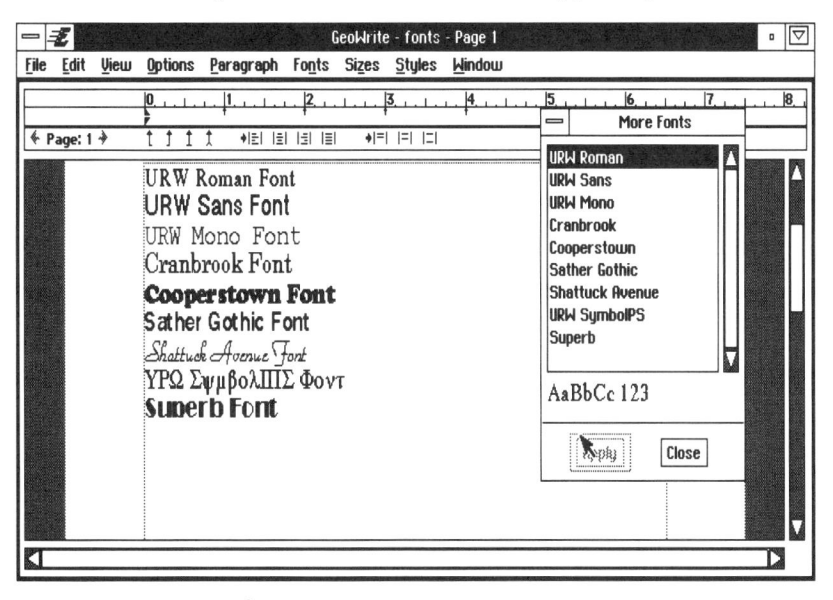

Figure 8.15. Font Samples.

Sizes Menu

Use the Sizes menu to change the font size of selected text, or to set the font size for new text. Figure 8.15 shows the URW Roman font in eight sizes. See the Pin Symbol section of the File Menu, discussed earlier in the chapter.

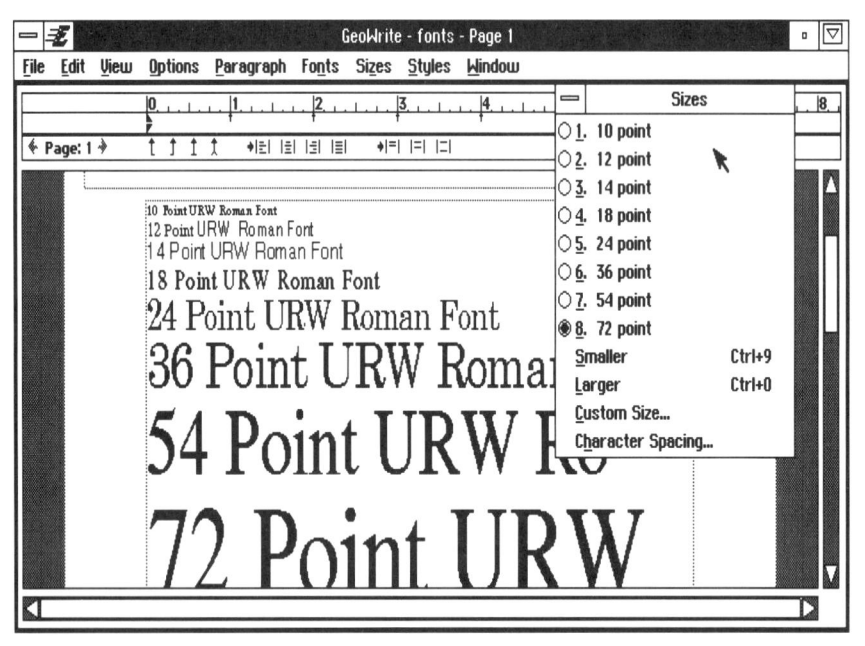

Figure 8.16. The Sizes Menu and Font Size Examples.

Standard Font Sizes

The Sizes dialog box lists eight point sizes from 10 to 72 points (72 points is equal to approximately one inch). The menu indicates the active point size by a filled circle next to it.

Make Existing Text Font Smaller or Larger

Select the text you want to change, then open the Sizes menu. Select **Smaller** to activate the next-smaller standard font size, or choose **Larger** to activate the next-larger font size.

You can also use the Smaller hotkey, **Ctrl-9**, or the Larger hotkey, **Ctrl-0**, to change font sizes from the keyboard.

Make New Text Smaller or Larger

Position the text cursor where you want to begin typing with the new font. Open the Sizes menu, then select **Larger** or **Smaller**.

You can also use the Smaller hotkey, **Ctrl-9**, or the Larger hotkey, **Ctrl-0**, to change the active font size from the keyboard.

Custom Size

To use a size other than a standard font size, select the **Custom Size** option. Click on the **UpArrow** or **DownArrow** to increase or decrease the displayed font size, or position the text cursor in the font size box and type a font size. You can specify from 4 points to 792 points. (A 792-point font is 11 inches tall—it will fill an 8-1/2-x-11-inch page although very few printers can print to the actual edge of page.)

Click the **Apply** button to view the font change in your document. When you are satisfied with your selection, click the **Close** button.

Character Spacing

Select Character Spacing to vary the amount of space between characters in a word. When you select Character Spacing, the program displays the Degree of Spacing dialog box.

Highlight the text you want to affect, or position the text cursor at the point where you want to begin typing with the new character-spacing value. Select the **Character Spacing** option from the Sizes menu.

Click on the up and down arrows to increase or decrease the amount of space, or position the text cursor in the spacing box and type the value you want.

Click the **Apply** button to see the character spacing in your document. When you are satisfied with the character spacing, click the **Close** button to return to the document.

Styles Menu

Use the Styles menu, shown in Figure 8.17, to display different typefaces: bold, underline, italic, bold and italic, etc.

You can select more than one typeface at a time so you could combine bold and italic, for example. The only exception is the Plain Text option, which turns off all other typefaces.

See the Pin Symbol section of the File Menu, discussed earlier in the chapter.

Plain Text (Ctrl+P)

Select Plain Text to turn off all other typefaces.

Bold (Ctrl+B)

Use Bold for thicker, darker text than Plain Text. Bold is usually used for headings and word emphasis.

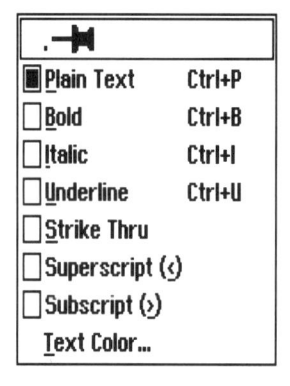

```
■ Plain Text      Ctrl+P
☐ Bold            Ctrl+B
☐ Italic          Ctrl+I
☐ Underline       Ctrl+U
☐ Strike Thru
☐ Superscript (<)
☐ Subscript (>)
  Text Color...
```

Figure 8.17. The Styles Menu.

Italic (Ctrl+I)

Use Italic to slant text to the right. Italic is usually used for word emphasis or for titles of books, works of art or court cases.

Underline (Ctrl+U)

Use Underline to place a line under each character. Underline is usually used for word emphasis.

Strike Thru

Use **Strike Thru** to place a line through each character. Strike Thru is usually used in editing to indicate text that should be removed from a document.

Superscript (<)

Use Superscript to write characters smaller and above the normal baseline of the text. Superscript is usually used for footnotes, algebraic exponents and other types of technical notation.

Subscript (>)

Use Subscript to write characters smaller and at or below the normal baseline of the text. It is usually used for mathematical subscript notations and other types of technical notation.

Text Color

Selecting this option displays the dialog box similar to that of the paragraph color dialog box of the Paragraph menu.

To change the color of text, select the text, or place the typing cursor in the paragraph you want to color. Select **Text Color** from the Styles menu.

To use the Text Color dialog box, follow the steps covered in the Paragraph Color section earlier in this chapter.

Window

Select the Window menu to display the dialog box shown in Figure 8.18.

188 • *Teach Yourself GeoWorks Pro*

```
┌─────────────────────────────────┐
│  .-📍                           │
│  Go to Beginning      Ctrl+A    │
│  Previous Page        Ctrl+V    │
│  Next Page            Ctrl+N    │
│  Go to Page...                  │
│  Redraw               Shift+Ctrl+R │
│  Overlapping          Ctrl+F5   │
│  Full-Sized           Ctrl+F10  │
│ ● Write Untitled 3 - Page 1     │
└─────────────────────────────────┘
```

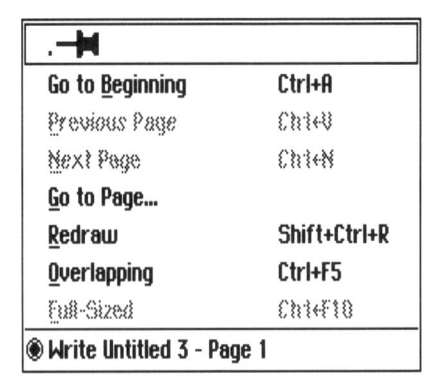

Figure 8.18. The Window Menu.

The Pin Symbol

See The Pin Symbol section of the File menu discussed earlier in this chapter.

Previous Page (Ctrl+V)

Select this option to go to the previous page in the document.

Next Page (Ctrl+N)

Select this option to go to the next page in the document.

Go to Page

Select this option to jump to a specific page in the document. Selecting this option shows the Go to Page dialog box.

Position the text cursor in the Go to Page box. Then type the page number you want to go to. Or you can click on the up and down arrows to specify the page number. Click the **OK** button to jump to the selected page.

Redraw (Shift+Ctrl+R)

Select this option when you want to redraw (refresh) the screen.

Overlapping

Select this option to display multiple pages in overlapping format on the screen. You can also display multiple documents in overlapping format. Figure 8.19 shows three documents in overlapping format.

Note that the title bar of each documents is visible. You can select any title bar to make it the active document.

Full-Sized (Ctrl+F10)

Use this option to change from an overlapping display to a full-sized display of the active document.

Page Listing and Select Page

The bottom portion of the Window menu lists the pages in your document. When you select a page from the list, the menu closes and you return to the document on the selected page.

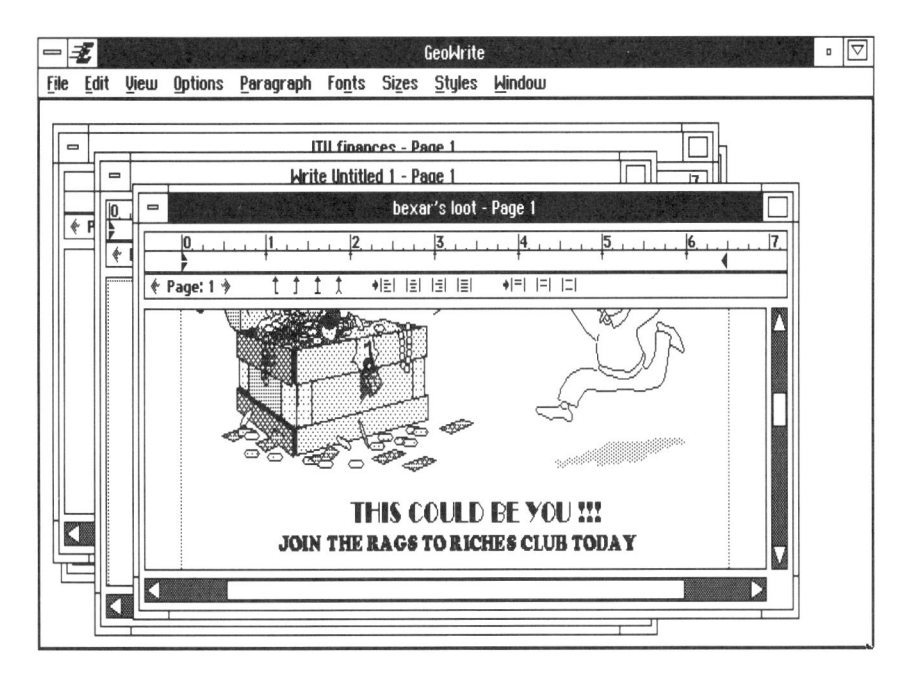

Figure 8.19. Overlapping Document Windows.

Summary

In this chapter you learned how to use the options on the nine GeoWrite menus. Each menu option was discussed in detail.

Chapter 9

GeoWrite Operations and Tutorial

In this tutorial chapter you will practice using some of the major features of the GeoWrite application. After completing this chapter you will be sufficiently acquainted with GeoWrite to apply the other features to your work on your own.

During the three exercises in this tutorial you will:

- Create a document
- Practice formatting techniques
- Insert a graphic image into the document
- Create and format a table
- Enter numbers into the table
- Copy the table
- Re-space and format the copied table
- Reset first-line indent and paragraph margin markers.

Accessing GeoWrite

Start the GeoWorks Pro program in the usual way. Select the **Advanced Workspace** icon from the GeoWorks Pro Welcome screen. If the GeoManager Information Line does not read \GEOMANAGER\WORLD, single-click on the **World** button at the bottom of the GeoManager window. Then double-click on the GeoWrite icon.

The program displays the GeoWrite window. The document title reads GeoWrite-Write Untitled-Page 1. The typing cursor is in the upper left corner of the typing panel.

Exercise 1

In this exercise you will:

- Create a document
- Enter text
- Format text
- Create a header
- Insert a GeoDraw drawing into the header
- Save the document.

Create and Save a Document

1. Type: `Declaration of Independence`
   Press: **Enter** to start a new line.
   The typing cursor moves to the beginning of the second line.

2. Open the File menu and select **Save**. The program displays the Select Directory and Enter New Filename dialog box.

3. Save the new document in the \GEOWORKS\DOCUMENT subdirectory. Change the subdirectory, if necessary, so that the Select Directory information line in the dialog box reads \GEOWORKS\DOCUMENT.

GeoWrite Operations and Tutorial • **193**

4. Position the text cursor in the New Name box. Type the name of the new document: `Declaration of Independence` Select: **Save**. The dialog box will close and you will return to the GeoWrite window. The Title bar should now read: `GeoWrite-Declaration of Independence-Page 1`.

Setting Options

5. Open the Options menu.
   Toggle on the following options (a filled square indicates the option is toggled on):

   - Draw Graphics
   - Align Ruler With Page
   - Snap to Ruler Marks
   - Show Ruler Top
   - Show Ruler Bottom
   - Show Horizontal Scroll Bar
   - Show Vertical Scroll Bar

6. Select: **Save Options**. The Options menu closes and you return to the document with the typing cursor at the beginning of the second line.

Setting a Center Tab

7. Set a center tab at the 4-1/4-inch position on the ruler. (Refer to Chapter 7, Tabs section.) Move the mouse cursor to the center tab symbol. Drag the center tab symbol to the 4-1/4-inch position on the ruler.

Figure 9.1. The Center Tab Symbol.

194 • *Teach Yourself GeoWorks Pro*

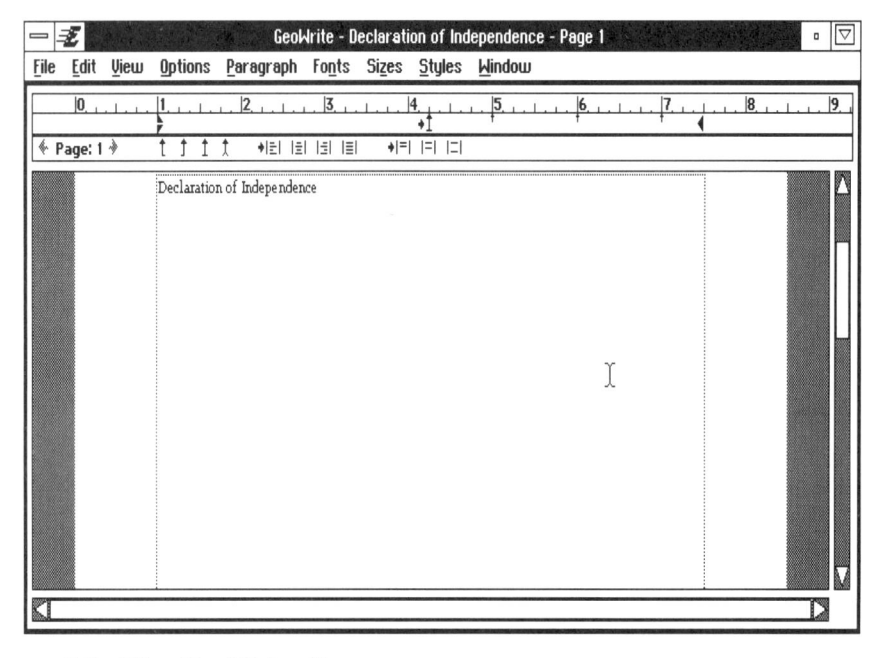

Figure 9.2. The GeoWrite Document.

       The program removes the one-inch tab symbols to the left of the center tab. The one-inch tab symbols to the right of it remain. Your screen should resemble that shown in Figure 9.2.

       Note the horizontal arrow pointing to the center tab you placed on the ruler. This indicates that it is the currently selected tab.

8. Press: **Tab**. The typing cursor moves to the 4-1/4-inch position.
   Type: `Declaration of Independence`
   Press: **Enter** to start a new line.
   The program centers the second line of text at the 4-1/4-inch center tab. The typing cursor moves to the third line.

Selecting Text

9. Position the cursor on the beginning of the first line of text. Select the first line by pressing and holding the left mouse button while dragging to highlight the entire line, then release the left mouse button. The text remains highlighted, as shown in Figure 9.3.

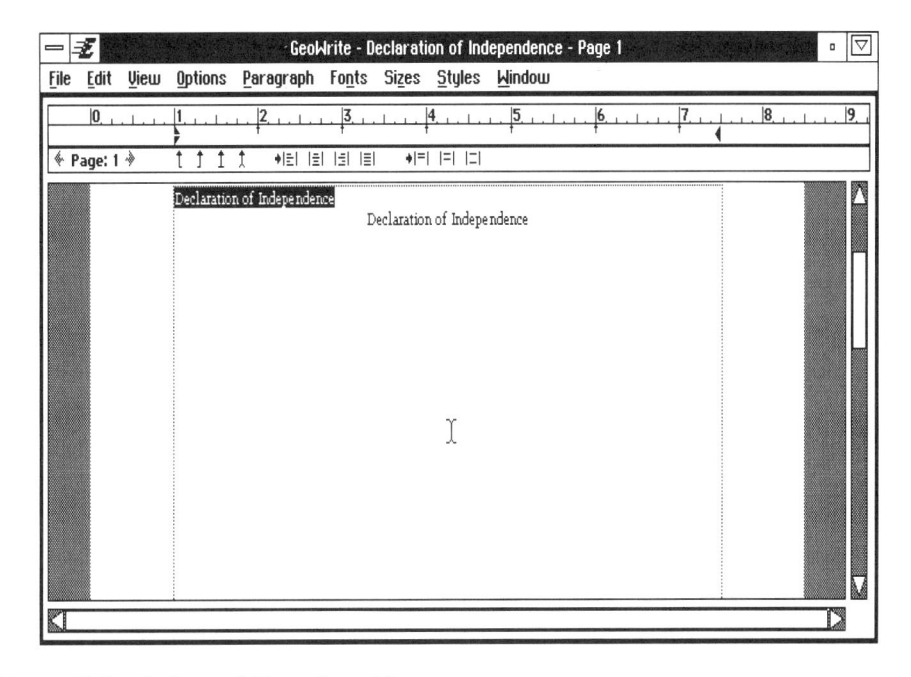

Figure 9.3. Selected Text in a Document.

Changing Font of Existing Text

10. Open: Fonts menu by pressing **Alt-N**.
    Click: **Pin** symbol to pin open the Fonts menu.
    Move: Mouse cursor to the title bar of the menu.
    Click and hold the right mouse button and drag the menu to the right side of the screen.

11. Select: Cooperstown font. The program displays the highlighted text in Cooperstown. The text remains highlighted and the Fonts menu remains open.

12. Select: Shattuck Avenue font. The program displays the highlighted text in Shattuck Avenue. The text remains highlighted and the Fonts menu remains open.

Changing the Size of Existing Text

13. Open the Size menu by pressing **Alt-Z**.
    Click: Option **4** (or press the number **4**) to select 18 point. The

program displays the highlighted text in 18-point Shattuck Avenue and closes the Size menu.

Changing Text Styles of Existing Text

14. Open: Styles menu by pressing **Alt-S**. Click on **Bold**. The program displays the highlighted text in bold 18-point Shattuck Avenue and closes the Styles menu.

15. Open: **Styles** menu again and pin it open.
    Move it to the right as described in step 10.
    Click on **Underline**. The program displays the highlighted text in bold and underline style. The pinned Styles menu remains. Your screen should resemble Figure 9.4.

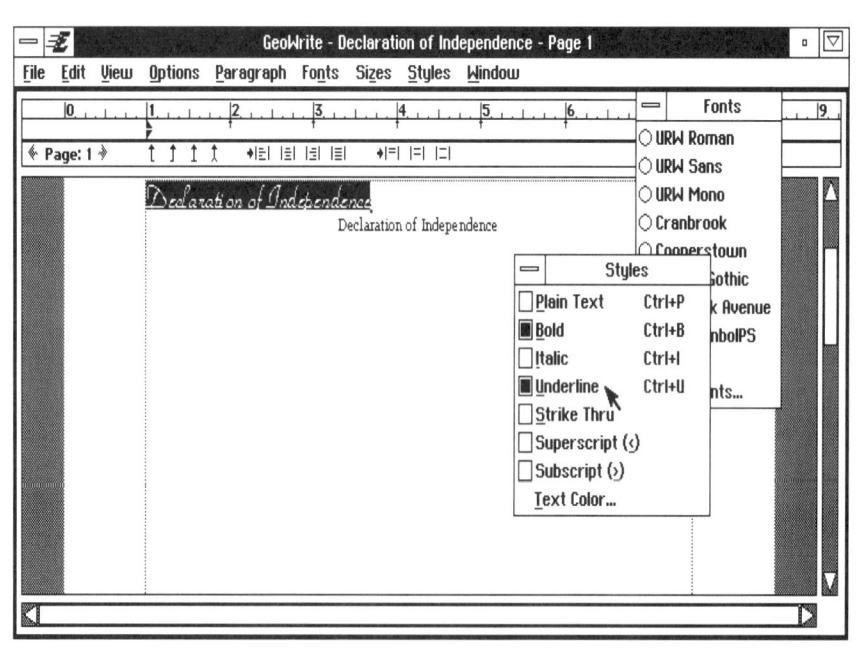

Figure 9.4. Changing Text Font and Style.

Closing Pinned Menus

16. Close the pinned Styles menu by double-clicking on its **Control** button. Then close the Font menu the same way.

Removing Text Highlighting

17. Click: Left mouse button anywhere on the typing area below the third line of the document. The program removes the highlighting and positions the text cursor at the end of the document (the beginning of the third line).

Creating a Blank Line

18. Position the text cursor at the end of the first line.
    Press: **Enter**. The program inserts a blank line between the first and second lines of text, and the cursor moves to the new blank line. The text after the new blank line moves down one line.
    Press: **Enter** again. The program inserts a second blank line, and the cursor moves to the new blank line.

Changing Font, Size, and Style for New Text

19. Open: Fonts menu and select the URW Sans font. The program closes the Fonts menu.

20. Open Size menu and verify that the size is set to 18 point. Close the Size menu by clicking anywhere off the Size menu.

21. Open: Styles menu and select Plain Text to toggle off all text style options. The program closes the Styles menu.
    You are ready to type using 18-point URW Sans font plain (no bold, underline, etc.).

Typing Text

22. Type: `Declaration of Independence`
    Press: **Enter**.
    Press: **Enter**.
    Type: `The Continental Congress in Philadelphia, on July 4, 1776 adopted the Declaration of Independence. John Hancock was president of the Congress at that time.`
    Press: **Enter**.
    Press: **Enter**.

Type: `IN CONGRESS, July 4, 1776.`
Press: **Enter**.
Press: **Enter**.
Type: `A DECLARATION`
Press: **Enter**.
Press: **Enter**.
Type: `By the REPRESENTATIVES of the UNITED STATES OF AMERICA,`
Press: **Enter**.
Press: **Enter**.
Type: `In GENERAL CONGRESS assembled`
Press: **Enter**.
Press: **Enter**.
Type: `When in the Course of human Events, it becomes necessary for one People to dissolve the Political Bands which have connected them with another, and to assume among the Powers of the Earth, the separate and equal Station to which the Laws of Nature and of Nature's God entitle them, a decent Respect to the Opinions of Mankind requires that they should declare the causes which impel them to the Separation.`

Your screen should resemble Figure 9.5.

Making a Header

23. Scroll to the top of the document until the screen displays the header box. Position the text cursor in the upper-left corner of the header box.

24. Type: `The MARK of the Scribe...`
    Press: **Enter**.
    Type: `MOTS`

25. Highlight the letters MOTS and change the size to 72 point. Your screen should resemble Figure 9.6.

    Note that the 72-point characters do not fit in the header box.

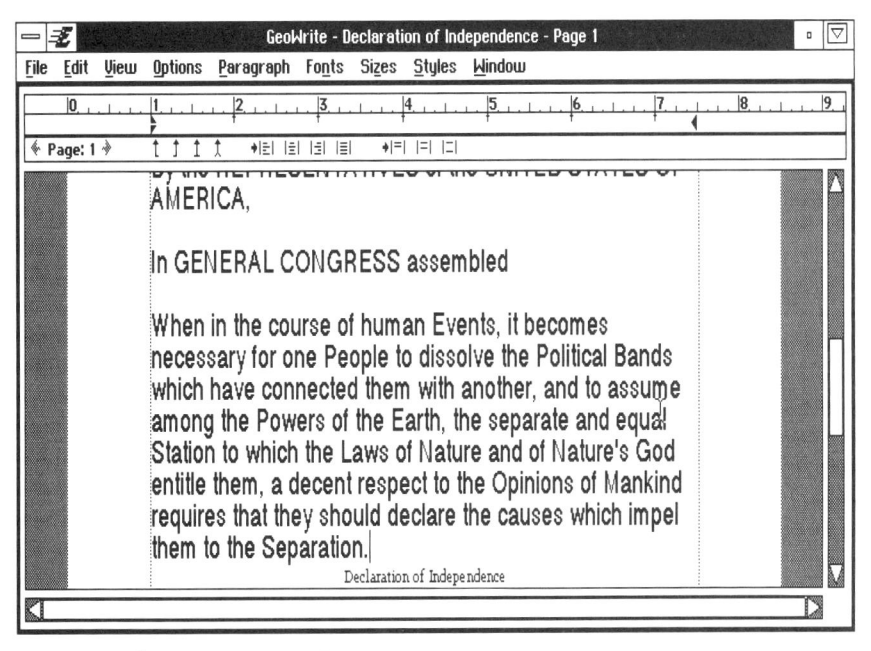

Figure 9.5. The Document Screen.

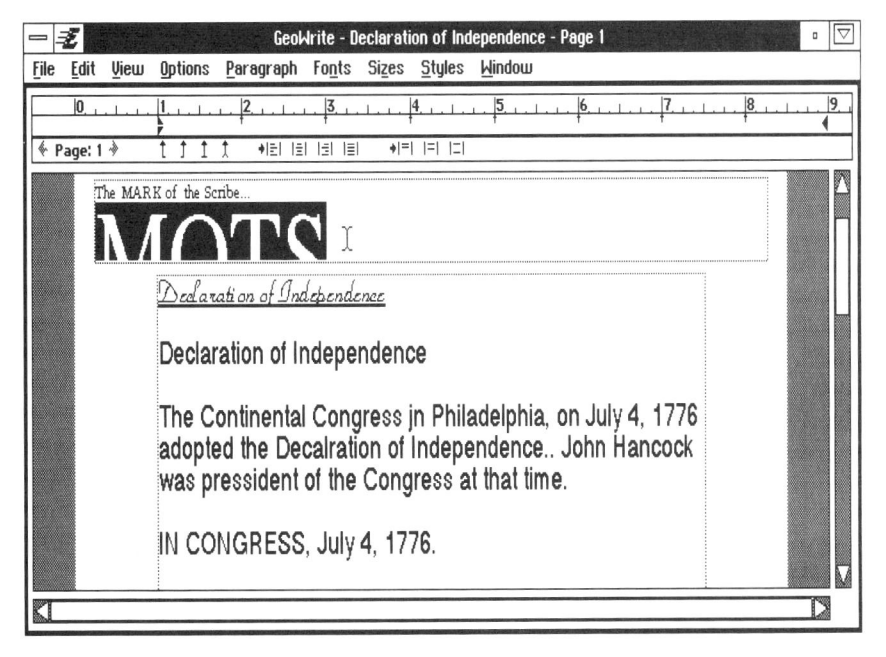

Figure 9.6. Creating a Header.

Changing Header Size

26. Select: **Page Setup** on the File menu.
    Change the Top Margin setting to 1.5 inches. Select the **OK** button to close the dialog box. Your screen should resemble Figure 9.7.

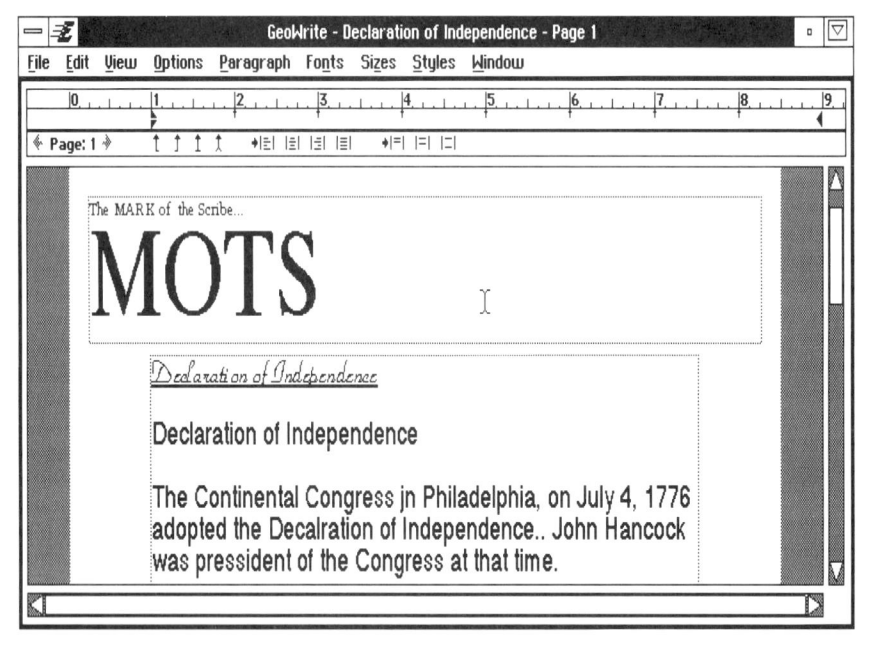

Figure 9.7. Re-sized Header.

Inserting a Graphic Image in the Document

To insert a graphic image in a GeoWrite document requires these basic steps:

- Open the graphics application (in this case, GeoDraw)
- Display the graphic image
- Copy the graphic image to the clipboard
- Resize the graphic
- Switch to the GeoWrite document

- Paste the graphic image into the GeoWrite document. In this tutorial you will place the graphic image into the header so that it will appear on all pages of your document.

Open a Graphic Image File in the Intermediate Workspace

27. Open: Express menu and select **Welcome** from the Startup menu. The program opens the Welcome screen, which is now the active window.
    Click: **Intermediate** button. The File Cabinet window appears.

28. Double-click: **CLIPART directory** icon in the File Cabinet window to open that directory. The contents of the CLIPART directory are displayed.

29. Double-click: **Clipart file** icon. The Read-Only message is displayed.
    Click on **OK** to proceed and open the file.

30. Click: **Go to Page** button to display the Go to Page dialog box.
    Click: **4. Pen & Ink** to select it.
    Click: **View Page** button. The drawing is displayed.

31. Click: **Close** button to remove the dialog box. Your screen should resemble that shown in Figure 9.8.

Open a GeoDraw Window and Copy the Graphic to the Clipboard

32. Select: **Copy** from the Edit menu. The program places a copy of the Pen & Ink drawing on the Clipboard.

33. Open: Express menu and click on **Welcome**.
    Click: **Advanced** button. You return to the GeoWrite screen (shown in Figure 9.7).

34. Open Express menu again.
    Select: **GeoDraw** from the Startup cascading menu. The GeoDraw window appears.

35. Select: **New** from the File menu.
    Click: Mouse cursor in a blank part of the screen.
    Select: **Paste** from the Edit menu. The Pen & Ink drawing is placed in the GeoDraw window. The program has placed handles around the drawing, as shown in Figure 9.9.

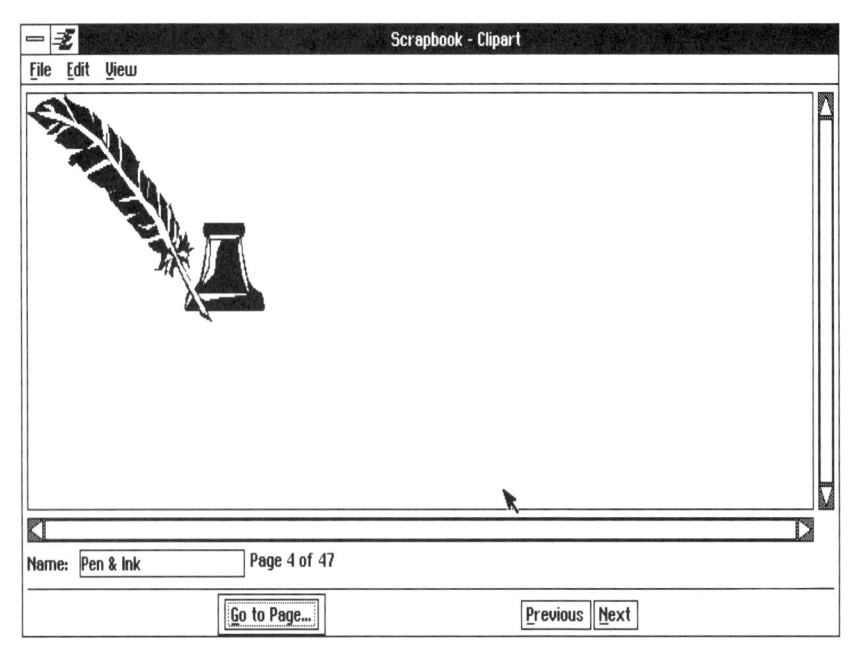

Figure 9.8. The Pen & Ink Drawing.

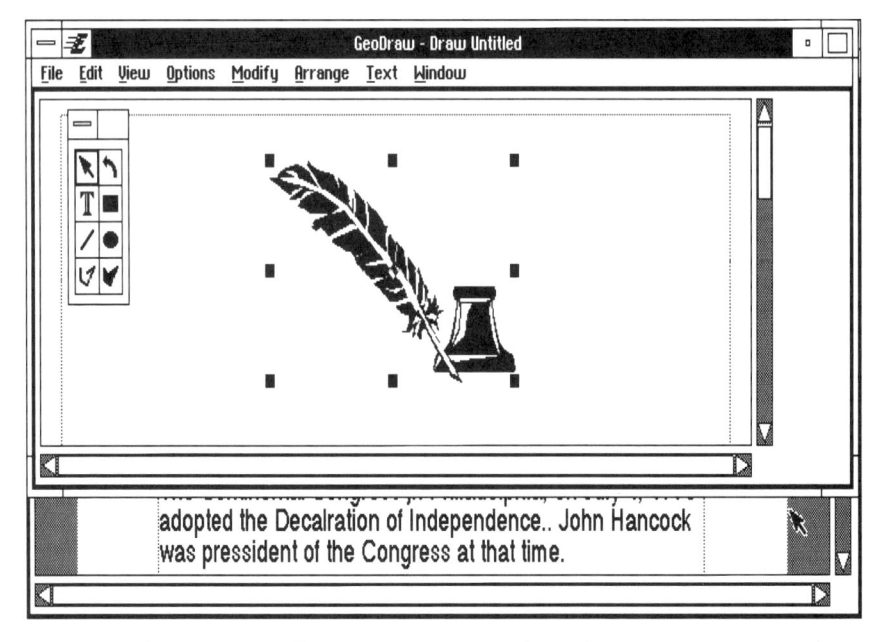

Figure 9.9. The Pen & Ink Drawing Copied to the GeoDraw Window.

Resize the Graphic

36. Press and hold the left mouse button on one of the image handles. Drag the image to make it smaller. Repeat with other handles as necessary to make the image approximately one-inch square. Use the handle in the center of the image if you want to relocate the image in the window. Your screen should resemble the one shown in Figure 9.10.

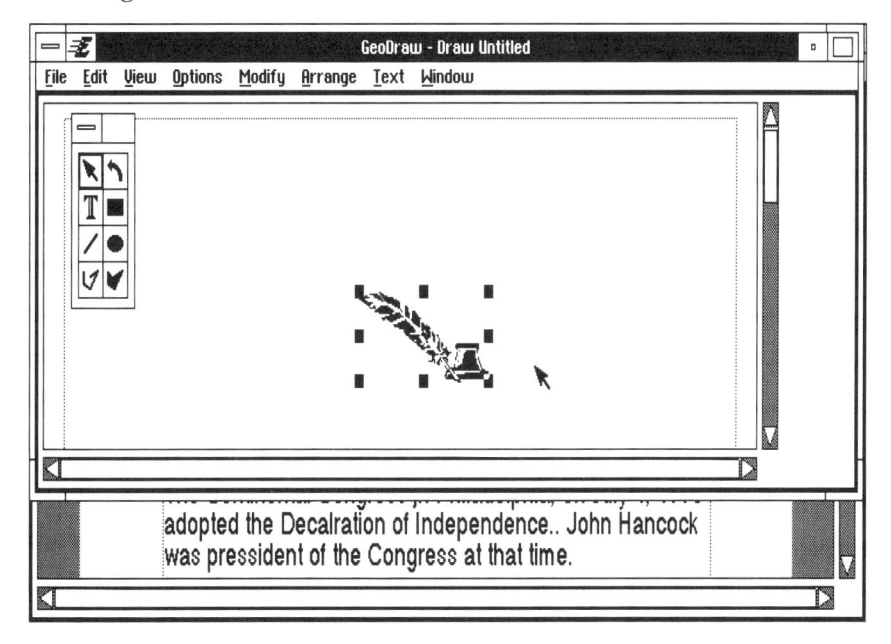

Figure 9.10. The Resized Pen & Ink Drawing.

Copy the Graphic to the Clipboard Again

37. Select: **Copy** from the Edit menu. The program copies the small drawing onto the Clipboard.

Exiting GeoDraw

38. Select: **Exit** from the File menu to close GeoDraw. Click the **Yes** button. Save the changes as the Miscellany file. The GeoDraw window closes and you return to the GeoWrite document. The drawing remains on the Clipboard.

Pasting the Graphic into GeoWrite.

39. Position the text cursor after the word MOTS.
    Press: **Spacebar** seven times.
    Select: **Paste** from the Edit menu. The program copies the Pen & Ink drawing into the header box at the cursor location. Your screen should resemble Figure 9.11.

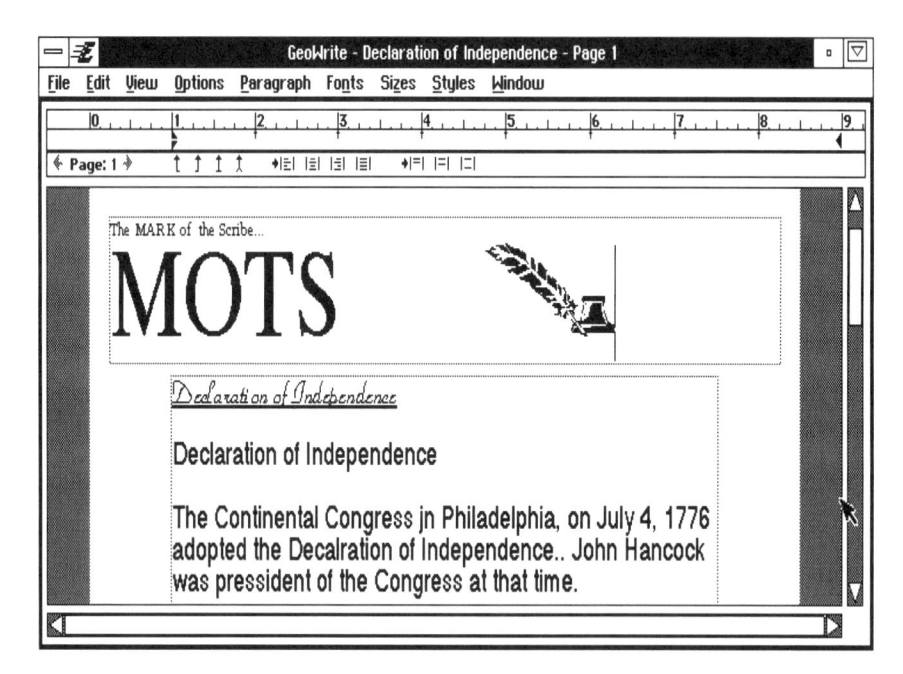

Figure 9.11. A Graphic Image in a Header Box.

This header with the Pen & Ink drawing will appear on all pages of your document.

Saving the Document

40. Save the document by selecting **Save** on the File menu.

Exercise 2

In this exercise you will:

- Create a page break in the document
- Create a table
- Set tabs and margins for the table
- Draw vertical lines in the table
- Enter text in the table
- Format the text
- Format the table
- Copy the table
- Re-space the table
- Save the document.

Creating a Page Break

1. Position the text cursor at the bottom of the document.
    Select: **Insert Page Break** from the Edit menu. The program inserts a page break and positions the cursor at the top of page 2. Notice that the header box remains and that the page number at the upper left has changed to 2.

You can also press **Enter** until the page number has changed to 2, indicating a new page.

NOTE

Creating a Table

A table is a collection of data presented in rows and columns. In this exercise you will create a two-column table with vertical lines between the columns and place the table in a double-line border box.

You use the tabs to create a table. In the exercise you will align numbers using the decimal tab option.

2. Press: **Enter** four times to create four blank lines.

Setting the Table Margins

3. Drag the left margin symbol. To do this, press and hold **Shift** while dragging the symbol with the left mouse button to the 2-1/2 inches position on the ruler line. The left margin is set at 2-1/2 inches.

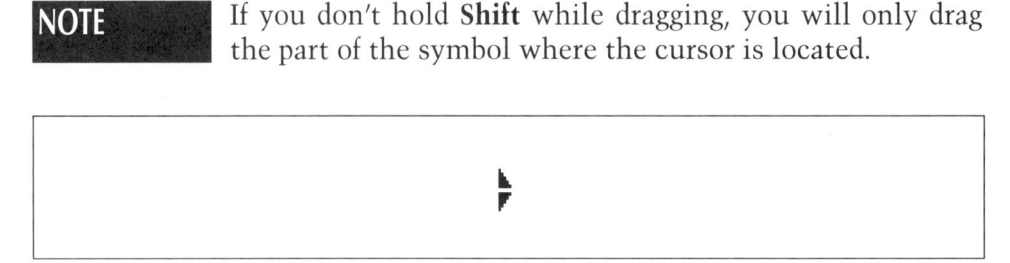

NOTE If you don't hold **Shift** while dragging, you will only drag the part of the symbol where the cursor is located.

Figure 9.12. The Left Margin Symbol.

4. Drag the right margin symbol. Press and hold **Shift** while dragging the symbol with the left mouse button to the 4-1/2 inches position on the ruler line. The right margin is set at 4-1/2 inches.

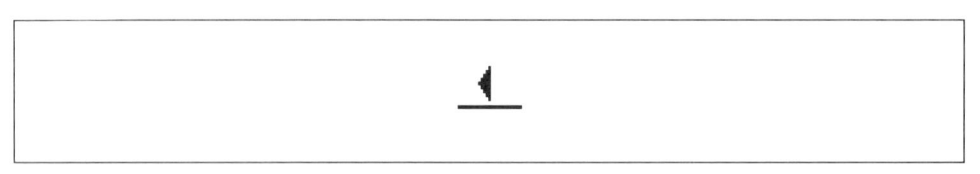

Figure 9.13. The Right Margin Symbol.

Drawing Vertical Lines with a Left Tab Marker

5. Drag a **Left Tab** symbol to 3-1/2 inches on the ruler line. The program sets a left tab at 3-1/2 inches and displays a horizontal arrow beside the new tab, indicating it is the currently selected tab.

6. Double-click on the selected tab or select **Tab Attributes** from the Paragraph menu. Pin the menu and move it to the right side of the screen.

Figure 9.14. The Left Tab Marker.

7. Select: Tab Lines **On**.
   The program displays a vertical line next to the selected tab on the ruler line to indicate that it will draw tab lines, and draws a vertical line at the tab position in the typing panel. The left vertical line above the Tab Attribute dialog box is the typing cursor; the right vertical line is the Tab vertical line.

8. Set the Tab Line Width option to 2 points by clicking the up arrow. The allowable range is 1 to 3 points.

9. Set the Tab Line Spacing to 2 points by clicking the up arrow. The allowable range is 1 to 3 points.

10. The Tab Attributes dialog box should resemble Figure 9.15. Click on **Apply** to make the changes.

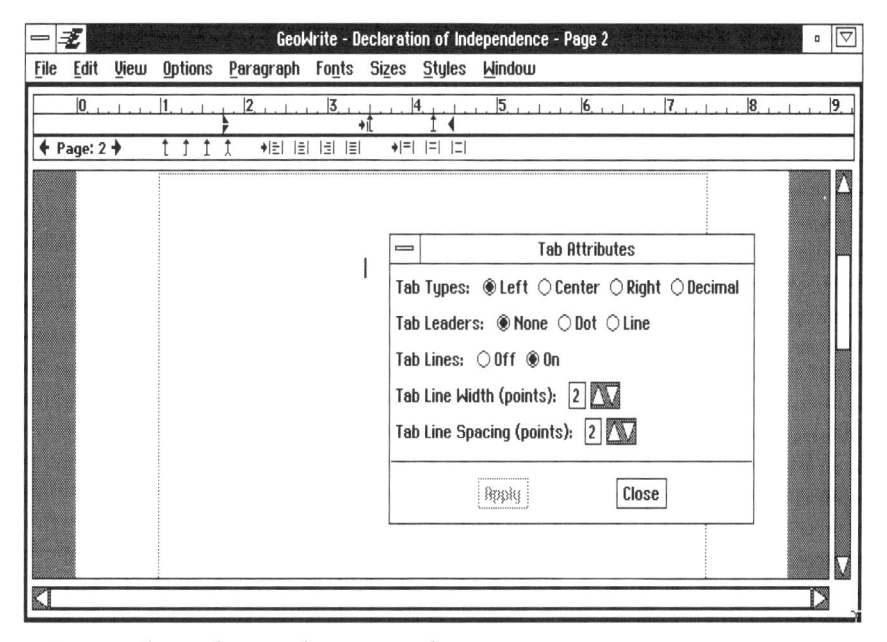

Figure 9.15. The Tab Attributes Dialog Box.

11. Click the **Close** button. The program closes the Tab Attributes dialog box, and you return to the document.

Setting Decimal Tabs

12. Drag the decimal tab symbol to the 3 inches position on the ruler line. Copy the new decimal tab (press **Ctrl** while dragging the new decimal tab symbol) to the 4 inches position on the ruler line. The program displays decimal tab symbols at 3 inches and 4 inches on the ruler line. Your screen should resemble that shown in Figure 9.17.

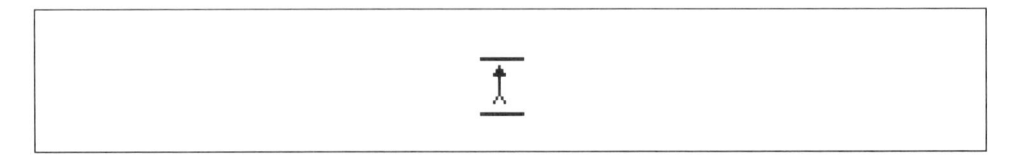

Figure 9.16. The Decimal Tab Symbol.

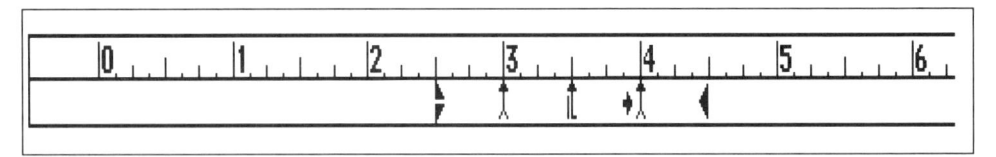

Figure 9.17. The Ruler Line with Tabs Set.

Entering the Table Text

13. Follow these steps to enter the table text:
    Press: **Tab** to position the text cursor on the decimal tab at 3 inches.
    Type: `456.987`
    The decimal point aligns on the decimal tab at 3 inches.
    Press: **Tab** to portion the text cursor.
    The text cursor moves to a position immediately after the vertical line at position 3-1/2 inches.
    Press: **Tab** to position the text cursor on the decimal tab at 4 inches.
    Type: `444.88`

The decimal point aligns on the decimal tab at 4 inches.
Press: **Enter** to start a new line.
The vertical line at 3-1/2 inches extends one line.
Press: **Tab** to position the text cursor on the decimal tab at 3 inches.
Type: `3.765`
The decimal point aligns on the decimal tab at 3 inches.
Press: **Tab** to position the cursor.
The text cursor moves to a position immediately after the vertical line at position 3-1/2 inches.
Press: **Tab** to position the text cursor on the decimal tab at 4 inches.
Type: `876.087`
The decimal point aligns on the decimal tab at 4 inches.
Press: **Enter** to start a new line.
The vertical line at 3-1/2 inches extends one line.
Press: **Tab** to position the text cursor on the decimal tab at 3-1/2 inches.
Type: `876.909`
The decimal point aligns on the decimal tab at 3 inches.
Press: **Tab** to position the text cursor.
The text cursor moves to a position immediately after the vertical line at position 3-1/2 inches.
Press: **Tab** to position the text cursor on the decimal tab at 4 inches.
Type: `76.987`
The decimal point aligns on the decimal tab at 4 inches.

Underlining Table Entries

14. Highlight: Both table entries in the last line (position the cursor at the beginning of the line, then press **Shift** while clicking the left mouse button to extend the highlight to the end of the line).
    Select **Underline** from the Styles menu. The program underlines both numbers.

15. Click the mouse at the end of the highlighted line to remove the highlighting and position the text cursor at the end of the line.

16. Select: **Plain Text** from the Styles menu.

Continuing Table Text Entry

17. Continue entering table text.
    Press: **Enter** to start a new line.
    Press: **Tab** to position the cursor on the decimal tab at 3 inches.
    Type: `1336.661`
    The decimal point aligns on the decimal tab at 3 inches.
    Press: **Tab** to position the text cursor.
    The text cursor moves to a position immediately after the vertical line at position 3-1/2 inches.
    Press: **Tab** to position the text cursor on the decimal tab at 4 inches.
    Type: `1397.954`
    The decimal point aligns on the decimal tab at 4 inches.
    Press: **Enter** to start a new line.

Removing Tab Maker

18. Remove the vertical line table (the left tab located at 3-1/2 inches) from the ruler line by moving the symbol to a bank area outside the ruler. This removes the last part of the vertical line.

Drawing a Border Around a Table

19. Select the entire table, but *do not include the last blank line*.

NOTE If you include the line where the text cursor is located in the highlighted portion, you will be trapped in the table. You will not be able to move the cursor outside the border to continue typing.

20. Select: **Border** from the Paragraph menu to display the Border cascading menu.
    Select: **Two Line border** option.
    Click: Left mouse button to remove the highlight. The program draws a two-line border around the table, as shown in Figure 9.18.

NOTE You can add lines to or delete lines from the table within the border by pressing **Enter**, **Del**, or **Backspace**, as appropriate.

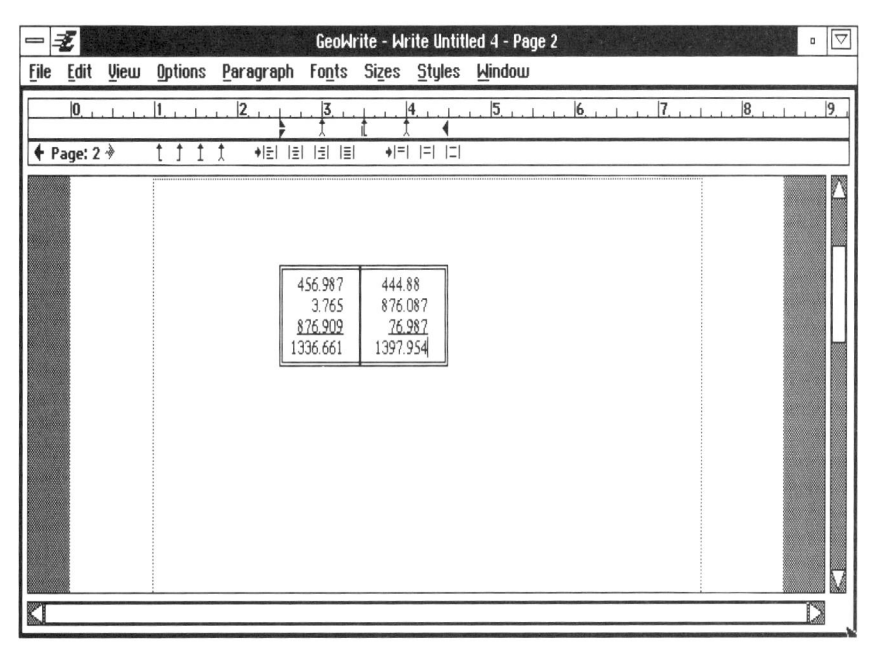

Figure 9.18. A Table with a Two-Line Border.

21. Highlight: Entire table.

22. Position the mouse cursor anywhere in the highlighted area, then press and hold the right mouse button. The cursor changes to the Quick Copy cursor, as shown in the highlighted area of Figure 9.19.

23. Drag the Quick Copy pointer to the location where you want to place the table copy. Release the mouse button. The program displays the table and the copy of the table. Your screen should be similar to Figure 9.20.

You can also use Copy on the Edit menu to copy the table to another document (or to a different location in the same document). Highlight the text, then select **Copy** from the Edit menu. The program copies the table to the Clipboard. Position the typing cursor in the new document (or in a new location in the same document). Select **Paste** from the Edit menu. The program places a copy of the table at the cursor location.

NOTE

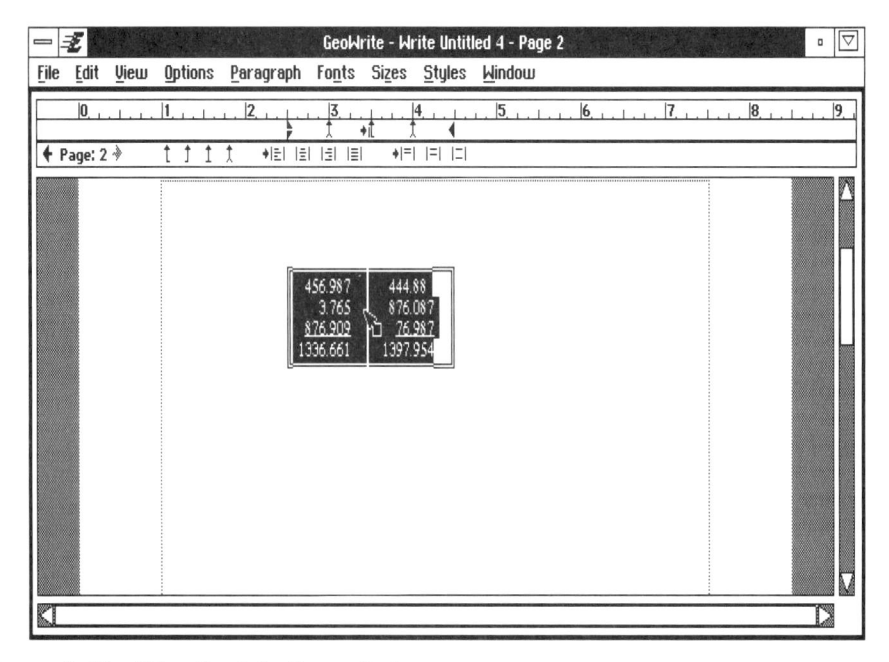

Figure 9.19. The Quick Copy Pointer.

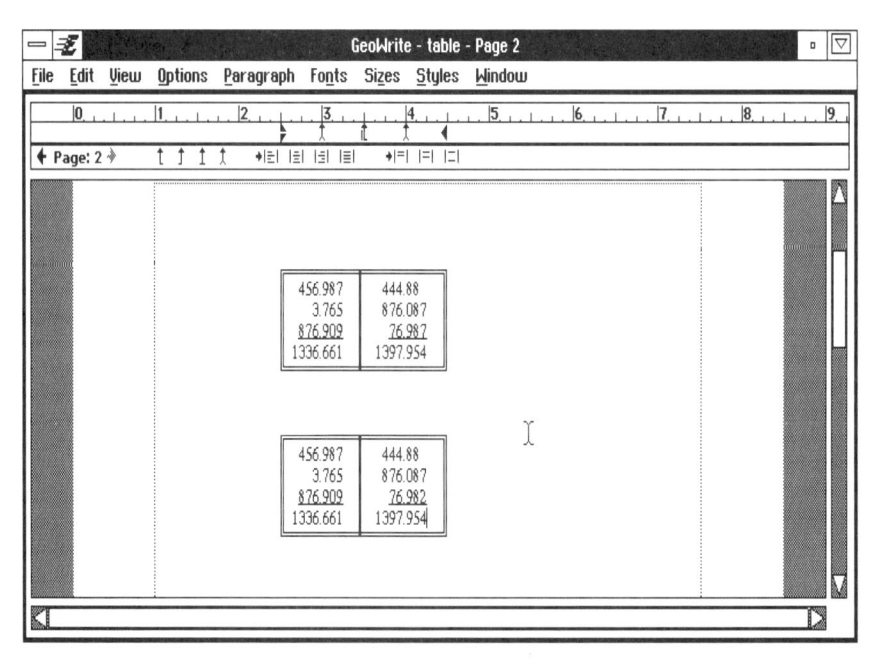

Figure 9.20. A Copied Table.

Re-spacing a Table

24. Highlight the entire lower table. Select the double-spacing icon (the last icon on the right of the line just above the main window). The program changes the table line spacing.

Saving the Document

25. Save the modified document by selecting **Save** on the File menu.

Exercise 3

In this exercise you will practice changing the margins of an existing paragraph to create:

- First-line indent paragraph
- Indented margin paragraph
- First-line outdent paragraph (hanging paragraph).

You can adjust the left and right margins of any paragraph in the text without affecting any other paragraph. The left margin marker looks like a split arrowhead. The top portion controls the indent of the first line only; the bottom portion controls the left margin of the paragraph. Depending on the relative positions of the indent and margin markers, you can create a paragraph with no indents, a first line indent, or a first line outdent (hanging paragraph), as shown in Figure 9.21.

1. Scroll to the top of page 1.
2. Position the text cursor anywhere in the paragraph that begins: "The Continental Congress in Philadelphia..."
   The current paragraph has no first-line indent or outdent.

Creating a First-line Indented Paragraph

3. Drag the **indent marker** (the top portion of the split arrowhead) to the right of the margin indent marker on the ruler line. The first line of the text moves right to the indent marker position. Your text should resemble that in the top paragraph in Figure 9.21.

Creating an Indented Margin Paragraph

4. With the cursor still placed in the same paragraph, drag the **left margin marker** (the bottom of the split arrowhead) to the right so it aligns with the first-line indent marker. The paragraph text displays with a new indented left margin but without a first-line indent. Your text should now look like that in the middle paragraph in Figure 9.21.

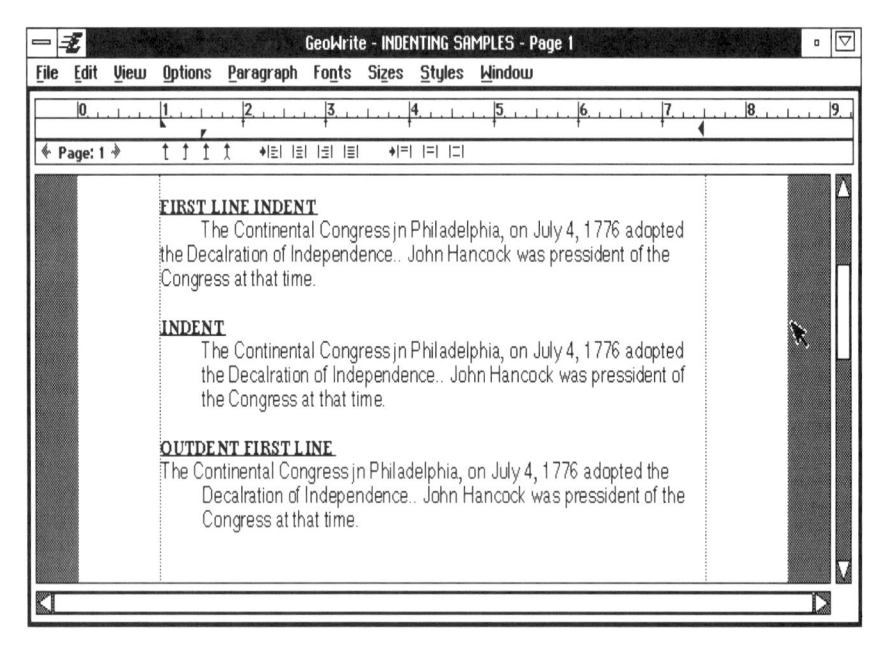

Figure 9.21. Paragraph Indent and Left Margin Options.

Creating a First-line Outdent Paragraph

5. Now, drag the **indent marker** to the left of the margin marker along the ruler line. The first line of text moves to the left, to the new indent marker position. Your text should now resemble the third paragraph in Figure 9.2.1.

Saving the Document

6. Save the modified document by selecting **Save** on the File menu.

Using Documents Created in Quattro Pro SE or Lotus 1-2-3

You can not only look at spreadsheets and graphs that you have created in Quattro Pro SE or Lotus 1-2-3, but you can incorporate them into GeoWorks Pro documents and even export them to other documents.

Any document you can view in the Quattro Pro viewer can be imported into either GeoWrite, GeoDraw or the Scrapbook. The spreadsheet viewer is explained in Chapter 19.

Importing a Document from the Spreadsheet Viewer

The following procedure allows you to bring spreadsheets or graphics from the viewer into GeoWorks applications:

1. Open: **Quattro Pro Viewer**. The Choose Document to View dialog box is displayed.

2. Double-click: Quattro directory to open it.

3. Select: Type of Document format from the list: Quattro Pro spreadsheet (.WQ1 file), Quattro Pro chart (.EPS file), or Lotus spreadsheet (.WK1 file). A list of the appropriate files is displayed.

4. Double-click: Name of the file you want to view. The file appears in the viewer.

5. If the document is a spreadsheet, you must select (highlight) the specific items you want to import (or choose **Select All** from the Edit menu to select and import all the items in the spreadsheet). If the document is a graph (.EPS file), you don't have to select it; just go on to step 6.

6. Choose: **Copy** from the Edit menu.

7. Open: Application into which you want to import the selected spreadsheet or graph by selecting **Startup** from the Express menu and choosing the application you want.

8. Position the cursor where you want to place the imported document.
   Select: **Paste** from the Edit menu. The item is copied.

Sending a Text Document by Modem via GeoComm or America Online

Once the document is copied to one of the GeoWorks Pro applications, you can send it by modem (if your computer has one installed) once the document is converted to a text file. Text files have most of the formatting symbols removed—they are ASCII files.

Note that you cannot send a graphics file by modem.

1. Choose: **Save as Text File** from the File menu to convert the document to a text file.

2. Open: GeoComm or America Online.
   Select: **Open** from the File menu.
   Open the file you want to send. Follow the procedure for sending a document by modem. These procedures are described in Chapters 16 and 17.

Sending a Document as a Fax

If your computer has a fax board installed, you can send both text and graphics files. A text file can be sent directly, but a graphics (.EPS) file must first be converted to a TIFF file.

1. Import the document as described above.

2. If the file is a text file, follow the procedure for sending a fax as explained in your fax board's manual.

3. If the document is a graphics file, convert it to a TIFF file. Many fax boards can transmit TIFF files, but not EPS files. To transmit an EPS file, you must first capture it using the Screen Dumper. This creates a TIFF file of the displayed EPS file. See the Screen Dumper section of Chapter 6.
   Then send the TIFF file using the procedure described in your fax board's manual.

NOTE If you have a fax machine, you will have to print the file before you send it. If you want to print a graphics file, you may need a PostScript printer to print it.

Summary

In this tutorial chapter you practiced creating a document with a header, inserting a GeoDraw graphic image in the GeoWrite document, creating and formatting a table, entering table text, drawing a border around the table, copying and re-spacing the table, and changing the first-line indent and paragraph margin markers. A brief discussion of importing documents from the Quattro Pro Viewer into GeoWorks Pro applications was included, as well as an outline of the procedure for sending documents by modem or fax.

Chapter 10

The GeoDraw Application

In this chapter you will learn how to use the GeoDraw application, a drawing program that allows you to create graphic images, import graphic images from other graphic programs, and display graphics with text. This chapter discusses most of the options (some were discussed in earlier chapters) in the eight pull-down menus on the Menu bar:

- File menu
- Edit menu
- View menu
- Options menu
- Modify menu
- Arrange menu
- Text menu
- Window menu.

You will be referred to earlier chapters in the book for discussions about some menu options. You might want to review the Chapter 4 section called, Accessing the GeoDraw Window that discusses the elements of the GeoDraw window.

Accessing the GeoDraw Application

Start GeoWorks Pro in the usual way. Select the **Advanced Workspace** icon from the GeoWorks Pro Welcome screen. If the GeoManager Information Line does not read **\GEOMANAGER\WORLD**, click the **World** button at the bottom of the GeoManager window. Double-click on the **GeoDraw** icon. The program displays the GeoDraw main screen, as shown in Figure 4.1 (Chapter 4).

File Menu

The GeoDraw File menu is similar to the GeoWrite File menu discussed in Chapter 8 with a few exceptions:

- GeoDraw has an Import option instead of the GeoWrite Insert as Text option
- GeoDraw does not have a Spell Check or a Save as Text File option
- The GeoDraw Page Setup option is different from GeoWrite's.

Import

Use this File menu option to import an image saved in other formats. GeoDraw treats an imported image as an object you can work with as you would any other object.

- **TIFF format files** which have a .TIF extension (one of the most universally acceptable bit-mapped file formats).
- **PC Paintbrush files** which have a .PCX extension.
- **EPS format files** (Encapsulated PostScript files), which is a format used to save graphs and slides. This format is used in Quattro Pro.

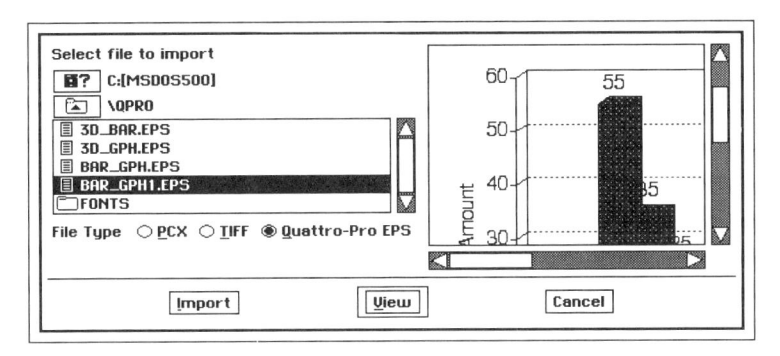

Figure 10.1. The Select File to Import Dialog Box.

Follow these steps to import a file:

1. Select: **Import** from the File menu. The program displays the Select File to Import dialog box, as shown in Figure 10.1.

2. Specify the File Type you want to import. In Figure 10.1, a Quattro Pro EPS file is specified.

3. If the image you want to import is not in the current subdirectory, double-click on the name of the subdirectory that contains the image file. (See Chapter 4, Creating and Saving Documents (Files) for a discussion about moving around subdirectories and selecting files.)

4. Select: File you want to import from the list in the left panel of the dialog box. In Figure 10.1, the BAR_GPH1.EPS file in the QPRO directory on drive C: is the selected file.

5. Click: **View** button to preview the selected image before importing it. Use the scroll bars to scroll the image in the right panel of the dialog box. Notice that only a small part of the file can be seen at one time in the view box on the right.

6. Click: **Import** button when you are satisfied that the correct file is selected. The program closes the dialog box and copies the image into the document window. (Large images may take several minutes to import.)

7. Repeat the process for each image you want to import.
   Click: **Cancel** button to close the Select File to Import dialog box without importing a file.

Edit Menu

You use the Edit menu in all GeoWorks Pro applications to copy graphics or text from one document to another, or from one section of a document to another section of the same document. In GeoDraw, the Edit menu also includes options selecting all the objects in the window, for deleting selected objects, and for manipulating graphic images—combining two or more images into a single object (fusing) and separating combined objects (defusing).

Figure 10.2 shows an Edit menu pinned in the lower left of the window with multiple objects selected.

See the Edit Menu section in Chapter 8 for a discussion about the Pin, Cut, Copy, Paste, and Delete options Edit menu. If you choose the Select All option, all the objects in the window are selected.

You can manipulate GeoDraw images in a variety of ways: rotate, flip, stretch, shrink, etc. When you select a graphic image by clicking on any portion of it, the program displays handles around the entire object—small squares around the margins and a diamond in the middle.

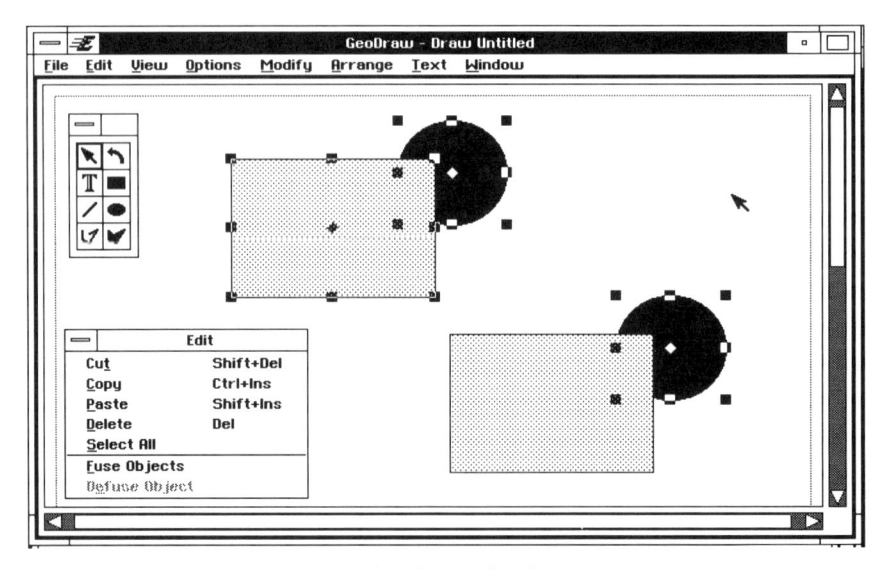

Figure 10.2. The Edit Menu and Selected Objects.

To select an object, be certain that either the Arrow Tool or the Rotation Tool is selected from the Tool Box. It is easy to forget to change pointers and find you are drawing in the window instead of selecting an object.

NOTE

Use the object handles to move the image (center handle) or manipulate its shape (margin handles) by pressing the mouse pointer on a handle and dragging. You must select an object before you can apply a menu function to the image.

Fuse Objects

Combining two or more separate objects into a group object is called fusing objects. Select the objects (see below) then select **Fuse Objects** from the Edit menu. Fused objects lose their individual status and cannot be selected separately. When you position the mouse cursor over any portion of the group object and then click, the entire group is selected as a single object.

The way to determine whether objects are fused is to select them. Figure 10.3 shows two fused objects in the upper portion and two unfused objects in the lower portion. Notice the difference in the way the handles appear. The handles on the upper object are treating the object as a single item. Separate handles for each object in the lower portion of Figure 10.3 are displayed, indicating there are two objects in the figure.

Selecting Objects by Dragging

You can select an object—or multiple objects—by using a *selection box*. As you look at the GeoDraw window, imagine a rectangle large enough to cover the objects you want to select. Position the arrow pointer or rotation pointer at a corner of the imaginary rectangle.

Click and hold the mouse button while dragging diagonally to the opposite corner of the imaginary rectangle. As you drag, a dotted selection box circumscribes the dimensions you set with the starting and ending drag points. When the dotted selection box surrounds all the objects you want to select, release the button. The program displays object handles for each of the selected objects. If you miss an object, you can repeat the process, or use the Ctrl method described next to add the item.

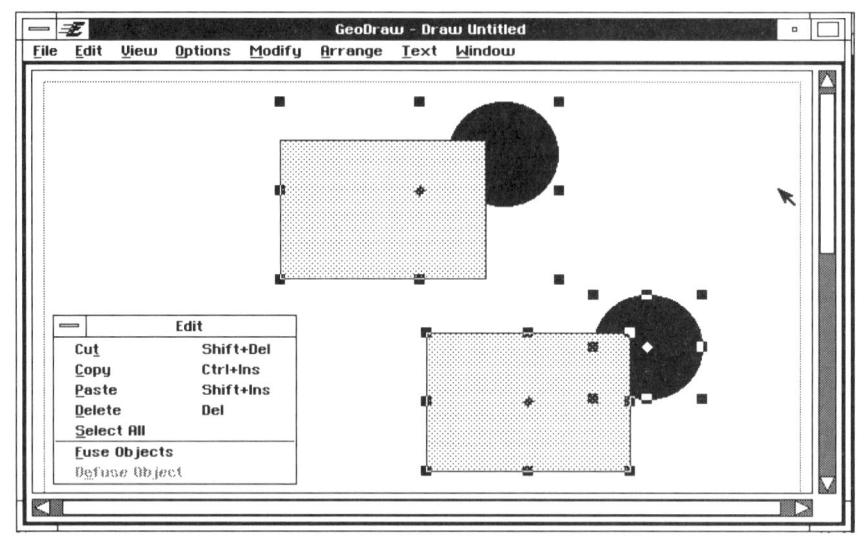

Figure 10.3. Selecting Fused and Unfused Objects.

Selecting Objects Using Ctrl

When you click on an object with the arrow pointer or rotation pointer, the object is selected. If you then position the arrow over another object and click, the second object becomes selected and the first object becomes deselected. To select more than one object at once, hold down **Ctrl** while clicking the mouse button. When you release Ctrl, the object is added to the selection group.

Defuse Object

A group object is made up of two or more **fused objects**. Fused objects can be *defused*—separated and returned to their individual status. To defuse a group, select it, then select **Defuse Object** from the Edit menu. The defused objects can again be selected and manipulated individually.

View Menu

The View menu allows you to change the size of the displayed image. Use increased magnification to align objects accurately; use reduced magnification to see more of the document and its layout. You can change the display size from 12.5% of actual size to 400% of actual size.

To select a View menu item, click on the item or press the item number. For example, press 5 to enlarge the display to 400%.

Correct for Aspect Ratio

See the View Menu, Correct for Aspect Ratio section in Chapter 8 for a discussion about this command.

Options Menu

Use the Options menu to select dragging options (by outline or by rectangle), and to display the Tool Box if you've closed it using the Control button in the Tool Box window.

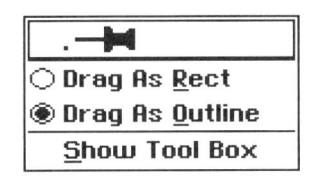

Figure 10.4. The Options Menu.

Drag As Rectangle

When dragging one or more selected objects with Drag As Rect turned on, a dotted rectangle moves with the pointer showing the new location of the objects. Release the mouse button to anchor the objects in the new location. The Drag as Rect command allows you to drag objects more quickly than the Drag As Outline command.

Dragging with the Left Mouse Button

Click and hold the left mouse button on the center handle of one of the selected objects. Release the mouse button to anchor the selected objects in the new location.

Dragging with the Right Mouse Button

Click and hold the right mouse button over any portion of one of the selected objects (it does not have to be over a center handle). Release the mouse button to anchor the selected objects in the new location.

Drag As Outline

When dragging one or more selected objects with Drag As Outline turned on, a dotted outline moves with the pointer showing the new location of the objects. Release the mouse button to anchor the objects in the new location. The Drag As Outline command operates more slowly than the Drag As Rect command.

Show Tool Box

You might want to view your drawing without the Tool Box obscuring part of the image. To close the Tool Box, click on the **Control** button, then select **Close** (or double-click the Control bar). To display the Tool Box again, select **Show Tool Box** from the Options menu.

Modify Menu

You can change the way objects are positioned and displayed in the window using the Modify menu. Figure 10.5 shows a pinned Modify menu with the Nudge cascading menu displayed.

Nudge

Use this option for precise object positioning—moving the object one pixel at a time. (A pixel is the smallest dot that can be displayed on your screen.) The Nudge cascading menu offers four directions in which you can nudge the selected object: up, down, right, and left.

It is a good idea to pin the Nudge cascading menu because positioning an object frequently requires more than one nudge.

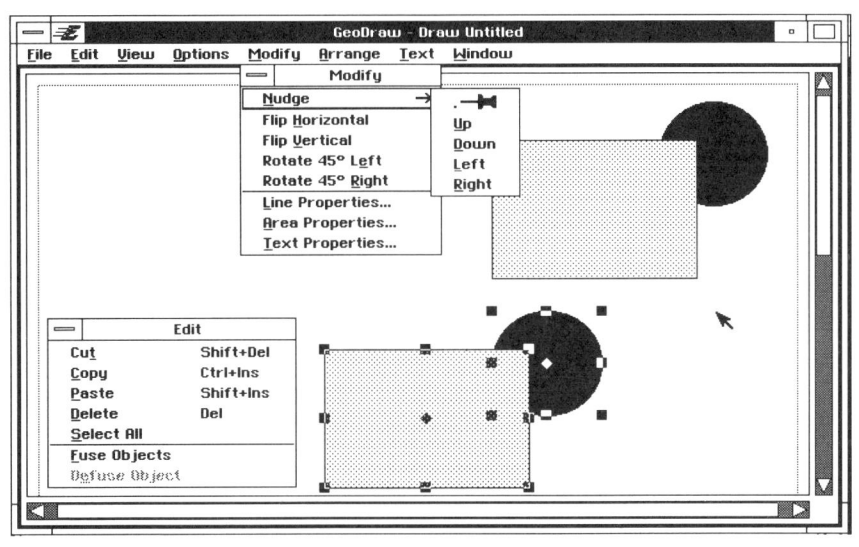

Figure 10.5. A Pinned Modify Menu with the Nudge Menu Displayed.

Flip Horizontal

Use this option to flip a selected object horizontally—spin the object 180° around the vertical axis. To edit text that has been flipped horizontally, you must flip it back to its original position, edit it, then flip it again.

Flip Vertical

Use this option to flip a selected object vertically—spin the object 180° around the horizontal axis.

To edit text that has been flipped vertically, you must flip it back to its original position, edit it, then flip it again.

Rotate 45° Left

Use this option to rotate selected objects 45° counterclockwise. Circles, ovals, and images imported from another application cannot be rotated.

To edit text that has been rotated, you must rotate it back to its original position, edit it, then rotate it again.

Rotate 45° Right

Use this option to rotate selected objects 45° clockwise.

To edit text that has been rotated, you must rotate it back to its original position, edit it, then rotate it again.

Rotate to Any Degree

To rotate an object more or less than 45°, select the rotate pointer from the Tool Box. Select the objects you want to rotate. Position the rotation pointer over a corner handle. Click and hold the mouse button while dragging the corner clockwise or counterclockwise to rotate the objects to the desired position. Release the button to anchor the objects in the new position.

Line Properties

Use this option to change the width, style, pattern, and color of the lines in your drawing. When you select Line Properties, the Line Properties dialog box shown in Figure 10.6 is displayed.

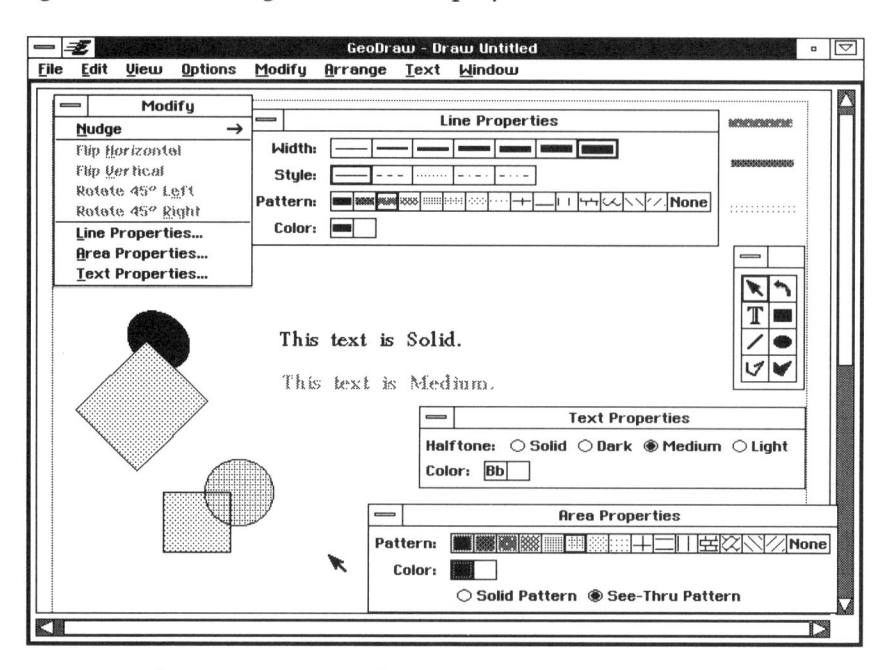

Figure 10.6. The Properties Dialog Boxes.

Line Width

To change a selected object's line width, click on the desired width in the Line Properties dialog box. To the right of the Line Properties dialog box in Figure 10.6 are three lines that have been drawn using the maximum width (and different patterns).

Line Style

To change a selected object's line style, click on the desired style in the Line Properties dialog box.

Line Pattern

To change a selected object's line pattern, click on the desired pattern in the Line Properties dialog box.

Color

To change a selected object's line color, click on the desired color in the Line Properties dialog box. If you do not have a color monitor, only black or white is available.

Double-click on the Control button to close the Line Properties dialog box.

Area Properties

Use this option to change the pattern, color, and see-through characteristics of the interior of selected objects. When you select Area Properties, the Area Properties dialog box, shown in the lower right of Figure 10.6 is displayed.

Pattern

You can choose one of 16 patterns to display in an object. First select the object, then click on the pattern you want in the Area Properties dialog box.

Color

You can choose to display an object's area in black, white, or a color (if you have a color monitor). First select the object, then click on the selection you want in the Area Properties dialog box.

If you do not select an object before you select a pattern or color, the pattern or color will apply to the next object you draw. The object must be a closed object before you can fill it with a pattern. For example, the square, circle, and polygon tools in the Tool Box create objects that can be filled.

Solid/See-Through Pattern

Use this menu option to display a selected object as solid—obscuring any objects behind it, or as transparent—displaying any objects behind it. Notice the two objects in the lower-left of Figure 10.6. One has been made with a see-through pattern, the other was not.

Text Properties

Use this option to change the properties of text in a GeoDraw window. You can change the text color and set a solid, dark, medium, or light halftone for the selected text.

- **Solid** displays all pixels in the text
- **Dark** displays 75% of the pixels
- **Medium** displays 25% of the pixels
- **Light** displays 15% of the pixels.

The center portion of Figure 10.6 shows text displayed with the Halftone set to solid and below that, text with the Halftone set to medium.

Arrange Menu

Use this menu to change the display order of overlapping objects, moving them front to back or back to front. You can display multiple levels of overlapping objects.

Bring To Front

When you select an object at any level in an overlapping display and then select **Bring to Front** on the Arrange menu, the selected object becomes the top object.

To rearrange overlapping objects in a fused group, defuse the group, then rearrange the individual objects.

Send To Back

When you select an object at any level in an overlapping display and then select **Send to Back** on the Arrange menu, the selected object becomes the bottom object.

Move Forward

Use this option to move a selected object one level up from its current position. For example, assume you have three overlapping objects. You select the bottom object, then select **Move Forward** on the Arrange menu. The selected object moves one level higher, becoming the middle object.

Move Backward

Use this option to move a selected object one level down from its current position. For example, assume you have three overlapping objects. You select the top object, then select **Move Backward** on the Arrange menu. The selected object moves one level lower, becoming the middle object.

Text Menu

You can use the Text menu to change the font, size, style, and justification of GeoDraw text. (Use the Edit menu to copy, cut and paste text.) See Chapter 8 for a discussion of the Pin, Fonts, Sizes and Styles commands on the Text menu.

Figure 10.7 illustrates the use of the Fonts, Sizes and Styles commands in drawing.

You can only pick one command from the Fonts and Sizes dialog boxes, but you can select more than one from the Styles dialog box.

Justification

Use this option to set right, left, center, or full justification for selected text. Figure 10.8 illustrates the four justification settings. A pinned Justification menu is shown on the right.

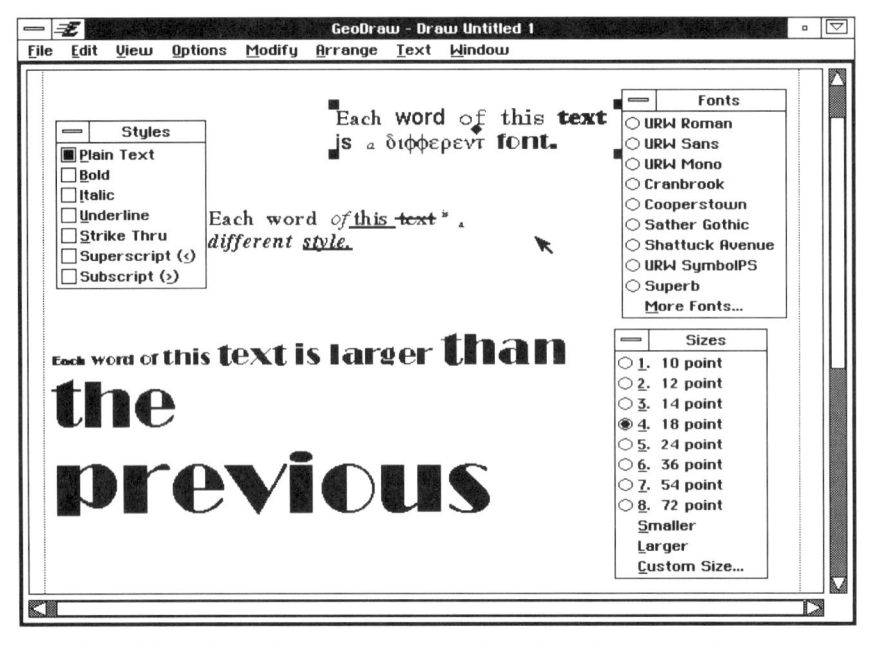

Figure 10.7. Use of the Fonts, Sizes, and Styles Commands.

To change the justification of text, select the text you want affected by the new justification. Then select a justification option from the Justification cascade menu. You can pin the Justification cascade menu for repeated selections.

Left

Use this option to align text along the left margin with a ragged-right margin.

Right

Use this option to align text along the right margin with a ragged left margin.

Center

Use this option to center text lines, regardless of line length, between the left and right margins.

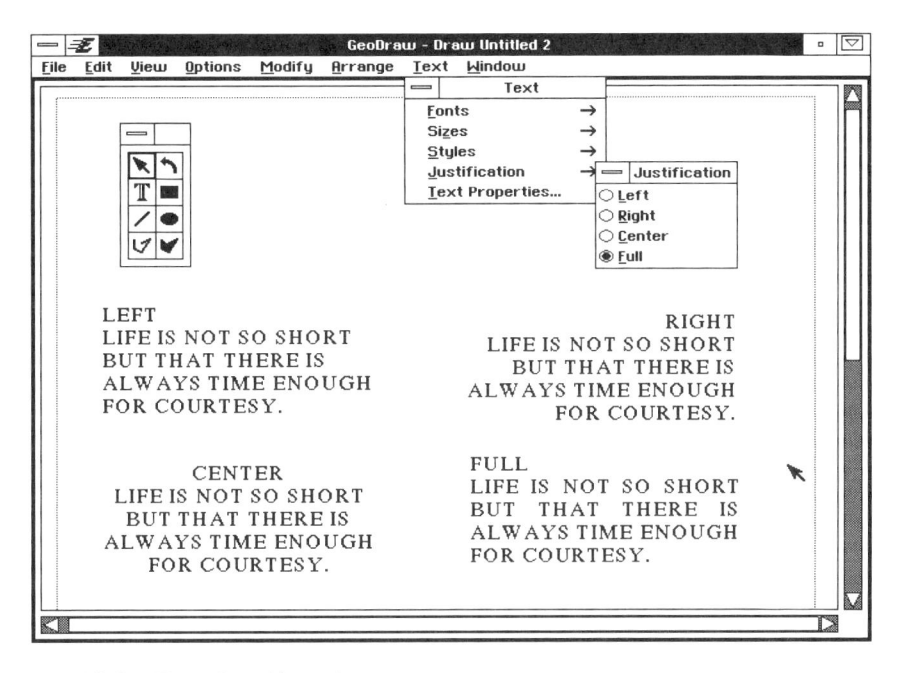

Figure 10.8. Text Justification.

Full

Use this option to add space between words to justify text along both the left and right margins.

> **NOTE:** Before starting to type text make sure the text box is sized the way you want it. The left and right edges of the text box determine the left and right margins of the text you will put in the box.

Text Properties

See the Modify Menu, Text Properties section earlier in this chapter for a discussion about this option.

Window Menu

GeoDraw is one of the GeoWorks Pro applications that allows you to open more than one document at a time. As you open documents using the Open command on the File menu, the default setting is for the new document to fill the entire GeoDraw window, covering previous documents.

The Window menu allows you to switch between full documents and overlapping display of those documents.

Overlapping (Ctrl+F5)

Use this option to display open documents as overlapping windows. When overlapping, all window title bars are visible and selectable so you can activate any window without using the Window menu to do so.

See the Menu Bar section in Chapter 5 for a review of window menu functions.

Full-Sized (Ctrl+F10)

Selecting this option achieves the same result as clicking the Maximize/Restore button to maximize a document display.

Document Listing

At the bottom of the Window menu is a list of currently open documents. When you select an open document from the Window menu, it becomes the active document. In overlapping display, the program places the selected document on top of other open windows. In full-sized display, the selected document fills the document area, covering any other open documents.

Tool Box

To select a Tool Box item, position the cursor over the desired tool icon and click the left mouse button. The program highlights the selected icon. A selected tool remains selected until you specifically choose another icon, allowing you to use the same tool repeatedly.

Any objects you create using the Tool Box can be manipulated and modified using the GeoDraw menu options described earlier.

The appearance of the GeoDraw cursor changes depending on the tool you select.

- **Arrow pointer cursor.** The arrow pointer is the default cursor when you enter GeoDraw. Use it to select objects.
- **Crosshairs cursor.** When you use any of the drawing tools, the cursor changes to crosshairs over the drawing area. The intersection of the crosshairs indicates where the shape will begin when you start to draw.
- **I-beam cursor.** When you select the text tool, the cursor changes to an I-beam cursor over the drawing area. Click the mouse to position the I-beam where you want to begin typing.
- **Rotate pointer cursor.** When you select the rotate tool, the cursor changes to a curved arrow. The rotate pointer is similar to the arrow pointer, except that it can also rotate objects.

Arrow Pointer Tool

When you enter GeoDraw, the arrow pointer is selected automatically. Use this tool to select items you want to manipulate.

Text Tool

Select the text tool to enter text into a GeoDraw document. The text you type becomes an object that can be moved, reshaped, rotated, and flipped just as you can any other object. It can also be edited, cut, copied, and pasted.

Creating a Text Object

Before you begin typing, you can create a text object to define the margins of the text. Position the text cursor where you want to place the first character. Single-click to produce a text object three inches wide (the default width).

To create a wider object for longer text lines, position the I-beam cursor at the desired left margin. Then drag the I-beam cursor to the desired right margin. Release the mouse button.

NOTE If the page is wider than the window, continue dragging when you reach the right edge of the window. The page will scroll, allowing you to set the right text margin to the right of the original window display.

As you enter text in the text object, it will wrap automatically at the right margin (just as text wraps in GeoWrite). Press **Enter** only when you want to start a new paragraph or to insert blank lines. As you type, text displays in the currently selected font, size, style, and justification settings.

Text Tool Editing

You can select a text object for editing in two ways: dragging and clicking.

To use the dragging method, select the text tool from the Tool Box. Position the text cursor to the left of the text you want to edit. Drag the text cursor to highlight the text you want to select.

To use the clicking method, select the text tool from the Tool Box. Position the mouse cursor to the left of the first character you want to select. Click the mouse to anchor the text cursor. Position the mouse cursor at the end of the block of text you want to edit. Press and hold **Shift**, then click the mouse button. Release **Shift**. The program highlights the text between the first and second mouse clicks. To change the selected range of text while it is still highlighted, press **Shift** and click the mouse button where you want to reset the end of the selected text. Release **Shift**. The program adjusts the highlighted text to the new range.

NOTE To edit more than one text object at a time, press and hold **Ctrl** as you click and drag the cursor over the other items you want to select. To remove an item from the highlighted group, press and hold **Ctrl**, then click again on the item you want to remove from the group. Release **Ctrl**. The program removes the item from the group.

See appropriate sections in Chapter 7 for more on typing text, selecting text, and editing with keyboard commands.

Line Tool

Select this option to draw a straight line in any direction. When Line Tool is the active option in the Tool Box, the cursor changes to crosshairs. Position the cursor where you want the line to begin, then press and hold the mouse button while dragging the crosshairs to the point at which you want to end the line. When you release the mouse button, the program displays the line with object handles.

Line Handles

You can use the three line object handles (one at each end of the line and one in the center) to move or modify the line.

To move a line, select the pointer tool, then position the cursor over the center handle. Press and drag the mouse button to move the line to another location. Release the mouse button to anchor the line in the new location.

To change line length, select the pointer tool, then position the cursor over one of the end handles. Click and hold the mouse button while dragging the end point to its new location. Release the mouse button to anchor the line.

To select a line object, double-click the pointer cursor over the line to select it, displaying the handles. Click the pointer cursor over the line again to deselect it, removing the handles.

Connect Line Tool

You can use the connect line tool in much the same way as the line tool. Select the connect line tool, then position the crosshairs cursor where you want the connected lines to begin. Click the left mouse button to anchor the starting point. Move the crosshairs to the point at which the first line segment will end and the second segment will begin. Click to anchor the junction point. Reposition the crosshairs and click to anchor successive junctions. Double-click on the last point or press **Esc** or press the right mouse button to end the line. When you end the line, the program displays line object handles.

Connected Line Handles

You can use the handles to move the connected segments as a unit, or to stretch or shrink the object.

To move a connected line, select the pointer tool, then position the cursor over the center handle. Press and drag the mouse button to move the connected line object to another location. Release the mouse button to anchor the object in the new location.

To stretch or shrink a connected line object, select the pointer tool, then position the cursor over one of the margin handles. Click and hold the mouse button while dragging the handle. Release the mouse button to anchor the object. Dragging either the top or bottom handles stretches (or shrinks) the object vertically. Dragging left or right handles stretches (or shrinks) the object horizontally. Dragging the corner handle stretches (or shrinks) the object both vertically and horizontally.

To select a line object, double-click the pointer cursor over the line to select it, displaying the handles. Click the pointer cursor to deselect a line, removing the handles.

Rotate Pointer

You can use the rotate pointer to move an object (as you can with the arrow pointer). You can also use the rotate pointer to rotate an object clockwise or counterclockwise. When you select the rotate tool, the cursor becomes a curved arrow.

Rectangle Tool

You can draw a rectangle of any size with the rectangle tool. Position the crosshairs where you want one corner of the rectangle. Drag the crosshairs diagonally in any direction. As you drag, the program displays an outline of the rectangle. Release the mouse button to anchor the rectangle and display the object handles.

See the Connected Line Handles section for a discussion about moving and stretching an object.

Circle Tool

You can draw a circle of any size with the circle tool. Position the crosshairs where you want to begin the circle. Drag the crosshairs in any direction to create the circle. As you drag, the program displays an outline of the circle (or oval). The outline may be a circle or a rectangle, depending on which option is active in the Options menu: Drag As Rectangle or Drag As Outline. Release the mouse button to anchor the circle and display the object handles.

See the Connected Line Handles section for a discussion about moving and stretching an object.

Polygon Tool

You can draw a polygon of any size using the polygon tool. Select the polygon tool, then position the crosshairs cursor where you want to begin the first line. Click the left mouse button to anchor the starting point. Move the crosshairs to the point at which the first line segment will end and the second segment will begin. Click to anchor the junction point. Reposition the crosshairs and click to anchor successive junctions. When you double-click on the last point to finish the polygon, the program draws a line between the last point and the first point, closing the polygon. The program displays object handles.

See the Connected Line Handles section for a discussion about moving and stretching an object.

Summary

This chapter showed you how to use the GeoDraw application to create graphic images, import graphic images from other graphic programs, and display and edit text. It covered most of the options in the eight pull-down menus on the GeoDraw menu bar.

Chapter 11

The GeoPlanner Application

The GeoPlanner application combines a calendar and an appointment book in one handy program. While it is similar to the Planner in the Beginner Workspace, you will find that it is more powerful and flexible. With GeoPlanner you can:

- Schedule events for any time of day
- Quickly switch to any date (day, month, or year) to view or schedule events
- Set alarms to notify you of upcoming events
- Schedule repeating events
- Search for a string of text (for example, if you don't remember when an event is scheduled, but you do remember what the event is)
- Copy or move text within GeoPlanner or to other applications
- Link with GeoDex to access the card file.

Using GeoPlanner

As with any GeoWorks Pro application, you can access GeoPlanner in one of the following ways:

- Double-clicking on its icon in the GeoManager window
- Choosing **Startup** from the Express menu and then selecting GeoPlanner from the cascading menu
- Clicking the DOCUMENT directory on the GeoManager screen, then clicking a GeoPlanner document icon.

When you open GeoPlanner, the program displays a window similar to the one in Figure 11.1.

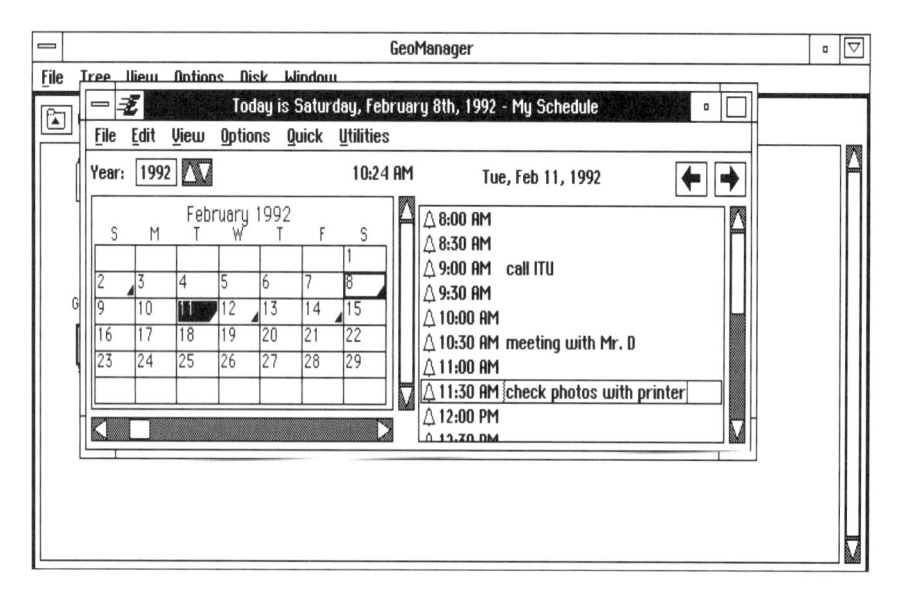

Figure 11.1. The GeoPlanner Window.

The program displays the current day, current date, and the document name in the top line of the window. In Figure 11.1, the day is Saturday, February 8, 1992. The open GeoPlanner document is titled My Schedule.

The standard GeoWorks Pro menu bar is displayed on the second line of the window.

The third line of the GeoPlanner window displays the selected year on the left followed by up and down arrows, the current time in the middle, and the selected day and date on the right (in this case it is Tuesday, February 11, 1992).

Selected Year

The year box displays the currently selected year. Every click on the small up arrow advances one year; every click on the small down arrow moves back one year. In Figure 11.1, the calendar displays February for 1992. If you click on the year box up arrow, the calendar display will change to February for 1993.

Current Time

The program displays the current time as set in your computer. If the displayed time is incorrect, you can reset the computer clock using the Preferences application. (See Chapter 6, Date & Time section.)

Selected Day and Date

The program displays the day of the week and the date of the highlighted calendar day. In Figure 11.1, February 11 is highlighted (shown in black). You can select a different day in two ways:

- Click on a day in the calendar. The highlight moves to the new day and the selected day and date display changes.
- Scroll through dates by clicking on the Previous Day arrow and the Next Day arrow at the far right of the third line.

Calendar

The large panel on the left displays a one-month calendar. When you first start GeoPlanner, the calendar displays the current month for the current year. The current day is highlighted on the calendar.

To select another day on the calendar, click on the day box. The highlight moves to the selected day.

If you select a different day, the current day becomes surrounded by a heavy outline and the newly selected day is highlighted. In Figure 11.1, the current date is February 8, and that day is shown outlined in the calendar. The selected day is February 11; it is highlighted on the calendar.

A small triangle in the lower-right corner of a day box indicates one or more scheduled events for that day.

At the bottom of the calendar is a scroll bar. Use the scroll bar to scroll through the months of the year.

Schedule of Events

The large panel on the right displays a list of times and any scheduled events. The default list of times is from 8:00 AM to 6:00 PM, incremented every half hour. When you enter an event into the list, you can accept a default time setting, or specify your own (for example, 10:50 AM or 8:45 PM). Use the vertical scroll bar on the right to scroll through the events list.

Scheduling an Event

Follow these steps to schedule an event:

1. Click on the day in the calendar panel that you want to schedule. The program displays the schedule list for that day in the right panel.

2. Click on or scroll to the time (or the nearest time) you want to schedule in the list of events.

3. Select **New Event** from the Edit menu. The program displays a blank event in the Event window.
   Type the time you want to schedule for the event (for example, 11:15 A. or 11:15 PM). If you do not want the event to start at any particular time, leave the time area blank.

4. Press: **Tab**. The cursor moves to the event description area. Type the event description—you can enter more than one line.

If you enter an event out of time sequence, GeoPlanner reorders the display the next time you open the schedule. **NOTE**

Viewing Scheduled Events

To view the events schedule for the previous day, click on the Previous Day arrow above the events window. To view the events schedule for the next day, click on the Next Day arrow.

You can view the events for several days at a time. Press and hold the mouse button as you drag the mouse cursor over the days you want to select. The program highlights the selected days and displays the range of dates above the events window. View the events schedules for the range of days by scrolling through the list.

Click on the Next Day arrow or Previous Day arrow above the events window to display additional blocks of days. For example, if you highlight five days in the calendar, clicking the Next Day arrow changes the list of events to the five days following the highlighted days.

The Menu Bar

The Menu Bar, the second line in the window, contains six menus. You can access the menu option by holding down **Alt** while pressing the underlined letter in the menu name, or by clicking on the menu name with the left mouse button.

Access the options on the menus by typing the underlined letter in the option name or by clicking the mouse button.

File Menu

See the File Menu section in Chapter 8 for a discussion about the New, Open, Close, Save, Save As, Revert, and Exit File menu options.

Page Setup

Use this option to specify how you want to print a schedule or calendar. When you select this option, the program displays the Document Options dialog box.

You can scroll the list to choose the size paper or envelope you want. If you choose Custom, the program displays two boxes in which you enter the width (from 2" to 45") and height (from 2" to 45") for your paper. You can then select whether you want the calendar or events schedule to print landscape (the long edge of the paper at the top and bottom) or portrait (the long edge of the paper at the left and right).

Print

When you are ready to print, select this option from the file menu to display the Printer Options dialog box.

The currently selected printer is listed at the top left of the dialog box. Click on the **Change Options** button beside the printer name to:

- Select a different printer, if you have installed more than one printer for GeoWorks Pro
- Select a different paper size
- Specify the paper source: tractor feed or manual.

The second panel in the Printer Options dialog box allows you to specify Document Options: which print quality—high, medium, or low (fastest option), whether to print text only, and the number of copies to print. See the Print subsection of the File Menu section in Chapter 8 for a discussion about print-quality settings.

The third panel in the Printer Options dialog box, the GeoPlanner Print Options panel, allows you specify what to print. You can choose to print:

- The Events window
- A calendar for the selected month(s)
- A calendar for the selected year.

To include scheduled events when printing a calendar, select the **Include Events** option. The month to print is selected by clicking on any day box in that month.

When you are satisfied with your selections, click on the **Print** button to begin printing.

Edit Menu

The Edit menu contains options that allow you to move or copy text, enter new events, delete events, and set alarms.

See the Edit Menu section in Chapter 8 for a discussion about the Undo, Cut, Copy, and Paste options.

Quick Copy and Move

You can also use Quick Copy or Quick Move to place text in another application.

Figure 11.2 shows selected text being copied and shows the Quick Copy pointer. In Figure 11.3, you see selected text being moved and you can see the Quick Move pointer.

Figure 11.2. The Quick Copy Pointer.

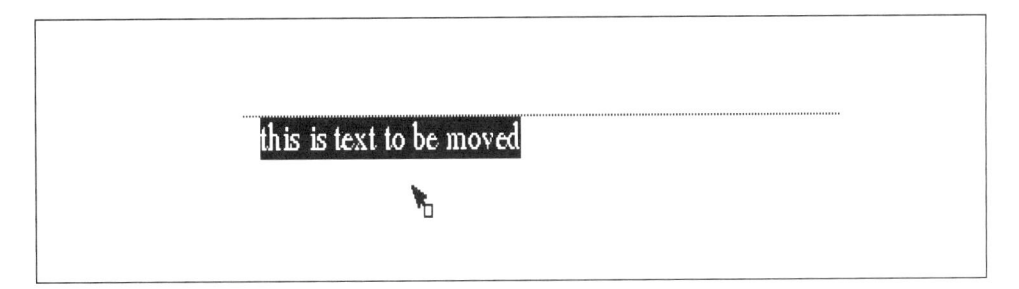

Figure 11.3. The Quick Move Pointer.

To use Quick Copy or Quick Move, first resize the window to make it smaller. To do this, click the Maximize/Resize button to display the screen with the double resizing border. Move the mouse cursor to a corner and, when the pointer changes, drag the window to reduce its size.

Next, open the other application you want to work with (for example, GeoWrite). Repeat the resizing procedure. Then drag each window (by its title bar) so they both can be seen.

Now, select the text you want to copy or move. Position the mouse cursor over the highlighted text. For Quick Copy, press and hold the right mouse button (the pointer changes to the Quick Copy pointer). For Quick Move, press and hold **Alt** then press and hold the right mouse button (the pointer changes to the Quick Move pointer).

Move the pointer to the target location. Release the button. The program copies or moves the selected text.

The program bypasses the Clipboard in a Quick Copy or Quick Move operation. Any text already saved on the Clipboard remains intact.

New Event

You can use this option to insert incremental times into the events list. When you click on **New Event**, a box containing the new time is inserted with a blinking cursor positioned in the box.

If you did not previously click on a specific time, the inserted time begins with 8:00 AM (duplicating the 8:00 AM entry). If you click **New Event** again, the program inserts a new time halfway between the currently chosen time and the next time on the list. In this case, the program would insert 8:15 AM. If you click **New Event** seven more times, the program inserts these time increments: 8:27, 8:29, 8:30, 8:45, 8:53, 8:57, 8:59, and 9:00 AM. The 8:30 AM and 9:00 AM times duplicate existing times on the list.

You can enter events for any of the new times by pressing **Tab** after the time entry to type the event description.

If you click on a time before clicking New Event, the new time is inserted just after the selected time. For example, if you select 1:00 PM, the inserted time is 1:15 PM (halfway between 1:00 PM and the next entry, 1:30 PM).

The shortcut for inserting new times is **Ctrl-N**.

Delete Event

This option allows you to remove an event from the schedule. When you click on the event to select it, the program draws a box around it. When you select **Delete Event** from the Edit menu, the program deletes the selected event from the list.

GeoPlanner does not have a shortcut for this operation.

Alarm Settings

Use this option to set an alarm as an event reminder. Click on an event in the events list to select it. The program draws a box around the event. Select **Alarm Settings** from the Edit menu to display the Event Information dialog box. The dialog box displays the date, time, and description of the selected event.

Setting an Alarm

Enter the date and/or time that you want the alarm to go off. Click the **Alarm On** button to activate the alarm. Click the **OK** button to close the dialog box. The program fills in the bell next to the event to indicate the alarm is set.

When the alarm goes off, the program displays a dialog box telling you the event and time for which you set the alarm. You can turn off the alarm or set the Snooze option. If you turn off the alarm, the program closes the dialog box. If you select Snooze, the program closes the dialog box temporarily, then sounds the alarm and displays the dialog box again after five minutes.

Read the Reminder Precedes Event Time By section under the View menu to see how to set the alarm to go off in advance of the scheduled event.

View Menu

Use the View menu to modify the way GeoPlanner displays the events window or the calendar.

Calendar Only

When you select this option, the program displays only the calendar window, using a full window display. You cannot view or enter events, although the alarm feature still works if you have set the alarm for any events. You can use the scroll bars at the bottom or at the right to view other months. Depending on your setting, you can scroll through one month at a time, or a block of four months at a time.

Events Only

This option displays the events window only. You can add, change or delete events. To change the displayed day, click the **Next Day** or **Previous Day** buttons at the top right of the window.

Both

When you select this option (the program default setting), the calendar and events windows display side by side. You can scroll through the months using the bottom and right scroll bars on the calendar. You can also scroll through the list of events using the scroll bar at the right of the events window.

Single Month

When you select this option (the program default setting), the calendar displays only one month.

Full Year

This option displays two months at a time, or, if Calendar Only is selected, four months at a time. Scroll through the months using the scroll bars at the bottom and right of the calendar.

Options Menu

Select this menu to change the way GeoPlanner displays, to vary the start and end times in the events list, and to set how far in advance the alarm should go off before an event's scheduled time.

Change Preferences

When you select this option, the program displays the Change Preferences dialog box, shown in Figure 11.4.

Day Template

When you activate this option, the events window shows the entire day in small (usually half-hour) time increments (the default setting), whether or not an event is scheduled for that day. If Day Template is Off, the program displays only scheduled events.

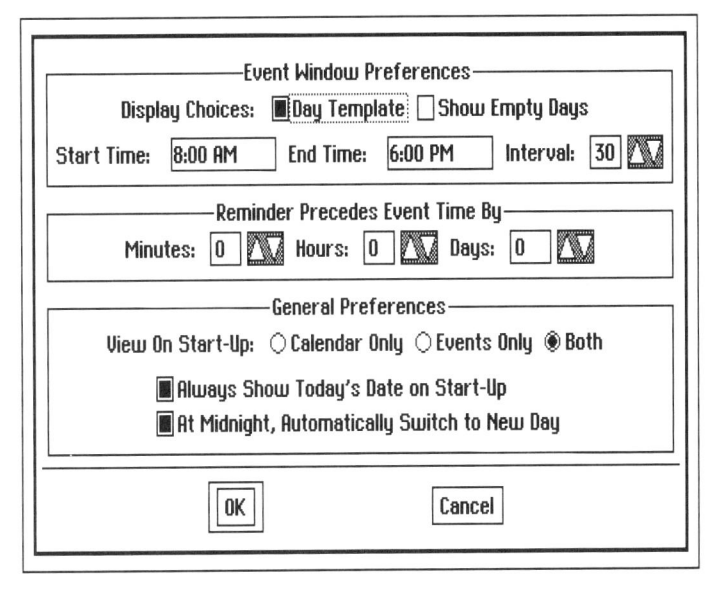

Figure 11.4. The Change Preferences Dialog Box.

Show Empty Days

When Show Empty Days is active (the default setting) and you select a range of days on the calendar to display in the Events window, the program displays all days, whether or not events are scheduled. When Show Empty Days is off, the Events window displays only days with scheduled events when you select a range of days on the calendar.

Start Time

Enter the time of day to begin the events list in the Start Time box. The default is 8:00 AM.

End Time

Enter the time of day to end the events list in the End Time box. The default is 6:00 PM.

Interval

You can click on the up and down arrows to change the interval between times in the events list. The default is 30 minutes.

Reminder Precedes Event Time By

You can use this option to set a buffer time between when the alarm goes off and the event's scheduled time. Click on the up or down triangles to set the minutes, hours and days options for the buffer. The default settings are 0, which means that the alarm goes off at the time the event is scheduled. The new settings become the program default.

> **NOTE** You can use the Alarm Settings option on the Edit menu to set the alarm buffer for a specific event, overriding the program default for that event.

Set options in the General Preferences section of the dialog box to determine how GeoPlanner displays when you start the program.

View On Startup

You can select one of three options for the initial display: Calendar Only, Events Only, or Both. See the View Menu section earlier in this chapter for a discussion about these display options.

Always Show Today's Date on Startup

When you turn on this option, the current day's date is always shown. When you turn it off, the date is not shown.

At Midnight, Automatically Switch to New Day

When you turn on this option, the program switches the next day's date at midnight. When you turn off this option, the program will not switch automatically to the next day's date.

When you are satisfied with your selections in the Change Preferences dialog box, click on **OK** to activate the settings and return to the Options menu. Any changes become effective immediately for the current session.

Save Preferences

To save permanently any changes in the Change Preferences dialog box—setting them as the new program defaults—select **Save Preferences** from the Options menu.

Quick Menu

Select this option when you want to quickly display event schedules.

Today

Select this option to display the events scheduled for the current day.

This Week

Select this option to display events scheduled for the entire week. The program does not display days for which no events are scheduled.

This Weekend

Select this option to display events scheduled for the weekend.

This Month

Select this option to display events scheduled for the entire month. The program will not display days for which no events are scheduled.

Utilities Menu

The Utilities menu options allow you to schedule repeating events, to search for a text string, and to link with the GeoDex application.

Repeating Events

Selecting this option displays the Repeating Events dialog box, which lists all your scheduled repeating events as well as holidays, as shown in Figure 11.5. If there are none, the box displays the words "No events." At the bottom of the dialog box are four buttons: New, Change, Delete, and Close.

New

Clicking on the **New** button displays the Type of Event dialog box. Select the frequency of the event (weekly, monthly, or yearly). Then select how the event is identified (by date, or by day of the week). Depending on your selection, some of the following options will be dimmed (unavailable).

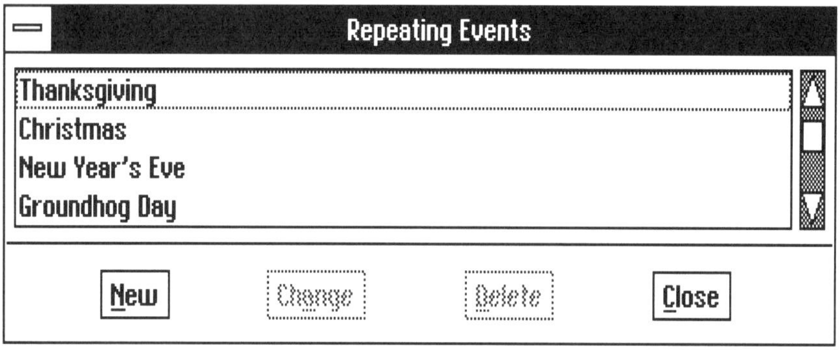

Figure 11.5. The Repeating Events Dialog Box.

Use the **Select Day(s)** option to specify the day(s) of the week on which the repeating event occurs. This option is active when you choose Weekly in the previous section.

Use the **Day of Month** option to specify the day on which the repeating event occurs (if you selected Monthly or Yearly and Specify by Date earlier). If you selected Yearly, you can also enter a month in the box labeled Month.

Use the **Day of Week** option to specify which week in the month (first to fifth) the repeating event occurs, and which day in the week. This option is available when you select Monthly or Yearly and also select Specify by Day of Week. For example, if an event always happens on the third Tuesday of the month, enter third and Tuesday in the respective boxes.

Click on the **Time** box to enter a time for the event.

Enter a description (required) of the repeating event in the Event box.

Use the **Repeat** option to select the frequency of reoccurrence. For example, select Forever if the event always occurs. If there is a specific time limit for the event, choose **From**. The first box now displays the current date. The To box displays the last day of the current year. You can change the dates in these boxes to whatever dates you want.

When you are satisfied with your selections, click the **OK** button to save your choice and return to the GeoPlanner window. Click the **Cancel** button to return to the GeoPlanner window without making changes.

Change

When you select this option, the program displays the dialog box described in the New section. Make whatever changes you want, then click the **OK** button to save the changes.

Delete

Select this option to delete a repeating event. Highlight the event and select **Delete**; the program removes the event from the list.

Close

Select this option to close the Repeating Events dialog box and return to the GeoPlanner window.

Search

You can use this option on the Utilities menu to search for a string of text. When you select this option, the program displays the Search dialog box. The text string you enter can be a word, part of a word, or a group of words.

GeoPlanner is case-sensitive. You must enter the string exactly as it occurs in the event listing. **NOTE**

When you are satisfied with the text string, click the **Start Search** button. The search begins at the current day and continues through the list of future events. If the program cannot match the string, a message asks if you want to search past events also. If the program finds the text string, it displays the text in the event window.

To find the next occurrence of the string, click the **Find Next** button to continue the search. When no further matches can be found, the program displays a message saying the search is complete.

GeoDex Lookup

Suppose you want to telephone a person mentioned in an event description for whom you have a card in the GeoDex address book. From within GeoPlanner you can search GeoDex for the name, then have

GeoDex dial the number for you. (GeoDex is explained in detail in Chapter 15.)

Follow these steps to look up a GeoDex card from within GeoPlanner:

1. Start GeoDex from the Express menu if it is not already running.

2. Switch back to the GeoPlanner window by clicking anywhere in the GeoPlanner window or by selecting it from the Express menu.

3. Select (highlight) the text (name, address, or any other identifying text string) you want to locate in GeoDex.

4. Select **GeoDex Lookup** on the Utilities menu. The program searches the GeoDex cards for a matching text string and displays the first card containing a match in the GeoDex window.

5. Switch to the GeoDex window by clicking anywhere in the GeoDex window or by selecting it from the Express menu.

6. Scroll to the appropriate phone number and have GeoDex dial it for you.

If the displayed card is not the one you want, or if you want to look at more cards that match the text string, follow these steps to continue the search:

1. Select the **GeoDex View** menu.

2. Select the **Both View** option. The left side of the window displays the first card containing the text (shown highlighted). The right side of the window displays all the entries in your card file listed alphabetically. At the bottom of the window is the text you selected in GeoPlanner. You can enter a different text string if you wish.

3. Click the **Find Next** button to continue the search. Continue clicking until you find what you want.

You can confine the search to only Index entries by clicking the **Confine Search To Index** button. Otherwise, the search includes all the text.

You can click the **Clear** button to remove the text string and stop the search.

From the GeoDex application you can search for a text string in GeoPlanner. After selecting the search text in GeoDex, use the **GeoPlanner** button in the bottom right of the GeoDex window to perform the search.

Summary

The GeoPlanner application is a combination calendar and date book. You can enter events in the date book and easily switch to any day, month, or year you want to view on the calendar. It is also easy to view events for a day, week, or the entire month. You can change some GeoPlanner settings to your preference and set an alarm to remind you of events. The Utilities menu allows you to schedule repeating events, and conduct a search for text within GeoPlanner or GeoDex.

Chapter 12

The Calculator Application

This application works much like a hand-held calculator. You can perform addition, subtraction, multiplication and division, calculate percentages, and store numbers in memory.

In this chapter you will learn:

- How to perform calculations
- How to switch between Standard and Hewlett-Packard Reverse Polish Notation (RPN) configurations
- How to set order of precedence for formula calculations in the Standard configuration
- How to calculate using RPN notation
- How to use the menu options.

Using the Calculator

You can access the Calculator application by:

- Double-clicking on the **Calculator** icon in the GeoManager window
- Selecting **Calculator** from the **Express menu/Startup** option.

When you start the Calculator application, the program displays a window similar to Figure 12.1.

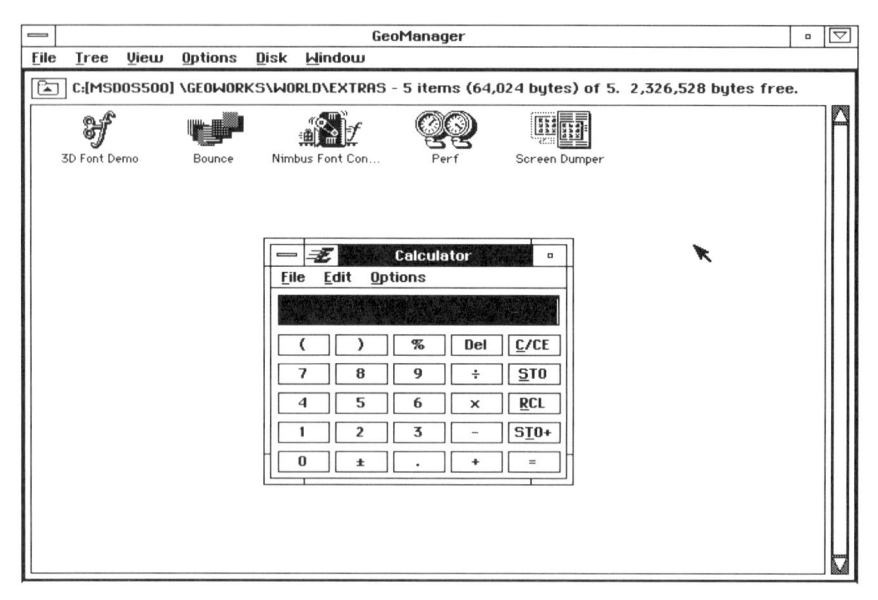

Figure 12.1. The Calculator Window.

The Calculator application is similar to the Calculator appliance in the Appliances section. You will find, however, that the Calculator application is more flexible and powerful. You can operate the calculator by clicking the mouse cursor on the calculator buttons or by pressing keys on the keyboard. Table 12.1 sets out the calculator functions and their corresponding keyboard keys.

Table 12.1. Calculator Functions.

Function	Click Button(s)	Press Key(s)
Digits (0 to 9)	0 to 9	0 to 9
Decimal point	. (period)	. (period)
Add	+	+
Subtract	-	-
Multiply	x	x or *
Divide	÷	/
Equals	=	= or Enter
Change sign	±	N
Clear	C/CE	C
Delete	Del	Backspace
Store in memory	STO	STO
Display memory	RCL	RCL
Add to memory	STO+	STO+
Percent	%	%
Parentheses	(or)	(or)

You can use the regular typing keys, or you can use the numeric keypad if *Num Lock* is on.

Delete

This function erases the last (leftmost) digit in a number.

Parentheses (Standard Configuration)

You can use parentheses to group numbers together so that they are operated on as a unit. Parentheses change the order of operations—the value inside the parentheses is calculated before any other operation. See Order of Operations in this chapter for information about the order of precedence in calculations.

Clear

You can click the **C/CE** button once to clear the displayed number. When you double click the **C/CE** button, the program clears everything, including any calculations in progress. To clear the memory from the keyboard, press **0**, then press **S** to store the value of zero.

Error

If you try to divide by zero, or if your result is a value greater than the calculator can handle, the program displays an error message. A result cannot be greater than 2,147,483,647 or less than -2,147,483,647. Click on **C/CE** or press **C** to clear the error message.

Order of Operations (Standard Configuration)

The Calculator application in Standard configuration follows this order of precedence when performing calculations:

First:	Quantities in parentheses
Second:	Multiplication and division
Last:	Addition and subtraction.

Arithmetic operations with the same order of precedence (multiplication and division, or addition and subtraction) are performed in the order they occur from left to right. The following example illustrates the order of operation. Suppose you enter the formula:

```
4 + 5 x 6 =
```

You may expect 54 as the answer (4 + 5 = 9; 9 x 6 = 54). However, the answer you get is 34. The reason is that the multiplication operation has precedence over addition. Therefore, the first calculation is 6 x 5 (= 30), then 4 is added to 30, with a result of 34.

To ensure that the sum of 4 + 5 is the value multiplied by 6, you must enter the formula like this:

```
(4 + 5) x 6 =
```

or like this:

```
6 x (4 + 5) =
```

The calculator first evaluates the sum in the parentheses, then multiplies the sum by 6 for a result of 54.

Memory Use

You can store a frequently used number in the calculator memory so you can call it up with a single click. You can also use the memory function to keep a running total when performing a series of calculations.

STO   This button stores the currently displayed number in memory, replacing any previously stored value.

STO+   This button adds the currently displayed number to the value stored in memory.

RCL   This button displays the value stored in memory. You can then use this number in a calculation.

The Calculator Menu Bar

At the top of the calculator display is a menu bar with three menu options: File, Edit, and Options.

File Menu

The only option on the Calculator File menu is Exit. Select this option to close the Calculator application and return to the GeoManager window.

Edit Menu

You can cut and paste or copy and paste numbers from the calculator into other applications using the Edit menu. See the Edit Menu section in Chapter 8 for a discussion of Cut, Copy, and Paste. After you have cut or copied, switch to the other application to paste.

Quick Copy and Quick Move

In addition to the Cut and Paste or Copy and Paste operations on the Edit menu, you can use Quick Copy or Quick Move to place text (or the Calculator display) in another application. See the Edit Menu section of

Chapter 11 for a full discussion of Quick Copy and Quick Move. In the Calculator, the operation of Quick Copy and Quick Move are the same. The Calculator results remain displayed after either operation.

Options Menu

You can use this menu to specify the number of decimal places for the calculator to display. You can also switch the calculator between Standard operation (the default) and Reverse Polish Notation (RPN), which is used by Hewlett-Packard calculators.

Decimal Places

Select this option to display the Decimal Places dialog box. Click on the small triangles to increase or decrease the number of decimal places shown. The range is 0 to 8 decimal places.

NOTE When a value includes more decimal places than the number specified for display, the calculator will round off the number for display purposes only. The actual value used in calculations retains its full number of decimal places. For example, if you have the number 223.463 and have set the decimal places to 1, the number will display as 223.5, but the calculator will use 223.463 in its calculations.

Standard

Select this option to configure the calculator as a standard hand-held calculator. The operations of the Standard configuration are described earlier in this chapter.

RPN

When you select this option, the calculator is reconfigured, as shown in Figure 12.2, and operates using Reverse Polish Notation (RPN). Unlike standard calculators, RPN calculators perform operations in the order they are entered, not according to an order of preference.

In general, the buttons on Standard and RPN calculators are the same, with the following exceptions:

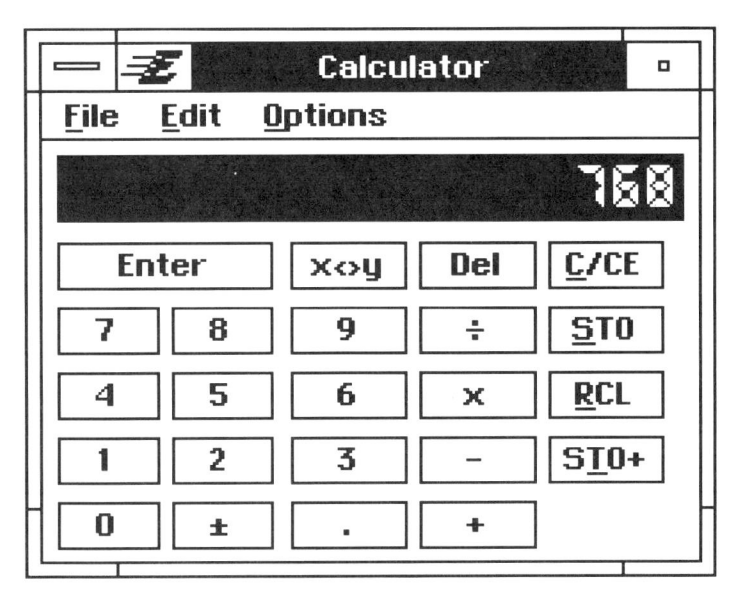

Figure 12.2. The RPN Calculator.

Enter Button

Use this button to separate the first and second numbers, storing the first number in a register so it can be recalled automatically for the calculation. RPN notation can use up to four registers and the displayed number in its calculations. Note that there are no parentheses and no equal sign buttons on the RPN calculator.

Exchange Button

Use the **Exchange** button to reverse the order of two numbers entered in the calculator. For example, suppose you want to divide 8 by 4, but you inadvertently entered the 4 first, then the 8. Click the **Exchange** button, or **Enter** on the keyboard, - to reverse the numbers.

Performing RPN Calculations

Click these buttons to perform the calculation 768 ÷ 16:

7	displays **7**
6	displays **76**
8	displays **768**
Enter	stores displayed number in first register
1	displays **1**
6	displays **16**
÷	divides value in register by displayed number: **768 ÷ 16**

The calculator displays the result: **48**

To erase the last displayed digit, click the **Del** button.

To switch the displayed number from negative to positive (or positive to negative), click the ± button.

What happens if you click the **Enter** button after entering the second value in this calculation: 8 x 4?

8	displays **8**
Enter	stores displayed number in first register
4	displays **4**
Enter	moves value in first register to second register, then stores displayed number in first register
x	multiplies value in first register by displayed number: **4 x 4**

The calculator displays the result: **16**. The value 4 in the first register (which has been used) is deleted. The value 8 in the second register moves down to the first register.

To add 9 to the displayed result of 16:

9	moves value in first register, **8**, up to second register. Stores displayed number, **16**, in first register. Displays **9**.
+	adds value in first register and displayed number: **16 + 9**

The calculator displays the result: **25**. The value 16 in the first register (which has been used) is deleted. The value 8 in the second register moves down to the first register.

To divide the displayed value by the value in the first register:

| x<>y | switches displayed value and value in first register |
| ÷ | divides value in first register, **25**, by displayed number, **8**. |

The calculator displays the result: **3.125**. The value in the first register (which has been used) is deleted.

Unlike standard calculators, RPN calculators perform operations in the order they are entered, not according to an order of preference. In other words, the same numbers entered in the same order do not necessarily give the same answers on the two calculators. The following example illustrates this.

Standard calculator: 6 + 2 x 4 = 14

> Performed as 2 x 4 = 8, 8 + 6 = 14 because multiplication takes precedence over addition.

RPN calculator: 6 + 2 x 4 = 32

> Performed as 6 + 2 = 8, 8 x 4 = 32 because the calculation is done as entered.

There is no need to use parentheses in RPN calculations. For example, to perform the calculation 50 x (6-4), first calculate 6 - 4 = 2, then calculate 2 x 50 to get the answer, 100.

Memory Functions

The memory register is separate from the calculation registers, so calculations will not affect the number stored in memory unless you click a memory-function button.

To store the displayed number in memory, click the **STO** button.

To add the displayed number to the value in the memory register, click the **STO+** button.

To display the value in the memory register, click the **RCL** button. You can then use that value in a calculation.

For example, suppose you want to divide the number 3 by the value in the memory register (5):

3	displays **3**
Enter	stores displayed number in first register
RCL	displays value in memory register: **5**
÷	divides value in first register, **3**, by displayed value: **5**

The calculator displays the result: **0.67**.

Now suppose you want to divide the value in the memory register (5) by the number 3:

RCL	displays value in memory register: **5**
3	stores displayed value in first register: **3**
÷	divides value in first register, **5**, by displayed value: **3**

The calculator displays the result: **1.67**.

Summary

This chapter explained how to access and use the Calculator application in the Advanced Workspace. You can perform calculations the same way you would with a hand-held calculator. In addition, you can cut, copy, and paste numbers to other application documents. You can switch the calculator from a Standard configuration to the Reverse Polish Notation configuration.

Chapter 13

The Notepad Application

In this chapter you will learn how to use the Notepad application in two ways:

- as a pad for jotting down notes to yourself
- as a DOS (ASCII) text editor.

Unlike GeoWrite, which creates GEOS-type documents, Notepad documents are saved as DOS-type documents.

Accessing the Notepad Application

You can access the Notepad application by:

- Double-clicking on the **Notepad** icon in the GeoManager window
- Selecting **Notepad** from the **Express menu/Startup** option

NOTE You cannot start Notepad automatically by opening one of its documents from the GeoManager/Document directory.

When you enter Notepad the first time, the program creates a blank NOTES.TXT file. The file is stored in the DOCUMENT subdirectory.

If a Notepad document was open when you last exited, the same document opens when you return to the application. If a NOTES.TXT file exists but was not displayed when you last exited, the program displays "Notepad - No File" in the title bar.

Using Notepad for Notes

You can use the Notepad application as a free-form pad for jotting and saving notes that do not require the special formatting features available in GeoWrite. When you save a Notepad document, you can choose to follow GEOS filename conventions or DOS filenaming conventions. (See the DOS and GEOS Files section in Chapter 4 for details.)

To help you decide which application is more appropriate for a task, the following table summarizes the differences between the Notepad and GeoWrite:

Table 13.1. Comparison of the Notepad and GeoWrite.

The Notepad	GeoWrite
Only one document can be open at a time	Multiple documents can be open at once
Creates and uses DOS-type documents	Creates and uses GEOS-type documents
Does not safeguard documents	Safeguards documents
No choice of fonts	A selection of fonts
No rulers, formatting or justification options	A variety of formatting and justification options

Using Notepad as a DOS Text Editor

You can use the Notepad to create and edit DOS text files, such as your AUTOEXEC.BAT file or other DOS batch files. Although editing DOS files in the Notepad is quite similar to working with GEOS files in GeoWrite, it is important to realize that all Notepad files are DOS files—they are not interchangeable with GEOS documents.

When saving a DOS batch file, you must use the DOS filenaming conventions or DOS will not recognize the file as one it can use.

The Notepad Menus

The menu bar at the top of the Notepad screen contains three menus: File, Edit, and Sizes.

File Menu

The File menu contains eight options, not all of which are available all the time.

New

When you select **New**, the heading at the top of the Notepad screen changes to Notepad—Notes. You can enter any text you want in the Notepad window. Edit notes using the same techniques you use to edit any document.

Open

Use this option to open an existing Notepad file or other DOS (text) file. Selecting **Open** displays a standard Select Document to Open dialog box.

On opening some files you may see a warning that the file contains non-ASCII characters that will be deleted if the file is opened. If you select **Yes**, the file is opened anyway.

Close

Select this option to remove a file from the Notepad window. If you modified the file since the last save—or if the file has never been saved—

the program displays this message: "Note has been changed. Do you wish to save it?" You can choose Yes, No, or Cancel.

If you select **No**, the program closes the file without saving your changes. If the file had never been saved, it is deleted entirely.

If you select **Cancel**, the program takes you back to the file window.

If you select **Yes**, one of two things will happen. If the document had been saved before, the program saves the file immediately and closes the file. If the file was never saved, then the program displays the standard Select Directory and Enter New Filename dialog box.

Save

When you select this option to save a note the first time, the program displays the standard Select Directory and Enter New Filename dialog box.

> **NOTE** Unlike most other GeoWorks Pro applications, the Notepad does not safeguard your changes as you work. Every time you make important changes to a file, select Save to preserve the changes.

Save As

You can use this option to save a previously named file under a different name. The program saves a copy of the file under the new name, preserving the original file. You can select the subdirectory and filename for the new document.

Revert

If you are working in a previously saved document and you decide you don't want to keep the changes made since the last save, select **Revert** from the File menu. The program displays a dialog box asking you to confirm that you want to revert to the last-saved version of your document. If you select **Yes**, the program deletes the changes.

Print

You can print your note using this option. When you select **Print**, the program displays the Printer Options dialog box, shown in Figure 13.1.

Figure 13.1. The Printer Options Dialog Box.

See the Print and File Menu/Print sections of Chapter 8 for discussions about this option.

Exit

Select this option to exit Notepad and go to the Welcome screen. The shortcut keystroke for Exit is **F3**.

Edit Menu

See the Edit Menu section in Chapter 8 for a discussion about the Notepad Edit menu options: cut, copy, and paste. See the Edit Menu section in Chapter 11 for a discussion about using the Quick Copy and Quick Move commands.

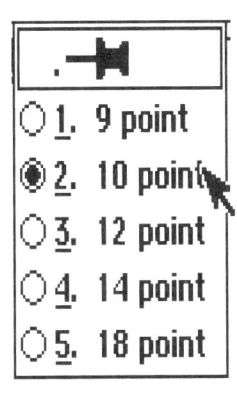

Figure 13.2. Sizes Menu.

Sizes Menu

When you select this option to change the size of displayed text in the Notepad window, the program displays the dialog box shown in Figure 13.2.

You can click on a size to select it, displaying all text in the Notepad in the selected point size. You can choose only one size at a time: 9 point, 10 point, 12 point, 14 point, or 18 point. Select a smaller size to display more text in the window at a time; select a larger size for readability.

NOTE The size of text on the screen does not affect the way the document will print.

Summary

In this chapter you learned how to use the Notepad to jot down quick notes that don't require the formatting capabilities of GeoWrite. You can print these notes, save them, or copy them to other documents. The Notepad is also ideal for creating DOS files or for editing DOS files from other sources, for example, your computer's AUTOEXEC.BAT file.

Chapter 14

The Scrapbook Application

In this chapter you will learn how to :

- use the Scrapbook application to collect your favorite graphics and text items
- create multiple scrapbooks
- cut and copy items from one scrapbook to another or from one application to another.

While the GeoWorks Pro Clipboard is a handy way to transfer text and pictures from one document to another, it can hold only one item at a time. Use the Scrapbook for permanent storage of the items you use frequently, such as a company logo or a favorite drawing.

One Scrapbook file can contain as many "scraps" of text or graphics as you wish, each on its own page. You can also create multiple scrapbooks, perhaps organizing your text and graphics by topic.

Accessing the Scrapbook

You can access the Scrapbook in several ways:

- Double-click on the **Scrapbook** icon in the GeoManager window
- Select **Scrapbook** from the Express menu/Startup option
- Click on a Scrapbook document icon in the GeoManager DOCUMENT directory.

The Scrapbook Window

When you open the Scrapbook application, the program displays the Scrapbook window shown in Figure 14.1.

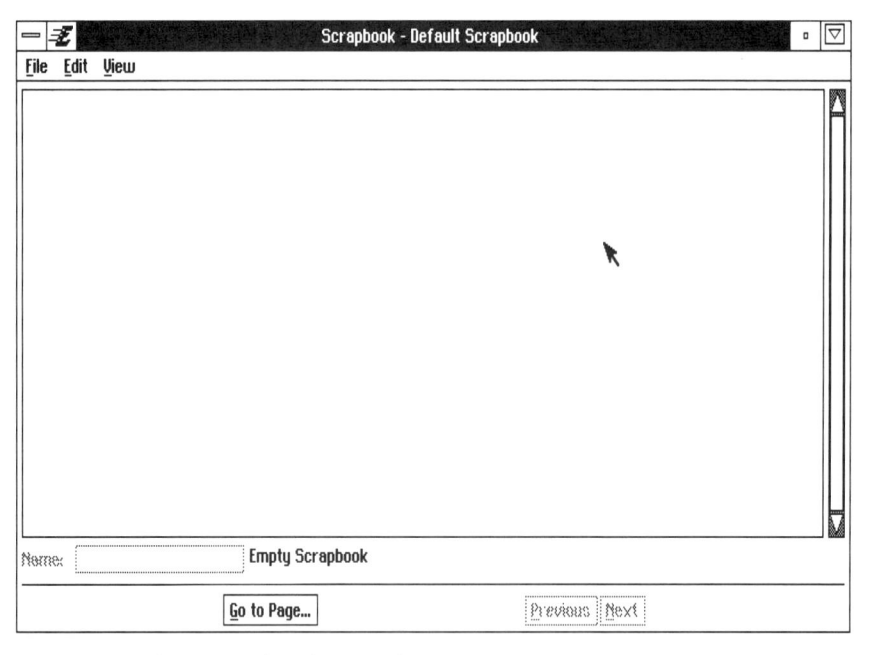

Figure 14.1. *The Scrapbook Window.*

The title bar displays the document name: Default Scrapbook. The first time you open Scrapbook, the program creates the file Default Scrapbook and displays it for you. Even if you have more than one

Scrapbook, the file Default Scrapbook will always appear when you open the program.

Two menu options display on the menu bar: File and Edit.

Below the menu bar is the Scrapbook window, where you can view the contents of the Scrapbook. If the contents of a page are larger than the window area, scroll the page using the scroll bar at the right of the window.

Below the window is a box labeled Name. You can name each page in the Scrapbook by entering a name in this box. The program displays the page name in this box if the page is already named.

If you have not yet saved anything in the Default Scrapbook file, the window area is empty and the notation **Empty Scrapbook** displays at the bottom of the window.

If you have saved images, the program displays the current page number and the total number of pages. (For example, Page 1 of 2.)

Go to Page Button

Below the Name box is the Go to Page button. You can select any page in the Scrapbook by clicking this button to display the Go to Page dialog box, shown in Figure 14.2. The dialog box displays a list of pages and page numbers in the Scrapbook, with the current page highlighted.

You can view any page you want by highlighting it and clicking the **View Page** button. Click the **Close** button to close the dialog box. The program displays the selected page in the Scrapbook window.

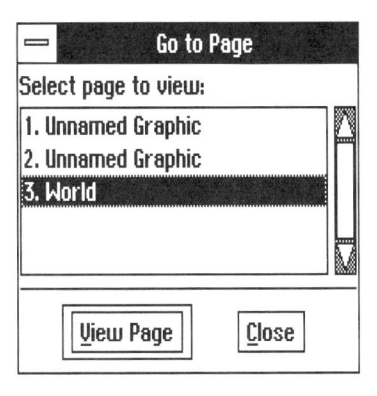

Figure 14.2. The Go to Page Dialog Box.

Previous and Next Buttons

To the right of the Go to Page button in the Scrapbook window are the Previous and Next buttons. Clicking the **Previous** button takes you to the previous page in the Scrapbook. If you are viewing the first page, the Previous button takes you to the last page. Clicking the **Next** button takes you to the next page. If you are viewing the last page, the Next button takes you to the first page.

The Menu Bar

The two menus on the Scrapbook menu bar, File and Edit, work in much the same way as they do in other GeoWorks Pro documents.

File Menu

When you select File from the menu bar, the program displays the File menu shown in Figure 14.3.

Figure 14.3. The Scrapbook File Menu.

The New, Open, Close, Save, Save As, and Revert options work in the standard way. See File Menu in Chapter 8 for a full discussion of these features.

Import

Use this menu option to import an image saved in one of these other formats:

- TIFF format files, which have a .TIF extension (one of the most universally acceptable bit-mapped file formats)
- PC Paintbrush files, which have a .PCX extension
- EPS format files, which are Encapsulated PostScript files—a format used to save graphs and slides in Quattro Pro SE.

GeoDraw treats an imported image as an object that you can work with as you would any other object.

Follow these steps to import a file:

1. Select: **Import** from the File menu. The program displays the Select file to import dialog box as shown in Figure 14.4.

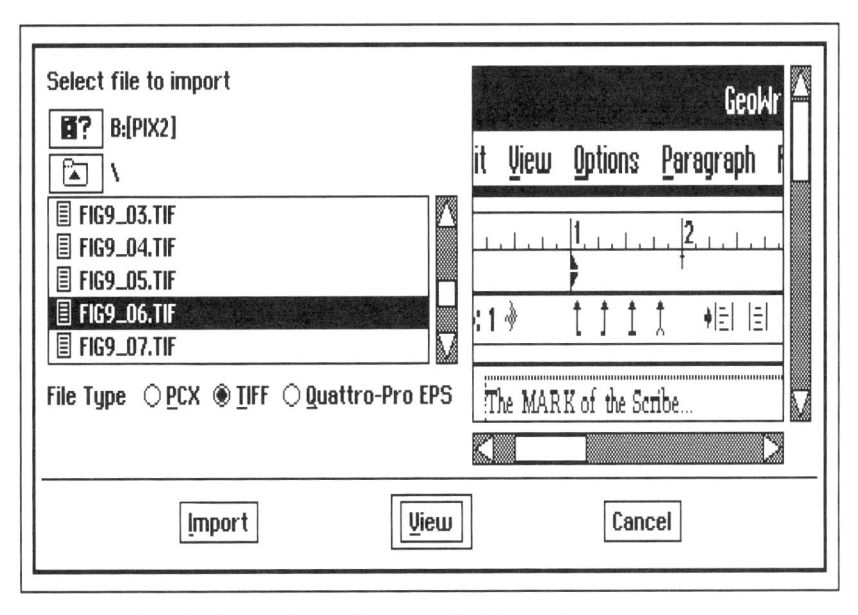

Figure 14.4. The Select File to Import Dialog Box

2. If the image you want to import is not in the current subdirectory, double-click on the name of the subdirectory that contains the image file. (See Chapter 3, Creating and Saving Documents, for a discussion about moving around in subdirectories and selecting files.)

3. Select: File you want to import from the list in the left panel of the dialog box. In Figure 14.4, the file named FIG9_06.TIF on the disk in drive B: (volume label PIX2) is the selected file.

4. Click: **View** button to preview the selected image before importing it. This particular image was a GeoWrite screen display "captured" for use as a graphic figure in this book. Use the scroll bars to scroll the image in the right panel of the dialog box.

5. Click: **Import** button when you are satisfied that the correct file is selected. The program closes the dialog box and copies the image into the document window. (Remember that large images may take several minutes to import.)

6. Repeat the process for each image you want to import.
Click: **Cancel** button to close the Select File to Import dialog box without importing a file.

Edit Menu

When you select this option, the program displays the Edit menu, shown in Figure 14.5.

This menu contains six options that allow you to add text or graphics to your Scrapbook, either on a new page or on the page you select. You can move or copy from a Scrapbook to another application or delete a page from the Scrapbook. You can also copy a page in a scaled display, i.e., smaller or larger than normal size.

Cut

You can use this option to move (cut) text or graphics from another application to the Scrapbook, or from the Scrapbook to another application. In either case, the transfer goes by way of the Clipboard. The shortcut for this option is **Shift-Del**.

Select (highlight) the text or graphics you want to move from an application to the Clipboard. Select **Cut** from the Edit menu in the application. The program removes the selected item from the application and places it on the Clipboard. Paste the item from the Clipboard to the Scrapbook.

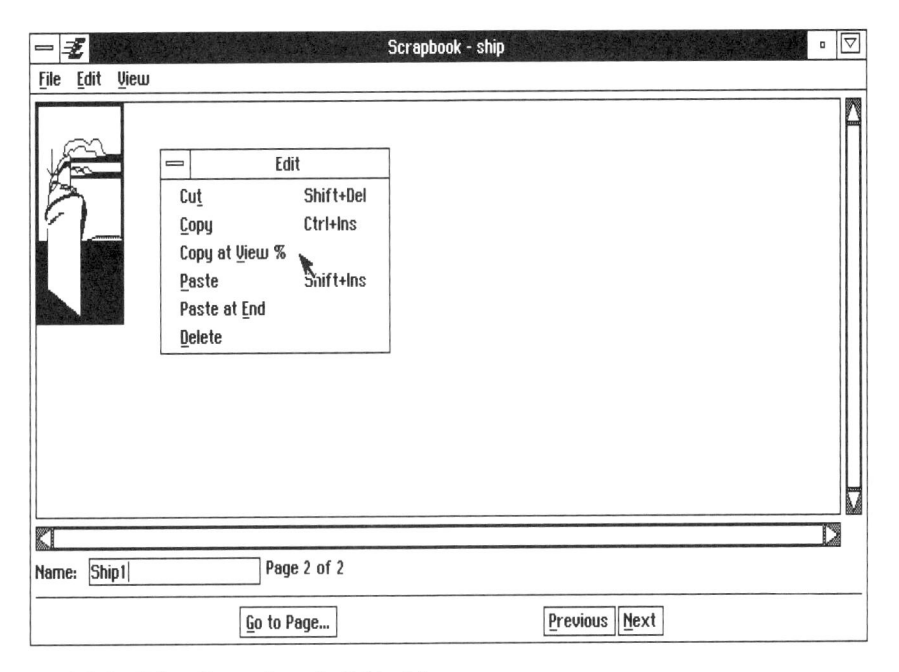

Figure 14.5. The Scrapbook Edit Menu.

When moving an item from the Scrapbook to the Clipboard, it is not necessary to highlight it first. Selecting **Cut** from the Scrapbook Edit menu automatically selects the contents of the displayed page and moves it to the Clipboard. The program renumbers any pages that follow the cut page.

Copy

This option works the same as Cut, except that the original material remains intact and a copy is placed on the Clipboard. The shortcut for this is **Ctrl-Ins**.

Copy at View %

If you have selected a display view at a scale other than normal, you can copy the display to the Clipboard in the scale you have selected. For example, if you chose a 125% scale for the display, you could copy the 125% display to the Clipboard by selecting **Copy at View %**.

In Figure 14.5, the ship image is reduced to a 50% view. To copy the image in its reduced size, use **Copy at View %** from the Edit menu. If you select **Copy** instead, the image is copied at normal size.

Paste

Select **Paste** from the Edit menu to copy the Clipboard contents into the Scrapbook. The program inserts a page in the Scrapbook at the current location and places the item on the page. For example, if page 2 is displayed when you select Paste, the program inserts a new page 2, renumbers the original page 2 as page 3, and renumbers subsequent pages. The shortcut for this is **Shift-Ins**.

Paste at End

This option places Clipboard material on a new page at the end of the Scrapbook. If you had five pages in the book, it pastes the material on a new page 6. No shortcut exists for this option.

Delete

This option deletes the contents of the displayed page. The contents are not copied to the Clipboard, so they cannot be retrieved. There is no shortcut for this command.

WARNING The program does not prompt for confirmation before deleting the material—as soon as you select Delete, the program removes the contents.

View Menu

This menu offers three choices for viewing a reduced display, a normal display, and four choices for viewing an enlarged display. There is also an option for Customizing the view.

NOTE The options on the View menu are dimmed and unavailable if you have a text display.

Refer to Chapter 10, "The GeoDraw Application" for a discussion of the options on the View menu, except Custom view.

Custom View

This option allows you to set the size of the display exactly. By clicking the up or down pointing arrowheads, you can change the setting from 1% to 140%. Click **Apply** to view the display at the setting you choose. In Figure 14.6, the ship is shown at a custom view of 112%.

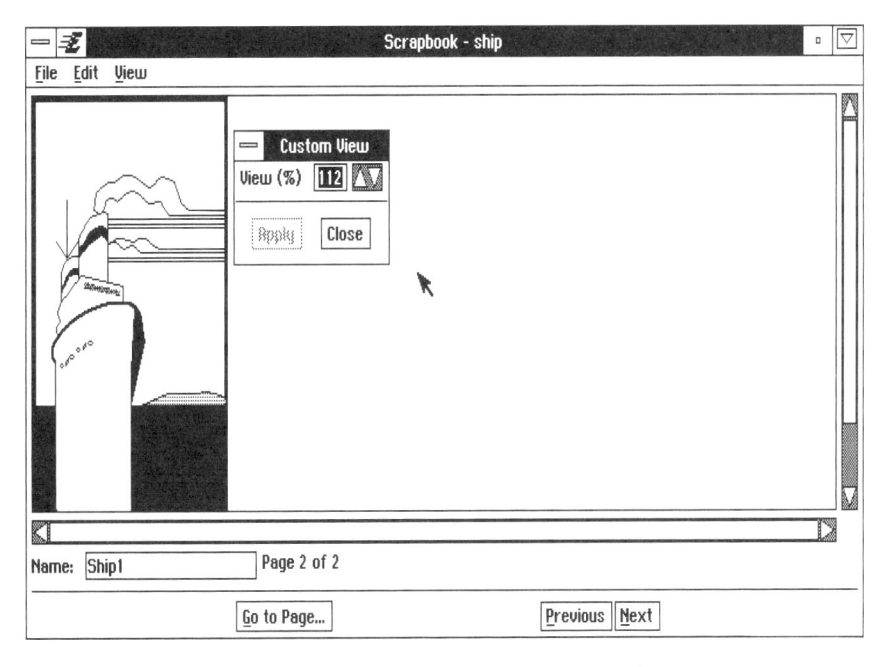

Figure 14.6. View of Picture at Custom View Size of 112%.

Changing the Default Scrapbook

Because the program opens the file Default Scrapbook every time you run the application, you might want to change the file Default Scrapbook to the scrapbook that you use most often.

Follow these steps to change the file Default Scrapbook:

1. Exit the Scrapbook application.
   If you return to the Welcome screen, select the **Advanced Workspace** icon to go to the GeoManager window.

2. Activate the DOCUMENT directory by clicking on the **Document** icon at the bottom of the window.

3. Highlight: Document called Default Scrapbook.

4. Rename: Document to some other unique name.

5. Highlight: Scrapbook document you want as the default.

6. Rename: Highlighted Scrapbook file as Default Scrapbook.

The next time you start the Scrapbook application, the new Default Scrapbook file will open automatically.

NOTE You must name the file exactly as shown, otherwise the Scrapbook application will not recognize the name.

Opening More Than One Scrapbook at a Time

There are two ways to open more than one Scrapbook at a time:

- From the GeoManager window, you can click the **Scrapbook** icon each time you want to open another document
- From the Express menu/Startup option, you can click the **Scrapbook** icon each time you want to open another document.

In either case, if the program displays a message that the Default Scrapbook is already in use, click the **OK** button. Then select **Open** from the File menu to open another Scrapbook.

You can display the open Scrapbooks in an overlapping format on the screen, as shown in Figure 14.7.

1. To do this, first open a saved Scrapbook and reduce it to an icon.

2. Then, open the Express menu and select **Scrapbook** from the Startup menu. The Default Scrapbook file opens.

3. Go to the File menu and select **Open**.

4. Choose: Scrapbook file you want and click on **Open** in the dialog box.

5. Next, resize the window (see Resizing a Window in Chapter 5) and position it where you want it.

6. Click: **Scrapbook** icon and resize that window also. Move it into an overlapping position. You can repeat this procedure if you wish.

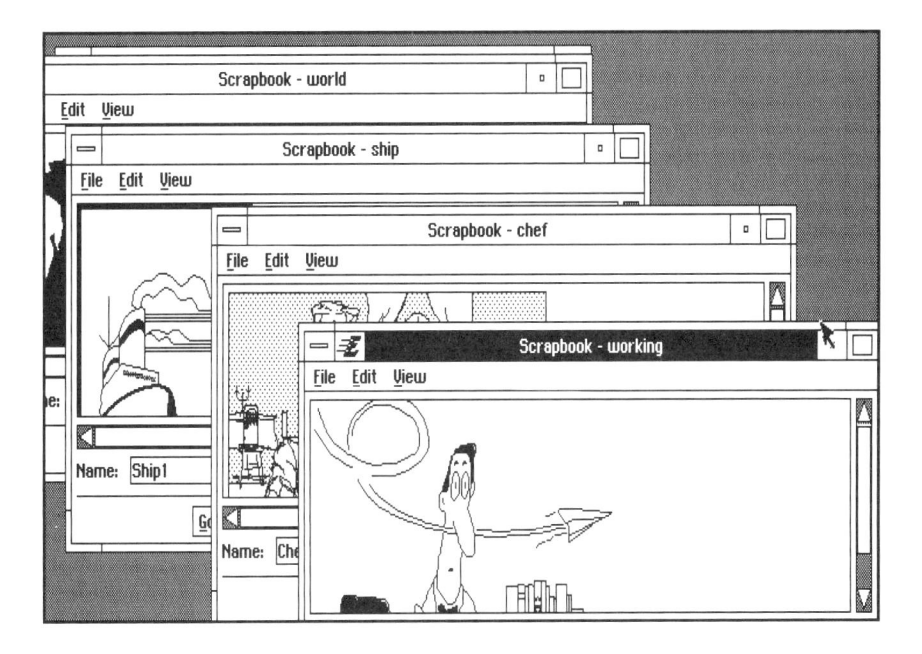

Figure 14.7. Overlapping Scrapbook Windows.

You can also resize and position the Scrapbook windows so they display side by side, as shown in Figure 14.8.

Cutting or Copying Between Scrapbooks

Follow these steps to cut or copy between open scrapbooks:

1. Click: **Maximize** button (the rectangle in the upper-right corner of the window) of the Scrapbook that contains the item you want to cut or copy. The program displays the Scrapbook as a full-size window.

2. Display: Scrapbook page that contains the item.

3. Select: **Cut** (or **Copy**) from the Edit menu. The program cuts (or copies) the item, placing it on the Clipboard.

4. Click: **Minimize** button (same as the **Maximize** button). The program displays the Scrapbook as an overlapping window again.

5. Click: **Maximize** button on the Scrapbook *into* which you want to paste the item. The program displays the Scrapbook as a full-size window.

6. Select: **Paste** (or **Paste at End**) from the Edit menu. The program copies the item from the Clipboard into the Scrapbook.

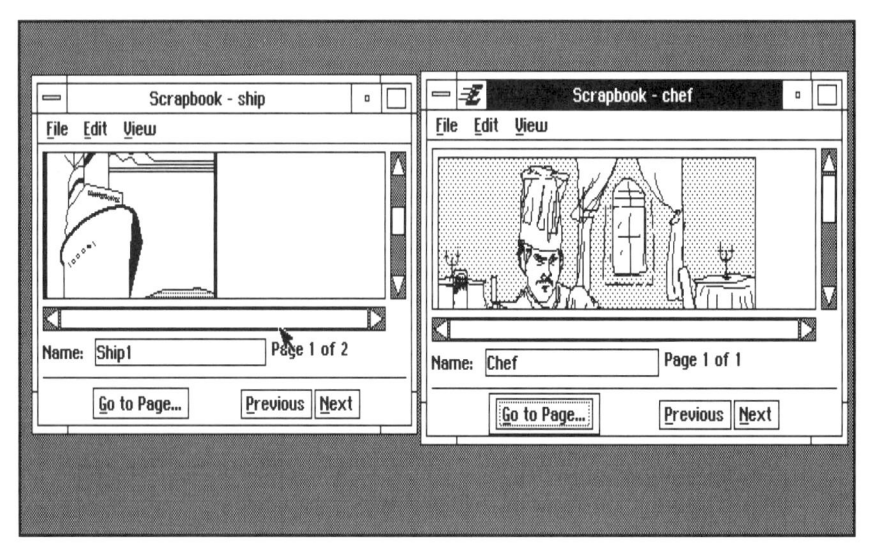

Figure 14.8. Resized Scrapbook Windows.

NOTE You can also reduce the Scrapbooks to icons, selecting and reducing them as necessary to move between them to cut (or copy) and paste.

Summary

The Scrapbook application is a handy way to store frequently used text or graphics. You can create multiple Scrapbooks, each with as many pages as you want. You can cut (or copy) items from one Scrapbook to another, from a Scrapbook to another application, or from another application to a Scrapbook.

Chapter 15

The GeoDex Application

In this chapter you will learn how to use the GeoDex application, a combination card file and automatic phone dialer. GeoDex is convenient for keeping track of names, addresses, and other notations. You can print lists of names and phone numbers. If you have a modem, you can use the GeoDex phone-dialing feature.

Accessing the GeoDex Application

The GeoDex program can be accessed in several ways:

- Double-click on the **GeoDex** icon in the GeoManager window
- Select: **GeoDex** from the Express menu/Startup option
- Click: a **GeoDex document** icon in the GeoManager DOCUMENT directory.

The GeoDex Window

When you open the GeoDex application, the program displays the window shown in Figure 15.1.

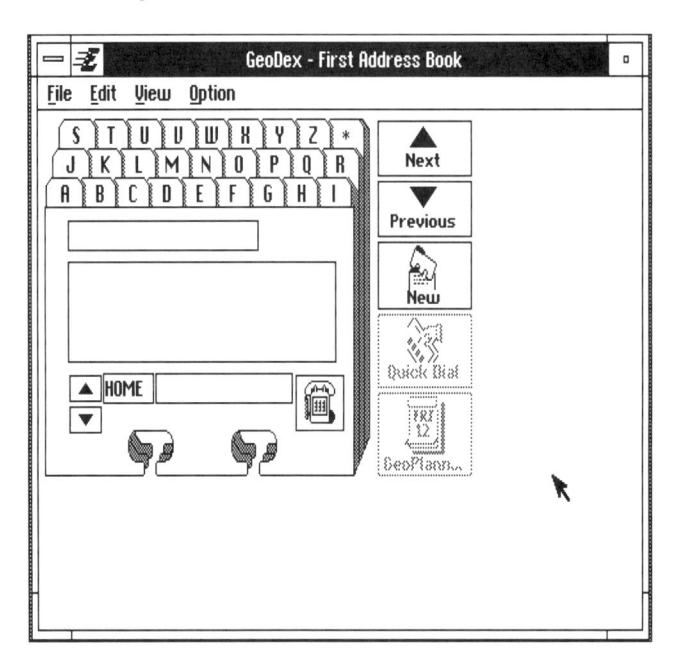

Figure 15.1. The GeoDex Window.

The GeoDex title bar displays the default file name, Address Book, or the name you have given the displayed card file. In Figure 15.1 the card file is named First Address Book.

The menu bar contains four options: File, Edit, View, and Option. The GeoDex menus are described later in this chapter. The program displays the card files on the left in the GeoDex window. Above the top card are letter tabs from A to Z and an * (asterisk) tab. You can click on a letter tab to flip to the cards listed under that letter. When you click the * tab, the program flips to cards that are not grouped under a letter. The program highlights the selected tab.

The top card is the GeoDex work area. Enter into the index field (the small box at the top of the work area) the word or words by which you want to identify the card. Remember that GeoDex alphabetizes according to the first word, so when entering a name, type the last name first.

You can enter the name, address, and other information in the large box. Use the scroll bar at the right of the large box to scroll the contents.

Below the large box is the phone number box. Each card can store up to seven phone numbers. The default phone number display is HOME. You can click the up and down triangles to switch to OFFICE, CAR, FAX, and three blank areas in which you can enter custom phone number designations. Enter the phone number in the box beside the designation.

The program displays five buttons to the right of the card window: Next, Previous, New, Quick Dial, and GeoPlanner.

Next

You can click this button to display the next card in alphabetical sequence. If you are viewing the last card in the file, the program flips to the first card in the file.

Previous

You can click this button to display the previous card in the alphabetical sequence. If you are viewing the first card in the file, the program flips to the last card in the file.

New

You can click this button to create a new card. The program files the card alphabetically for you.

Creating a Card

Follow these steps to create a new card:

1. Enter in the index field the word or words that identify the card. If you are entering a person's name, type the last name followed by a comma, then type the first name.

2. Press: **Enter**. The program copies the index field contents into the address area below.
Press: **Enter** again to move down a line.
When the identifying text is the way you want it, type the address

information, pressing **Enter** each time you want to begin a new line.

Press: **Backspace** to correct any mistakes.

3. Press: **Tab** to move to the phone number area. Select the appropriate number designation (home, office, car, or fax) or create your own designation.

4. If you will be using the Dial or Quick Dial features, enter the phone number following the guidelines outlined in the following section, Entering Phone Numbers.

5. Click: **New**, **Next**, **Previous**, or **Tab**. Clicking any of these buttons will insert the new card in the index.

Entering Phone Numbers

Follow these guidelines when entering phone numbers:

- You can insert a hyphen (-) or a space within the number to make it easier to read
- Omit the area code for local numbers
- Include any number that you must dial to place a call manually. For example, if you must always dial 9 to access an outside line, include the 9 like this: 9-555-1212
- Include any necessary access number for your long distance service
- For a long distance number, include the 1 and the area code. For example: 1-508-555-1212
- If your modem software supports it, you can place a comma anywhere in the number to pause the dialing procedure briefly. This is sometimes necessary to make a modem connection. For example, you could enter 1-505,-555-1212. Check your modem manual for information about this feature.

You can configure GeoDex to insert preliminary numbers automatically for every number dialed. It is then not necessary to include these numbers in every phone listing. See the Option Menu section later in this chapter.

To use the Quick Dial and Dial features, you must have a Hayes-compatible modem that shares the same line as your telephone. You should refer to your modem manual for instructions on installing and setting up the modem.

NOTE

Use the Preferences application to configure GeoWorks Pro for your modem.

See the Dialing a Phone Number section later in this chapter for information about dialing a number.

Quick Dial

Select this option to display two lists: the most frequently called and the most recently called names and phone numbers, as shown in Figure 15.2.

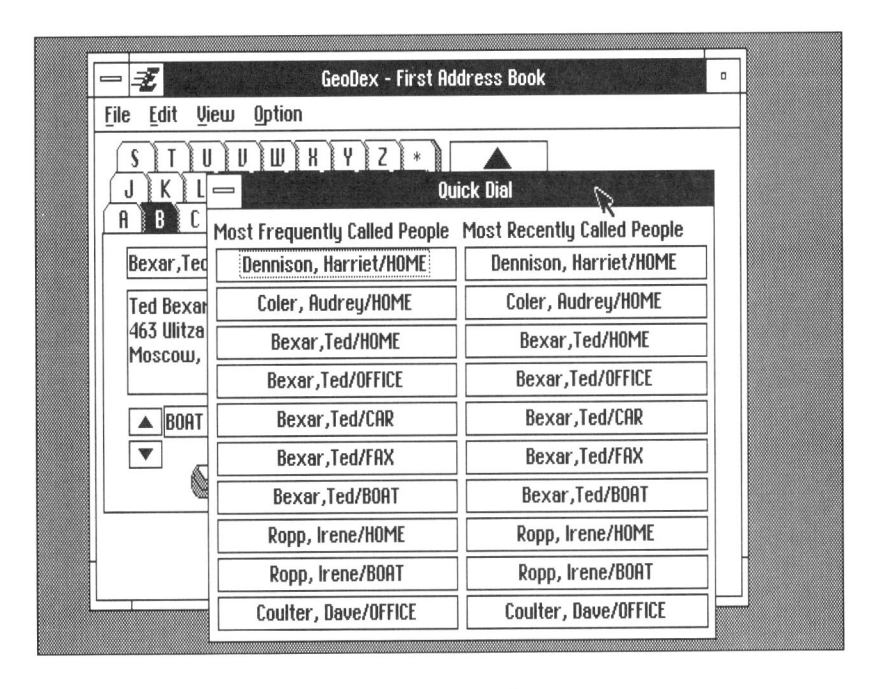

Figure 15.2. The Quick Dial Phone Number Listings.

The program updates the lists every time you make a phone call from GeoDex, modifying the lists to reflect your calling pattern.

See the Dialing a Phone Number section later in this chapter for information about dialing a number.

GeoPlanner

This item is shown dimmed unless you have selected **Both View** from the View menu (or double-clicked on a letter tab) and are conducting a search for a text string. You can then click this button to search GeoPlanner for the text string. See Chapter 11 for a discussion about searching for text strings in GeoPlanner and GeoDex.

The Menu Bar

Two of the four menus on this bar, File and Edit, work in much the same way as they do in other GeoWorks Pro documents.

See the File Menu section in Chapter 8 for a discussion of the options on the File menu.

Edit Menu

This menu contains six options that allow you to delete cards, move or copy text from a file card to another card or to another application. See the Edit Menu section in Chapter 8 for a discussion about using the Cut, Copy, and Paste options. See the Edit Menu section in Chapter 11 for a discussion about using the Quick Copy and Quick Move commands.

Undo

You can select this option when you change your mind about an alteration to a card—whether you added, deleted, or edited text. When you select **Undo**, the program returns the card to its former contents, as they were before you made the change. The shortcut for this is **Alt-Backspace**.

Clear

If you have created an address card but have not inserted it in the card file, you can remove the card by clicking **Clear** on the Edit menu. The program removes the card immediately, without confirmation.

Delete

You can select this option to get rid of a previously saved file card. The program removes the card immediately, without confirmation.

View Menu

The View menu allows you to select three options for viewing the information in the GeoDex file: Card View, Browse View, and Both View.

Card View

This option displays the default card file view. You can flip through cards by clicking the **Next** or **Previous** buttons, and you can display the cards for a specific letter of the alphabet by clicking on a letter tab.

When Card View is active, you can create new cards or edit existing cards.

Browse View

When you select this option, the display changes to a list of names sorted alphabetically. You can scroll through the list to find the name you want. At the bottom of the list is a box for a phone number. When you click on a name to highlight it, the program displays that person's phone number in the box. You can click the up and down triangles to scroll through the list of phone numbers for the selected card.

You can dial the displayed phone number following the dialing instructions in the Dialing a Phone Number section later in this chapter.

Both View

When you choose this option, the display shows the Card View and the Browse View side by side, as shown in Figure 15.3.

You can double-click on a letter tab to change the display to the Both View option.

NOTE

Searching for Text

At the bottom right of the Both View display is a Search For box, in which you can enter a text string to search for. You must enter the text exactly as it occurs, including uppercase and lowercase, in the card or cards you want to match.

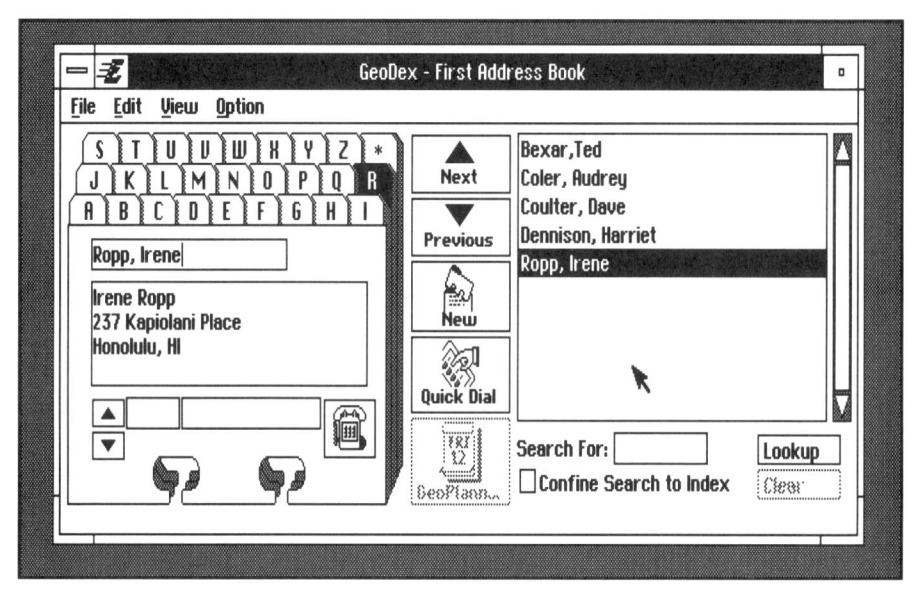

Figure 15.3. The GeoDex Both View Display.

Click the **Find Next** button to search for the text. If GeoDex finds an exact match, the program highlights the match in both views. When you begin a search, the **GeoPlanner** button on the left view becomes available. This means that you can open a GeoPlanner window and search the Events listings for the text string.

Continue clicking the **Find Next** button to search for more occurrences of the text string.

You can confine the search to the Index entries only and omit searching the address and phone number fields. Click on the **Confine Search to Index** button to select this option.

Click the **Clear** button to remove that text string and terminate the search request.

Option

This menu has one option: Dialing. You can use this option to set a default prefix or area code for every phone number you dial in the

GeoDex application. When you select the Option menu, the program displays the Dialing dialog box shown in Figure 15.4.

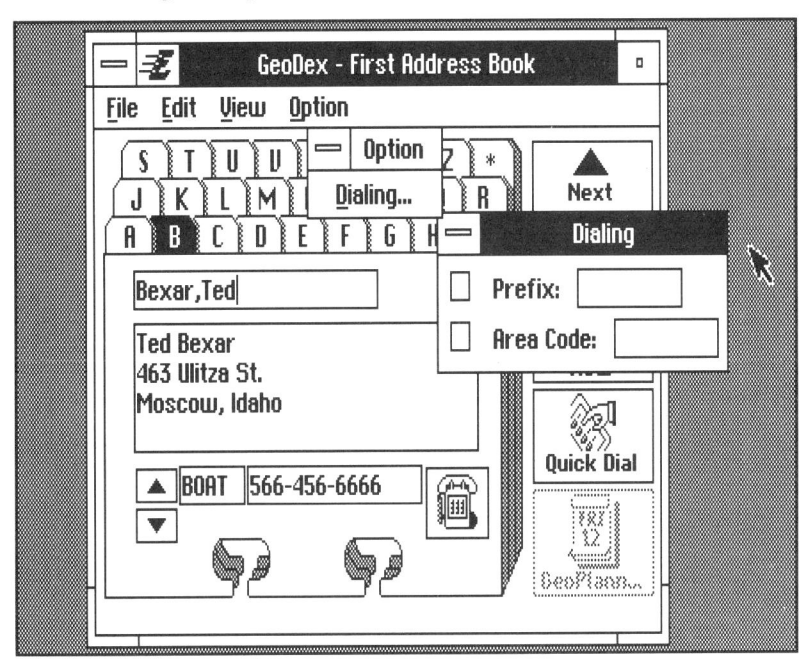

Figure 15.4. The Dialing Dialog Box.

The Prefix and Area Code buttons are toggles—they appear highlighted when they are turned on.

Prefix

You can enter any often-used or mandatory access code in this field. When the **Prefix** button is turned on, every phone call will be dialed with the prefix number. (See the procedure for entering phone numbers earlier in this chapter.)

Area Code

This option is handy if you take your computer on trips. Enter your area code and turn on this option to convert your otherwise local calls to long distance calls. Remember to include the number 1 with your area code.

The area code field can accept up to 10 numbers, making it easier to dial overseas numbers.

Dialing a Phone Number

Follow these steps to dial a phone number:

1. Make sure your phone is hung up correctly.

2. Flip through the index cards to display the card you want, or click the **Quick Dial** button and scroll to the name and number you want in the Quick Dial list.

3. Click: **Dial** button (which looks like a telephone) beside the displayed phone number. The program displays the Dialing message box to tell you that GeoDex is dialing the number. You will hear the modem dialing the number.

4. As soon as the modem finishes dialing, pick up the telephone and click the **Talk** button to reset the modem before it emits the loud connect tone.

Summary

You can use the GeoDex application to keep track of names, addresses, and phone numbers on separate index cards, creating more than one address book to organize your cards, if you wish. If you have a Hayes-compatible modem, you can also use GeoDex as a handy phone dialer to call local, long distance, or overseas numbers. You can move or copy text to other cards or other GeoWorks Pro applications. A search capability allows you to search GeoDex index cards and GeoPlanner Events lists for a string of text.

Chapter 16

America Online

GeoWorks Pro gives you convenient access to America Online, the bulletin board service. You must be a registered member of America Online to use it, and there is a monthly charge for the service. You can become a member of America Online directly from within GeoWorks Pro.

America Online offers a variety of services, including:

- Writing and receiving messages
- Receiving GeoWorks Pro updates and information
- Chatting online with other subscribers
- Getting answers to your computer problems
- Accessing public-domain and shareware programs
- Access to stock market prices
- EasySabre access, allowing you to make airline reservations
- Reading current news items
- Fax capabilities without a fax board
- Using the online Grolier's encyclopedia.

The GeoWorks Pro information and support available on America Online is particularly helpful. In addition to downloading program updates from the bulletin board, you can download other useful programs. There are many programs available for downloading that you will find practical in many areas of your computer operations. You can post any questions about GeoWorks Pro on the bulletin board and receive your answers within a day or so.

The interface for accessing and using this bulletin board is similar to that for other GeoWorks Pro applications. This makes America Online exceptionally easy to learn and use.

America Online Installation

America Online requires a Hayes (or Hayes-compatible) modem. America Online performance improves if your computer has 640K of memory, a hard drive, a mouse, and an EGA or higher-resolution monitor. (If you have a Tandy 1000, select CGA during installation.)

As America Online is installed as part of the GeoWorks Pro program, all that remains is for you to set up your system parameters. The usual way to start the America Online application is from the GeoManager World screen. When you double-click on the **America Online** icon, the America Online opening window is displayed, as shown in Figure 16.1.

See Chapter 4 for a discussion about using the features on a GeoWorks Pro application window, including the Control button, Express menu, and the Minimize and Maximize/Restore buttons.

The Menu Bar

The offline Menu bar contains seven menus: Help, File, Edit, Go To, Mail, Members, and Window. These menus are available whether you are online or offline, but there are some minor differences in the online and offline menu bars.

NOTE *Online* means that you are connected to and actively communicating with the service. *Offline* means the connection has not been made or has been terminated.

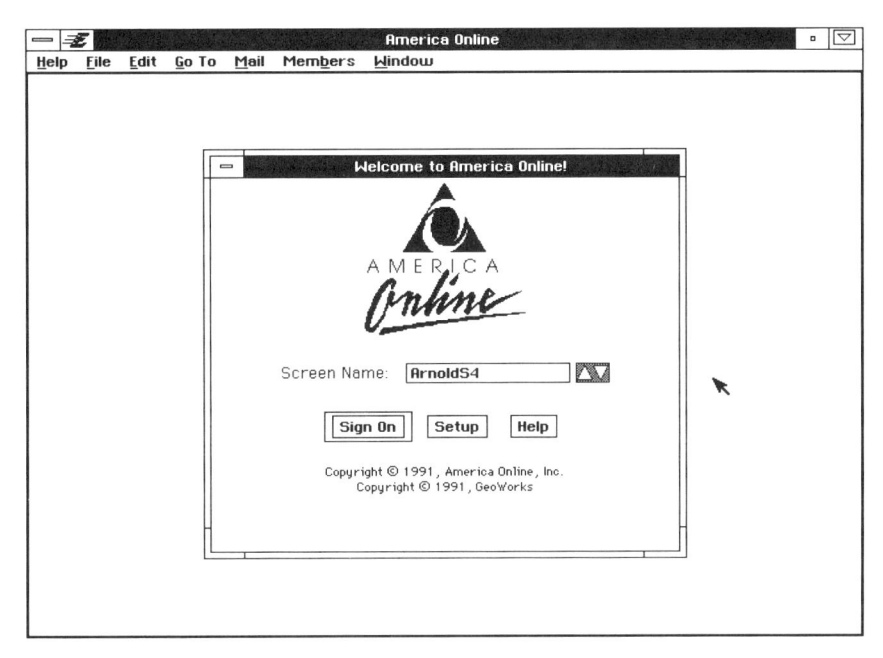

Figure 16.1. The America Online Opening Window.

Help Menu

The Help menu on the Welcome screen and Help menus on other windows offer immediate help about the America Online service.

Get Help

You can select this option to display the Get Help dialog box. When you click on a topic in the Topic panel, information about the topic displays in the Description panel.

About America Online

Select this option to view copyright information and the software version number of your America Online program.

File Menu

The File menu, shown in Figure 16.2, like other GeoWorks Pro File menus, allows you to create a new file, open, save or print an existing file, and exit the application. In addition, the America Online File menu allows you to open a communication log, perform DOS functions, and cancel an action.

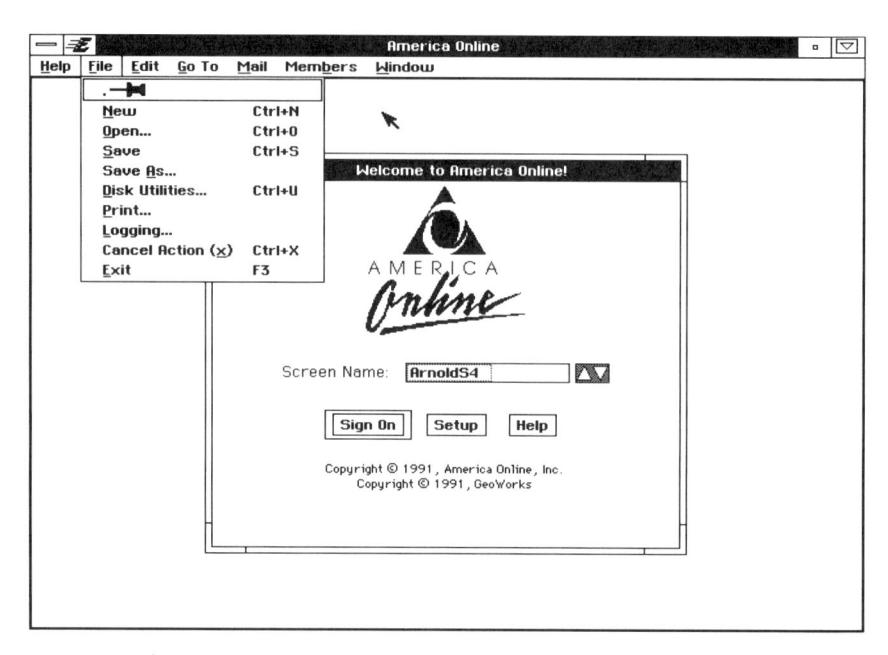

Figure 16.2. The America Online File Menu.

The Pin Symbol

See Chapter 8 for a discussion about the Pin Symbol on the File menu.

New

When you select this option, the program opens a new blank window named Untitled, overlaying any other open window. You can type mail memos in this window while you are offline, then post the message when you are online. This can save you considerable time online and the associated online charges.

When you are online and select **New** from the File menu, you can type the new document, or use **Paste** from the Edit menu to place online text into the new document. You can then save and print it. You can also attach text to a different document. See Chapter 8 for a full discussion of Edit menu functions like Paste.

Open

You can use this option to access other files (or conference logs), including those you create in America Online (using New from the File menu). You can read these while online, or, to limit connection charges, read them after you leave the service.

Save

This command allows you to save a document, e-mail (electronic mail), or a message you are reading online. You can specify the drive, directory and filename for the saved file. See Chapter 8 for a discussion about the Save option on the File menu.

Save As

This command allows you to duplicate an existing file and save it with a new filename. You can specify the drive, directory, and filename for the new file. See Chapter 8 for a discussion about the Save As option on the File menu.

Disk Utilities (Ctrl-U)

When you select this command from the File menu, the dialog box shown in Figure 16.3, Select a Drive, Directory, and File, is displayed. You then have a choice of the following:

- Opening the selected file
- Getting information about the file (i.e., filename, path to file, bytes in the file, file attributes, and last modification date)
- Deleting the selected file or directory (if the directory is empty)
- Renaming the selected file
- Modifying the file. Allows you to specify a new filename. You can also specify one of the following attributes for the file: read-only, archive, system, or hidden.

The free space of the drive is also displayed, and you can elect to have hidden files displayed. In addition, you can create a new directory, obtain help, or cancel any action and close the dialog box.

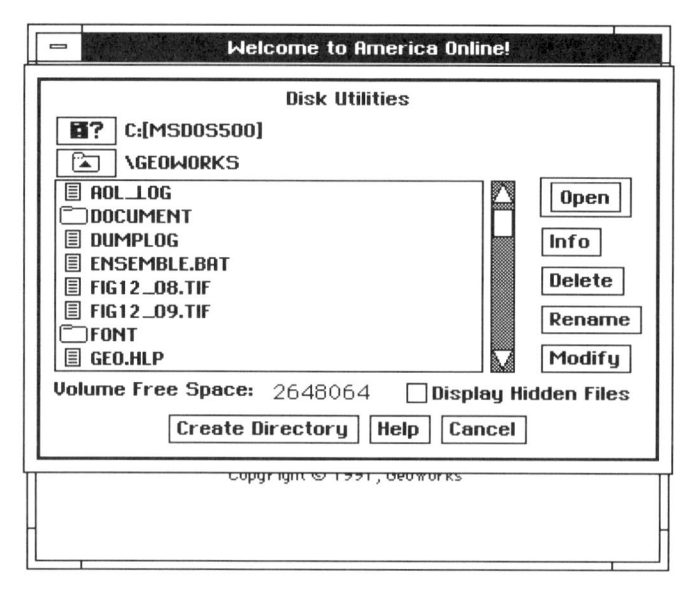

Figure 16.3. *The Disk Utilities Dialog Box.*

Print

This menu option allows you to print files, including those you have saved online, such as conference logs or encyclopedia articles. In order to use this command you must have your printer set up. See Chapter 8 for a discussion about the Print option on the File menu.

If you have not previously installed a printer or want to select a different one, you must terminate your America Online connection (if you are online) and select **Setup** from the offline menu to change your printer setup.

Logging

You can log your online activities, saving to disk a copy of the materials you read (for example, encyclopedia articles), or record your chat sessions with other America Online subscribers. You can edit the log offline, save the portions you want as a separate document and discard the original log. You can activate two types of logging: Conference and Session.

Conference Log

The conference log saves all text from all chat areas, including classrooms, forums, conference rooms, and America Online rooms.

Session Log

The session log saves information, such as encyclopedia articles, from all areas of America Online except the chat areas.

Opening a Log

Follow these steps to open a conference or session log:

1. Select: **Logging** from the File menu. The dialog box shown in Figure 16.4 is displayed.

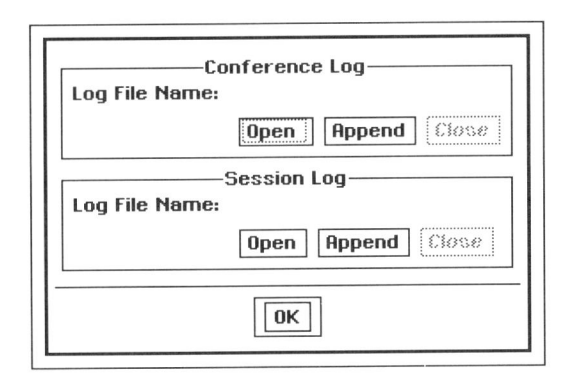

Figure 16.4. The Logging Dialog Box.

2. Click: **Open** button in the Conference Log panel or the Session Log panel in the dialog box. The dialog box shown in Figure 16.5 is displayed.

3. Select: Drive and subdirectory in which you want to save the log. The default filename shown is LOGFILE.TXT. You can change this filename and its extension if you want.

4. Click: **Save** to accept the specified path and filename.

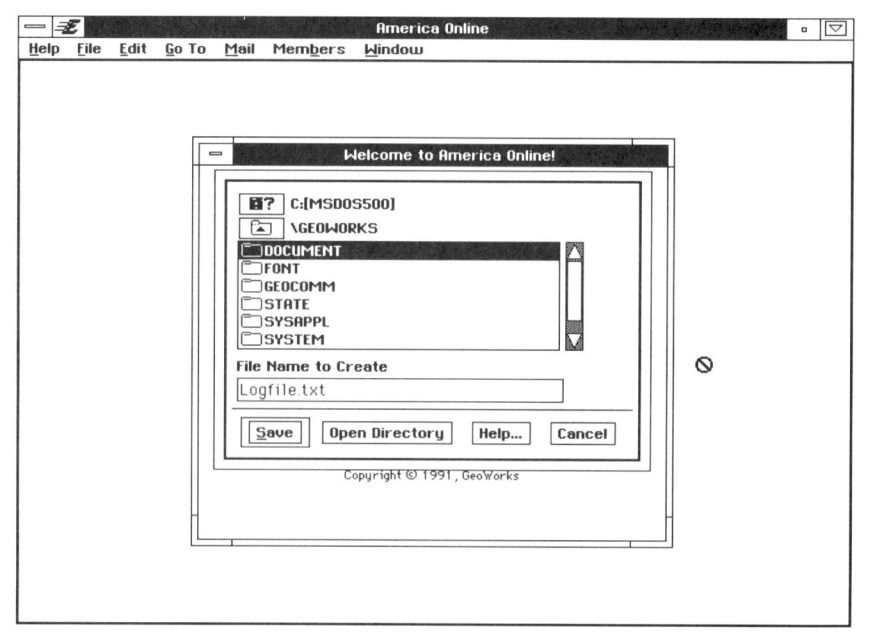

Figure 16.5. The Logging File to Open Dialog Box.

5. The program displays the specified Log File Name in the log window. Click **OK** to accept the file name.

6. When you want to close the log, select **Logging** from the File menu, then click the **Close** button.

NOTE If you exit America Online without closing the Log file, the program will open the log (and start recording again) the next time you go online.

WARNING Conference and Session logs can use a great deal of disk space. If you are saving to a floppy disk, be careful to close the log before you run out of disk space. You can then replace the disk with a new floppy and open a new log.

Reading a Log

Follow these steps to read a log file:

1. Exit America Online (if you are online).
2. Select: **Open** from the File menu.
3. In the File to Open dialog box, select the drive and directory where you saved the log, then select the file you want to read.

Cancel (Ctrl+X)

Select this option to cancel any action in progress (e.g., canceling a file transmission).

Exit (F3)

Select this option to exit America Online (go offline). When you select **Exit**, the program asks you to confirm that you want to exit. When you select **Yes**, you return to the Welcome to America Online window, and the program terminates the telephone connection.

You can also double-click the **Control** button at the top left of the America Online window to go offline.

Edit Menu

See the Edit Menu section in Chapter 8 for a full discussion about using the Cut, Copy, and Paste options on the Edit menu.

Go To Menu

When you are online, this menu allows you to go directly to any area of service and to perform a variety of tasks relating to America Online. Figure 16.6. shows the Go To menu. Many of the Go To menu commands are dimmed when you are offline. Dimmed items are not available until you go online. These items provide quick access to a variety of information sources in America Online.

Set Up & Sign On

When you create a message offline and you are ready to send it, use the **Set Up and Sign On** command on the Go To menu to go back to the opening screen (Figure 16.1). Your message remains open, and when you access the bulletin board, the Send button becomes undimmed, allowing you to send the message.

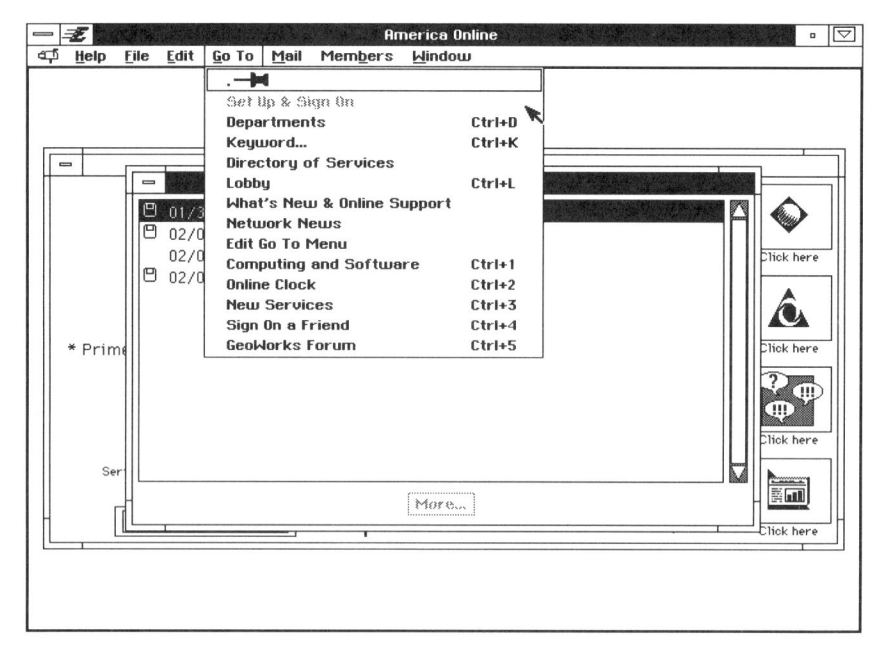

Figure 16.6. The Go To Menu.

Set Up

If you select this button from the Opening Screen, a setup dialog appears, as shown in Figure 16.7.

This dialog box allows you to specify your phone type, either tone or pulse. Click on the appropriate radio button to select it. Next, specify the port where your modem is connected. Click on the correct choice from the list.

You can now set up the information required to connect with two phone numbers—a First Try and a Second Try. Enter the phone numbers, the baud rate for your modem, and the network service that you have.

The next two sections let you enter a prefix for reaching an outside line (if that is necessary) and a code for disabling call waiting if you have that service. The items are dimmed if they do not apply. See the Dialing a Phone Number section in Chapter 15 for more information about phone numbers.

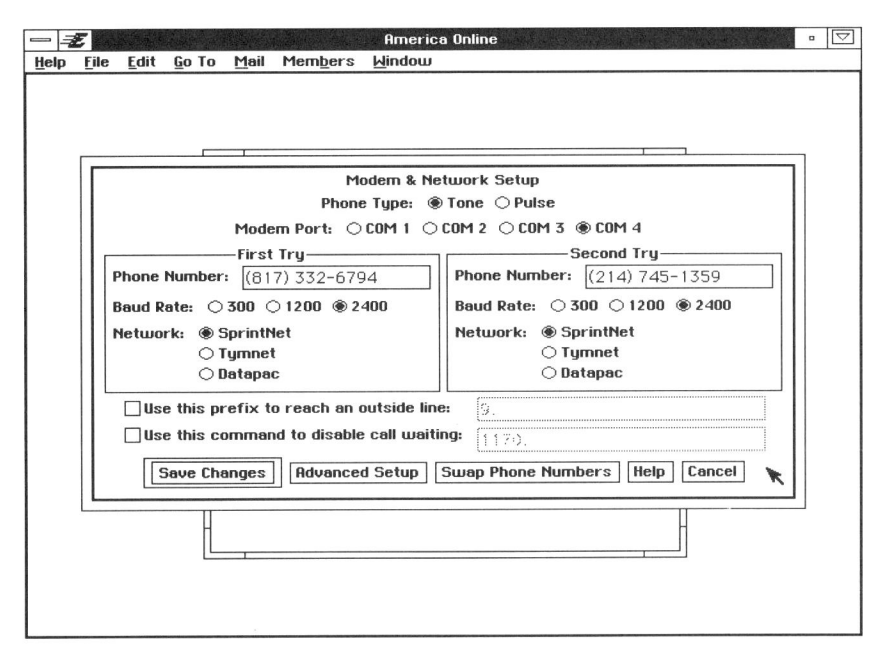

Figure 16.7. The Setup Dialog Box.

After you make your selections, you have a choice of five buttons. Click on **Save Changes** to put your choices into effect. Selecting **Cancel** returns you to the previous screen.

Clicking the **Swap Phone Number** button switches the information contained in the First Try and Second Try boxes.

If you click on the **Advanced Setup** button, a second dialog box appears as shown in Figure 16.8.

This dialog box allows you to enter a Pre-Modem String and a Post-Modem String. There are three buttons to choose from on this box. Select **OK** to accept your entries. **Cancel** takes you back to the previous screen. Clicking on **System Preferences** displays the Preferences Application window. This is exactly the same as the window discussed in Chapter 6. Refer to that chapter for information on all the options in the Preferences window.

If you need further information on setting up, select the **Help** button. This displays a screen with a list of seven relevant topics. Choose the one you want and click the **Help** button to display the help topic. Click **Cancel** when you have finished.

308 • *Teach Yourself GeoWorks*

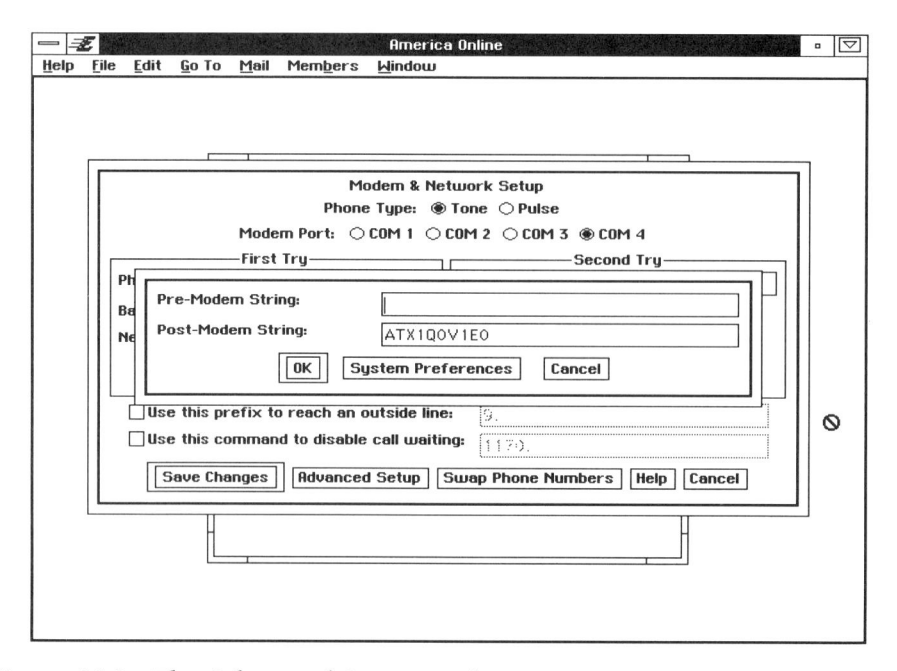

Figure 16.8. The Advanced Setup Dialog Box.

NOTE You can also click on the **Help** button at the bottom of the America Online display (see Figure 16.1). This help screen has a much more extensive list of help topics.

Sign On

Selecting **Sign On** from the Opening Screen displays a series of screens that guide you through the sign-on/registration procedure. The first screen in the sign-on process displays the telephone number you are trying to access. You can press **Cancel** to terminate the Sign-on process.

After you have accessed the network, the next screen prompts you for your password. Figure 16.9 shows a password being entered. Notice the password is not displayed; each letter is shown as an asterisk.

After your password is accepted, the Welcome opening screen shown in Figure 16.10 is displayed.

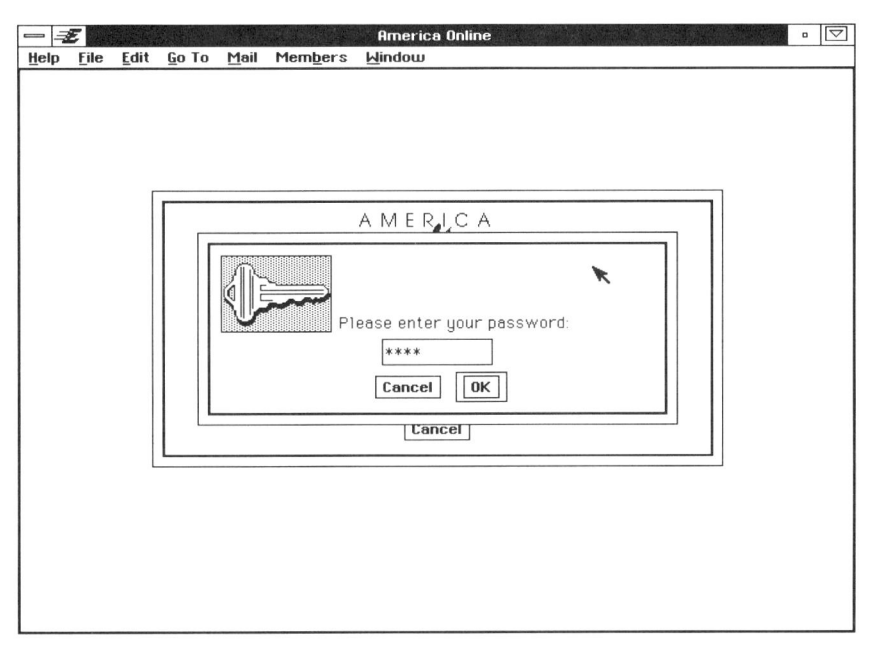

Figure 16.9. Entering a Password.

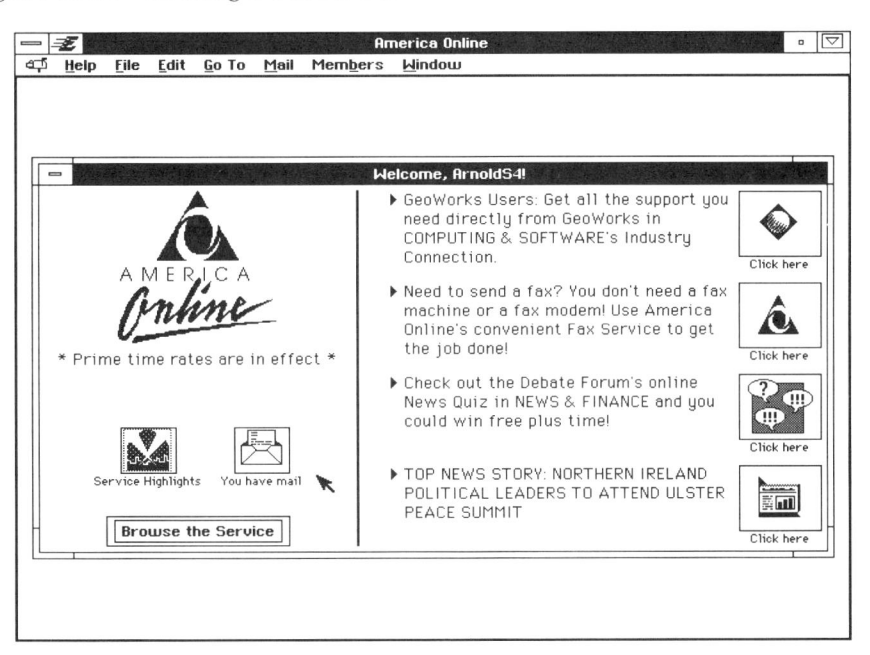

Figure 16.10. The America Online Welcome Opening Screen.

If you have mail waiting for you, you are notified by two short computer beeps and the envelope symbol in the lower-left section of the screen is not dim. You have several choices from this Welcome screen. For example, clicking on **Service Highlights** displays the screen shown in Figure 16.11.

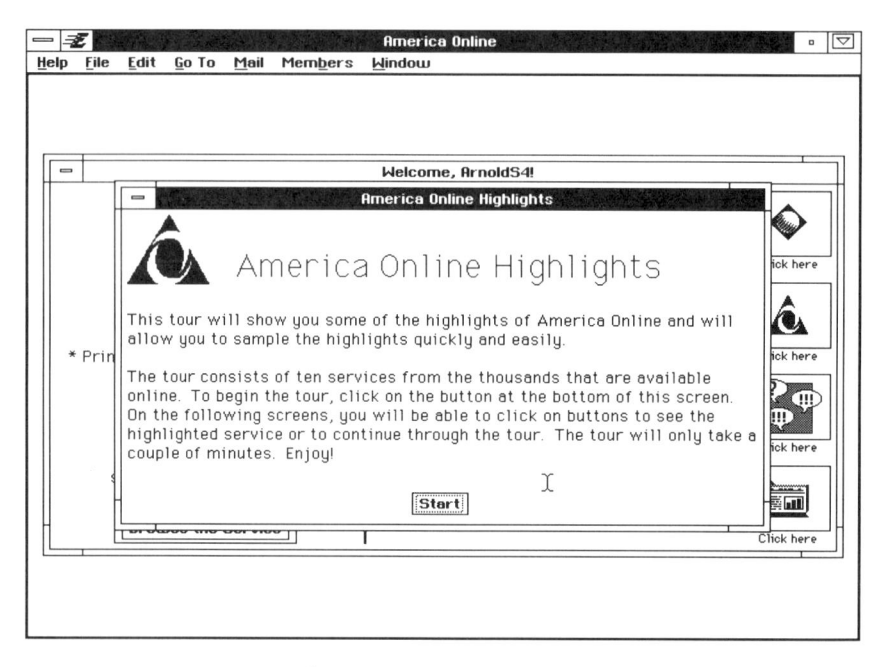

Figure 16.11. America Online Highlights.

If you click on the envelope **You have mail**, a New Mail Dialog Box is displayed. A typical New Mail Dialog Box is shown in Figure 16.12.

Notice that a mailbox has been added to the extreme left of the menu bar at the top of the screen. If you choose not to immediately display your waiting mail you can quickly access your mail at any time you want to by clicking the Mailbox symbol.

With the New Mail Dialog Box displayed, you can double-click (or highlight and click) a mail item to display it. When your mail is displayed there are four buttons on the left side and scroll bars on the right side. If the mail item is long, use the scroll bars to display all of it.

America Online • 311

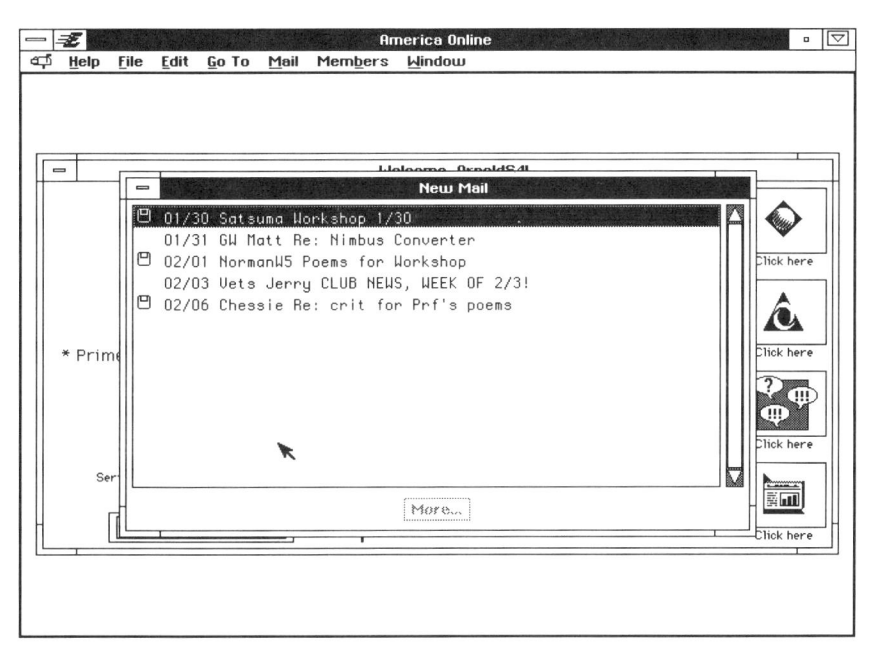

Figure 16.12. A Typical New Mail Dialog Box.

When a mail item is displayed, four buttons appear on the left side of the mail item window, as shown in Figure 16.13:

Reply Click this to display a form with the To box filled in with the name of the person who sent you the mail.

Forward Click this to forward the message to another person. You will have to specify the person to whom you want to forward the message

Reply to All Click this to reply to all recipients of the original letter.

Download File Click this to download a file "attached" to the mail. You must specify the drive and directory into which you want the file downloaded. You can also change the suggested name of the downloaded file.

In Figure 16.13 a message containing an attached file is displayed. The **Download File** button has been clicked and 21% of the file has been downloaded. Before the downloading starts you can click the Sign off after transfer box. This will immediately initiate the sign-off (going offline) process after the file is downloaded to disk. Often, you may sign on just to download a single file, and this reduces your online time.

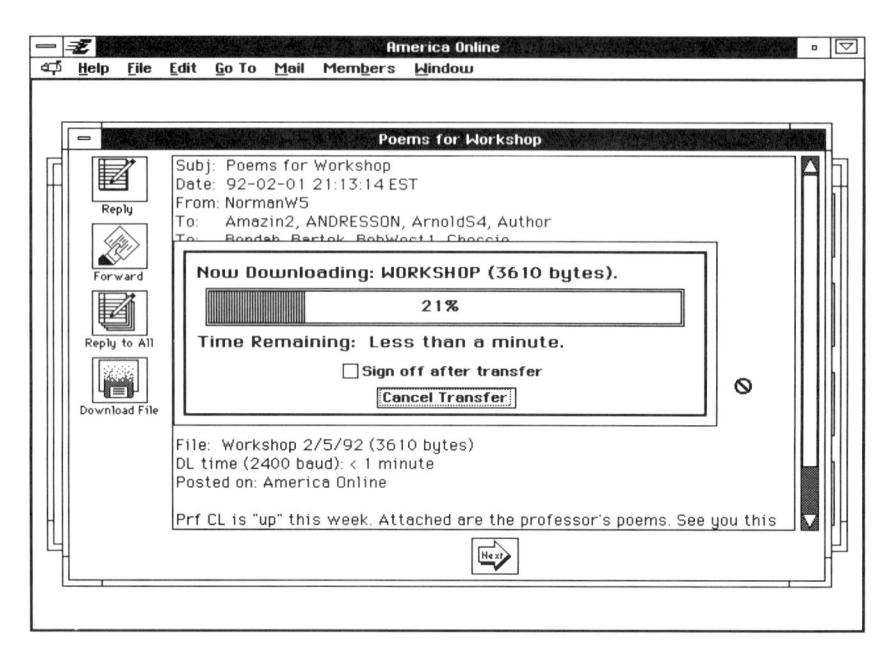

Figure 16.13. Downloading An Attached File to a Message.

After the attached file is downloaded, if you did not click the Sign off after transfer dialog box, you can click **More** at the bottom of the New Mail dialog box (as shown in Figure 16.12) to display the next item. If you have read all the new mail and click **More**, a dialog box indicating there is no new mail is displayed. Click **OK** to close the dialog box and return to the New Mail Dialog Box. Double-click the **Control** button on the New Mail Dialog Box to close it.

Departments (Ctrl+D)

Selecting this option from the Go To Menu displays the Browse the Service dialog box shown in Figure 16.14. A similar screen is displayed when you click the Browse the Service button in the America Online Welcome screen (see Figure 16.10). Buttons on the top of the panel display available departments.

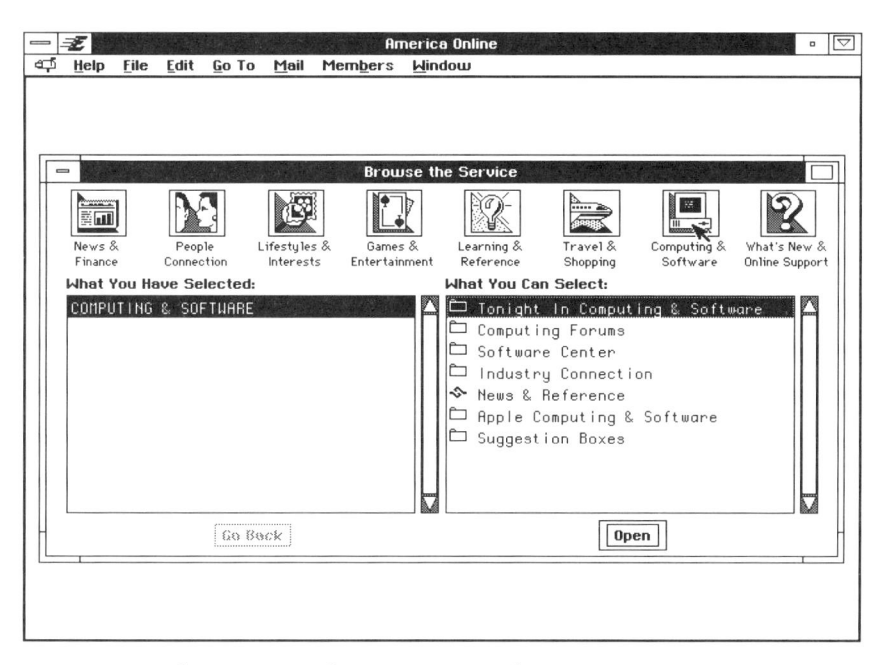

Figure 16.14. The Browse the Service Dialog Box.

Below the row of buttons are two panels. When you select a department button, your selection is listed in the left panel. In Figure 16.14 the Computing & Software button was selected. In this case the left panel shows only one item. The right panel displays the contents of the highlighted option in the left panel. In the right panel the symbol at the left of each item indicates the item type.

Select an item in the right panel to search through the program directories. Double-click on an item to display its contents. You can go back to previous levels or select other options in the department by clicking on the appropriate items in the panels.

Keyword (Ctrl+K)

You can use Keyword for shortcut access to various areas of America Online. Select the **Keyword** option from the Go To menu, type a keyword, then click the **OK** button. To see a list of department-specific keywords, select **Keyword Help** from the Keyword window.

Directory of Services

Select this option to learn about the America Online services. The information on each service includes: the service name, keywords (if applicable), search words (if applicable), access path to the service, and a description of the service.

Lobby (Ctrl+L)

Selecting this option gives you access to a large selection of conversation areas where you can chat with other members currently online, or receive information left by other members.

What's New & Online Support

This option removes you from online status and places you in a free-of-charge area which gives you access to information relating to America Online.

Network News

This option gives you access to current information relating to the Network.

Edit Go To Menu

This option gives you quick access to editing the last five menu items on the Go To menu. The ones currently listed are suggested areas you might want to access quickly. They are shown in Figure 16.6 together with their shortcuts. You can change these menu entries to list areas you use often. If you do this, you must also change the associates Keyword entry to correspond to your new menu entry. The shortcut keys do not change.

Mail Menu

The Mail menu shown in Figure 16.15 allows you to write mail, check mail you've read, check mail you've sent, send a fax or paper mail, and edit your address book.

Compose Mail (Ctrl+M)

You can use this option to compose and send electronic mail to another America Online member.

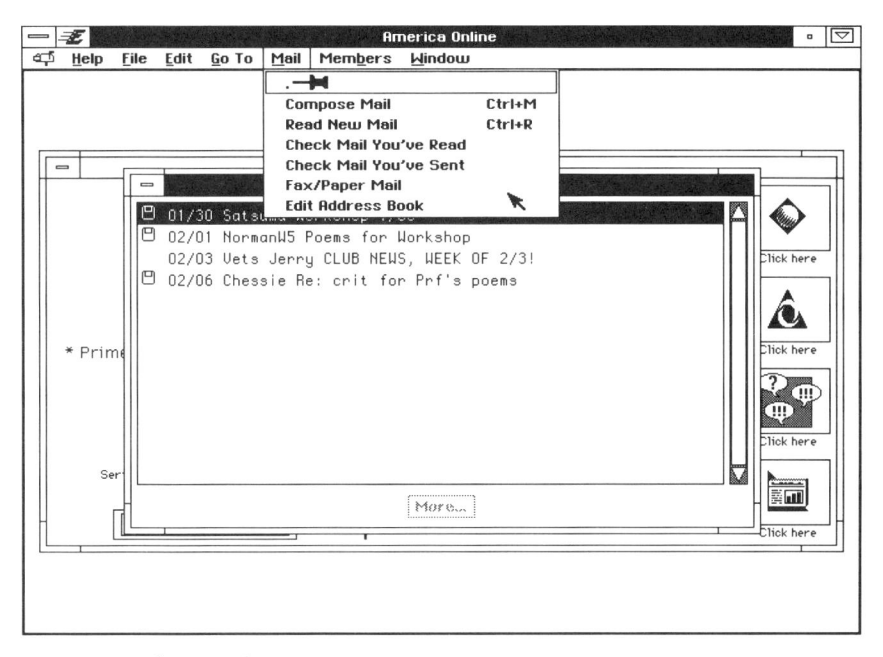

Figure 16.15. The Mail Menu.

1. When you choose **Compose Mail** from the Mail menu, the Compose Mail dialog box shown in Figure 16.16 is displayed.

2. Address the mail memo by typing in the screen name(s) of the member(s) to whom you want the mail sent in the To: box. If you are addressing the mail to more than one person, separate each screen name with a comma, but don't put spaces between names. Use CC: (carbon copy) to enter the screen names of any others to whom you want to send a copy of the mail.

3. Type the subject of your mail memo in the Subj: field. You must complete this field.

4. Type your mail message in the large File panel.

To reduce your connect time, use **Compose Mail** while offline. The Send button is dimmed while offline, but when you sign on you will be able to send your mail.

NOTE

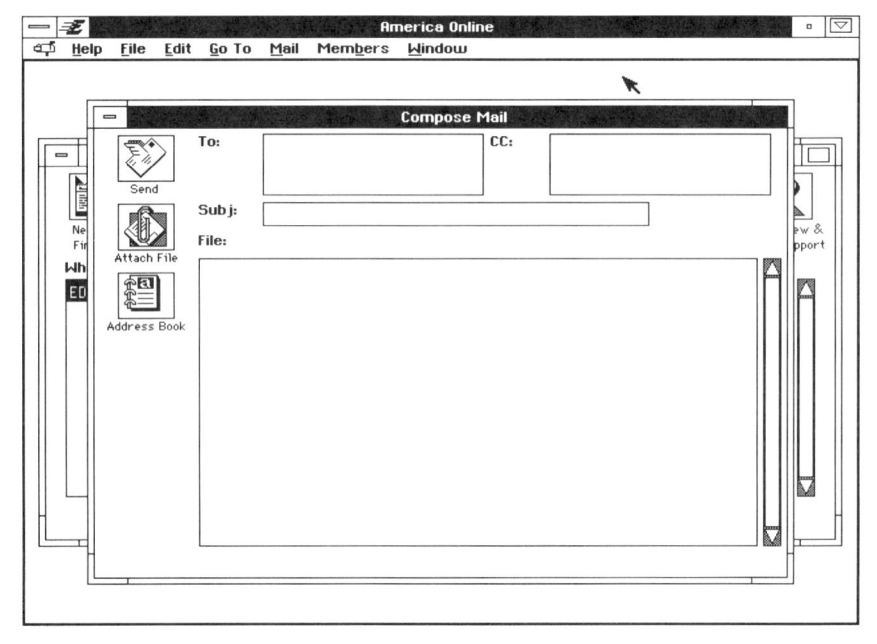

Figure 16.16. The Compose Mail Dialog Box.

The three buttons to the left of the message area are used as follows:

Address Book

The Address Book button can be used to paste names into the proper fields. You do this by clicking the **Address Book** button on the left to display your saved addresses. Highlight the recipient's name, and click **To:** or **CC:** to paste the name in the field.

Attach File

The Attach File button can be used to attach files to your mail. You do this by clicking the **Attach File** button, and then specifying the drive, directory, and filename of the file you want to attach. Click **Open** and the name of the selected file is displayed in the File field, and the Attach File symbol changes to Detach File. The Detach File symbol allows you to change your mind about sending the file.

Send

Clicking the **Send** button immediately sends your mail.

Read New Mail

If there is mail you have not read you can elect to immediately read it by clicking the **You have mail** button (see Figure 16.10) when you sign on. If you elect not to immediately read your unread mail you later access it by choosing **Read New Mail** from the Mail menu. You can also access your unread mail by clicking on the mailbox symbol on the menu bar.

Any of these methods displays a New Mail Dialog box with a list of your unread mail. Double-click on the message you want to read.

Reply Button

With your new mail displayed you can easily reply to it. You can use the Reply button on the left of the message area to respond to the sender of the message, (see Figure 16.13.) When you select this option, the program automatically addresses the reply to the person who sent you the currently displayed mail. The program inserts the name of the person who sent you the mail into the To: field, and the same subject in the Subj: field preceded by Re:. You can change these fields if you wish. Type your reply, attaching a file if you want to, then click the **Send** button.

Download Attached File

The program displays a diskette symbol next to the title of new mail that has a file attached to it. The program also displays the approximate time required to download the attached file (copy it from the America Online service to your hard disk or a floppy disk).

To download the attached file click the **Download File** button. The program displays a dialog box in which you select the drive, subdirectory and filename for the saved file. To rename the file, highlight the filename and type the new filename. Click the **Save** button to save the file.

Check Mail You've Read

Select this command in the Mail menu to reread mail you've already received. When you select this option, an Old Mail dialog box is displayed. Double-click on the title of the mail you want to reread.

The program automatically deletes any mail sent to you that is over seven days old. You can read or reread your mail any time within the seven days.

Check Mail You've Sent

Select this command to reread mail you've sent. When you select this option a Check Mail You've Sent dialog box is displayed. Double-click on the title of the mail you want to reread.

The program deletes any outgoing mail that is over seven days old.

Fax/Paper Mail

To send a fax (facsimile transmission) or send paper mail using the America Online service, select **Fax/Paper Mail** from the Mail menu. The program displays the Browse the Service window with the current price structure and instructions for these communications.

When you are ready to proceed, click the **Send Fax/Paper Mail** button and follow the procedures described earlier in the Compose Mail section. You can send only one kind of message at a time: paper mail, electronic mail, or fax.

Fax

You can compose your fax in the mail window or copy a saved memo file into the mail window. You cannot attach a file to a fax transmission. If you want to send mail created with a word processor outside the GeoWorks Pro program, make sure to save the file as an ASCII file (DOS text) before opening America Online.

The To: field for a fax communication requires a name and fax phone number (including area code), for example, Deitz Bexar@800-555-1212. You can use up to 20 characters in the name, including uppercase or lowercase characters, blank spaces, and punctuation marks (except commas and parentheses). The fax charge is displayed and you can confirm or cancel the action.

Paper Mail

For paper mail you must type the name and address using the following format: `Deitz Bexar@usmail`. Type the message and click the **Send** button. A dialog box is displayed prompting you for the recipient's street address and your return address. The charge is displayed and you can confirm or cancel the action. If you confirm the action, your letter is printed and mailed in a standard #10 envelope within 24 hours.

Edit Address Book

The Address Book saves you time by allowing you to quickly enter an address or group distribution list. To enter an address in the Address Book, click the **Create** button. To edit an existing address, highlight it and then click the **Modify** button. To delete an address, highlight it and then click the **Delete** button.

Group Name Field

To create a group address, click in the **Group Name** field and type the name you want in your Address Book. Next click in the **Screen Names** field and enter the names you want associated with the group name. Press **Enter** to complete the entry in the Address Book.

Members Menu

The Members menu shown in Figure 16.17 allows you to contact other members currently online and obtain information about them.

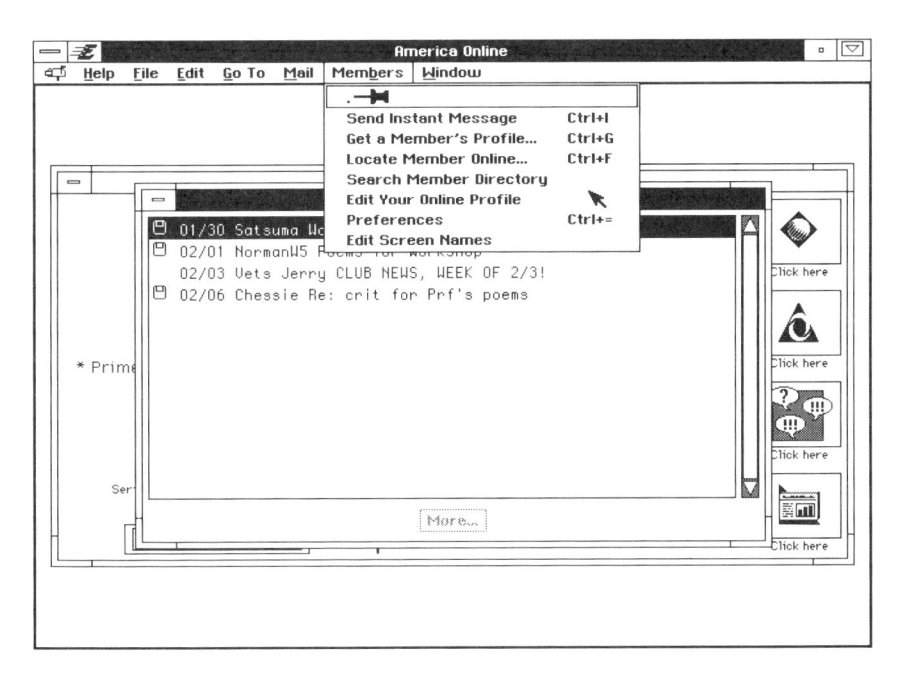

Figure 16.17. The Members Menu.

Send Instant Message (Ctrl-I)

Use **Send Instant Message** to send a quick message to another member who is currently on the bulletin board. The program displays a dialog box in which you enter the recipient's screen name. You can then verify whether the member is currently online by clicking the **Available** button. If the member is online, type the message to send in the window, then click the **Send** button.

To respond to an instant message you receive, click the **Respond** button, type your response, and then click the **Send** button.

Get a Member's Profile (Ctrl-G)

The Get a Member's Profile command permits you to access personal profiles of America Online members so you can find members with interests similar to yours.

Enter the screen name of the member you want in the dialog box that appears and click **OK**. The member's profile is displayed.

Locate Member Online (Ctrl-F)

The Locate Member Online command allows you to find the location of a member who is currently on the bulletin board. Type the screen name of the member you want to locate, then click the **OK** button. The program displays a message indicating if the member is online and in which chat area. Click **OK** to continue. Double-click on the **Control** button (or select **Cancel**) to close the window.

Search Member Directory

This command allows you to search for a member by his or her real name or screen name. A dialog box using the same format as that of Figure 16.14 allows you to conduct the search.

Edit Your Online Profile

This option allows you to enter information about yourself for other members to access.

Edit Screen Names

This option allows you to create five screen names your yourself. You can change four of these at any time (one is permanent).

Preferences

When you select this command, the dialog box shown in Figure 16.18 is displayed.

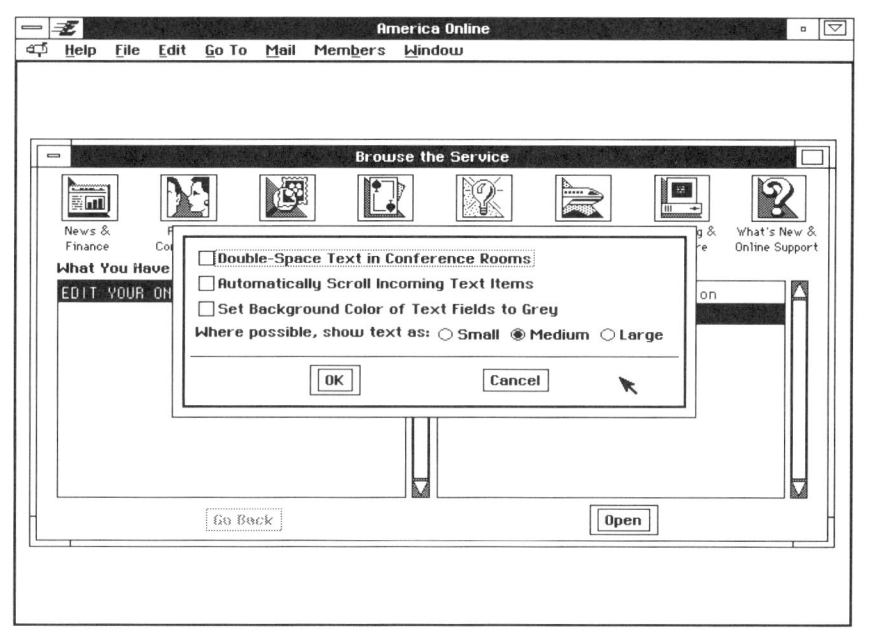

Figure 16.18. The Preferences Dialog Box.

The Preferences dialog box allows you to specify the way you want your displays to be formatted in America Online.

Window Menu

The Window Menu allows you to close or hide windows and also indicates all open windows.

Hide

Choose this command to hide a window. The window remains open, but is not displayed in the viewing area. To re-display the window, choose the title of the hidden window from the bottom of the Window menu.

Close (Ctrl-F4)

Choose this command to close the active window. You can also close the window by double-clicking the **Control** button in the upper-left corner of the window.

Close All Windows (Ctrl-F9)

Choose this command to close all displayed windows. Remember you can move or resize windows with double borders to allow you to see other information. To move a window, drag the title bar. To resize a window, place the mouse pointer on a double border. When it changes to a double headed arrow, click the left mouse button and drag the border to resize the window.

Bottom Section of Window Menu

The bottom section of the Window menu lists all open windows. Select a window to make it the active window.

Summary

This chapter described the services and features available in the America Online bulletin board service. If you have a modem, you can subscribe to and use the America Online service from within GeoWorks Pro.

Chapter 17

The GeoComm Application

In this chapter you will learn how to use the GeoComm application to communicate with bulletin boards, online services such as America Online, or other personal computers. You will learn how to:

- Create text or retrieve a file to send to the remote computer
- Retrieve text, saving it to the hard disk
- Configure GeoComm for your hardware
- Write scripts to automate repetitive communication tasks, such as logging onto a bulletin board you use frequently.

The GeoComm application allows you to communicate through a modem over telephone lines with other computers. A modem is a computer translation device. It translates information from your computer into a form that can be sent over telephone lines. At the other end of the telephone line a modem then translates the information back to a form that the other computer can understand.

Accessing the GeoComm Application

You can access the GeoComm application two ways:

- Double-clicking the GeoComm icon in the GeoManager World directory
- Selecting GeoComm from the Express Menu/Startup option.

Except for the title bar and menu bar, the opening GeoComm window is blank when you open the program.

See Chapters 4 and 5 for discussions about the features and functions of application windows.

Figure 17.1 shows a pinned File menu from the GeoComm application with three cascading menus displayed.

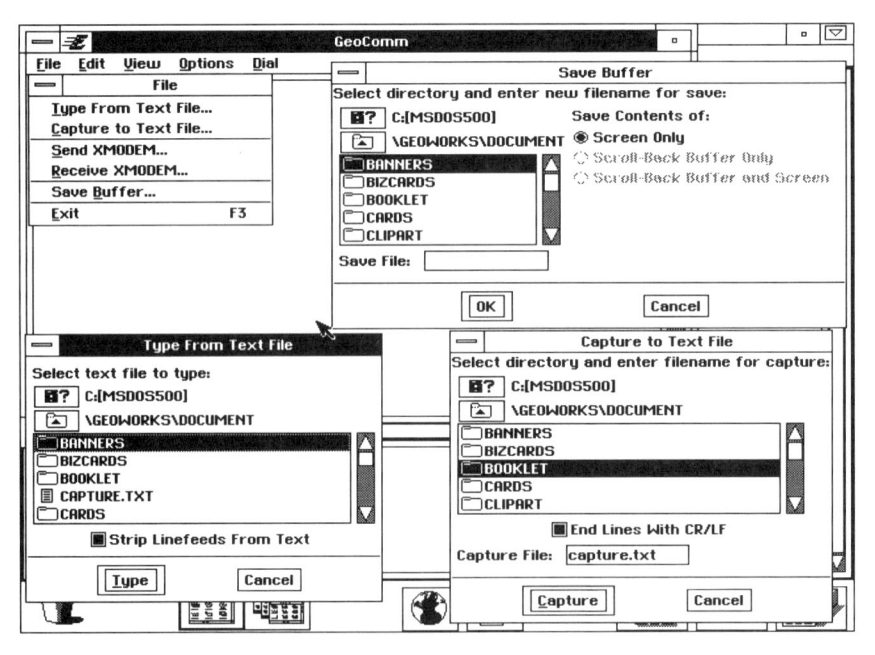

Figure 17.1. Pinned File Menu and Three Cascading Menus.

Figure 17.2 shows the same pinned File menu and the remaining two cascading menus that are accessible from the File menu.

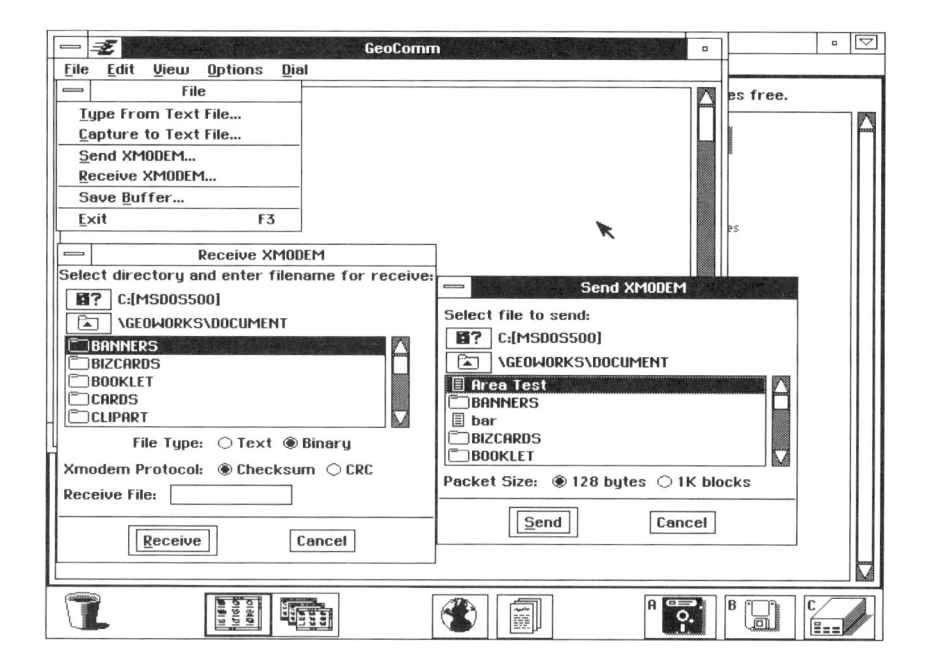

Figure 17.2. The GeoComm File Menu and Two Other Cascading Menus.

When the GeoComm window is active, the cursor displays as a solid black rectangle. When the GeoComm window is not active, the cursor displays as an outline (not filled). Click on the GeoComm window to make it the active window; the cursor displays as a solid rectangle. When the GeoComm window is active, the program immediately sends to the remote computer anything you type in the GeoComm window.

The following describes the GeoComm menus.

File Menu

You can use the File menu, as shown in Figure 17.1 and Figure 17.2, for file-related functions.

Type From Text File

Once you establish communication with a remote computer (you are *online*), you can then exchange information. When you disconnect from the remote computer you are *offline*. Some bulletin boards determine your charges by the number of minutes you are online. When you are online, the program sends whatever you type in the GeoComm window to the remote computer (or bulletin board). The program places information you receive from the remote computer in your window at the cursor position.

You can reduce your online time by composing messages offline. You can send files from other applications, send DOS text files, or copy text from other documents into the GeoComm window. Select the **Type From Text File** option to copy DOS text files into GeoComm.

When you select this option, the program displays the Type From Text File dialog box. This dialog box is shown in Figure 17.1 in the lower-left corner of the window. The dialog box shows drive C: as the current drive and the current directory as \GEOWORKS\DOCUMENT. See Chapter 8 for a discussion about selecting subdirectories and files.

GeoComm works only with DOS files. As you move around subdirectories you will not see any GEOS-type documents listed in the subdirectory contents window when you use the Type From Text File option. For example, the program will not display any GeoWrite documents, which are GEOS-type files.

You can, however, open a GeoWrite text window on your screen, select (highlight) text that you want to transmit, then copy it to the GeoComm window. You can use Quick Copy or Quick Move to copy the highlighted text to the GeoComm window for transmission.

The following outlines the procedure for sending (transmitting) a DOS text file.

1. Select the **Type From Text File** option on the File menu. The program displays the Type From Text File dialog box.

2. Select the drive, subdirectory, and filename of the file you want to send.

3. Click the **Strip Linefeeds From Text** option to remove linefeeds. Normally you want this option turned On. Contact the computer service you are calling to determine whether the service requires this option.

4. Click the **Type** button on the Type From Text File dialog box. The program displays a status window indicating the name of the file you are transmitting and the contents of the file.

5. Click the **Stop** button in the status window to stop the transfer of data.

Capture to Text File

Select this option to store data as you receive it, specifying a drive, subdirectory, and filename for the data. You can also decide when to start and stop recording data. The following steps outline the procedure for saving incoming data to a file.

1. Select the **Capture to Text File** option from the File menu. The program displays the Capture to Text File dialog box.

2. Select the drive and subdirectory in which you want to save the file.

3. Enter a DOS filename in the Capture File: box (one to eight characters followed by a period and an optional one to three characters as an extension) for the file. The program displays the default file name CAPTURE.TXT.

4. Select the **End Lines With CR/LF** option to have linefeeds after each carriage return. Normally you want this option turned On.

5. Select the **Capture** button. The program displays the Capture Status window. Everything you send or receive is saved to disk in the file you specified.

6. Click the **Done** button in the Capture Status window when you want to stop recording data.

Send XMODEM

When you type into the GeoComm window or transmit a DOS file using the Type From Text File option, the program does not check for errors in the transmitted data. On noisy telephone lines, errors can be so severe that the received text is incomprehensible. The XMODEM technique uses error checking to ensure essentially error-free transmissions, even on noisy telephone lines.

When you send or receive files using XMODEM, the program transfers the file in blocks of data. Each block is tested to make sure it transferred properly and without error. If the program detects an error, it retransmits the faulty block.

Both the local and remote computers must use the XMODEM operation. You can use XMODEM to send DOS files or binary files such as GEOS documents. The following outlines the steps required to send a document using XMODEM.

1. Make sure the remote computer or bulletin board is set up to receive XMODEM. To do this, you must specify whether you are sending a text file or a non-text file (a binary file). Usually the instructions for setting up a remote computer to receive XMODEM are listed on the bulletin board you are calling. If not, contact the computer service.

2. Select the **Send XMODEM** option from the File menu. The program displays the Send XMODEM dialog box, which is shown in Figure 17.2 in the lower-right corner of the window.

3. Locate the file you want to send by selecting the drive, subdirectory, and filename.

4. Select a Packet Size of **1K blocks** (1,000 bytes) if your telephone connection is relatively good and the remote computer accepts 1K blocks. If not, select 128 bytes.

5. Click the **Send** button. The program displays the Send Status window indicating that the file is being transmitted and noting any errors encountered during the transmission.

6. Click the **Cancel** button if you want to stop the file transmission.

Receive XMODEM

Receiving XMODEM files is similar to sending them. The following steps outline the procedure for receiving XMODEM files. You might use this mode to download files or programs from a bulletin board.

1. Prepare the remote computer or bulletin board for XMODEM transmission. To do this, specify that you want to receive an XMODEM transmission. The instructions for setting up the remote computer to send XMODEM are usually listed on the bulletin board you are calling. If not, contact the computer service.

2. Select the **Receive XMODEM** option from the File menu. The program displays the Receive XMODEM dialog box, as shown in Figure 17.2 in the lower-left corner of the window.

3. Specify the drive and subdirectory in which you want to save the file.

4. Enter a DOS filename (one to eight characters followed by a period and an optional one to three characters as an extension) for the file.

5. Select the **File Type** option: Text or Binary. Select **Text** to receive a DOS text file. Select **Binary** to receive a GEOS document or a program file. (Some bulletin boards allow you to download software programs that are either shareware or in the public domain.)

6. Select **CRC** if the remote system uses CRC checking (Cyclic Redundancy Check). Select **Checksum** if the remote system doesn't allow CRC. CRC is a better error-checking method than the Checksum method. Both methods, however, should produce the same results: error-free transmissions. If you are not sure which setting to use, select Checksum.

7. The **Receive** button. The program displays the Receive Status window, indicating the name of the file you are receiving and any errors occurring during the transmission. To stop receiving the file, click the **Cancel** button.

If the program dims the Cancel button, it means you cannot interrupt the file transfer.

NOTE

Save Buffer

As you transmit or receive a file, the program displays the data on the screen. The program scrolls text upward as the data fills the screen. The program stores the most-recently displayed 175 lines in a special display buffer (storage device) called the scroll-back buffer.

Use the vertical scroll bar to view lines that have scrolled off the screen, up to the last 175 lines. To view the currently active screen again, move the vertical scroll bar to the bottom.

The program stores the text in the scroll-back buffer in DOS text format. You can save the contents of the scroll-back buffer as a DOS text file by following these steps:

1. Select the **Save Buffer** option on the File menu. The program displays the Save Buffer dialog box, shown in Figure 17.1.

2. Select the drive and subdirectory in which you want to save the buffer contents.

3. Select the **Save File** button. Type a DOS filename for the buffer file (one to eight characters, followed by a period and an optional one-to-three characters as an extension).

4. Select one of the save options on the right side of the Save Buffer dialog box:

    - **Screen Only** Use this option to save only the contents of the currently displayed screen

    - **Scroll-Back Buffer Only** Use this option to save the information that has scrolled past the top of the screen

    - **Scroll-Back Buffer and Screen** Use this option to save both the contents of the scroll-back buffer and the contents of the currently displayed screen.

5. Select the **OK** button to create the file and save the text.

Exit

Select the **Exit** option to close all open documents and exit the application. If any documents contain unsaved changes, the program will ask if you want to save the changes before you exit.

Edit Menu

You can use the Edit menu to copy text from other applications or to other applications using the Clipboard.

See Chapter 8 for a discussion about using the Edit menu to cut and paste or copy and paste text using the Clipboard.

Use the Clipboard to copy all or portions of a GEOS file (such as a GeoWrite file) into the GeoComm window.

You do not need to use the Clipboard to place DOS text files (such as files created in Notepad) in the GeoComm window, because GeoComm uses DOS files. However, you might consider using the Clipboard for DOS-type text files if you want only a portion of the DOS document.

Follow these steps to send (transmit) text copied from the Clipboard:

1. Use the **Cut** or **Copy** commands (in any application) to place the text you want to send on the Clipboard.

2. Activate the GeoComm window by clicking on it, or if GeoComm is not already running, open it using the **Startup** option in the Express menu.

3. Select **Paste** from the Edit menu. The program copies the contents of the Clipboard into the GeoComm window and transmits the text to the remote computer.

Message

Use the Message option in the File menu to edit messages before sending them. The following outlines the procedure for editing messages and then sending them.

1. Select the **Message** option. The program displays the Message window. Figure 17.3 shows a pinned Edit menu and a Message window.

2. Type the message you want to send, editing it as necessary.

3. When you are satisfied with the message, select the **Send** button on the Message window. The program sends the message to the remote computer. The main GeoComm window displays the portion that has been transmitted.

4. You can continue transmitting by first typing (and correcting) the message in the Message window, and then selecting the **Send** button when you want to transmit.

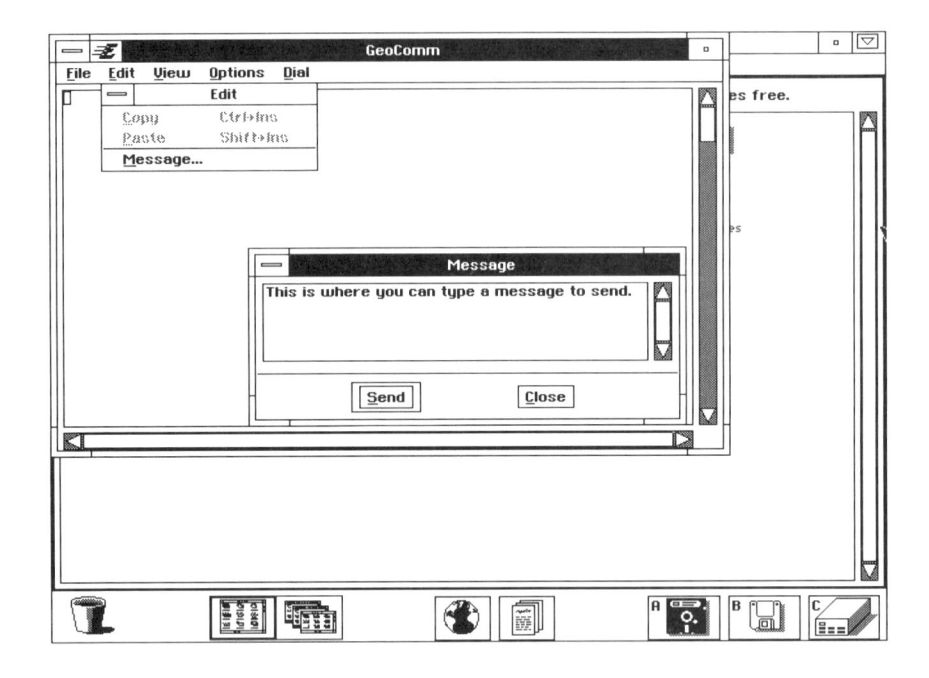

Figure 17.3. The Edit Menu and Message Window.

NOTE Each time you click the **Send** button, the program transmits the entire contents of the Message window. Press **Backspace** to delete the previous contents before typing your next message.

5. Select the **Close** button to return to the main GeoComm window. You can continue typing responses to incoming messages directly in the GeoComm main window, but remember that everything you type is transmitted immediately, without an opportunity to edit the message.

View Menu

You can change the appearance of the screen display using the View menu. Figure 17.4 shows a pinned View menu and the Window Size dialog box (selected from the View menu).

Small/Large Font

Select one of these options to change the size of text in the GeoComm window. Changing the size of the displayed font does not change the number of lines or columns displayed unless the window becomes too large for the screen. In that case, the program reduces the number of displayed lines and columns.

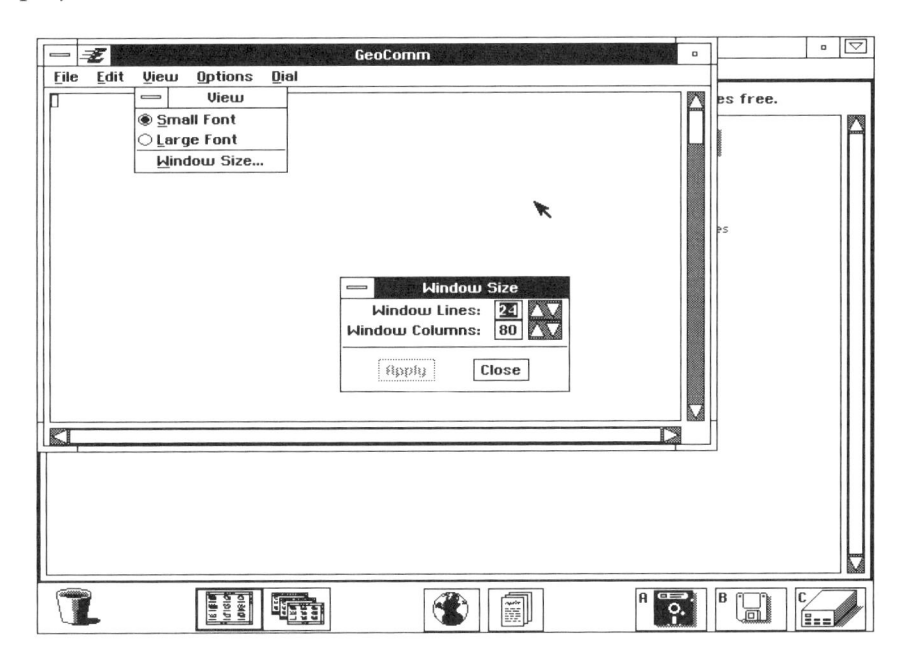

Figure 17.4. The View Menu and the Window Size Dialog Box.

Window Size

When you select the Window Size option, the program displays a dialog box showing the current number of lines and columns in the display. You can click the arrow buttons to change the number of lines and columns in

334 • *Teach Yourself GeoWorks Pro*

the display. After you make your selection, click the **Apply** button. The program changes the display to reflect your selections. When you are satisfied with the window size, click the **Close** button to return to the GeoComm window.

NOTE The maximums are 80 columns and 24 lines. If your screen cannot display these maximums, the program reduces them.

Options Menu

Use the Options menu to specify how you will display, store, and transfer data matching your system with the remote system configuration.

Figure 17.5 shows a pinned Options menu in the lower left of the window. The Protocol, Terminal, and Modem dialog boxes are also shown.

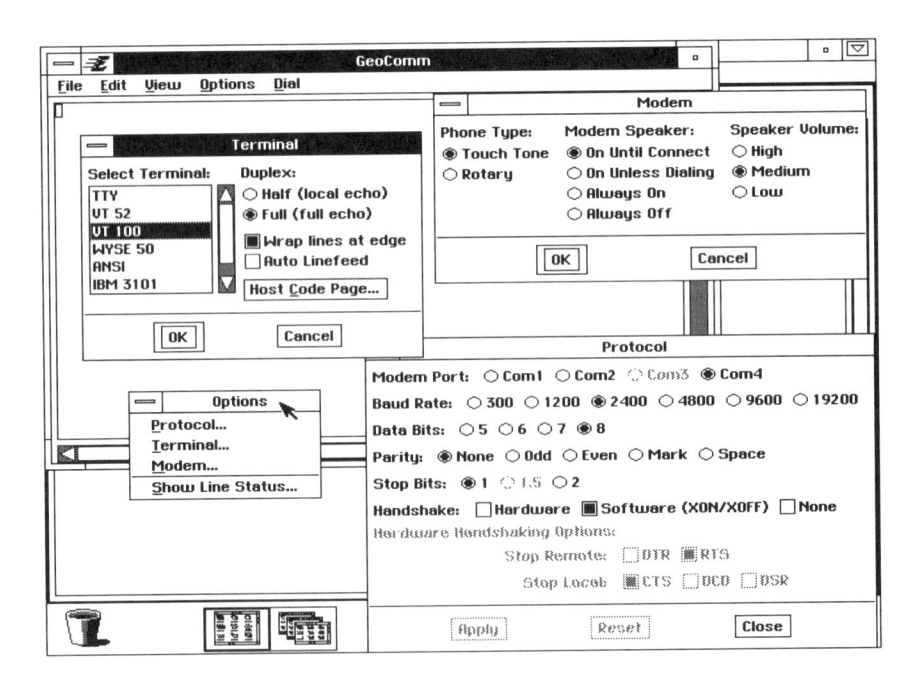

Figure 17.5. The Options Menu and the Protocol, Terminal, and Modem Dialog Boxes.

Before you can communicate with another system, you must set certain GeoComm parameters:

Protocol   The transmitting and receiving settings
Terminal   The settings for displaying and decoding the data
Modem   The settings required to operate your modem.

Protocol Settings

In order for your computer to communicate with a remote computer, the protocol settings of both systems must match. You set your system default settings in the Preferences application (see Chapter 6). You can change the settings for the current session by selecting Protocol. The program displays the Protocol dialog box shown in Figure 17.5.

Any selection you make in the Protocol dialog box will override settings in the Preferences application—for the current session only. The next time you start GeoWorks Pro, the program re-establishes the Preferences default settings for GeoComm. The following sections describe the Protocol settings:

Modem Port

Configuring your modem for your computer usually involves setting switches on the modem to select the proper communication port (COM port). Each COM port has a number. The COM port number is a conventional way of telling the software where to send and receive information. Before you can make your software (GeoComm) work, you must set your modem to one of the valid COM ports, and then tell the software which COM port to use. Most modems can be set to COM1, COM2, COM3, or COM4.

Some computers have a built-in serial port set up as COM1. If your computer has a built-in serial port, you may need to set your modem to COM2, COM3, or COM4.

The COM ports and IRQ (Interrupt Request) settings are related. The settings for these are usually determined by jumper blocks or DIP switches on the modem or serial port. Most modems can be set to use IRQ2, IRQ3, IRQ4, and IRQ5. These settings are reserved for particular devices, as follows:

IRQ2	Interrupt Controller
IRQ3	Secondary asynchronous device (COM2 and COM4)
IRQ4	Primary asynchronous device (COM1 and COM3)
IRQ5	Hard disk controller.

Communications software usually supports IRQ3 and IRQ4. This means you must be careful not to share an IRQ setting with a mouse or other device whose software is memory-resident—it stays in memory, even when the device is not active. (Often you can share an IRQ setting with a device if it is not driven by a memory-resident program).

A mouse device is usually set on COM1. If so, you should not set your modem to either COM1 or COM3 (they both use IRQ4 and would interfere). In this case COM2 or COM4 would be reasonable choices.

A bus mouse (one that comes with an electronic card you install in the computer) does not have a COM port address, but does have an IRQ setting. You must make sure that its IRQ setting does not conflict with your modem IRQ setting.

Your transmission settings for baud rate, data bits, parity, and stop bits must match those of the remote system.

Baud Rate

The *baud rate* is the number of changes per second in the electrical state of the output line from the modem. This is generally understood to be the same as the number of bits per second that can be transmitted by the modem. (A baud rate of 2400 implies 2400 bits per second, which may or may not be the case. At higher speeds, the bits per second can be higher than the baud rate.)

Data Bits

This signifies the amount of data the computer can store and process at one time (called a *word*). Most PCs process eight bits at one time (8 bits = 1 byte = 1 word). However, in some cases the word length is different. Specify the number of data bits for your system.

Parity

This item specifies the type of error-detection technique used to check the integrity of the binary data transmission (1 or 0 bits). In some parity systems, an extra bit is added to the block of bits (word) to do this checking. You can select the following types of parity: none, odd, even, mark, and space. Specify the one that applies to your system.

Stop Bits

Use this option to set the number of stop bits to insert in the transmission to mark the end of each word.

Handshake

The local and remote computers send *handshake signals* back and forth to establish a valid connection. You can select two handshake options: Software and None.

Select **Software** (XON/XOFF) from the handshake options. If you select None, you can lose portions of your incoming data.

Accepting Protocol Changes

When you are satisfied with the protocol settings, click the **Apply** button to accept the settings, then click the **Close** button to return to the GeoComm window.

Terminal Settings

Some remote systems may expect your system to be a specific type of terminal that will be able to translate certain codes and text sequences. GeoComm provides seven terminal emulations, settings that make your computer act and respond as if it were a specific type of terminal, so it can speak the same language as the remote computer.

Select Terminal

GeoComm emulates (simulates) the following types of terminals:

- TTY
- ANSI
- VT 52
- IBM 3101

- VT 100
- TVI 950
- WYSE 50.

Usually you use a standard TTY (teletype) terminal emulation. If you connect to a system requiring some other type of terminal, you must select the emulation from the list.

Duplex

The duplex setting determines the direction of data flow. Full duplex allows data to flow in both directions (to and from your computer) at the same time. Half duplex allows data to flow in only one direction at a time.

- **Half (local echo).** If the characters you type do not appear on your screen, then choose **Half**.
- **Full (full echo).** If the characters you type appear twice on your screen, select **Full**.

Wrap Lines at Edge

Set this option when you want GeoComm to wrap any text lines that are too long to fit in the display window. GeoComm will automatically split long lines into shorter ones. If you do not select this option, GeoComm will not display the portions of the lines that do not fit in the window.

Auto Linefeed

This option replaces a received carriage return with a carriage return and a linefeed. Turn off this option if the lines on your display are double-spaced. Turn on this option if each new line on your display overwrites the previous line.

Host Code Page

Because computers are used in many countries, and therefore with different languages, the host computer may be using a different set of character codes (code page). For example, if you press the key closest to the left Shift key, a U.S. keyboard layout produces a Z. If the keyboard layout is French, pressing that key produces a W, while on a German keyboard the same key would produce a Y. Each of these keyboards is using a different code page.

Whenever you want to communicate with another computer (for example, via GeoComm) you must be sure the two computers are "on the same wavelength." If your computer is using a different code page than that being used by the recipient's computer you must tell your computer what code page the other computer is using.

To do this, select the correct code page from the list of code pages displayed.

Accepting Terminal Settings

When you are satisfied with the terminal settings, click the **OK** button to return to the GeoComm window. Click the **Cancel** button to return to the GeoComm window without making any changes.

Modem Settings

Your computer must have a modem in order for you to use GeoComm to communicate over telephone lines with other computers.

The term *Hayes-compatible* indicates that a modem accepts the same command language as modems made by Hayes Microcomputer Products, Inc. Hayes developed the intelligent modem for first-generation personal computers in 1978. This command language (Hayes Standard AT Command Set) for modem control is now the industry standard. Use a Hayes or Hayes-compatible modem with the GeoComm application.

The command modem has two states: *command* and *online*. In the command state the modem accepts instructions (commands). In the online state the modem can dial, answer calls, and transmit and receive data.

Once a modem is connected to a remote modem, it performs the *handshaking procedure*. This is quite similar to someone on a phone saying, "Hello." Then the remote end responds with, "Hello, this is..." If you have the modem speaker turned on, you will hear the harsh sounds of the modem handshake. When the handshake is complete, the two computers are online and can communicate (transmit data to each other).

To change your modem settings select **Modem** from the Options menu. The program displays the Modem dialog box shown in Figure 17.5.

Phone Type

There are two basic types of phone systems in use today, the touch tone and the rotary. Select the type of phone service you have.

- **Touch Tone.** Select **Touch Tone** if you hear different tones as you dial your phone.
- **Rotary.** Select **Rotary** if you hear a series of clicks as you dial your phone.

Modem Speaker

Modems are constructed with a built-in speaker, allowing you to hear the telephone operations as they happen. You can select one of the following options for the modem speaker:

- **On Until Connect.** Select this option to hear the dialing operation. Your speaker remains on until the other modem answers.
- **On Unless Dialing.** Select this option to turn on the speaker only while you are waiting for the other modem to answer.
- **Always On.** Select this option to keep the speaker turned on throughout the transmission.
- **Always Off.** Select this option to keep the speaker turned off throughout the transmission.

Speaker Volume

Some modems do not come with their own internal volume controls. Use the **Speaker Volume** option to select a comfortable volume level for your modem speaker output.

Show Line Status

GeoComm lets you monitor the occurrence of transmission errors, allowing you to verify that your Protocol settings are correct. To display the line status, select **Show Line Status** from the Options menu. Figure 17.6 shows the Show Line Status window.

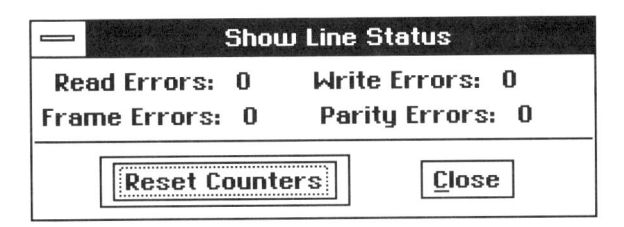

Figure 17.6. The Show Line Status Window.

GeoComm displays a count of four types of transmission errors: read, write, frame, and parity. Click the **Reset Counters** button to reset the four counters to zero. Click the **Close** button to close the window and return to the GeoComm window. GeoComm continues to monitor the errors. The next time you open the Show Line Status window (during the current session), GeoComm displays the updated error counts.

Dial Menu

The Dial menu contains three potions: Scripts, Quick Dial, and Hang Up.

Scripts

You can use the Scripts option to automate many of the repetitive communication tasks you perform regularly. For example, if you call a certain bulletin board frequently, you can set up an automatic log file so you do not have to remember the log-on sequence. GeoComm provides several script files that you can use as examples for creating you own scripts.

Creating a Script File

Figure 17.7 shows the Scripts dialog box in the upper-right corner. In the lower left is a Notepad display of a portion of the COMPU.MAC script file. In the lower right is another Notepad display of the GENIE.MAC script file.

Script files are DOS files, the type of file Notepad can display and edit. You can use Notepad or another DOS text editor to create a new file and save it, or you can modify a supplied script file, then use the **Save As** option on the File menu to rename and save the file. You must use a DOS filename with the extension .MAC, or the program will not recognize the file as a script file.

It is a good idea to save all script files in the \GEOWORKS\GEOCOMM subdirectory.

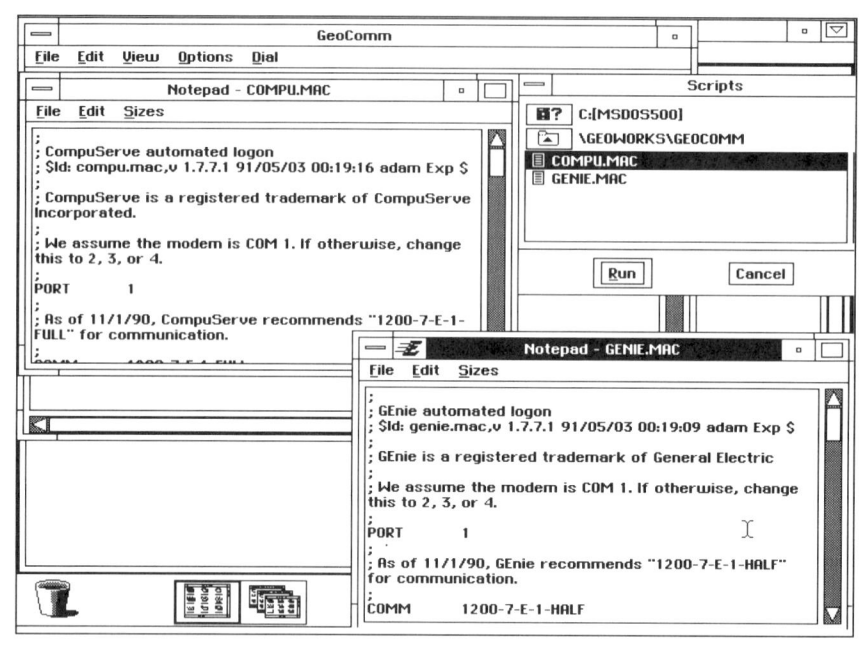

Figure 17.7. The Scripts Dialog Box and Notepads with Script Files.

See the Script Commands section later in this chapter for a discussion about writing a script.

Running a Script File

Follow these steps to run a script file:

1. Select **Scripts** from the Dial menu to display the Scripts dialog box.

2. Locate the script file you want to run. If the script file is not in the \GEOWORKS\GEOCOMM subdirectory, select the drive, subdirectory, and filename of the file you want. You can avoid these additional steps by saving all script files in the \GEOWORKS\GEOCOMM subdirectory.

3. Select the **Run** button. The program displays the Script Display window, which shows you the script as it plays. Click the **Stop** button to stop the script.

Script Commands

A script file is essentially a small program to perform repetitive tasks. For example, you can write a script to log onto a bulletin board. GeoComm provides a language of script commands for you to use when writing the script.

You must type script commands in uppercase. You can type labels in uppercase, lowercase, or a mixture of the two, although all labels must be typed consistently throughout the script. For example, GeoComm views these labels as inconsistent in format:

:Start :START   :start :STarT.

In Table 17.1, the words you must replace with text specific to your situation are enclosed in < > (angle brackets). You do not type the brackets.

Table 17.1. GeoComm Script Commands.

Command	Description
:<label>	A label is a line beginning with a colon. The GOTO command (discussed later) forces the program to jump to a label to begin processing from that point.
:ABORT	:ABORT is a special label that must be in uppercase (the colon is required). If the user clicks the **Stop** button while the script is running, GeoComm jumps to the :ABORT label and ends the script.
BELL	Sounds a beep to alert the user.
CLEAR	Clears the Script Display window.
COMM <baud-data bits-	Sets the communication settings. You can use these values in the script:

Table 17.1. continued...

Command	Description
parity-stopbits-duplex>	Baud: 300, 1200, 2400, 4800, 9600, 19200 Bits: 5, 6, 7, 8 Parity: N, O, E, M, S Stop bits: 1, 1.5, 2 Duplex: HALF, FULL. For example: COMM 2400-8-O-2-FULL in a script file means a 2400-baud line with eight data bits, odd parity, two stop bits, and full duplex.
DIAL	Dials the number specified (tone or pulse does not matter here).
<number>	To dial 9 for an outside line and then dial 555-1212, enter the following in the script file: `Dial 9,555-1212`
END	Stops the script and returns control to the user. It does not use the :ABORT label.
GOTO <label>	Forces the program to jump to the line starting with :<label>. For example, when the program reaches the command GOTO ITU, the program searches for a line starting with :ITU. When the program finds the line, it jumps to the label and continues running the script program from that point.
MATCH<"text"> GOTO<label> PROMPT<number>	Use the MATCH and PROMPT commands together when you want to wait a specific length of time while the program examines incoming data for a match with the <"text"> string. You must enclose <"text">in double quotes. If you want to match an Enter keystroke, use "CR" as the text string. You can use more than one MATCH command before the PROMPT command.

Table 17.1. continued...

Command	Description
	The PROMPT command pauses the script for a specific length of time while waiting for the MATCH command to be satisfied. When the program finds a match, the script uses a GOTO command to jump to a specified label. If no match is found in the specified time, then the program continues with the command following the PROMPT command.
	The MATCH command(s) must come before the PROMPT command, and you must have both the MATCH command(s) and the PROMPT command.

	You specify time in sixtieths of a second. For example, suppose you want to wait 60 seconds (60 x 60 = 3600) for a text string from the remote computer asking for your last name, or specifying that there are thunderstorms and the system is offline. Write the following in the script file:
	`MATCH "Last name?",CR GOTO ITU`
	`MATCH "Thunderstorms. System Offline!`
	`"GOTO Hqrs PROMPT 3600`

PAUSE<number>	The PAUSE command temporarily halts the script for a specific length of time. The <number> is in sixtieths of a second. If you do not specify a number, the program pauses for one second. For example, to pause the program for one minute (60 seconds) use the following command in your script: `PAUSE 3600`
PORT<port>	Specifies the COM port to use for communicating with the remote computer. For example, to use COM port 4, use the following command in your script: `PORT 4`

Table 17.1. continued...

Command	Description
PRINT<text>	Use this command to display text on your computer screen. This text is not sent to the remote computer. For example, to display the message "Signing on" while you are signing onto the remote computer, use the following command in your script file close to where the actual sign-on command is issued: `PRINT "Signing on",CR,CR`
PULSE	Use this command if your phone uses pulse dialing, not tone dialing.
SEND<"text">	This command sends <"text"> to the remote computer. For example, to send the word "password" followed by Enter, use the following command in your script: `SEND "password",CR`
TERM <terminal type>	Use this command to make GeoComm emulate a specific terminal type. The <terminal type> must be one of the following: TTY, VT 52, VT 100, WYSE 50, ANSI, IBM 3101, or TVI 950. For example, to make GeoComm emulate an ANSI terminal, use the following command in your script: `TERM ANSI`

Quick Dial

You can connect your computer to a remote computer by either calling (dialing) the remote computer or answering a call. To dial a number with your modem, select **Quick Dial** from the Dial menu. The Quick Dial option works only with Hayes-compatible modems. If you have a different type of modem, you will probably have to dial the number manually.

Dialing a Number

To dial a number, position the text cursor in the Phone # box. Type the phone number you want to dial. Select the **Dial** button. The program dials the phone number.

Telephone Number Format

You can use almost any format to enter the telephone number. For example, you can use the number format 1-555-555-5555 for long distance calls. Here a 1 is placed before the area code.

If you need to use a special dialing sequence to access a long distance service, enter the sequence before the regular number. For example, the sequence 12345.1.555.555.5555 dials the long distance service access code (12345), then the long distance number.

Inserting a comma briefly pauses the dialing sequence to accommodate connection delays. For example, if you use 9 to access an outside line, enter the phone number like this: 9,555-1212. The program will dial 9, pause briefly to access the outside line, and then dial 555-1212.

Hang Up

If you are on a bulletin board or connected to another computer and decide you want to quit, you should first use the logoff procedure for the remote system. (Logging off formally tells the remote computer that you are leaving.) After you log off, select **Hang Up** from the Dial menu. The program displays the Hang Up dialog box asking you to confirm that you want to break the connection and hang up. Select the **Yes** button to terminate the connection (equivalent to hanging up your phone) and close the dialog box.

Summary

In this chapter you learned how to configure the GeoComm application for your system and how to use GeoComm to communicate with a remote computer, sending and receiving data. You also learned how to create scripts to automate the communication process.

Chapter 18

The Games Applications

I n the Games Applications chapter you will find the rules and options for two popular games. You will learn:

- How to play the Solitaire game
- How to set Solitaire options
- How to play the Tetris game
- How to get Tetris options, including two-person play.

The Solitaire game, Klondike, in the Advanced Workspace is a more versatile version of the same game included the Beginner Workspace. You can change the settings for several aspects of the game, such as how many cards to draw, the type of scoring to use, which game level to play, and a timer for the game.

Probably the most popular of all solitaire games, Klondike is known by a variety of other names, including Demon and Fascination.

Tetris, found in the Intermediate and Advanced Workspaces, is a popular and possibly addictive new game designed by two Russian programmers. It is a game of skill, so the more you play, the better your scores will be (theoretically at least).

The following paragraphs will refresh your memory on the rules and menu options for these games.

The Solitaire Application

When you select Solitaire from the GeoManager window, the program displays the Solitaire window shown in Figure 18.1.

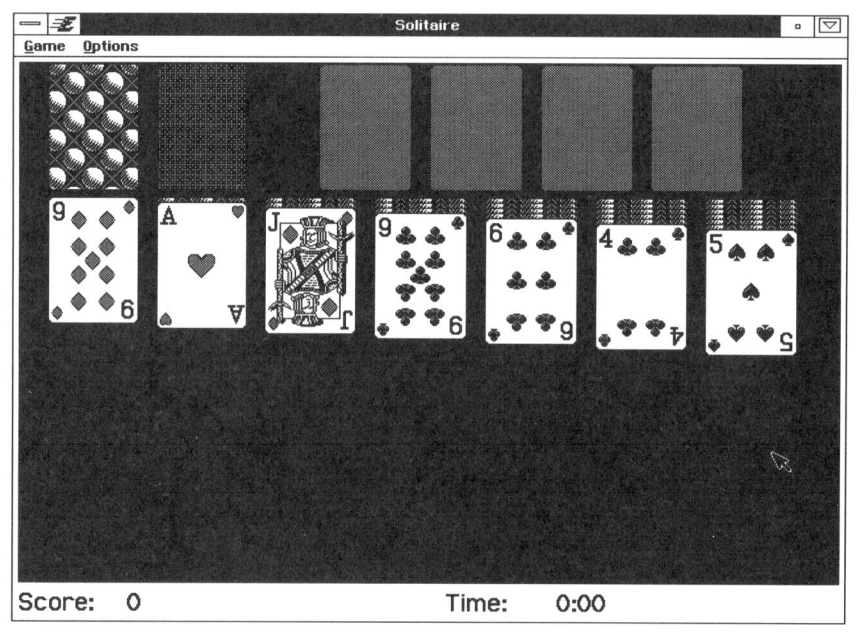

Figure 18.1. The Solitaire Opening Window.

NOTE The on-screen black-and-white image uses a fade for the red cards, making them easy to distinguish from the black cards. The captured images show only black or white.

The Solitaire menu bar contains two options, Game and Options.

Game Menu

The Game menu contains three options: Re-Deal, Undo, and Exit.

Re-Deal (Ctrl+R)

Select this option to deal the cards again and begin a new game. The shortcut for Re-Deal is **Ctrl-R**.

Undo

Select this option if you want to back out of a move, returning to the previous display. There is no shortcut for this item.

Exit (F3)

Select this option to exit the Solitaire application and return to the GeoManager window.

Options Menu

The Options menu shown in Figure 18.2 contains eight items that allow you to customize the game.

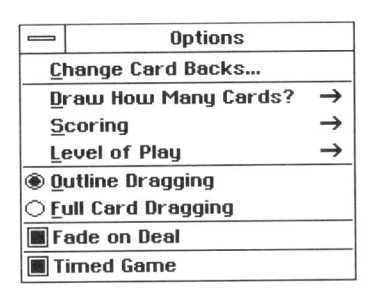

```
┌─────────────────────────────┐
│            Options          │
├─────────────────────────────┤
│ Change Card Backs...        │
│ Draw How Many Cards?      → │
│ Scoring                   → │
│ Level of Play             → │
│ ● Outline Dragging          │
│ ○ Full Card Dragging        │
│ ■ Fade on Deal              │
│ ■ Timed Game                │
└─────────────────────────────┘
```

Figure 18.2. The Options Menu.

Change Card Backs

You can choose from three designs for the backs of the cards. Select the one you want and then click the **Apply** button to see how the selection looks. When you are satisfied, click the **Close** button to return to the Solitaire window.

Draw How Many Cards?

You can specify drawing either one card or three cards at a time from the deal stack. When you select the option you want, the program returns you to the Solitaire window.

Scoring

You can choose standard scoring, Vegas scoring, or none.

Standard Scoring

In standard scoring, the program resets the score to zero whenever you Re-Deal. The point system is:

- 10 points for playing a card on a suit stack
- 5 points for exposing (turning face up) a card in one of the seven play stacks
- 5 points for playing a card from the discard stack
- -1 point for every 10 seconds of play.

If you are turning over three cards at a time, the program penalizes you every time you reach the end of the deal stack:

- -10 points for each of the first three times. The fourth time you reach the end of the deal stack, the program penalizes you $(n-3)$ x -10, where n is the number of times you reach the end of the deal stack.

If you are turning over one card at a time, the penalty is:

- -30 the first time you reach the end of the deal stack. From then on, the penalty is $(n-1)$ x -30, where n is the number of times you reach the end of the deal stack.

Vegas Scoring

In Vegas scoring, the program follows these scoring rules:

- -52 points for re-dealing (score is not zeroed)
- 5 points for playing a card on a suit stack.

Level of Play

There are three levels of play: beginner, intermediate, and advanced. When you select the level you want, the program returns you to the Solitaire window.

Outline Dragging

Select this option to display an outline of a card as you drag it from one pile to another.

Full Card Dragging

Select this option to display the full card as you drag it.

Fade on Deal

Select this option to determine how the program displays face-up cards following a deal or re-deal. When this option is on, the program draws face-up cards from left to right. When this option is off, the program displays all face-up cards simultaneously.

Timed Game

You can set the timer to keep track of how long you take to complete a game or how long you take for each move.

Card Layout

The program places cards face down in seven play stacks. The first play stack on the left contains one card, the next contains two cards, the third contains three cards and so on, with the last play stack on the right containing seven cards. When the seven stacks are made, the program turns face up the top card on each one. Above the seven stacks on the right are the four suit stacks. (A suit stack is empty until you can place an ace face up on it.)

The program places the remaining (undealt) cards face down at the top left in the deal stack, with room for discards beside it. Figure 18.3 shows the arrangement of the cards for a game in progress.

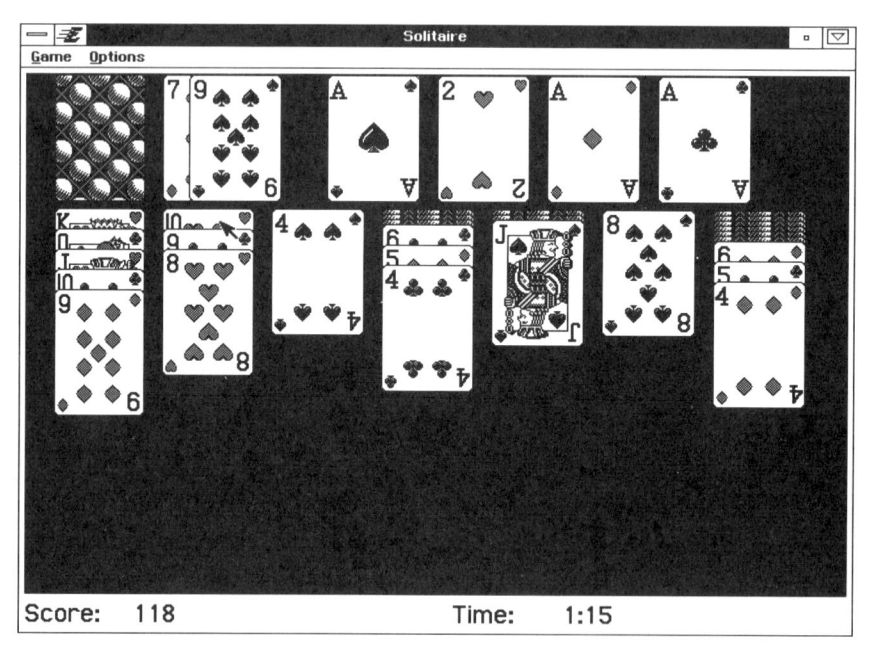

Figure 18.3. A Solitaire Game in Progress.

Playing the Game

The object is to build up the suit stacks with a complete sequence of cards, ace through king, of the same suit.

To play a card, position the cursor over the card, press the left mouse button, then drag the card to the new location. Release the mouse button to anchor the card.

To turn over a card, double-click on it with the left mouse button.

The top face-up card in any stack, except those in the suit stacks, can be played.

You can move a face-up ace on a play stack to a suit stack. You can then play the 2 of the same suit by placing it on the ace when it becomes available. The 3 of that suit is placed on the 2.

You can move face-up cards on the play stacks from one stack to another following this rule: a card can be placed only on the next higher-ranking card of the opposite color. For example, you can place a black 10 only on a red jack. When you remove the last face-up card from a play stack, you then turn over the new top card of the play stack.

You can move a sequence of face-up cards on the play stacks. For example, suppose the top card of one play stack is the 9 of diamonds. On another play stack is the face-up sequence: 8 of spades, 7 of hearts, 6 of clubs. You can move the 8-7-6 sequence onto the 9 of diamonds. You cannot move just one card of a face-up sequence on a play stack—you must move the entire face-up sequence as a group.

If you move the last card in a play stack, leaving an empty space, you can fill the space only with a face-up king. Turn up the cards one at a time (or three at a time, depending on your Draw How Many Cards? setting) in the deal stack by clicking on the top card in the deal stack.

The program places the turned-up card face up on the discard stack. Play the top card in the discard stack, if possible, by placing it on the appropriate suit stack or on a play stack. When you play a card from the discard stack, the card under it becomes available for play.

When you can no longer play any face-up cards, turn up another card from the deal stack and place it face up on the discard stack.

When you have turned up all cards from the deal stack and you cannot make any other card moves, turn over the discard pile and use it as the new deal stack by double-clicking on the top card in the discard stack.

The Tetris Application

The game Tetris, like Solitaire, can be addicting. You can play Tetris as a solitaire game, or competitively against others. Either way, Tetris is a game of skill. Although Tetris is easy to learn, this does not mean you will soon tire of the game. Indeed, the more you play and the more skilled you become, the more you want to play.

The object of the game is to accumulate as many points as you can. To play the game you attempt to *completely* fill a row with blocks. Each row that is completely filled is removed from the screen. The rows on top (if any) are moved down to replace the completed row(s). This gives the dropping pieces more distance to drop, thereby giving you more time to react. If you leave spaces in a row it is not removed and other blocks can pile up above it. When the pile reaches the top the game is over.

As a block falls from the top you can rotate it and/or move it to a different column. Once you have the orientation of the block the way you want it, and its column location, you can cause it to drop rapidly to the bottom. Each time you drop a piece, you score; the sooner you drop it, the more points you score. This means the faster you play, the higher your score. For improved scores it is therefore desirable to orient and position a dropping piece as quickly as possible, and then cause it to rapidly drop to the bottom.

Moving Pieces

There are six different types of pieces that are used in Tetris. The following chart indicates how you can manipulate them as they fall from the top to the pile at the bottom. If you are playing a one-person game, then you can manipulate the dropping piece by using any of the three ways shown in the table.

Table 18.1. Tetris Keyboard Usage.

Action	Left player (Keyboard)	Right player (Numeric keypad)
Move piece to left	D or J	LeftArrow
Move piece to right	F or L	RightArrow
Rotate piece clockwise	G or K	5
Rapidly drop piece	Spacebar or , (comma)	DownArrow or Ins
Increase difficulty level	I or A	UpArrow

Scoring

Your score is determined by several factors. The higher the level of play, the more you score for each game piece.

Figure 18.4 shows a typical one-player Tetris screen in the middle of a game. This game displays a preview of the next piece to fall. The falling piece is shown headed towards the bottom pile. Above the game rectangle is a tally of the number of lines that have been cleared in the current game and the current score.

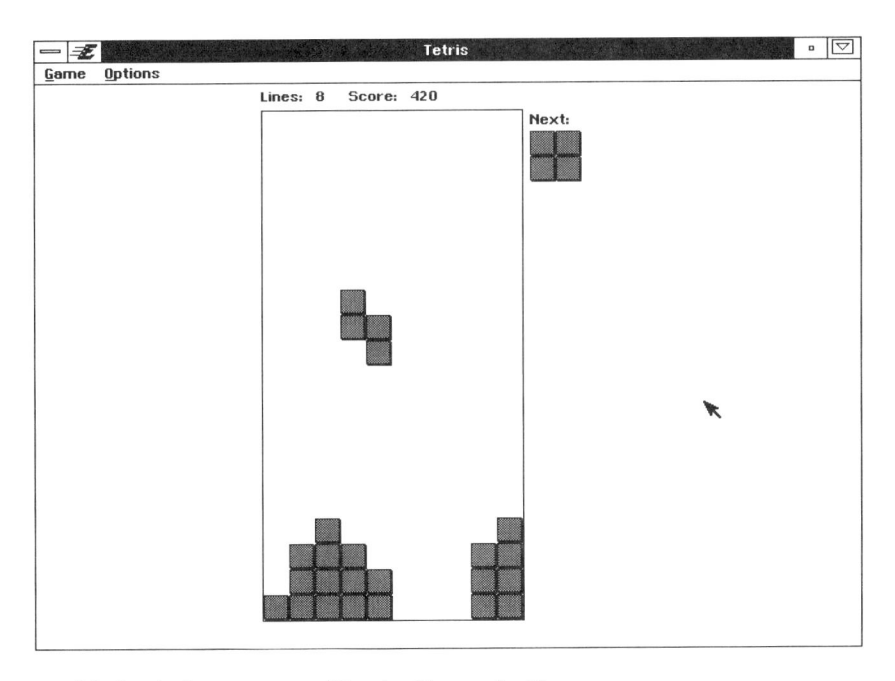

Figure 18.4. A One-person Tetris Game in Progress.

The Preview Pieces command in the Options menu allows you to see the next new piece before it appears in the game window. This gives you a little time to decide your plan of action for the next piece. Selecting this option, however, penalizes you by scoring you lower for pieces on the pile.

One of the reasons this game is so challenging is that you are continually fighting the clock. The faster you play, the higher your score. The higher your score, the faster the pieces drop. This gives you less time to orient and position the dropping pieces. As the game level increases, your score for each piece landing on the pile is increased.

You can score extra points by clearing more than one row at a time. For example, you get more extra points for clearing four rows at one time than you do for clearing three rows at one time.

Game Menu

The Game menu has the following commands:

About Tetris

This command displays a scrollable description of Tetris.

Start New Game (Ctrl+S)

This command allows you to start a new game.

To start Tetris:

1. Double-click on the **Tetris** icon in either the Advanced Workspace or Intermediate Workspace. The Tetris game window appears. Maximize it to fill the screen.

2. Choose the **Options** menu. Select **Two Players** if you are playing against an opponent. If you do not select this option a one-player game is displayed.

3. Specify any other options you want for the game, such as Preview Pieces or Players Get Identical Pieces (available only for a two-player game). You can also specify other options from the menu. Most of the other options are for setting the skill level of the game to be played.

4. To start a game choose **Start New Game** from the Game menu.

Abort Current Game (Ctrl+A)

This command aborts the current game. You can now start a new game, reset the skill level, or exit Tetris.

Pause Game (Ctrl+P)

Selecting this option allows you to pause (freeze) the action of the game. When you want to resume the game action, choose the **Continue Game** command from the Game menu. Pressing **P** also pauses the game.

Continue Game (Ctrl+C)

If you have paused the game, this option restarts the action. Pressing **C** also restarts the action.

Exit (F3)

This command closes Tetris and returns you to the screen you were in when you initiated the game.

Options Menu

A pinned Options menu is shown in Figure 18.5.

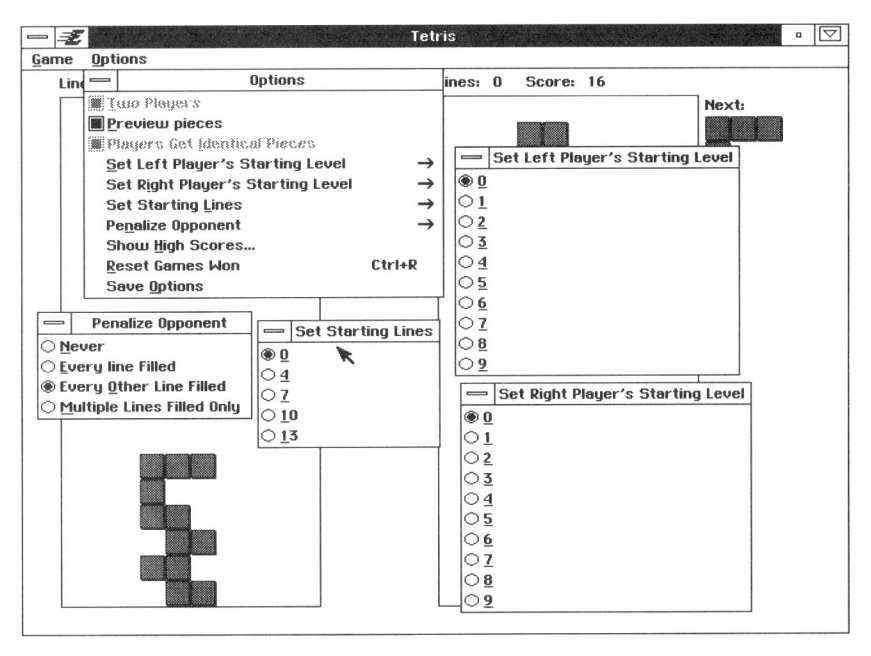

Figure 18.5. Pinned Tetris Options Menus.

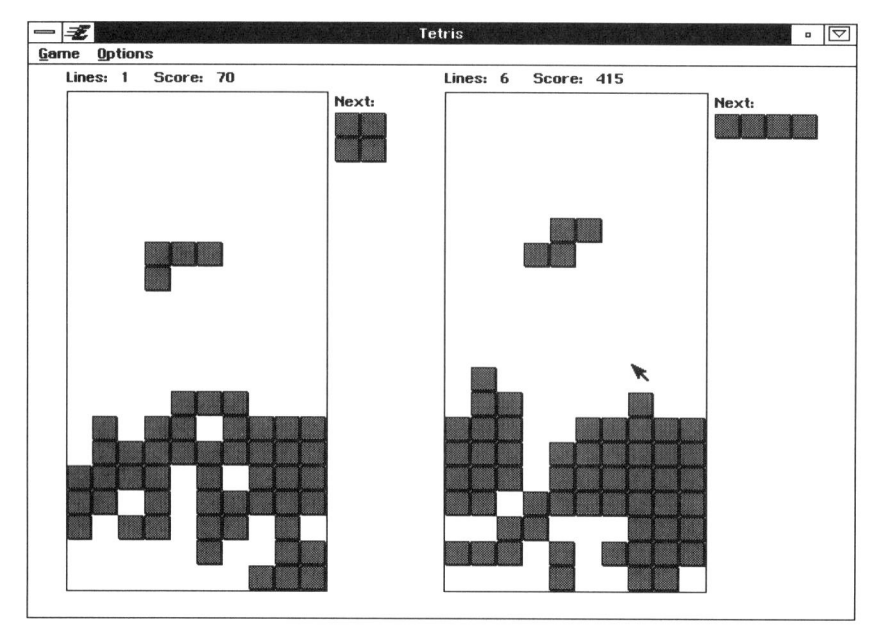

Figure 18.6. A Two-player Game in Progress.

Two Players

Selecting this option causes two game boards to be displayed on the screen. The keyboard can be used to control the left game board, and the numeric keypad controls the right game board. A two-player game in progress is shown in Figure 18.6. The options Preview Pieces and Players Get Identical Pieces was specified.

Although each player sees the same pieces, the faster player will see more of them (and score higher).

Preview Pieces

With this option selected a picture of the next game piece to drop is displayed to the upper-right of the game board. Using this option takes away some of the challenge of the game and reduces scores for each piece.

Players Get Identical Pieces

In a two-player game, selecting this option gives each player the same sequence of falling pieces. Using the **Spacebar**, **,** (comma), the **DownArrow**, or the **Ins** key can cause one player to play more pieces than the other. Nevertheless both players will be presented with the same sequence of falling pieces (although the faster player may see more of them).

Set Left Player's Starting Level

Figure 18.5 shows a pinned Set Left Player's Starting Level dialog box in the upper-right corner of the window. You can set any level from 0 (zero) to 9 as the starting level. Level 0 is the easiest and level 9 is the most difficult. The higher the level selected the faster the game pieces fall.

Set Right Player's Starting Level

In the lower-right of Figure 18.5 is the Set Right Player's Starting Level dialog box. This dialog box is the same as the Set Left Player's Starting Level dialog box, except it affects the right player's level of play.

Set Starting Lines

This option allows you to start the game with some lines partially filled in at the bottom. This option is used to increase the difficulty from the start of the game. A pinned Set Starting Lines dialog box is shown in the lower center of Figure 18.5.

Penalize Opponent

The control each player has over his opponent's game is increased by using this option. When you select this option a dialog box like the one shown in the lower-left of Figure 18.5 is displayed. This dialog box provides several ways to penalize an opponent.

Never	This option does not allow an opponent to be penalized.
Every Line Filled	This option causes a line to be added to the opponent's game board for each line that is cleared.
Every Other Line Filled	This option causes an extra, partially filled row to be added to the opponent's game board every *other* time a row is cleared.

Multiple Lines Filled Only This is a very challenging option. For each two lines cleared, the opponent is penalized by a single line (a line is added to the opponent's game board). If three lines are cleared, the opponent is penalized two lines. If four lines are cleared, the opponent is penalized four lines.

Show High Scores

This option causes the top 10 scores to be displayed. When you finish a game that is eligible for listing you are prompted to enter your name.

Reset Games Won (Ctrl+R)

When you are playing a two-player game, a record is kept of the total number of games each player has won. Choose this option to reset the count to zero.

Save Options

Use this option to keep the current options settings for your next session in Tetris. This makes the current selection the default selection. The next time you open Tetris these options will be in effect.

Summary

In this chapter you learned the rules for the Klondike Solitaire game and how to use the options on the two Solitaire menus that set various parameters for the game. You also learned how to set up Tetris for either a one-person or a two-person game. In addition, you learned how to use the keyboard to control the action of the game.

Chapter 19

The Spreadsheet Viewer

In this chapter you will learn:

- How to view a Quattro Pro SE or Lotus 1-2-3 spreadsheet or chart from within GeoWorks Pro
- How to paste all or part of Quattro Pro SE and Lotus 1-2-3 files into GeoWorks Pro applications.

The Quattro Pro Viewer allows you to view either Quattro Pro SE or Lotus 1-2-3 spreadsheets without leaving GeoWorks Pro. There are three types of files that can be viewed in the Quattro Pro Viewer. The three-letter file extension determines the type of file. The following are the types of files that can be viewed in the Quattro Pro Viewer:

Table 19.1. Files That Can Be Viewed in Quattro Pro Viewer.

File Extension	File Type
.WQ1	Quattro Pro SE or 2.0 spreadsheet
.EPS	Quattro Pro SE or 2.0 chart file in an .EPS file or slide .EPS format
.WK1	Lotus 1-2-3 file

Once you are viewing a spreadsheet in the Quattro Pro Viewer you can copy it to the Clipboard. From the Clipboard you can paste the spreadsheet in the Scrapbook, GeoDraw, or GeoWrite. If you want to view graphs or copy them, you must have saved them in an .EPS format. This chapter discusses these procedures.

The Quattro Pro Viewer imports only one page of a spreadsheet at a time. You can specify which page you want and what portion of the page is to be displayed in the viewer.

The Quattro Pro Viewer is just that—a viewer. You cannot edit a spreadsheet from within the viewer. Once you have pasted the spreadsheet into GeoDraw or GeoWrite, you can edit the image.

You can also use the Quattro Pro Viewer to display encapsulated PostScript (.EPS) files. This type of file can be created within Quattro Pro SE. It is used to save graphs in the .EPS format for later printing on a PostScript printer. The .EPS graphs displayed in the viewer can be pasted to the Scrapbook, GeoDraw, or GeoWrite. If you first paste an .EPS graph file to the Scrapbook you can then copy and paste a scaled version into GeoWrite (or GeoDraw).

Quattro Pro SE

Quattro Pro SE is separate from GeoWorks Pro and must be installed in its own directory. Both programs have their own sets of installation disks. Once installed, each program is independent from the other. The Quattro Pro Viewer provides a link to display Quattro Pro SE files. Although the Quattro Pro Viewer allows you to view the Quattro Pro SE files in GeoWorks Pro, the Quattro Pro SE program is not running when you do this.

You can use the Quattro Pro Viewer to exit GeoWorks Pro and start Quattro Pro SE. In fact, you can specify what file is to be displayed in Quattro Pro SE when it is opened. Then when you exit Quattro Pro SE you are returned to the Quattro Pro Viewer.

It simplifies matters if you install Quattro Pro SE in the \QPRO directory on the same hard disk drive as the \GEOWORKS directory. If Quattro Pro SE is installed in a different directory or drive, you must tell the Quattro Pro Viewer the location of the file you want.

If you used a directory name other than \QPRO or installed Quattro Pro SE on a different drive from the one where you installed GeoWorks Pro, then you only have to specify the Quattro Pro SE directory name and location once. After that the name and location is stored for later use by the Quattro Pro Viewer.

NOTE

Spreadsheet Viewing

There are several ways you can open a spreadsheet or chart for viewing. The usual way is to start from the GeoWorks World directory. The procedure is as follows:

1. Double-click on the **Quattro Pro Viewer** icon.

   The Quattro Pro Viewer window is opened with the Choose Document to View Dialog Box displayed, as shown in Figure 19.1. (Note: Your files or directories may be somewhat different.)

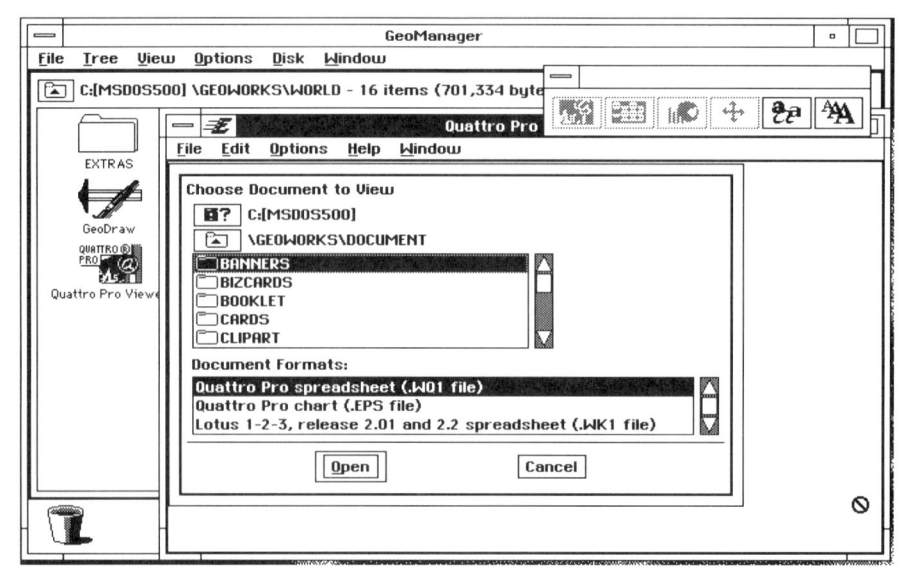

Figure 19.1. The Opening Quattro Pro Viewer Window.

2. Click the type of file you want to open in the Documents Formats dialog box.
   If no files are displayed in the file list box it means there are no files of the specified type in the currently selected directory.

3. Use the file list box to select the file to view. Figure 19.2 shows that the Quattro Pro directory has been selected. When you click on the Open button , it is added to the path statement and a list of Quattro Pro files is displayed, as shown in Figure 19.3. Compare this dialog box with the one in Figure 19.1. (Note: your drive and/or directory may be somewhat different.)

   To the right of the Drive button you can see drive C: is displayed with its label (MSDOS500) specified. Your drive and label may be different.

   The Directory button is directly below the drive button. Clicking on this button moves you up one level in the directory tree. In Figure 19.2, the back slash symbol (\) shows that the root directory is now the current directory.

4. Highlight the file you want to view in the files list and select **Open**.

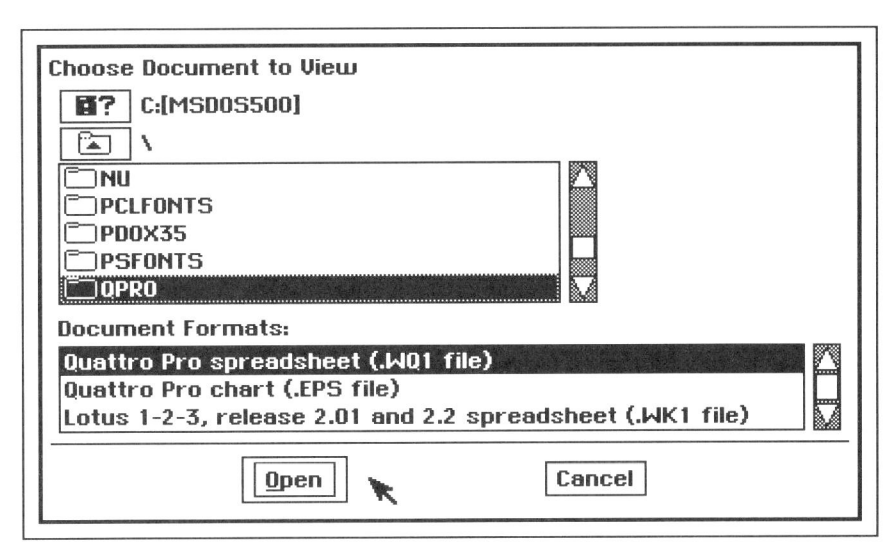

Figure 19.2. Selecting the QPRO Directory.

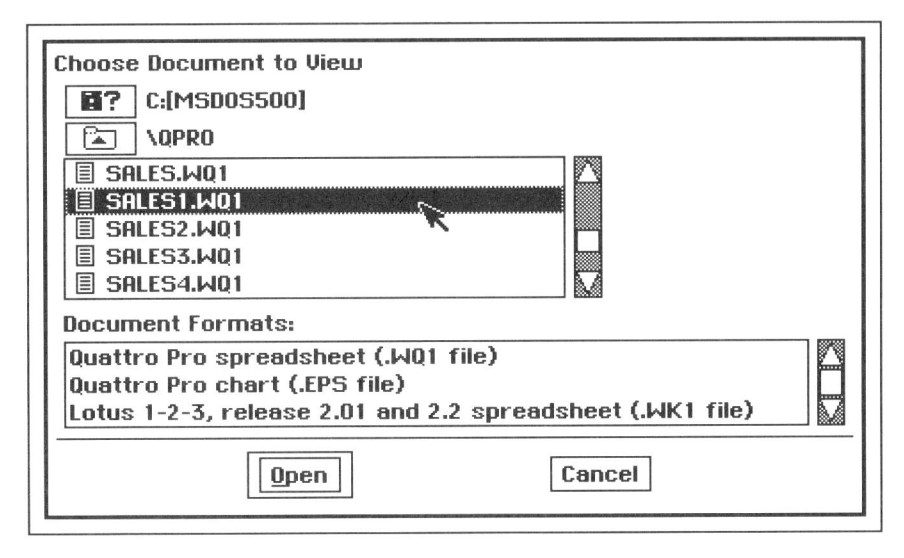

Figure 19.3. Files with a .WQ1 Extension in the QPRO Directory.

Specifying a File from GeoManager

You can specify from GeoManager the file to be displayed in the Quattro Pro Viewer. The following outlines the procedure:

1. Open the GeoManager window. The current directory should be \GEOWORKS\WORLD. If it is not, click the **World** button (Figure 19.4) at the bottom of the window.

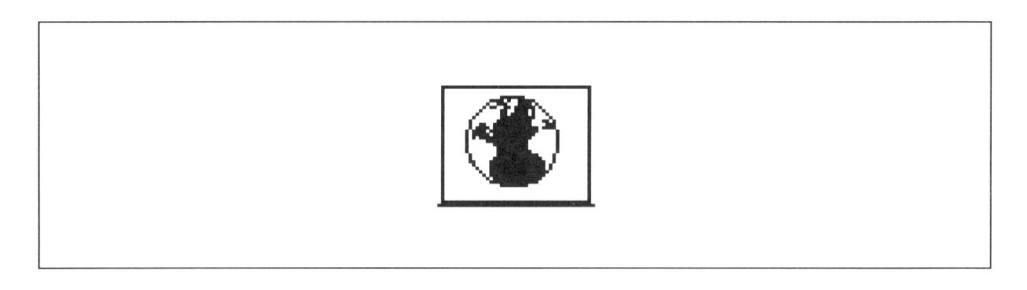

Figure 19.4. The World Button.

2. Click the **Document** button (Figure 19.5) to the right of the World button at the bottom of the window.

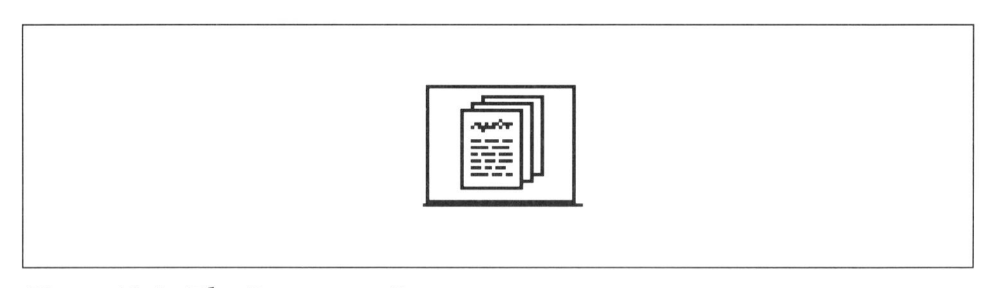

Figure 19.5. The Document Button.

3. Use the drive and directory buttons to specify the location of the file you want to view. Figure 19.6 shows the files in the \QPRO directory. (Your files may be somewhat different.)

    Notice the files with an .EPS or WQ1 extension are shown with a Quattro Pro icon. Files with a .WK1 extension would also be shown with a Quattro Pro icon. In Figure 19.6 the file BAR_GPH.WQ1 has been selected.

4. Double-click the Quattro Pro file icon you want to display. The Quattro Pro Viewer is opened with the selected file displayed.

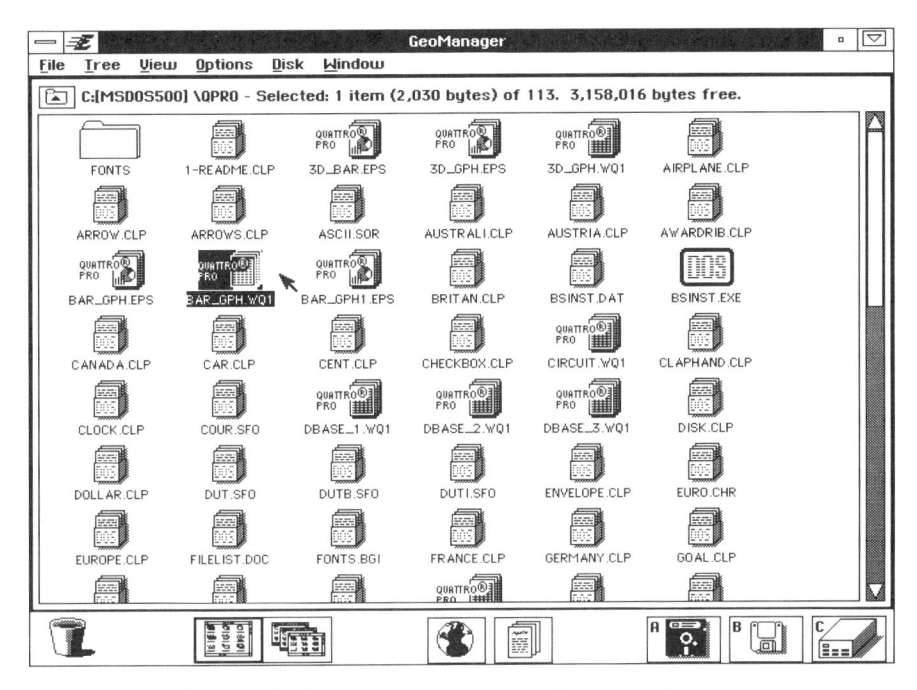

Figure 19.6. Files in the \QPRO Directory of Drive C:.

You can have access to two spreadsheets by reducing one to an icon before opening a second spreadsheet. By repeating this procedure you can have access to several spreadsheets at one time. You can also repeatedly open files without closing any previous file, and then select any one for viewing from the Window menu.

Quattro Pro Viewer Menus

The following is a description of the Quattro Pro Viewer menus.

File Menu

New

This menu command is used to close the Quattro Pro Viewer and open

Quattro Pro SE. Figure 19.7 shows the File menu and the dialog box displayed when the **New** option is selected.

You cannot create or edit a spreadsheet from within the Quattro Pro Viewer. You must do this in the Quattro Pro SE program. The following procedure outlines how to create a new spreadsheet if you are currently in the Quattro Pro Viewer.

1. Choose **New** from the File menu.
   A Select Directory and Enter Filename For New Document dialog box is displayed, as shown in Figure 19.7.

2. Specify the directory where you want Quattro Pro SE to save the new spreadsheet.

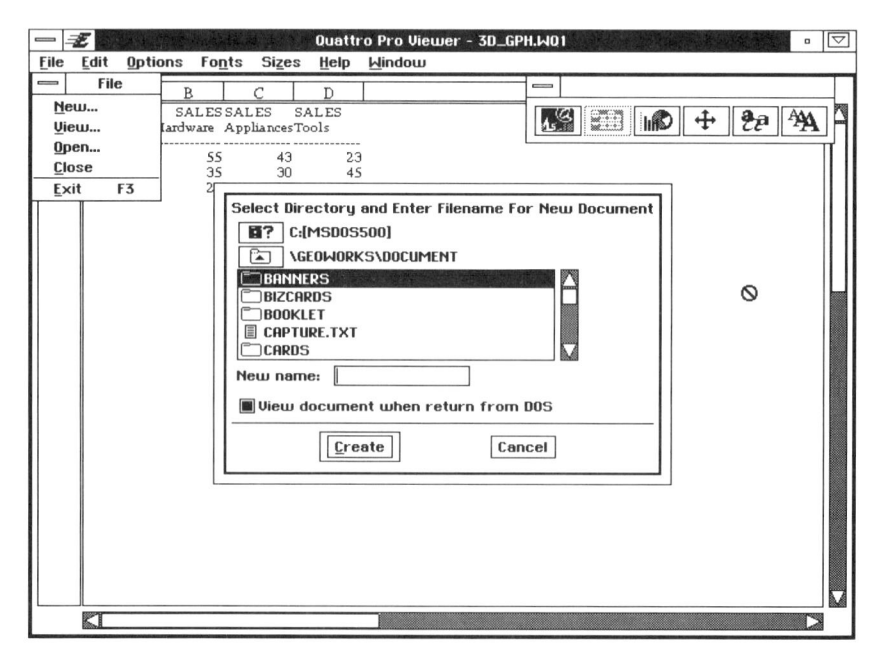

Figure 19.7. The Select Directory and Enter Filename for New Document Dialog Box.

NOTE Make sure the specified directory is displayed on the directories line (below the drive specifier) and not just highlighted in the directories box.

3. Type the filename you want to use for the new file. You do not have to specify the extension (.WQ1 will be used automatically).

4. Select **Create**.
   The Launch Quattro Pro dialog box is displayed, with the name of the new file you have specified. You have a chance to consider whether you really want to start Quattro Pro SE at this time. Select **Cancel** if you change your mind about creating a new file or decide you want to give it a different name.

5. Select **OK**.
   GeoWorks Pro closes and Quattro Pro SE is opened with a blank spreadsheet with the specified filename. After you make your entries in the new spreadsheet, you can save and exit Quattro Pro SE. You are returned to the Quattro Pro Viewer. Choose **View** from the File menu if the new file you created is not displayed.

View

This menu command is used to display a file in the Quattro Pro Viewer. It does not start Quattro Pro SE. You can change the file displayed in the viewer by using the File menu as follows:

1. Choose **View** from the File menu.
   The Choose Document to View dialog box shown in Figure 19.2 is displayed.

> **NOTE:** You can change the drive and/or directory if the file you want is not in the current directory.

2. Specify the type of file you want to view in the Document Formats dialog box.

3. Highlight the file you want to view and select **Open**.
   The dialog box is closed and the specified file is displayed.

You can have access to more than one spreadsheet by reducing one to an icon before opening a second spreadsheet. By repeating this procedure you can have several spreadsheets open at one time. You can also repeatedly open files without closing any previous file, and then select any one for viewing from the Window menu.

Open

This menu command is used to close the Quattro Pro Viewer and open Quattro Pro SE with a specified file displayed in the window. When you select this option, the dialog box shown in Figure 19.8 is displayed.

After you specify **Open** the Launch Quattro Pro dialog box is displayed. This gives you an opportunity to cancel the action.

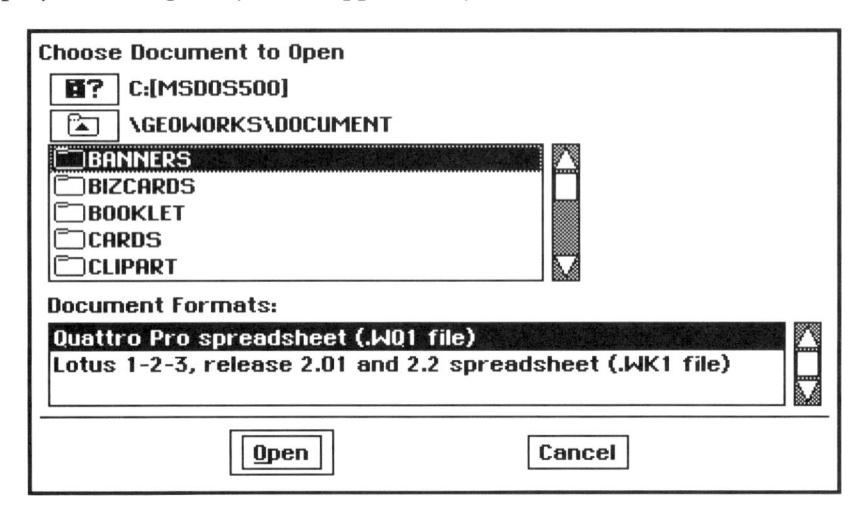

Figure 19.8. The Document to Open Dialog Box.

Close

This command is used to close the file currently displayed in the Quattro Pro Viewer.

Exit F3

This command is used to exit the Quattro Pro Viewer and return you to the previous window.

Edit

Copy (Ctrl+Ins)

This command is used to copy a portion of the displayed spreadsheet to the Clipboard. To use this command, click and drag the mouse to highlight the area you want copied to the Clipboard. After the area is highlighted choose **Copy** from the Edit menu. The highlighting is removed and the area is copied to the Clipboard. You can then go to another application, such as GeoWrite or GeoDraw, and use **Paste** from the Edit menu to paste the image in the application.

When you copy spreadsheet text to the Clipboard, it is copied with tabs separating the columns. If you paste this into GeoWrite the tabs are automatically entered in the ruler. You can change the tab stops and also edit the text after it is pasted in GeoWrite.

If you copy the spreadsheet to the Clipboard and then paste it in GeoDraw, it is copied as a text object you can edit. You can also rotate and stretch (change the size) of the pasted text object. You cannot change the tab stops in GeoDraw (as you can in GeoWrite).

You can also use the same procedure to copy charts (graphs) from the Quattro Pro Viewer to the Clipboard, and then paste them into GeoDraw or GeoWrite. When you do this the pasted graph is treated as a single graphic. If you want to rotate it or change its size, you must do it in GeoDraw. You can then copy the rotated or resized graphic to GeoWrite.

You can place titles on graphs in GeoDraw. This is sometimes a faster way to modify a graph than going back to Quattro Pro SE to do it.

NOTE

To copy a row you have to first select (highlight) it. You can select any row you want to copy by triple-clicking on any portion of the row. You can also select a row by clicking on the row number on the left of the window. To select several rows, triple-click on the first row and then drag to select the other rows.

In Quattro Pro Viewer, imported .EPS charts have a blue background. If you want a white background, you should select **Annotate** from the Graph menu and select **White** as the background choice. The default (gray) comes out as blue when importing a graph; then go ahead and import the chart.

Select All

This command is used to copy all of the displayed spreadsheet to the Clipboard. It is used in the same way as the **Copy** command.

> **NOTE** In the upper-left corner of the document window is the Select All button. Clicking this button selects (highlights) as much of the entire spreadsheet as will fit on a page.

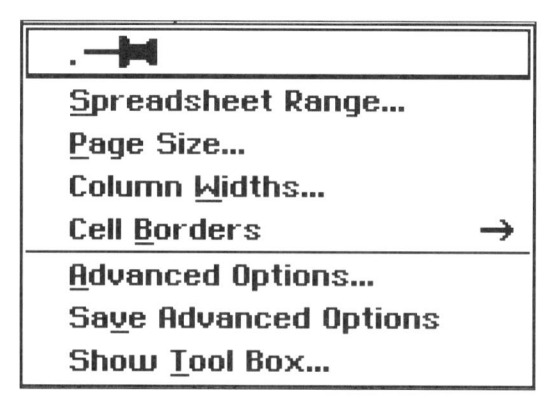

```
┌─────────────────────────────────┐
│         .──┤                    │
├─────────────────────────────────┤
│   Spreadsheet Range...          │
│   Page Size...                  │
│   Column Widths...              │
│   Cell Borders              →   │
├─────────────────────────────────┤
│   Advanced Options...           │
│   Save Advanced Options         │
│   Show Tool Box...              │
└─────────────────────────────────┘
```

Figure 19.9. The Options Menu.

Options

Figure 19.9 shows the Options menu. The Options menu contains the following items:

Spreadsheet Range

For practical purposes the Quattro Pro Viewer is limited to about 26 columns and 60 rows. For spreadsheets larger than this you can specify which part of the spreadsheet you want displayed. This is done by specifying which cell in the spreadsheet you want the Quattro Pro Viewer to use as the upper-left corner.

When you select this option, the dialog box shown in Figure 19.10 is displayed.

If you select **Display as much as possible given the current Page Size**, you are prompted to type the starting cell. The cell you specify becomes the upper-left corner of the spreadsheet in the viewer.

You can also limit the lower-right corner of the spreadsheet in the Quattro Pro Viewer. If you select Display a block of cells, then you can specify both the upper-left and lower-right limits for the block of cells to be displayed in the Quattro Pro Viewer.

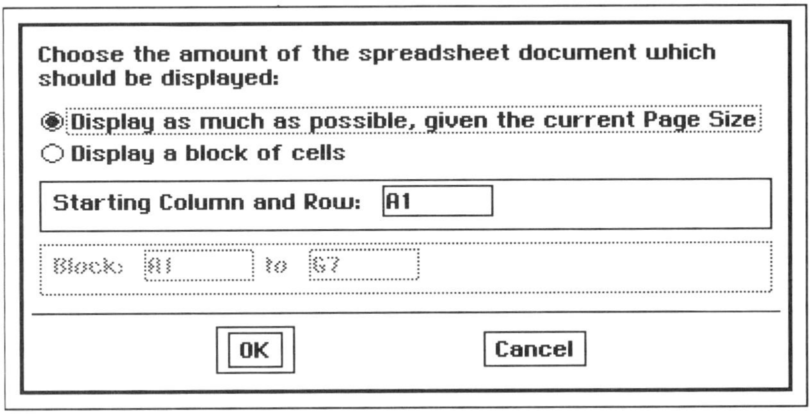

Figure 19.10. The Choose the Amount of the Spreadsheet Document Which Should Be Displayed Dialog Box.

Page Size

The Page Size option determines the size of the page you want. This determines how much of the spreadsheet is placed on a page. This in turn determines how much of the spreadsheet is displayed in the Quattro Pro Viewer. When you select this option, a dialog box similar to the one in Figure 19.11 is displayed.

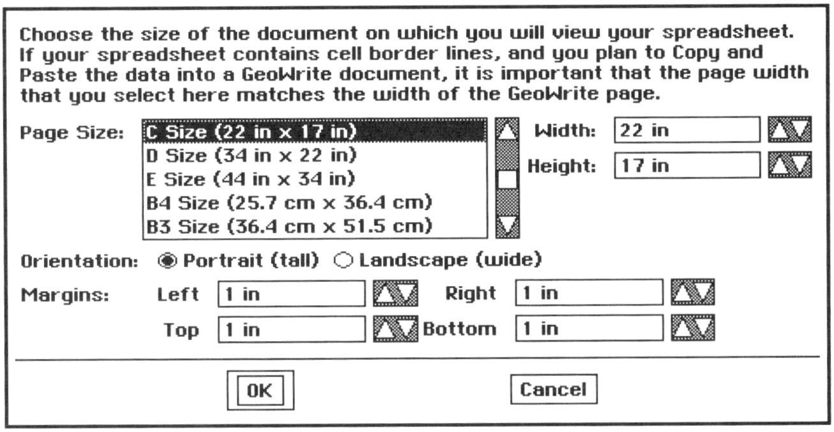

Figure 19.11. The Choose the Size... Dialog Box.

This dialog box allows you to specify the page size, orientation, and margins. Obviously, the larger the page size, the more of the spreadsheet you will see.

NOTE The Page Size option is not available when viewing a chart.

Column Width

Specifying **Fixed Column Widths** allows you to click one of the **Default Tab Spacing** choices. This will cause all the columns in the spreadsheet to have this width. If a cell in a column contains text that does not fit the width you specify, the end of the text is cut off. If a cell contains a number that does not fit, the number is replaced with asterisks (*).

Cell Borders

If you choose **None**, the borders in the displayed spreadsheet are removed. This display does not affect the actual Quattro Pro SE saved file. Choosing **As in File** returns them to the display.

Advanced Options

When you select this option, the dialog box shown in Figure 19.12 is displayed.

Figure 19.12. The Advanced Options Dialog Box.

If **Confirm before launching Quattro Pro SE** is specified, a Confirm dialog box is displayed each time you choose Edit Spreadsheet-New or Edit Spreadsheet Open. If the box on the left is gray (or white) the dialog box is not displayed.

Confirm before viewing matching document causes a confirmation prompt to be displayed before a matching document is displayed. The spreadsheet and chart should both be in the same directory.

As you become more familiar with the program you may elect not to have these confirmation dialog boxes displayed.

You can also elect to have warnings issued if:

- The spreadsheet is wider or taller than the viewer's page size
- The spreadsheet is too complex to view using proportional column widths
- The spreadsheet is too complex to view full height
- The spreadsheet has cell borders drawn and is copied to the Clipboard.

The box at the bottom of the dialog box allows you to start a program other than Quattro Pro SE. If you want to use the Quattro Pro Viewer to look at Lotus 1-2-3 files and use the View Matching Spreadsheet command (discussed below), you must change the Document Extension field to read .WK1. You will also have to change the Program field to read C:\LOTUS\123.EXE. This will cause the Quattro Pro Viewer to start Lotus 1-2-3 instead of Quattro Pro SE.

Save Advanced Options

Selecting this option saves any changes you have made in the Advanced Options menu so they will be the defaults for future sessions.

Show Tool Box

The Tool Box is shown in Figure 19.13.

Selecting this option displays the Tool Box. You can close the Tool Box by double-clicking its control button. If it is currently displayed, clicking this menu option has no affect. The Tool Box consists of six buttons as shown in the upper-right area of the window as shown in Figure 19.7. The Tool Box items are six commonly used commands that correspond to commands found on the menus. The following is a description of each of the Tool Box buttons.

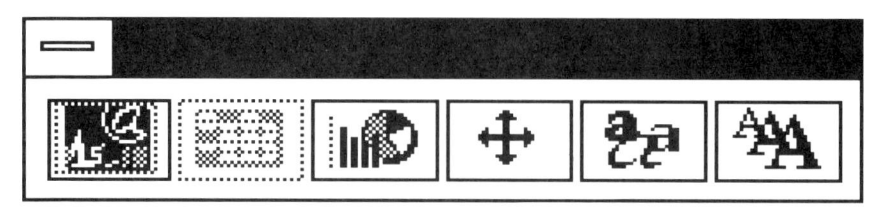

Figure 19.13. The Tool Box.

Edit Spreadsheet

Clicking the first button in the Tool Box opens Quattro Pro SE and displays the same current spreadsheet as the Quattro Pro Viewer. This is the same as selecting **Edit Spreadsheet** from the Window menu.

View Matching Spreadsheet

The View Matching Spreadsheet button is shown in Figure 19.14.

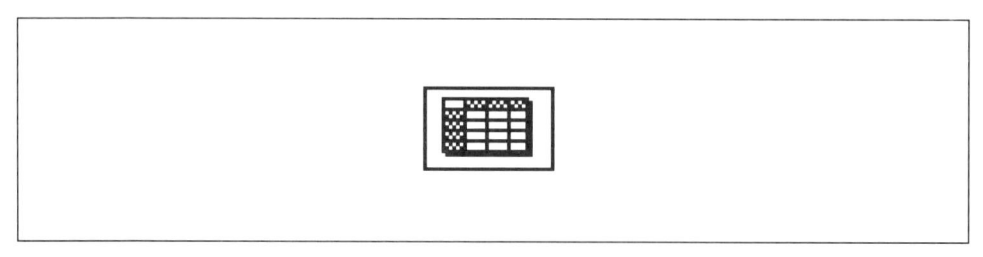

Figure 19.14. The View Matching Spreadsheet Button.

The only time this button is active is when you are viewing a chart. Clicking this button when you are viewing a chart in the Quattro Pro Viewer displays the spreadsheet corresponding to the chart. For example, if you are viewing the chart BAR_GPH.EPS and click this button, the spreadsheet BAR_GPH.WQ1 is displayed in the Quattro Pro Viewer. For this to work, both files must be in the same directory.

This button is the same as selecting **View Matching Spreadsheet** in the Window menu.

View Matching Chart

The View Matching Chart button is shown in Figure 19.15.

Clicking this button when you are viewing a spreadsheet in the Quattro Pro Viewer displays the corresponding chart. For example, if you are viewing the spreadsheet BAR_GPH.WQ1 and click this button, the chart BAR_GPH.EPS is displayed in the Quattro Pro Viewer. For this to work, both files must be in the same directory.

This button is the same as selecting **View Matching Chart** in the Window menu.

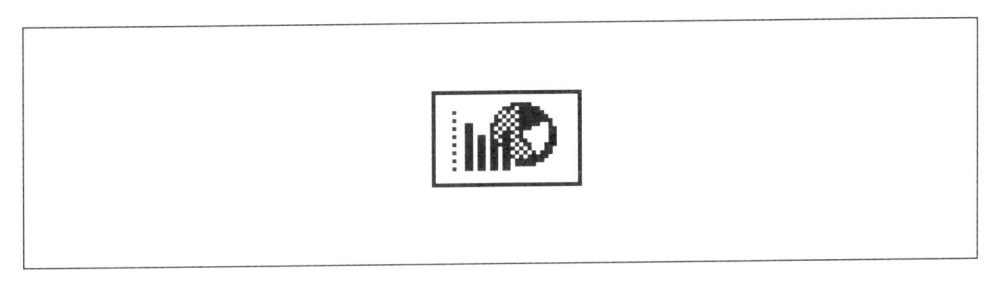

Figure 19.15. The View Matching Chart Button.

Set Spreadsheet Range

The Set Spreadsheet Range button is shown in Figure 19.16.

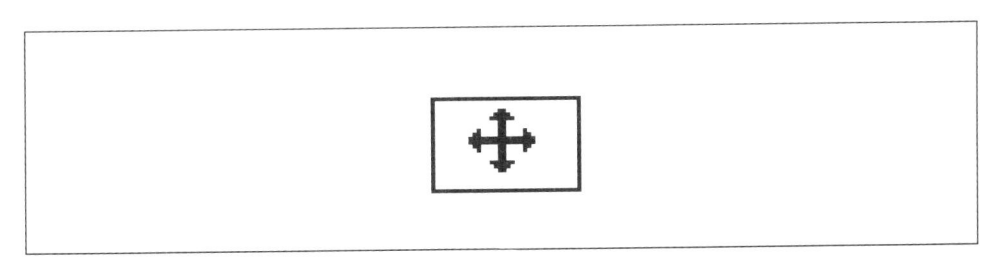

Figure 19.16. The Set Spreadsheet Range Button.

Clicking this button allows you to set the starting cell or range of cells in the Quattro Pro Viewer. Clicking this button is the same as choosing **Spreadsheet Range** on the Options menu.

Set Font

The Set Font button is shown in Figure 19.17.

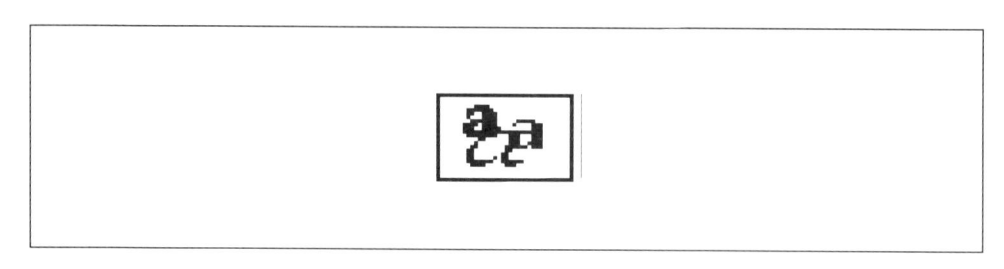

Figure 19.17. The Set Font Button.

Clicking this button displays the More Fonts Dialog Box. You can select (highlight) a font in this dialog box and select **Apply** to make it the font used in the spreadsheet. Selecting this button is the same as choosing **More Fonts** from the Fonts menu.

Set Font Size

The Set Font Size button is shown in Figure 19.18.

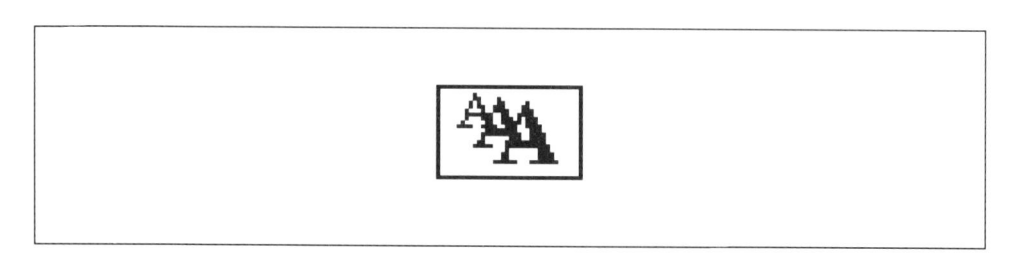

Figure 19.18. The Set Font Size Button.

Clicking this button displays the Custom Size Dialog Box. This dialog box allows you to change the font size used in the spreadsheet. When you change the font size the Quattro Pro Viewer changes the column widths and row heights to be consistent with the new font size. Clicking this button is the same as choosing the **Custom Size** command in the Sizes menu.

Fonts

The Fonts menu allows you to select the font you want used in the spreadsheet. Selecting **More Fonts** from this menu displays a dialog box that shows an example of the selected font below the font list.

When you click **Apply**, the font used in the spreadsheet changes to that specified.

Sizes

The Sizes menu allows you to change the spreadsheet font size. The Quattro Pro Viewer changes the column widths and row heights to be consistent with the new font size specified. If you select **Custom Size** from the Sizes menu, the Custom Size dialog box is displayed.

Help

The Help menu allows you to access help for the Viewer program. You can use the scroll bar or click the **Page Up** or **Page Down** buttons to view other information.

Window

The Window menu is shown in Figure 19.19.

Edit Spreadsheet

Selecting this menu command closes the Quattro Pro Viewer and opens Quattro Pro SE with the spreadsheet you were viewing. If you are viewing a chart in the Quattro Pro Viewer when you select this option, Quattro Pro SE is opened with the spreadsheet corresponding to the chart you were viewing.

View Matching Spreadsheet

This option is available if you are viewing a chart (the View Matching Chart command is dimmed). Clicking this menu command displays in the Quattro Pro Viewer the spreadsheet corresponding to the chart you are viewing.

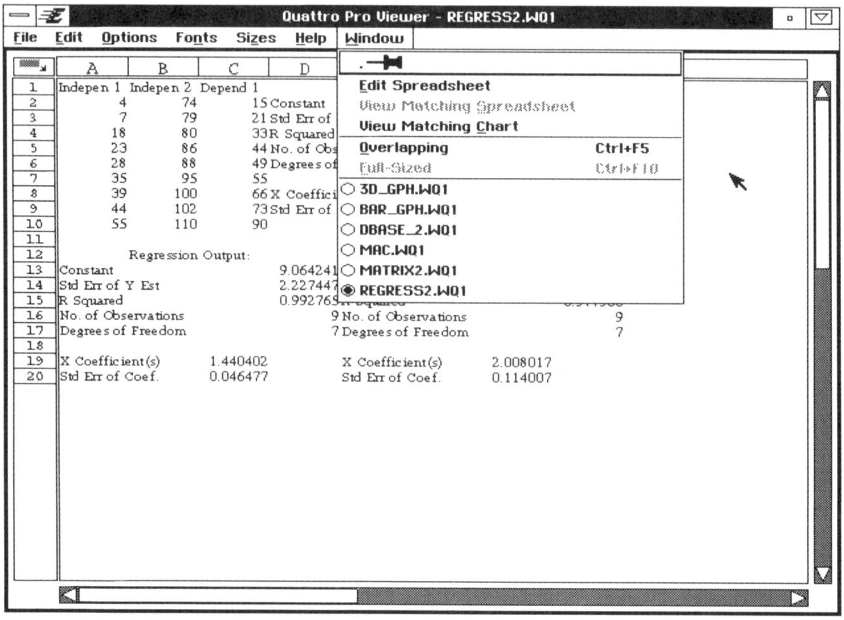

Figure 19.19. The Windows Menu.

View Matching Chart

This option is available if you are viewing a spreadsheet (the View Matching Spreadsheet command is dimmed). Selecting this menu command displays in the Quattro Pro Viewer the chart corresponding to the spreadsheet you are viewing.

Overlapping

If you have selected several files to view and you have not closed any, you can display them in an overlapping format, as shown in Figure 19.20.

You can select any file from the overlapping display by clicking anywhere on it. When you click on a displayed spreadsheet in the overlapping display it is selected and brought to the foreground. You can then move it (by dragging the title bar), and maximize it (by clicking on the **Maximize** button in the upper-right corner of the spreadsheet title bar). You can also maximize the spreadsheet by selecting **Full-Sized** from the Window menu.

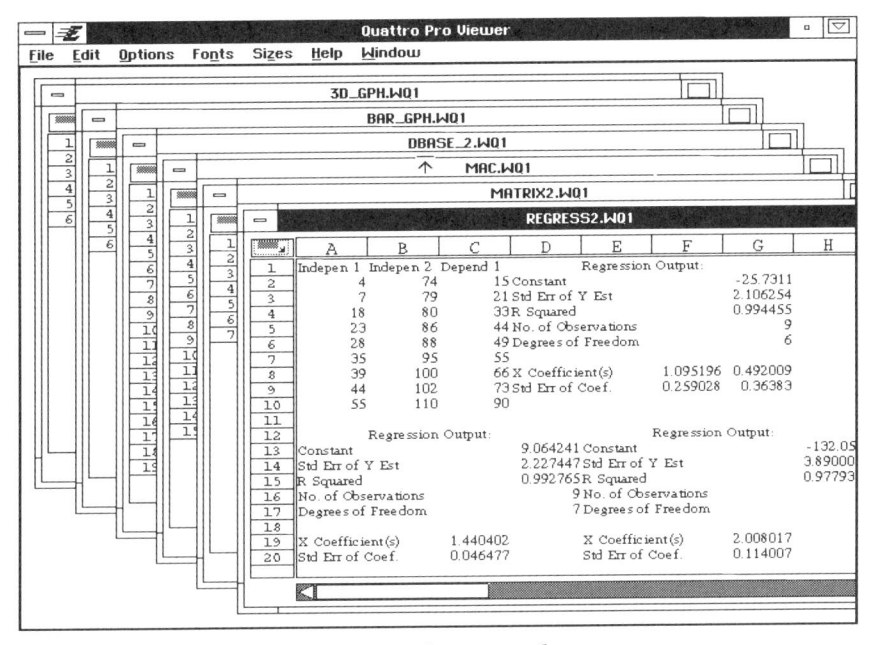

Figure 19.20. An Overlapping Window Display.

Full-Sized

Selecting this menu item causes the selected spreadsheet to be displayed full size. In the overlapping view the Maximize button is sometimes not visible. Using this Window command saves you the time of dragging the selected spreadsheet so you can see the Maximize button.

Listing of Open Files

At the bottom of the Window menu is a list of open files. You can click on a file to select it and have it displayed in the Quattro Pro Viewer.

Summary

In this chapter you have learned to use the Quattro Pro Viewer to view spreadsheets and charts without leaving GeoWorks Pro.

Chapter 20

The DOS Programs Application

The DOS Programs application gives you a convenient way to run DOS programs from within GeoWorks Pro. From the DOS Programs application you can:

- Create, modify, and delete buttons for DOS programs
- Go to the DOS prompt to enter DOS commands manually
- Create and edit DOS batch files.

Whenever you click on a DOS program button, GeoWorks Pro runs the program.

Accessing the DOS Programs Application

You can access the DOS Programs application by clicking on the **DOS Programs** icon on the Welcome screen. When you enter the application for the first time, the program displays only one icon, as shown in Figure 20.1. The Options menu is also shown in Figure 20.1, and is discussed later in this chapter.

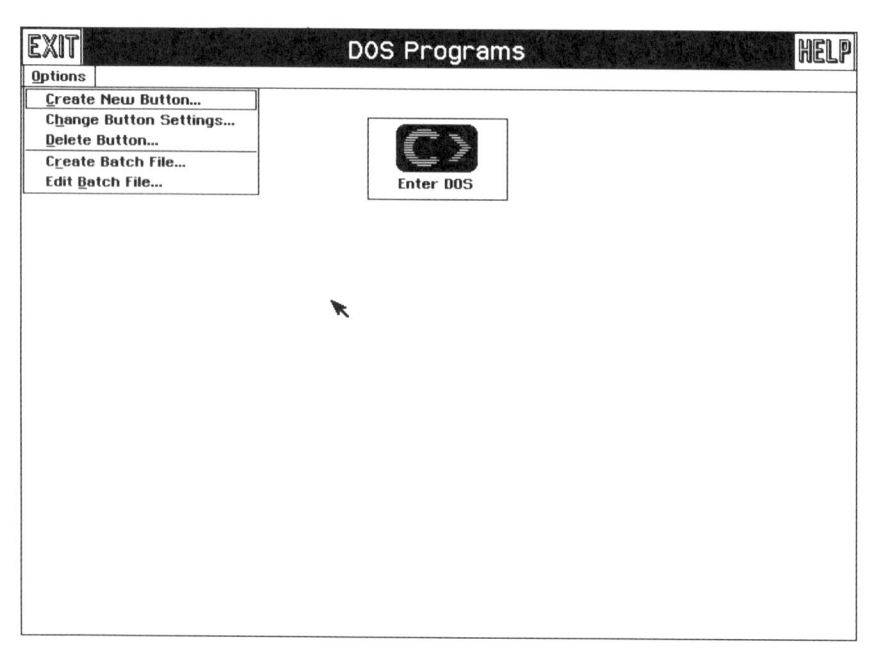

Figure 20.1. The DOS Programs Window with Options Menu.

The DOS Programs Window

At the top-left corner of the DOS Programs window is the EXIT button. Click **EXIT** to return to the Welcome screen. At the top right is the HELP button. Click **HELP** to display information about using the DOS Programs application.

When you click the **Enter DOS** icon, the program takes you temporarily to the DOS prompt, from which you can enter DOS commands. You can perform DOS functions, such as formatting disks, checking the amount of memory available, and copying data from one disk to another. You can also run small programs. When you are ready to return to GeoWorks Pro, type `Exit` and then press **Enter**.

Options Menu

The Options menu is the only menu available in the DOS Programs application. When you select this option, the program displays the Options menu shown in Figure 20.1.

The Options menu contains three sections and five items. Use the option in the top section to create a new DOS program button (icon). Use the options in the center section to change or delete buttons. Use the options in the third section to create or edit batch files.

Create New Button

You can run your DOS Programs and issue DOS commands without exiting GeoWorks Pro. When you create a DOS program icon, you set it up to run the sequence of commands you would type directly at the DOS prompt.

When you select the **Create New Button** option, the program displays the Select DOS file for button dialog box, shown in Figure 20.2.

In the top section are two buttons. Click the top button to change the default drive. The program displays the current (default) drive beside the drive button. In Figure 20.2 this top line shows drive C: and the drive label is MSDOS500.

The second button is the Move Up One Directory button, followed (on the same line) by the path and current directory. The path displayed is \NORTON. This indicates that the NORTON directory in drive C: is specified. When you first select the Create New Button option, the program displays the root directory (\).

The root directory is the top directory on the drive; you cannot move up another level on the drive. If you do click the **Move Up One Directory** button when the root directory is shown, a list of the computer's drives is listed in a display box.

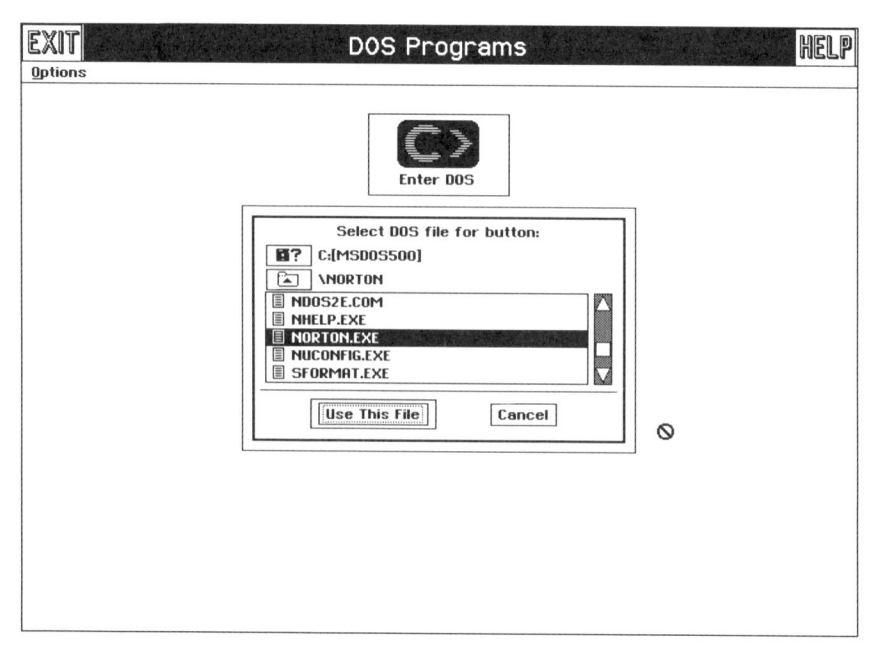

Figure 20.2. The Select DOS File for Button Dialog Box.

The display box below the buttons lists the subdirectories and files in the currently selected directory. To select a subdirectory (move down one level) double-click on a subdirectory name in the display box below the two buttons.

When the selected directory is the one you want, highlight the DOS program file in the display box you want to use. With the file highlighted in the display box, click the **Use This File** button to select it.

For example, assume you want to create a button to start the Norton Utilities program. First select the drive (using the top button and selecting the drive from the display) where you installed the program. Assume you installed the program on drive C:, in the directory \NORTON.

Scroll through the list of subdirectories under the root directory until you find the \NORTON subdirectory. Double-click on the NORTON subdirectory name to select it. The path (second line) changes to \NORTON, and the display box lists the files and subdirectories under the \NORTON subdirectory. Only DOS files with the extensions .COM, .EXE, and .BAT display in the box, as shown in Figure 20.2.

Highlight the program file that runs the program. In the case of the Norton program, the file is NORTON.EXE. Most of the time, a DOS program file has the extension .EXE, but some use the extension .COM. After you highlight the NORTON.EXE file, click the **Use This File** button. The program displays the Button Settings dialog box shown in Figure 20.3.

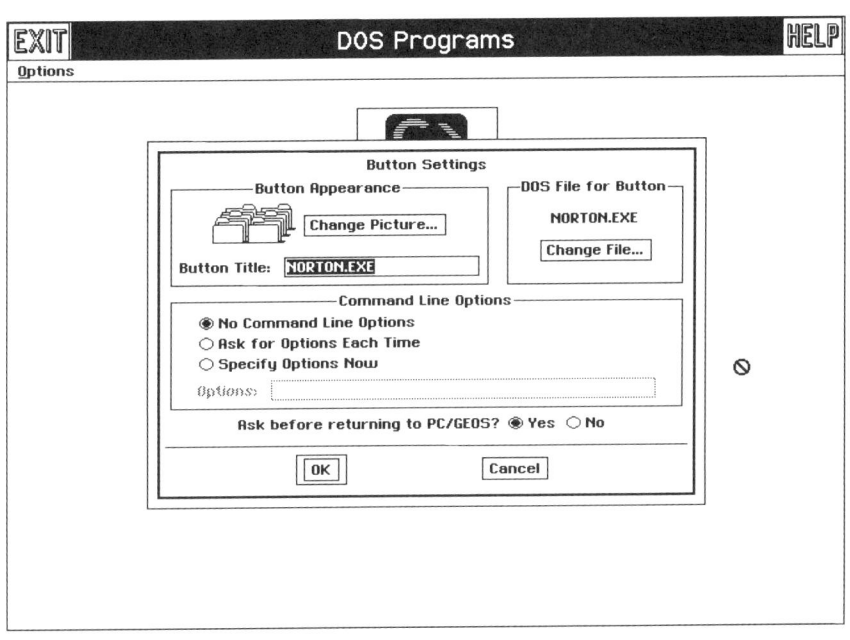

Figure 20.3. The Button Settings Dialog Box.

Button Appearance

At the top left of the dialog box is the Button Appearance area, which includes the Button Title field. Click the mouse cursor in the **Button Title** field to position the text cursor. Type the title you want for the button. You can edit this text if you want.

To change the picture for the icon you are creating, click the **Change Picture** button. The program displays a long list of the available buttons. The list is displayed over the Button Settings dialog box. You can use the scroll bars to view the buttons available.

Figure 20.4. An Added Button in the DOS Programs Window.

The list contains a wide choice, including a selection for popular software programs. Scroll through the list and highlight the one you want.

Click the **OK** button to close the scroll box and accept the selection. Figure 20.4 shows how the selected button appears in the DOS Programs window.

When you click the Norton Utilities button, GeoWorks Pro closes and the Norton Utilities program is open. When you close the Norton Utilities program you will automatically be given the choice of returning to DOS or to GeoWorks Pro.

DOS File for Button

The name of the DOS program file you selected is displayed in the DOS File for button area on the right. If you want to assign a different file to the button, click the **Change File** button under the filename. The program returns to the Select DOS file for button dialog box (see Figure 20.2). Choose the file you want and click the **Use This File** button. The program displays the new filename.

If the Button Title you selected is the name of the run file, you should go back to the Button Title field and change the title to correspond with your new file selection. To do this, click the **Button Title** field to position the text cursor, then type the new button title.

Command Line Options

Some DOS Programs and DOS commands accept options (switches, filespecs, or parameters) that specify something the program or command is to do. For example, if you were running the Norton Utilities FileFind program, you could enter a filespec such as *.* (specifies searching all files, the entire drive) and a switch such as /S (specifies including files in subdirectories).

DOS commands like CHKDSK and DIR also accept options. For example, with the DIR command, you could enter the filespec *.SPR to display all files with the extension .SPR. You could also add the switch /P to pause the DOS display after each screenful of files.

The Command Line Options area is located at the bottom of the Button Settings dialog box. You can choose one of three settings regarding command-line options:

No Command Line Options	Use this if you do not want to specify any options.
Ask for Options Each Time	Select this if you want to be able to enter options each time you use that program. This is useful if you often need to change the switches you use.
Specify Options Now	Select this option to use the same switches every time you use the program or command. Enter the options in the Options text box.

When you are satisfied with the Button Settings dialog box, click the **OK** button to accept the settings. The program displays the new button in the DOS Programs window. To run the program, click the button. The program will ask you for options if you specified Ask for Options Each Time in the Button Settings dialog box. The program will clear the screen and run the program. When you exit the DOS program or it finishes running, GeoWorks Pro re-establishes control and returns you to the DOS Programs window.

If you create more buttons than will fit on your screen, you can use the paging arrows at the bottom of the window to view additional buttons.

Change Button Settings

You can change any of the settings you specified for a button. When you select the **Change Button Settings** option, the program displays the Select Button to Change dialog box. Highlight the name of the button you want to change, then click the **Change Settings** button. The program returns you to the Button Settings dialog box, shown in Figure 20.3. Make whatever changes you wish, then click the **OK** button to activate the changes.

Delete Button

When you select this option to remove a button, the program displays the Select Button to Delete dialog box. Highlight the button name you want to delete, then click the **Delete** button. The program closes the dialog box and removes the button from the DOS Programs window.

Creating and Using Batch Files

You can create and edit batch files without leaving GeoWorks Pro. A batch file is collection of DOS commands contained in a text file. Rather than type the DOS commands every time you want to perform a frequent function, create a batch file that will enter the commands for you. When you run a batch file, DOS reads the commands one at a time, as if you were typing them at the DOS prompt.

Use the last two options on the Options menu to create and edit batch file.

Create Batch File

When you select this option, the program displays the Select Directory and Enter New Filename dialog box, shown in Figure 20.5.

This dialog box works much the same as the dialog box shown in Figure 20.2. See the Create New Button section earlier in this chapter for a discussion about moving around subdirectories.

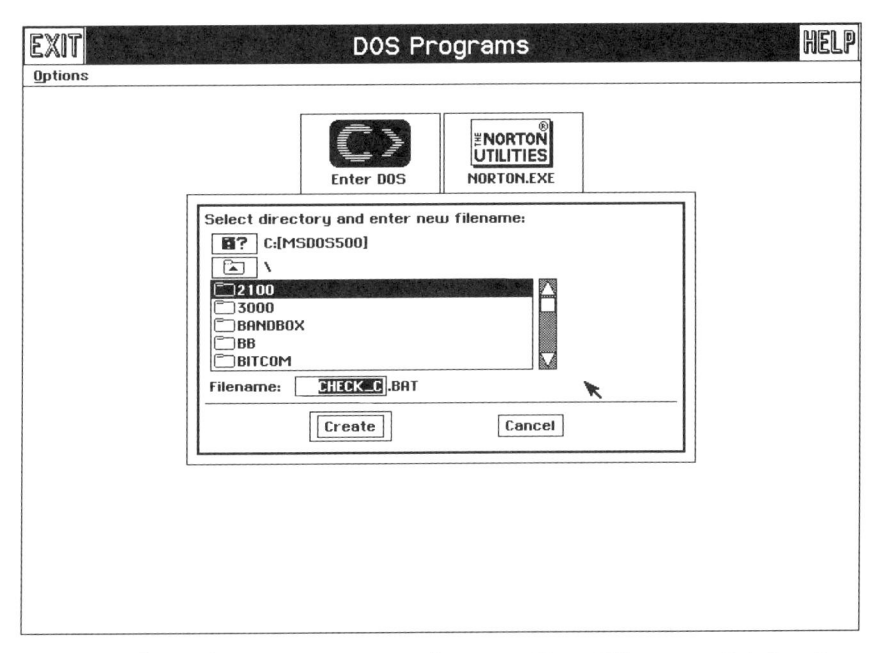

Figure 20.5. The Select Directory and Enter New Filename Dialog Box.

When you have selected the subdirectory in which you want to store the new batch file, click the **Filename** field to position the text cursor. Enter the filename you want to use. You must use a DOS filename (one to eight characters). The program automatically gives it the .BAT extension. Click the **Create** button to display the Batch File Text dialog box, shown in Figure 20.6.

Enter your DOS commands in the box, using a new line for each command. Press **Enter** to start a new line.

Edit Batch File

When you select this option to edit your batch files, the program displays the Select Batch File to Edit dialog box. Select the subdirectory that contains the batch file and highlight the file to edit. Click the **Edit File** button to display the batch file in the Batch File Text dialog box, as shown in Figure 20.6.

Position the text cursor on the line you want to edit. Use **Backspace** to delete characters, type the characters you want, and press **Enter** to start a new line.

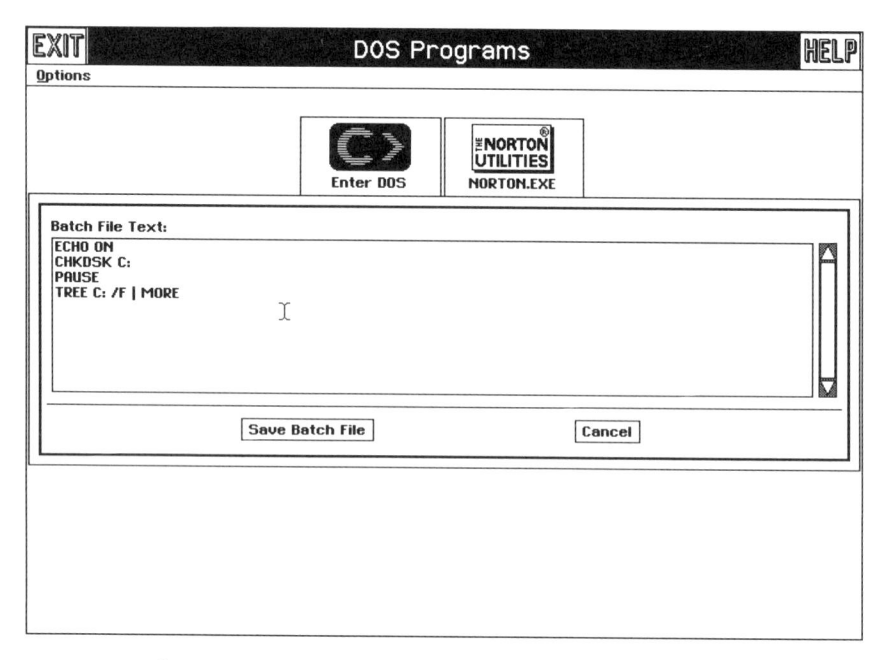

Figure 20.6. The Batch File Text Dialog Box.

When you are satisfied with the batch file, click the **Save Batch File** button to save your changes. Click the **Cancel** button to return to the DOS Programs screen without any changes.

Summary

The DOS Programs application allows you to temporarily exit GeoWorks Pro to the DOS prompt to perform DOS functions.

You can also create, change, or delete buttons to run DOS programs or DOS commands from the DOS Programs window. In addition, you can create and edit batch files to execute a sequence of DOS commands and create buttons for your batch files, as well.

Index

A

Acceleration, mouse 121
Address Book (AOL) 316
Address Book Appliance 17
Adjusting Range Selected 150
Advanced Workspace 53-71
    Control button 54
    Creating/Saving Documents 59
    Dialog Boxes 58
    Exiting 59
    Express Menu 55
    Icons 58, 60-61
    Maximize/Restore Button 56
    Menu Bar 57
    Minimize button 57
    Moving in 54,
    Windows 54
    Saving/Creating Documents 59
    Scroll Bar 57
    Subdirectories 61-62
    Title Bar 56
Alarm Settings 249
America Online Application 297-322
    Installation 298
    Menu Bar 298

Annotation Enable Option 134
Append Option 134
Appliances 9-24
    Address Book 17
    Banner 18
    Calculator 21
    Notepad 22
    Planner 15
    Solitaire 21
Appliances 9-24
    Selecting 13
Area Properties 229
Attributes, file 85
Auto Linefeed 338

B

Background 107-109
Banish Screen Dumper 134
Banner Appliance 18-20
Baud Rate 111, 123, 336
Beginner Workspace 11
Blinking cursor (Screen Dumper) 140
Border Menu (GeoWrite) 176-178
Bring to Front Option (GeoDraw) 230
Buttons, mouse 12

Buttons
   Cancel 42
   Close Dir 46
   Control 37, 54, 75
   Copy 42
   Delete 45
   Document 63, 100
   Documents 47
   Drive 47, 101
   Duplicate 42
   Exit 43
   Express Menu 37, 55, 76
   Format 43
   Full/Overlapping 100
   Help 49
   Maximize/Restore 56
   Minimize 57
   Move 40, 42
   Open 42
   Open Dir 45
   Rename 42
   World 63

C

Calculator Appliance 21-22
Calculator Application 259-268
   Functions 261
   Memory Functions 267
   Menu Bar 263
   Order of Operations 262
   RPN 264
   Using 260
Capture to Text File Option
   (GeoComm) 327
Changing
   Font 195
   Text Size 195
   Text Style 196
Check Spelling 166-170

Circle Tool (GeoDraw) 239
Clicking (mouse) 12
Close 76
Closing a Pinned Menu 196
Color
   Choices 136
   Dump 137
   Of Object (GeoDraw) 229
   Paragraph 174
   Text 187
COM ports 337
COMPU.MAC file (GeoComm) 65
Computer Configuration (Preferences)
   112-113
      Expanded memory 113
      Extended memory 113
      Managed Extended Memory 114
      Memory types 113
   Conference Log 303
Configuring GeoWorks Pro 6-8
Confirm Delete 84
Connect Line Tool (GeoDraw) 237
Connected Line Handles
   (GeoDraw) 238
Control Button 37, 54, 75
Control Menu 37, 55, 75-76
Copy Command 84, 164
Correct for Aspect Ratio 171
Create
   Batch file 392
   Directory 83
   New Button 387
Creating Documents 59
Currency formats 115
Cursor, types of 235
Custom borders, choosing 176
Cut Command 164
Cutting/Copying Between
   Scrapbooks 285

Index • 397

D
Data Bits 336
Date & Time (Preferences) 107
Default Tabs Menu 178-179
Delete
 by Dragging 85
 Command 84
 Confirm 84
Deleting selected text 150
Deselect All Command 87
Dial Menu (GeoComm) 341-347
Dialing a Phone Number 296
Dialog Boxes 26, 58
 Selecting from 27
Dictionary (User) 168
Directories
 Closing 46
 Creating 46
 Document(s) 47, 62
 Icons 29, 62
 Opening 45-46
 Root 61
 World 62
Disk Menu 95-97
 Copy Disk Command 95
 Format Disk Command 96
 Rename Disk Command 97
 Rescan Drives Command 97
Disks
 Floppy 47-48
 Formatting 43-44
Display
 Options 130
 Performance 129
Document Button 63, 368
DOS Files 60
DOS Programs Application 385-394
 Create a New Button 387
 DOS file for button 390

Double-clicking 37
 to Set time 121
Dragging with Mouse 13
 as Outline 226
 as Rectangle 225
 Left button 225
 Right button 226
 to Delete 85
Draw Graphics Option (GeoWrite) 171
Drive Icon 41
Dump color 137
Duplex Terminal Setting (GeoComm) 338
Duplicate 84

E
Edit a Batch file 393
Edit Menu 163-170
 (AOL) 305
 (GeoComm) 331-332
 (GeoPlanner) 247-249
Editing a text object (GeoDraw) 235
Encapsulated PostScript 133
Entering Phone Numbers (GeoDex) 290
Exit 34, 87, 163
 to DOS 80
Exporting/Importing Files 62-64
Express button 37, 55, 76
Express Menu 37-39, 55-56, 76-80
Extras Directory 126-140
 3D Font Demo 126
 Bounce 128
 Font Demo 126
 Nimbus Font Converter 128-131
 Perf 128-131
 Screen Dumper 131-140

F
Fax sending 216
 (AOL) 318

File Attributes (DOS) 85
  Archive 85
  Hidden 85
  Read-only 85
  System 85
File Cabinet (Intermediate Workspace) 28
    Buttons in 39, 45
    Control button 37
    Exit to DOS 39
    Express Menu 37
    Information Line 44, 99
    Preferences 38
    Printer Control 38
    Title Bar 39
    Window description 37
File Close Command 34, 156
File Menu
  (AOL) 299-305
  (GeoComm) 324-330
  (GeoManager) 81-88
  (GeoPlanner) 245-246
File Menu Commands 32
  Attributes 85
  Close 34
  Copy 84
  Create Directory 82
  Delete 84
  Duplicate 84
  Exit 34, 87
  Get Info 82, 154
  Move 83
  New 154
  Open 32, 82, 155
  Rename 85
  Revert 34, 157
  Save 33, 156
  Save As 157
File names

DOS 31, 60
GEOS 31, 60
File types 60
Files(s) 31
  Copying 42
  Creating 59
  Deleting 45
  DOS 60
  Duplicating 42
  GEOS 60
  Getting Info about 39
  Icons 60
  Importing/Exporting 62-63
  Moving 40-42
  Opening 39
  Renaming 42
  Saving 59
  Saving GEOS as DOS 69-70
First-line indented paragraph 213
Flip Horizontal/Vertical Option (GeoDraw) 227
Font Sizes Menu 184-185
Fonts Menu 182-185
Footers (GeoWrite) 147-148
Formats
  Encapsulated PostScript 133
  Full-page PostScript 133
  Long Date 118
  Number 116
  PC-Paintbrush 133
  Quotation Marks 118
  Raw Bit Map 133
  Short Date 119
  Time 119
  TIFF 133
Fuse/Defuse Objects (GeoDraw) 223

G

Games Applications 349-362

Index • 399

Solitaire 350-355
Tetris 355-362
GENIE.MAC file (GeoComm) 65
GeoComm Application 323-347
    Opening 64, 324-325
    Protocol Settings 335
    Save Buffer 330
    Send/Receive XMODEM 327
    Terminal Settings 337
GeoDex Application 287-296
    Accessing 287
    Entering Phone Numbers 290
    Menus 292-295
    Quick Dial 291
    Window 288-291
GeoDex Lookup 255
GeoDraw 219-239
    Accessing 54, 220
    Arrange Menu 230-231
    Edit Menu 222-225
    File Menu 220-222
    Modify Menu 226-230
    Options Menu 225-226
    Text Menu 231-234
    View Menu 224
    Window Menu 234
GeoManager 73-101
    Bottom Line Icons 100
    Control Line 75
    Express button 76
    Screen 74
    Window 99
GEOS Files 60
GeoWorks Pro
    Moving Around In 11
    Starting 10
GeoWrite
    Application 141-152
    Headers/Footers 147

Justifications 146-147
Line spacing 147
Margins 143-144
Menus 153-190
Mode 148
Opening 66
Operations & Tutorial 191-217
Paging arrows 144
Paragraph alignment 146
Ruler 143, 172
Tab types 145
Tabs 144
Window 142
Get Info 82
Go To Menu (AOL) 305-314
Go to Page Command 188
GeoPlanner Application 241-257
    Calendar 243
    Menu Bar 245
    Schedule of Events 244
    Using 242
Graphics
    Inserting in GeoWrite document 201-204
    Resizing 203
    Viewing in a document 171
Grayscale (Screen Dumper) 137

H

Handles 14
Handshake 125, 337
Headers (GeoWrite) 147-148
    Making 198
Height/Width of image (Screen Dumper) 136
Help Menu (AOL) 299
Hide All Option 173
Host Code Page 338-339

I

Icons 11, 26, 41, 58, 60, 62, 81, 100
   Repositioning 81
   Restoring 81
Image Name (Screen Dumper) 136
Importing/Exporting Files 62
Importing documents into GeoWorks
   Pro 215
Importing DOS files into GeoWrite 69
Information Line 99
Insertion mode (GeoWrite) 148
Installation (AOL) 298
Installation, GeoWorks Pro 1-8
   Monitor 6
   Mouse 7
   Printer 8
   Setup 4
   System requirements 2-3
Intermediate Workspace 25-51
   Directories 29
   File Cabinet Window 28
   File Menu 28
   Files 31
International Formats (Preferences)
   115-119
Interrupt Level Options (Preferences) 114
IRQ Settings for modem 335
Italic 186

J

Justification Settings (GeoWrite)
   146-147

K

Keyboard Option (Preferences)
   119-121
Keyboard editing 150-152
Keyboard, Menu Selection using 35

L

Line(s)
   Handles 237
   Properties 228
   Spacing 147, 180
   Tool 237
Log, Conference/Session (AOL) 303
Log Name (Screen Dumper) 134
Long Date Format 118

M

Mail Menu (AOL) 314-319
Maximize/Restore button 56
Measurement Units 116, 173
Members Menu (AOL) 319-321
Menu(s)
   Closing 36
   Control 55
   Disk 95-97
   Edit 163-166, 222-223, 247-248,
     273, 278, 292, 305, 331, 372-374
   Express 37, 55-56, 64-65
   File 32-34, 81-87, 154-163, 220,
     245, 271, 278, 299-304, 325-330
     369-372
   Hotkey Command 36
   Keyboard commands 35
   Mnemonic Command 35
   Mouse selection 34
   Moving 36
   Options 92-95, 171-173, 250, 294,
     334-340, 351, 359, 374-380, 387
   Pinning 36, 81
   Startup 78
   Tree 88-90
   View 90-92, 171, 224-225, 249, 282,
     293, 333
   Window 98-99, 188-189, 234, 321
Menu Bar 57, 81

Index • **401**

(GeoPlanner) 245
Minimize button 57, 76
Mode
   Insertion mode 148
   Overwrite 148
Modem 122-125
Modem Port 337
Modem Settings (GeoComm) 339-341
Monitor, Selections 6-7
Mouse 121-122
   Buttons 12
   Clicking 12
   Double-clicking 37
   Dragging 13, 40
   Pointers 11-12
   Right button 40
   Scrolling 13
   Selecting 7, 13
Move 76, 83
   Backward 231
   Forward 231
Move Up One Directory Level button 68
Moving in GeoWorks Pro 11
   Icons 11
   Pointers 11-12
Next Page Command 188
Nimbus-Q fonts 128

N

Notepad Appliance 22-24
   Copy 23
   Cut 23
   Paste 23
   Printing 23
   Text Size 24
Notepad Application 269-274
   Accessing 269
   Menus 271-274

Number Format/Measurement Units 116
Number of Copies 136, 161-162

O

Open Document, List of 234
Open (File Menu) 82
Options 135
   Save 173
   Screen Dumper 135-137
   Spell Check 173
Options Menu 171-173
   (DOS programs) 387-393
   (GeoComm) 334-340
   (GeoManager) 92-95
      Ask before Return Command 94
      Confirm Command 94
      Delete Command 94
      Minimize on Run Command 94
      Read-Only Command 94
      Replace Command 94
      Save Options Command 95
   (GeoPlanner) 250-252
Orientation 136, 161-162
Outdented paragraph 214
Overlapping Documents Display Option 189, 234
Overwrite mode (GeoWrite) 148

P

Page
   Go to 188
   Next 188
   Previous 188
Page break(s)
   Creating 205
   Inserting 165
Page listing/Select Page (Window menu) 189

Page numbers
  Inserting 165
Page Setup 161-162
Paging arrows (GeoWrite) 144
Paper size 136, 161-162
Paragraph(s)
  Color 174
  Indented 213
  Menu 173-175
  Outdented 214
  Spacing 181
Paragraph alignment
  Center 146
  Fully justified 147
  Left 146
  Right 147
Parity 112, 124, 336
Paste Command (Edit menu) 164
Path, file or directory 44, 62, 99
PC-Paintbrush 133
PC/GEOS (Preferences) 125
Performance display (Extras) 129
Pin symbol 81, 154
Pinning menus 81, 154
  Closing 196
Planner Appliance 15-16
Pointers in GeoWorks Pro 11-12
Polygon Tool (GeoDraw) 239
Preferences Application/Extras
  Directory 103-140
Preferences Icons 104-126
  Background 107-110
  Computer 112-114
  Date & Time 107
  International 115-119
  Keyboard 119-121
  Look & Feel 105-107
  Modem 122-125
  Mouse 121-122

PC/GEOS 1225-126
Printer 110-112
Sound 110
Video 114-115
Preferences Options
  Document Safeguarding 106
  Font Size 106
  Look & Feel 105
  Opening Screen 106
  Overstrike Mode 106
  Safeguarding documents 106
Previous Page Command (Window
  menu) 188
Print Command (File menu) 160
Printer 111
  Change Options 161
  Control Panel 79
  Document print 161
  Install New 111
  Page Setup 161-162
  Parallel/Serial port 111
  Selecting 8
Protocol
  Changes 337
  Settings (GeoComm) 335-337

Q

Quick Copy pointer 212, 247, 263
Quick Dial (GeoComm) 346
Quick Menu (GeoPlanner) 253
Quick Move pointer 247, 263
Quotation Marks format 118

R

Rectangle Tool (GeoDraw) 238
Relocating a Window 80
Rename file or directory 85
Reopen an Application 77
Repositioning an Icon 81

Resizing a Window 80
Restore 76
Restoring an Icon 81
Reverse Polish Notation (RPN)
    (Calculator) 264
RGB Color 136, 175
Rotate (Modify menu)
    45 Degrees Left 227
    45 Degrees Right 228
    Rotate to Any Degree 228
Rotate Pointer (GeoDraw) 238
Ruler 143
    Align 171
    Show 172
    Snap to 172

S

Saving
    a GEOS file as a DOS file 69
    Documents 59, 214
Scrapbook Application 275-286
    Accessing 276
    Cutting/Copying between 285
    Default Scrapbook, changing 283
    Menus 278-283
    Opening more than one 284
    Window 276
Screen capture 131-140
    Table of keys used in 138
Screen Dumper 131-140
    Annotation 133
    Base Name 132
    Blinking cursor 140
    Dump Number 132
    Formats 133
    Menu Bar 134
    Select Directory 132
    Starting 137, 140
    Using 137

Screen Redraw (Refresh)
    Command 188
Script Commands (GeoComm)
    343-346
Script file(s) 65
    COMPU.MAC 65, 341
    Creating 341-342
    GENIE.MAC 65, 341
    Running 342-343
Scroll Bar 13, 57
Select All Command 87
Selecting
    by Clicking 27, 34
    by Dragging 28, 34, 148, 223
    by Specifying 148
    Large units 149
    Lines 149
    Text 194
    with Hotkeys 36
    with Keyboard 35
    with Mouse 13, 34
    Words 149
Send to Back (GeoDraw) 231
Sending a document as a Fax 216
Session Log (AOL) 303
Set Font button (Spreadsheet
    Viewer) 380
Set Font Size button (Spreadsheet
    Viewer) 380
Set Up (AOL) 306
Setting a tab 193
Shadow border 176
Short Date Format 119
Show Options
    All 173
    Ruler 172
    Scroll Bar 173
Sign On (AOL) 308
Snap to Ruler marks (Options menu) 172

Solitaire 21, 350-355
  Layout 353
  Playing 354
  Scoring 352
Sound (Preferences) 110
Spacing
  Lines 180
  Paragraphs 181
Specifying to select 148
Spelling Checker 166-170
Spreadsheet
  Extensions 364
  Menus 369-383
  Page size 375
  Range 374, 379
  Specifying a file 367
  Tool Box 378
  View matching spreadsheet 378
  Viewer 363-383
  Viewing 365
Starting, Screen Dumper 137, 140
Starting GeoWorks Pro 10
Startup (Express menu) 78
Statistics, performance 129
Stop bits 112, 125, 337
Store/Recall Style 165
Strike Thru (GeoWrite) 187
Strip Linefeeds From Text 326
Styles Menu (GeoWrite) 186-187
Subdirectories 61, 67
Subscript 187
Superscript 187

T

Tabs 144-145
  Attributes Menu 178
  Decimal 208
  Left 206
  Remove 210

Types 179
Table, Creating 205-213
Table border 210
Telephone number format (GeoComm) 347
Templates 29
Terminal Settings (GeoComm) 337, 339
Tetris 355-362
  Moving pieces 356
  Penalize Opponent 361
  Scoring 357
  Two players 360
Text color 187
Text File Commands 158
  Import a Text File 158
  Insert From Text File 158
  Save as a Text File 159
Text Properties 230
Text Styles 186-187, 196
Text Tool 235
TIFF 133, 137
Time format (Preferences) 119
Title Bar 56, 80
Tool Box (GeoDraw) 234
Transmitting a Text document 216
Tree Menu (GeoManager) 88-90
  Collapse Branch Command 90
  Drive Command 88
  Expand All Command 88
  Expand Branch Command 90
  Expand One Level Command 90
  Show Tree Window Command 88
Typeface Styles Menu 186-187
Typing cursor movement 150

U

Underline 187
Underlining in Tables 209

Units, measurements
  (Preferences) 116
Utilities Menu (GeoPlanner) 253-255

V

Video 114-115
  Automatic screen blanking 115
  Video adapter 115
View Matching
  Chart 379, 382
  Spreadsheet 378, 381
View Menu (GeoComm) 333-334
View Menu (GeoManager) 90-92
  Compress Display Command 92
  Icons Command 91
  Names and Details Command 91
  Names Only Command 91
  Show Hidden Files Command 92
  Sort by Command 92
View Menu (GeoPlanner) 249-250
View Menu 171

W

Wastebasket 100
Welcome 77
Welcome Screen 10

Width/Height for printing 136, 161-162
Window(s), Advanced Workspace 26, 54
  Main display 99
  Relocating 80
  Resizing 80
Window menu 98-99, 187-189
  (AOL) 321-322
  Close All Command 98
  Close Command 98
  Full-Sized Command 99, 189, 234
  Listing/Selection Command 99
  Overlapping Command 98
Word Length in data trasmission 124-125
Workspace
  Advanced 53-71,
  Intermediate 25-51,
  Beginner 9-24
World button 63, 368

X

XMODEM files
  Receiving 328-329
  Sending 327-328